RAPHAEL PUMPELLY

History of American Science and Technology Series
General Editor, LESTER D. STEPHENS

Raphael Pumpelly
Gentleman Geologist of the Gilded Age

PEGGY CHAMPLIN

The University of Alabama Press
Tuscaloosa and London

Copyright © 1994
The University of Alabama Press
Tuscaloosa, Alabama 35487–0380
All rights reserved
Manufactured in the United States of America

∞

The paper on which this book is printed meets the minimum
requirements of American National Standard for Information
Science-Permanence of Paper for Printed Library Materials,
ANSI Z39.48-1984.

Library of Congress Cataloging-in-Publication Data

Champlin, Margaret Derby.
   Raphael Pumpelly : gentleman geologist of the Gilded Age / Peggy Champlin.
     p. cm.—(History of American science and technology series)
  Includes bibliographical references and index.
  ISBN 0-8173-0691-9 (alk. paper)
    1. Pumpelly, Raphael, 1837–1923. 2. Geologists—United States—Biography. I. Title. II. Series.
QE22.P8C48 1994
550'.92—dc20
[B]   93-4778

British Library Cataloguing-in-Publication Data available

*For Chuck
and
Chuck, Jr., Katy, John,
Judi, Susan, Nancy*

Contents

List of Illustrations	ix
Preface	xi
1. Education of a Geologist	1
2. Geology in America, 1835–1860	29
3. Exploring "Across America and Asia"	51
4. Economic Geologist of the Gilded Age	78
5. Gentleman Geologist	116
6. With the United States Geological Survey	141
7. Explorations in Turkestan	164
8. The End of Geology's Heroic Age	203
Notes	217
Bibliography	249
Index	265

Illustrations

Raphael Pumpelly at Freiberg, age nineteen	17
Eliza Shepard Pumpelly, age twenty, and Raphael Pumpelly, age thirty	88
The house at Newport, Rhode Island, 1881	100
Letter from Raphael Pumpelly to Bailey Willis, October 13, 1879	102
Raphael Pumpelly at age forty-seven, photographed by Marian (Mrs. Henry) Adams	134
Chronology of the culture strata at Anau showing relation to climatic cycles	191
Raphael Pumpelly at about age eighty	204

Preface

Raphael Pumpelly's *Reminiscences* are a charming account of his exciting life as a geologist and explorer, and many biographers and historians have cited passages from its pages. Even novelists have drawn from his stories, including Larry McMurtry, whose *Anything for Billy* contains a stagecoach ride in which the narrator gallantly surrenders his comfortable seat to a woman and takes the rear-facing place, as Pumpelly told of doing during his miserable journey to Arizona in 1861 to take his first job working a silver mine.[1] Pumpelly said little of his scientific work, however, and he has remained a rather shadowy figure in the history of American geology, even though he was an expert mining geologist, a consultant to the governments of Japan and China, a director of geological surveys, and leader of an important archaeological expedition to Central Asia.

Precisely because Pumpelly's career spanned such a variety of activities, his biography provides an excellent opportunity to look at the development of the profession of geology during the years spanned by his career, from 1860 to the early twentieth century. In this period, the practical applications of geology to resource development were of major importance, but geologists were also investigating new subjects, such as petrology, geomorphology, glaciology, and structural geology. These investigations resulted in an explosion of knowledge in these areas and in the growth of subdisciplines. Pumpelly did research in these fields but like others of his generation did not limit himself to any one of them; he remained a generalist in a time of increasing specialization, a transitional figure in a period of rapid change.

The post–Civil War years, when westward expansion, railroad building, and industrial growth were accompanied by almost unrestricted speculation in mines and land, have become known as the Gilded Age, a term taken from the book of that name by Mark Twain and Charles Dudley Warner. Those were days when people might "come into sudden opulence by some means which they could not have classified among any of the regular occupations of life" or when a man could not "get into Congress without resorting to arts and means that should render him unfit to go there," as Twain and Warner wrote.[2] Land grabbing, unscrupulous mining ventures, and political corruption did indeed abound, but wealth acquired legitimately in the Gilded Age also enabled many people to cultivate the arts and sciences, mount exploring expeditions, build museums, and establish research institutions. Pumpelly's investments allowed him to live at times as a "gentleman geologist," pursuing his own research interests. He traveled the world, collected art, belonged to gentlemen's clubs, and owned homes in Newport, Rhode Island, and Dublin, New Hampshire, where he and his wife were at the center of a cultivated social group. At the same time, he was deeply committed to his profession, keeping up with the latest developments in geology, contributing to scientific journals, and maintaining membership in a number of professional societies. So it is that Pumpelly's career enables us not only to see geology as a developing profession but also to see it in relation to the cultural life of his remarkable time, the Gilded Age.

This book, which began as a doctoral dissertation, owes much to the expert guidance of my adviser, Robert G. Frank, Jr., who encouraged me to persevere and suggested many paths to pursue. I am grateful to Gary S. Dunbar for his continuing interest in Pumpelly and for directing me to additional sources, to M. Norton Wise for his thought-provoking comments on the final draft of the dissertation, and to editor Lester Stephens for his careful reading of the manuscript and for his many helpful recommendations for improving it. Many thanks to Daniel Howe and Roy Porter, who read and commented on chapter 5, "Gentleman Geologist," and to Clifford M. Nelson for his useful comments and suggestions, especially relating to chapter 6, "With the United States Geological Survey." The late Seymour Chapin, to whom I owe my initial interest in the history of science, read an early version of chapter 1, "Education of a Geologist."

I received invaluable assistance from the staff of the Manuscript Reading Room at the Henry E. Huntington Library, where I spent many pleasant hours with the Pumpelly Collection and the papers of Pumpelly's friends Louis and Henry Janin. The staff and resources of the

Geology and Research Libraries at the University of California at Los Angeles made much of my research on the history of American geology possible. Thanks to a Smithsonian graduate student fellowship, I was able to spend ten weeks in Washington, D.C., doing research in the Smithsonian Institution Archives, the National Archives, the Library of Congress, and the archives of the Carnegie Institution of Washington and the National Academy of Sciences. The staffs of all these institutions were unfailingly helpful. I am grateful to Nathan Reingold for sponsoring the fellowship and to Marc Rothenberg and his staff at the offices of the Joseph Henry Papers for giving me a desk, suggesting new sources of material, and making me feel at home. I would also like to thank Clark Elliott, who provided me with material from the Harvard University Archives relating to Pumpelly's brief tenure as a Harvard professor, W. Keith Wedge, who sent copies of letters from the archives of the Missouri Department of Natural Resources, Division of Geology and Land Survey, and archivist W. Gregory Gallagher of New York's Century Club. I am especially thankful for Beverly Twitchell Denbow's meticulous editing of the manuscript.

I first became interested in Pumpelly long ago when my children were in a carpool with Raphael Pumpelly's great-grandchildren, and I learned from the children's mother Shirley what a family legend Pumpelly had become. Raphael Pumpelly III shared with me his childhood memories of his grandfather and he and his daughter Lisa have been enthusiastic supporters of this project. My husband, Charles, has backed me all the way, and to him and my children this book is dedicated.

Education of a Geologist

The Early Years

On a day in late winter, sometime in the mid-1840s, when the ice was breaking up on the Susquehanna River, a boy of about eight was balancing himself precariously on a block of ice in midstream and fast heading for a collision with a pier of the bridge downriver. What had started as a stunt to impress his friends had become a dangerous escapade, from which the pilot of a ferryboat rescued him at the last minute. Looking back on his life many years later, Raphael Pumpelly believed that boyhood adventures like this one helped him to develop the physical coordination and ability to think and act quickly that saw him through other risky situations later in life.[1]

"The stork chose well my destination," thought Pumpelly, as he recalled the river, creek, hills, and cliffs of his childhood, for there at the junction of Owego Creek and the Susquehanna River in southern New York State the glaciers of the last ice ages, which had given final shape to the landscape, had created a variety of natural formations to challenge an active boy.[2]

Pumpelly's love of adventure and lifelong fascination with exploration may have been inspired by his family's involvement with surveying. The region was still mostly wilderness when his forebears from Connecticut settled in the southern part of the state near the Pennsylvania border, where the soil and climate were good enough to attract settlers from the east and the pine forests supplied lumber for local needs as well as for export. Pumpelly's grandfather, John Pumpelly, who had run away to sea at age eleven and fought with Rogers's Rangers during the French and

Indian War, had been superintendent of the Salisbury ironworks before moving west in 1802 with his family of six children to a frontier farm near Ithaca.[3]

John's oldest son, James, became a surveyor, moved to Owego, and, seeing the opportunities that existed in land development, persuaded his younger brothers, William, Charles, and Harmon, to join him. The brothers played a major role in turning the village into a prosperous county seat. William and Harmon assisted James in surveying the village, dividing it into 2-acre lots and laying out the western part of the township as 143-acre farms. They also participated in the surveys that determined the New York–Pennsylvania boundary line. Aware of the need for good transportation through the Southern Tier, Harmon helped welcome a state surveying team that passed through Owego in 1825, laying out the route for a road from the Hudson River to Lake Erie. Working for the survey was the young Joseph Henry, later to become one of the country's leading scientists and the first secretary of the Smithsonian Institution. "The inhabitants along the route treat us with the greatest kindness," wrote Henry, adding that Harmon Pumpelly had lent him "his best compass and offered to furnish whatever funds we might want in completing the survey to Bath."[4]

The Pumpelly brothers made profitable investments in land and timber, built sawmills, acted as agents for a nonresident owner of large tracts of land, and became important contributors to the life of the community. James Pumpelly was the first village president, a member of the state assembly, a founder of Owego Academy, and president of the Susquehanna Steam Navigation Company, which built the first steamboat to attempt (unsuccessfully) in 1835 to navigate the Susquehanna down to Wilkes-Barre. Another brother, Charles, a lumberman and merchant, was town supervisor, member of the state constitutional convention of 1821, and member of the state assembly. Harmon Pumpelly, the youngest of the brothers, seems to have had the most acute business sense. Having prospered through his investments in land and timber, he moved to Albany in 1844, where he became involved in banking and insurance, participated in various cultural and civic enterprises, and exerted political influence on state and national levels. He traveled in Europe, had one of the best libraries in Albany, and was noted for his hospitality and "refinement of manner." Harmon took a particular interest in Raphael's career and was able to offer his nephew counsel and to exert influence on his behalf when necessary.[5]

William, Raphael Pumpelly's father, was about sixteen years old when he moved to Owego in 1805 to become a successful merchant and businessman. He owned retail stores, built lumber camps and sawmills, and was president of the First Bank of Owego. His investments in pine forests provded him with a "comfortable fortune," enabling him to retire in 1844 at age fifty-five. William was forty-eight when his youngest son Raphael was born on September 8, 1837. His other children were a daughter by a previous marriage, a son, John, born about 1827, and a daughter, Antoinette, born about 1832. Raphael Pumpelly remembered his father as a tall, dignified, conscientious man, devoted to family, church, and community, and as prosperous but abstemious in his habits and little inclined to indulge in luxuries such as foreign travel or unnecessary comforts. William often complained, especially during the years Raphael and his mother were abroad, that his wife's or youngest son's tastes would put them all in the poorhouse.[6]

Raphael's mother, Mary Welles Pumpelly, was descended from old Connecticut families: Welleses, Talcotts, and Pitkins, some of whom had been governors, legislators, chief justices, and treasurers of the colony. Her grandmother was a first cousin of Jonathan Edwards. Mary set strict New England standards of behavior for her children and enforced attendance at church and prayer meetings, which, like most small boys, "Raffy" hated, although he rather enjoyed Bible stories.

Mary Pumpelly was also a talented artist and poet whose work helped her to keep in touch with the world of culture from which she no doubt felt isolated there in the small upstate New York village. The popular Owego poet, N. P. Willis, who wrote the preface to Mary's volume of *Poems*, praised her ability to keep the "wings of her imagination high in the empyrean," even with a family of children and a life completely domestic. Willis attributed her inspiration to the natural beauty of the Susquehanna region, where there were "stream-banks and backgrounds of mountains . . . and primeval forests to which the world has scarcely a parallel. Does anyone suppose that such habitual surroundings have no effect in formation of the poetic character?" Her poems, however, were long, classical-religious epics: "Belshazzar's Feast," "Herod's Feast," and "Pilate's Wife's Dream," in which nature was not noticeably present. Raphael thought he got his "sense of responsibility and of charity in judgment of others" from his father, but it was to his mother that he attributed his "strong imagination and power of visualizing," qualities he thought essential to a scientist, especially to a geologist when applying observations to the formation of working hypotheses.[7]

Raphael's exploring instincts were aroused early, not only by listening to the talk of his surveyor uncles, but also by watching rafts loaded with lumber float downriver to distant places. Like most potential geologists,

Raffy loved the outdoors. He played by the river, fished, climbed mountains, and learned to ride. His mother was often ill with some unnamed nervous disorder, and although he learned to walk softly in the house, he seems to have been a daredevil in the open, evidently often free of parental supervision. When he was four years old, his older brother threw him in the river to teach him to swim. Unfortunately the experience only gave him a lifelong fear of the water, for which he compensated by showing his bravery in other ways, daring to go where other boys did not: climbing cliffs, searching out places where rattlesnakes were known to live, and riding cakes of ice in the river. With his friends, Raffy played at being pirates, with a lair in an underground cave. The boys pilfered food and supplies, confiscated a boat, and played hooky until their pranks were found out.

In spite of her illness, his mother was a strong presence in his life, tender and loving but also capable of administering a whipping and delivering affecting moral lectures when he was bad. Until he was about eight years old, she taught him at home, insisting on long hours of practice at reading and writing. He then entered Owego Academy, which he remembered chiefly for the frequently administered rod, no doubt for his truancy.[8]

Mary Pumpelly was responsible for first arousing her son's interest in natural history when she read aloud to the children from Hugh Miller's popular book on geology, *The Old Red Sandstone; or, New Walks in an Old Field*.[9] Pumpelly came to believe that hearing this book read to him as a child contributed to his eventual decision to take up a career in geology. His British contemporary, Archibald Geikie, later head of the Geological Survey of Great Britain, also called Miller's *Old Red Sandstone* the chief inspiration for his career.[10]

A Scottish quarryman who was self-taught in geology, Hugh Miller introduced his readers to a subject that had long been an avocation for physicians, country gentlemen, and clergymen. Miller suggested that the study of geology could be a source of intellectual satisfaction and profit for the ordinary working man, the stonemason in particular, who, he believed, was especially well placed to contribute to the science and thereby improve his position in society. *The Old Red Sandstone*, which was based on a series of articles Miller had written for a newspaper, was not only popular, it was recognized by such eminent geologists as Louis Agassiz and Roderick Murchison for its original contributions to geology and paleontology. Agassiz had thought the geological formation popularly known as the Old Red Sandstone did not contain any fish, but Miller had found a primitive species in this formation near his home in

Scotland. In his presidential address to the Geological Society of London in 1842, Murchison praised Miller's new book, which was dedicated to him, for its original contributions as well as for its value to the beginner to whom it was worth "a thousand didactic treatises."[11]

The book's strong appeal for young people is due to the fact that Miller wrote in vivid language about the kind of landscape he was familiar with and about his own introduction to geology. Not interested in a university education, he had apprenticed himself at age seventeen to a stonemason and by the second day of work had become excited by watching a gunpowder blast and discovering what lay under the loosened blocks of stone. A rock surface thus exposed

was ridged and furrowed like a bank of sand that had been left by the tide an hour before . . . the resemblance was no half resemblance—it was the thing itself; and I had observed it a hundred and a hundred times, when sailing my little schooner in the shallows left by the ebb. But what had become of the waves that had thus fretted the solid rock, or of what element had they been composed? I felt as . . . Robinson Crusoe did on his discovering the print of the man's foot on the sand.[12]

Like Miller, Pumpelly had probably seen strange things he did not understand in the rocks of the cliffs around Owego. He might have wondered, as Miller did, what could have caused loose surface stones to become smoothed and rounded "as if they had been tossed about in the sea, or the bed of a river, for hundreds of years." Or he might have separated thin layers of strata and been curious about the fossilized impressions he found there. Miller thought that turning over the leaves of the strata was like turning the leaves of a herbarium, finding "pictorial records of a former creation in every page."[13]

Miller's clear descriptions of the fossils that crowded his shelves at Cromarty inspired the young Pumpelly to search the hills around his home, hoping perhaps to find one of the cone-shaped belemnites Miller described or some of the fish "plated above and below, like the tortoise" or "bristling over with thorns." Members of the New York Natural History Survey had pointed out in their reports of 1842 that the Old Red Sandstone formation of the Catskills was probably the same as that of Britain and that some of it could be found on the tops of hills in New York's third district, in which Owego lay. As a child, Pumpelly could hardly have known of the survey's work, but he searched the hills, and his collections "were soon too numerous in our house for general comfort."[14]

That Pumpelly's mother should have thought *Old Red Sandstone* so suitable for reading to the children is not surprising, for Miller used his geology as a way of proving God's hand in nature, preparing creations in distinct, successive steps that culminated in man. The *American Journal of Science* reviewer commended the book not only for its admirable synopsis of geological formations but also for its "deep and healthful moral feeling, a perfect command of the finest language, and a beautiful union of philosophy and poetry."[15]

Miller painted an attractive picture of life as a geologist: "I have been an explorer of caves and ravines—a loiterer along sea-shores—a climber among rocks—a laborer in quarries. My profession was a wandering one."[16] It sounds like an adventurous life and is in fact the way of life that has always attracted geologists to the profession. But in the United States in the 1840s, most boys would not have thought of wanting to grow up to be a geologist; there were not enough role models, nor was geology a subject much taught in the schools in spite of the fact that since the 1830s geologists had been working on several state geological surveys, including that of New York.

Paths to a Career in Geology

Although a number of American scientists were supporting themselves as geologists in the 1850s and 1860s, they had prepared themselves in a variety of ways; no prescribed educational path to the profession yet existed. Some, like Pumpelly's contemporary and future director of the United States Geological Survey, John Wesley Powell, had a "homemade education" in natural history. At age ten, Powell's interest in science was stimulated by a self-taught natural philosopher, George Crookham of Jackson, Ohio, who had a small museum and a science library, gave free instruction to interested boys, and took them on field trips. Following Crookham's example, Powell became an avid collector and went alone on exploring expeditions through many parts of the Midwest. He took a few college courses and by his early twenties was teaching school and serving as secretary of the Illinois Society of Natural History. After the Civil War, with little other formal preparation, Powell became professor of geology at Illinois Wesleyan University.[17]

Nathaniel Southgate Shaler was the son of a Kentucky physician and amateur mineralogist whose extensive mineral collection helped to encourage the boy's early interest in natural history. Shaler was educated at home in a rather desultory way, and from the age of fifteen until he entered Harvard he was taught the classics and German *Naturphilosophie* by a private tutor. By the time he was ready for college, Shaler was interested enough in science to enroll in Harvard's Lawrence Scientific School, where he studied geology and paleontology with Louis Agassiz.[18]

A few schools had teachers who encouraged a student's interest in geology. As early as the late 1820s, James Dwight Dana was fortunate to have a science teacher at Utica High School, within fifty miles of Owego, who had studied at Amos Eaton's Rensselaer School. Eaton's school, which opened in 1825 at Troy, New York, with the support of wealthy Stephen Van Rensselaer, trained many future science teachers and members of state geological surveys in mineralogy, botany, geology, and chemistry. (It later became Rensselaer Polytechnic Institute.) Eaton emphasized fieldwork and encouraged students to participate in classroom lectures and demonstrations. Field trips along the route of the Erie Canal, then under construction, gave his students valuable opportunities to observe the exposed strata. One of Eaton's students, Fay Edgerton, became Dana's science teacher in Utica. Following Eaton's methods and using the textbooks that Eaton and Ebenezer Emmons had written for the Rensselaer School, Edgerton not only stimulated Dana's interest in science but also provided "his first role model of what it meant to be a scientist." Dana then went on to study with Benjamin Silliman at Yale in 1830.[19]

Pumpelly seems to have had no such encouragement in science early in his life, in or out of school—except from his mother. He did not remember any science being taught at Owego Academy, for example. After the pirate escapades and others apparently even more serious, his parents decided to send him to Mr. Harris's "rather exclusive" boarding school for boys in White Plains where he "came into an atmosphere of well-ordered discipline and study." His only exposure to geology was from a teacher who took the students on outings and pointed out various types of rocks and minerals.[20]

His mother intended that Raffy should go to Yale, following the tradition of her own forebears, so in 1853 she enrolled him in William Russell's New Haven Collegiate and Commercial Institute, a Yale preparatory school attended by students from various parts of the country and Latin America. His report for the term ending March 1854 shows that his studies included mathematics, English grammar and composition, Latin, Greek, and declamation. The only course that would have included natural science was Mental and Moral Science, which used as a text William Paley's *Natural Theology,* the popular work by the liberal English divine who demonstrated God's goodness with examples of design in nature. If the book made any impression on Pumpelly, he did not mention it in his *Reminiscences.*[21]

At midcentury, the curriculum at Yale still emphasized the classics, as did the preparatory course of study at the Russell school. Mathematics at Yale, as well as at most other colleges, was a means for training the mind, not for meeting the needs of America at a time when industry, inventions, engines, and railroads were remaking the country. Pumpelly and some other Russell students witnessed the antagonism of Yale students to mathematics when they attended "The Burial of Euclid," a yearly pageant put on by Yale sophomores. "We're free! Hurrah! We've got him fast; Old Euk is nicely caged at last!" the members of the class chanted, as they paraded in grotesque costumes and carried a symbolic copy of Euclid to the funeral pyre. Pumpelly's contemporary, Josiah Willard Gibbs, who became one of the most distinguished mathematical physicists of his generation, was a Yale sophomore in 1855, probably the only one to whom Euclid meant something more than a subject for ridicule. Years later, Pumpelly's friend and Russell classmate, publisher Henry Holt, would remember the Yale of this period as "probably at its worst in mind, body and estate. In mind it dated back for centuries."[22]

Although science was indeed a small part of the curriculum at Yale, Benjamin Silliman, one of the most influential early science educators in the United States, had been teaching natural history, mineralogy, and chemistry there since 1804. Silliman attracted a number of science students to Yale, including Amos Eaton and James Dwight Dana. Dana himself began teaching at Yale in 1856 as the first Benjamin Silliman Professor of Natural History.[23]

Realizing the need for more advanced and practical science training, Silliman and John Pitkin Norton had organized the Yale School of Applied Chemistry in 1847. Although originally founded to improve scientific agriculture, important additions to the curriculum were geology, paleontology, and mineralogy. Textile manufacturer Abbott Lawrence gave $50,000 the same year to endow Harvard's Lawrence Scientific School, which was to emphasize the teaching of science for industry. In 1852, while Pumpelly was at Russell, Yale Scientific School, as it came to be called, graduated its first six students. The scientific school was a poor relation of Yale, however, looked down upon by regular students. It struggled financially until 1861, when railroad builder Joseph Sheffield provided an endowment of $100,000 and the school was renamed Sheffield Scientific School. Patterned after the advanced technical schools of Europe with their research laboratories and staff of professors well trained in the sciences, it was one of the first schools in the United States to meet the needs of modern technology. In 1860 Clarence King, the first director of the United States Geological Survey, chose to go to Sheffield instead of attending Yale College as his uncle and grandfather had done. In the midsixties Pumpelly had coal samples from China analyzed in Sheffield's laboratory.[24]

In 1854, however, Pumpelly seems to have been unaware of any of the developments in science at Yale. No teacher at Russell encouraged his scientific interests and, in any case, geology was still little more than a hobby for him. At Russell he was more interested in sailing on the sound, finding where the Yale men did their drinking, and indulging in various prep school hi-jinks.

Pumpelly did not question his mother's plan that he should go to Yale until his last year at Russell, when his good friend George Dunham told him that he was thinking of going to school in Germany. Pumpelly, in his impulsive way, decided at once that he wanted to do the same. Picking the right moment, he made the suggestion to his mother and to his surprise she agreed. "We will go, let me arrange it," she told him. His father consented, and on June 4, 1854, Raffy and his mother sailed on the German half-clipper ship *Donau*, bound for Hamburg. Dunham went to Yale.[25]

The Search for an Education

The few American geologists of the 1840s and 1850s who were trained in Europe usually went there for advanced study after having had some college science or work experience at home. Josiah Dwight Whitney, for example, California's first state geologist, graduated from Yale in 1839 after attending Silliman's lectures in chemistry and mineralogy. He then worked on the New Hampshire geological survey before going to Europe to study at the École des Mines in Paris and in Karl Friedrich Rammelsberg's laboratory at the University of Berlin. Chemist and mineralogist George Brush graduated with the first class of the Yale Scientific School in 1852, spent a year at the University of Virginia as assistant in chemistry, and then went to Germany to study with Justus von Liebig at Munich and at the mining school at Freiberg, in Saxony. Eugene W. Hilgard, geologist, soil scientist, and University of California professor, began his studies at Homeopathic Medical College and the Franklin Institute in Philadelphia, with more advanced work later at the University of Heidelberg and at Freiberg.[26]

Pumpelly, however, went to Europe with no college work at all, almost no science preparation, only a vague notion of what he wanted to do, and with no particular school in mind. For more than two years he traveled from place to place with his mother, searching for a good school and acquiring a surprising amount of useful science through self-study, independent fieldwork, brief enrollment in lectures and classes, and the help of professionals whom he met along the way. He and his mother lived for a while in Hanover, then moved on to Paris, Naples, Rome, and Florence, their wanderings somewhat resembling the Continental grand tour once taken by English youths to complete their education.

Pumpelly enjoyed every new experience, as did his mother. For her the European trip was the fulfillment of a dream. Traveling with her son for the purpose of his education enabled her to enjoy herself without guilt, although in her letters home she always expressed concern for the welfare of her husband and of her other children. Her older son, John, seemed to have no feelings of resentment for this special treatment for his younger brother, but he did regret that he had not himself had better scientific training for his engineering job on the Delaware and Lackawanna Railroad. He wrote that he was happy for his brother's opportunity: "I can picture to myself Raffy upon the rigging of the ship, among the sailors, inquiring into everything new, going among the peasants of some little hamlet, looking with eyes wide open upon the many new sights and faces." John was also glad that his mother was able at last to realize so pleasantly her "life long presentiments" for European travel. Owego came to seem limited to Mary Pumpelly, who longed for a more stimulating life. While in Europe, she wrote to her husband that she would like to move "somewhere nearer New York," even wishing that he would "sell and already be moved when we return."[27]

To learn German, Pumpelly and his mother settled in Hanover, where, they had heard, the language was spoken with the best accent. Raffy learned languages by speaking and listening carefully to pick out the familiar words; he had little patience with learning from a grammar. On discovering similarities between English and German words, he became conscious of making an intellectual discovery for himself, learning for the first time to observe, make comparisons, and draw inferences. "The language no longer seemed a dry study but like the rocks . . . it was a store of fossils." It was the beginning of true education for him, the stage where "education becomes no longer the memorization of a mass of more or less related facts and ideas, but it enters into the far wider realm of . . . knowledge."[28]

In an almost completely unstructured way Pumpelly picked up a knowledge of geology that was probably better than anything he could have learned in college at home. Some of it was through classes, but most was through independent study and collecting excursions. At first he took an interest in technical subjects, possibly because of their relation to surveying, which his father and uncles had done, or because of his brother's encouragement to prepare for a career in engineering. He may have begun to realize the handicap he was under for coming to Germany without prior preparation in science when he went to Vienna to inquire about the entrance requirements to the technological institute there and found that he was not well enough prepared to take the entrance examinations. Because the polytechnical school at Hanover had no entrance requirements and he could attend any classes that interested him, he took courses there in chemistry, mineralogy, and industrial processes. At first he took the courses just to improve his understanding of German, but soon the content began to interest him, and before long he found himself taking notes during the lectures and studying the good collection of models used to illustrate the industrial courses. He even bought some chemicals and simple laboratory apparatus and tried doing experiments on his own, but he felt he learned little.[29]

From home, John wrote that he was pleased to hear of Raffy's new interests: "I think Raffy has hit upon the right course of study. It will fit him for engineering of which that connected with public works is only one of many branches." John thought that Raphael ought to "fix upon engineering" and then get practical experience in the field. John regretted that he himself had wasted time pursuing various "business schemes" and had never studied mechanics, chemistry, and mineralogy, which would have prepared him better for a career in engineering.[30]

Pumpelly's desire to learn more about geology began when, in a secondhand bookstore, he found a German translation of an introductory geology textbook by the French geologist, François-Sulpice Beudant. The chapters on the fossils characteristic of the successive geological formations inspired him to go on expeditions to nearby quarries, and from his expanding collections of ammonites, crinoids, and other fossils he taught himself something of the geological history of that part of Germany.[31]

The following year, Pumpelly was able to take advantage of the rich resources France offered for the study of geology when he and his mother moved to Paris with his sister Antoinette and her baby, who had joined them during the summer. He studied French on his own, haunted the shops that sold mineral specimens and fossils, and visited the libraries and the collections of the natural history museum. He also joined a small class in geology that met daily at the Jardin des Plantes, taught by Charles d'Orbigny, "a little gentleman covered with snuff" who was the brother of the well-known paleontologist, Alcide d'Orbigny. Charles d'Orbigny was on the Council of the Geological Society of France and published frequently in its bulletin on the geology and paleontology of the Paris region.[32] His lectures were rather dull, Pumpelly thought: "The course was not printed, but we each had a manuscript copy. It was extremely elementary, even for that time. Monsieur d'Orbigny read from his MS., which treated only of the rocks; then he showed specimens, closed his book and dismissed us."[33]

The occasional field trips on which d'Orbigny took his students were more profitable and a great pleasure. Pumpelly collected fossils, probably from the chalk pits of Montmartre, and returned through the streets of Paris "covered with chalk dust but reckless and happy in the possession of a load of fine fossils." As he may have realized, only about forty years had passed since Georges Cuvier and Alexandre Brongniart had first used fossils from the chalk to identify individual strata within the Tertiary formations, helping to establish paleontology as a major tool for working out the divisions of geologic time.[34]

Several practicing scientists encouraged Pumpelly in his geological studies during these *wanderjahre*. One was Dr. J. F. Noyes, whom he and his mother had met on the ship and with whom he shared his rooms in Hanover. Dr. Noyes was in Hanover to study German before going on for advanced study in ophthalmology in Berlin, but he had an interest in geology and mineralogy as physicians often did, because of the close connections between paleontology and mineralogy on the one hand and between anatomy and medicinals on the other. After moving to Berlin, Dr. Noyes wrote several times to Pumpelly's mother about Raffy's studies, urging that Pumpelly come there, calling Berlin "the Athens of Europe." He recommended Professor Karl Friedrich Rammelsberg of the University of Berlin, an outstanding mineralogist and crystallographer and author of several textbooks and many papers on the chemical analysis of minerals. Both Rammelsberg and a Dr. Sonnenschein gave private instruction in chemistry and mineralogy for geologists at reasonable prices, Noyes wrote.[35]

Pumpelly evidently never went to Berlin. Perhaps he was having too good a time in Hanover, for he had engaged a fencing teacher and riding master and had made friends with some of the German students and joined in their social activities, which included liberal amounts of beer drinking. Possibly his parents thought Berlin would be too expensive, for by the end of the first year Pumpelly and his mother had spent more than the $400 they had each been allotted. Mrs. Pumpelly admitted to her worried husband that Raffy was extravagant but that he had promised to economize.

In the spring of 1855, while still in Hanover, Pumpelly met a scientist who provided further incentive to continue his geological investigations. "Learning that there was a geologist at Hildesheim, I made bold to go there to see his collection of fossils, never having seen one before." This was Friedrich Adolph Roemer, who without formal training had made major contributions to the determination of the Devonian and Carboniferous stratigraphy of the Harz Mountains, following the work of England's Roderick Murchison and Adam Sedgwick.[36] Roemer received the boy kindly and showed him "drawer after drawer full of fine specimens of forms ranging through all the geological periods." When he saw that Pumpelly recognized a few fossils from the rocks of Hanover, Roemer took time to explain, "in a manner adapted to my understanding, the broad outlines of geological history, and, in a general way, the changes from certain older forms to younger ones in successive formations, and their interrelationships."[37] Roemer later took Pumpelly on an extended field trip and gave him letters of introduction to other European scientists. "You will not regret giving him a good chance," Pumpelly's mother wrote, when telling her husband of the impression their son had made on the eminent scientist.[38]

The greatest recognition of Pumpelly's ability, used by his mother to convince her husband that the European trip was worthwhile, was his induction into the Geological Society of France. Charles d'Orbigny was so impressed with the young man's ability that he proposed him for membership, introducing him at the meeting of December 17, 1855.[39] Mrs. Pumpelly had written to her husband, who was worrying about their expenses, of d'Orbigny's plan to make Raffy a member of the society, which, she said, included Élie de Beaumont, Louis Agassiz, Hugh Miller, Baron Alexander von Humboldt, and seven or eight Americans, "but no boys of eighteen. One other American commenced [study with d'Orbigny] when Raffy did but the professor said 'he walks and you fly.'" D'Orbigny, she said, predicted a promising future in geology for their son.[40]

A great part of Pumpelly's self-education came from his exploration of some of the most scenic and geologically interesting parts of Europe. He took one walking trip through the Rhine Valley, alone except for a newly acquired Newfoundland dog, and another in the Swiss Alps with his brother-in-law, Jeremiah Loder. The beauty of the landscape affected him deeply, but he was always intensely interested in what lay under the surface, aware that the Rhine was the romantic setting of the Siegfried legends but also aware of the volcanic rocks he saw for the first time in the cliffs of the Drachenfels. The Alps awed him, but he learned to observe the rock masses and the angles of stratification that were responsible for the surface appearances. In the Alps he saw his first glaciers, traced their courses and tributaries, observed moraines, and examined the surface scratches made by the rocks the glaciers had carried.[41]

By the end of 1855, Pumpelly felt fairly certain that geology was the field for him and he wrote his father asking to be allowed to stay longer in Europe, as he wanted to go to Italy. He told his father that through his own study and the work with d'Orbigny he had acquired a good background in theory but now needed practice. D'Orbigny had recommended a trip to Italy by way of the Auvergne in central France,

which is one of the most celebrated volcanic districts in the world. . . . Then in Italy are Vesuvius and Aetna as active volcanoes. Professor D'Orbigny . . . says it will be of the greatest importance to use in my after life. I beg of you dear Papa, that you will not disappoint me in this wish which is not to make a journey of pleasure but to practice myself in the determination of rocks and in mapping, etc.[42]

That winter he was ill with catarrh, and his mother was worried that it might lead to consumption. A lung specialist was called in who conveniently "ordered me off to Naples, with a big bottle of cod liver oil and quinine." William Pumpelly managed to provide the money and Raffy and his mother arrived at the Bay of Naples on February 23, 1856. There in the background, Vesuvius "rose from the crater of its vastly greater progenitor," the rising vapor creating "a pillar of cloud by day, and a pillar of fire by night." Vesuvius had been almost continually active since the great eruption of 1631 and would remain so until about 1944, providing a field laboratory for geologists from around the world.[43]

For a month Pumpelly explored the volcanic area without textbook or professional guidance, although his mother sometimes accompanied him and, as always, encouraged his interests. He compared the young active crater to the dying solfatara, traced old lava flows, and observed the differences in structure between old and newer ones. He noticed that escaping gases were causing changes in the surface material, in some places creating a coating of iron oxide crystals or other minerals. Thus he began to realize that rocks and minerals were not inert, dead matter but, like language, were in the process of being formed before his eyes. He learned a great deal, although he knew he needed to know more chemistry to understand completely the processes that were going on.[44]

Pumpelly's biggest adventure, which dramatically illustrates his impulsive nature and his urge to explore the unknown, was a trip to Corsica during the summer of 1856. He had seen the island from the ship on the way to Naples and was attracted by its wild and mountainous appearance. Intending to be gone only for a day or two, he left his mother a note and boarded a boat going to Bastia. There, a talk with the British consul about Corsica's history and the wildness of the interior incited him to set out with a guide to explore the island. He wrote of his adventures there in three of the most romantic chapters of his memoirs.[45] He sent letters back to his mother but she evidently never received them, and when he finally returned to meet her in Florence, he found that she had not known where he was or whether he was dead or alive.

This was Pumpelly's first real exploring expedition, a prelude to his later explorations in China. He learned how to travel rough, eating what his guides could provide and sleeping on the ground. He received guidance from Corsica's chief of the Forest Service and other experts, but he also learned valuable lessons from his native guides that would help him in future travels to deal tactfully with people of different cultures.

He became familiar with the main features of the island's geology. He noted the granitic core at the heart of the mountain ranges, so different from the stratified or volcanic formations he had seen before. He studied closely the intrusive dikes that had cut through older rock, some cutting through other dikes. He made sketches, collected specimens, and tried to determine the relative ages of the dikes.

Pumpelly's experience on Corsica gave him an opportunity to make his first original contribution to geology. In one of the valleys below Mount Baglia Orba, which he climbed, he discovered rocks that were polished in a way he had observed at the foot of a glacier in Switzerland. They were also scratched and grooved, with lines running in one direction. Although he did not entirely understand the significance of his find at the time, he returned to the island the following summer after having read Louis Agassiz's *Études sur les Glaciers*[46] and became convinced that he had discovered traces of former glacial action where glaciers had not been known to exist. At Freiberg, Pumpelly was encouraged to write a paper that was published in Germany's principal geological journal, *Neues Jahrbuch*, in 1858.[47] Just before leaving for home in 1859, Pumpelly delivered his paper, in French, to the Geological Society of France, and it was published in the society's bulletin.[48] This paper was an early contribution to the literature on glaciology. Agassiz's glacial theory had been received with considerable skepticism in Europe at the time it was published in 1841, but by the 1850s many American geologists had accepted the theory, at least in part, and were beginning to study and write on the subject. Pumpelly never published directly on glaciers again, although he later became interested in the relation of glaciers to rock disintegration and soil production as well as in the broader question of climatic change at the end of the ice ages. As in later life, he was quick to take up a new subject, but after mastering its main points and making what use of it he needed, he would go on to something else.

Pumpelly's explorations of the Alps, Vesuvius, and Corsica were important learning experiences. They gave him valuable exposure to fieldwork, helped him to develop an investigative technique, and taught him to observe, compare, note differences, and come up with tentative hypotheses. He later thought that he learned more by trying to form his own explanations, whether they were right or wrong, than he would have from formal instruction. Remembering this period in his life, Pumpelly felt that it was this continuing interest in geology that saved him from becoming "a forerunner of the army of boys who have been brought over there to lead desultory lives, losing the traditions of their country, and the chance of fitting themselves for useful careers."[49]

Although Pumpelly had accumulated considerable background in geology in his hit-or-miss fashion, he knew that a more systematic training was expected of a professional geologist in the mid-1850s and that he would have to find a school somewhere in Germany and begin to prepare seriously for a career. His father wanted him to return home, for there were signs of the impending depression of 1857. John had written to his mother in March of his father's loss of income due to a bank failure, and he reported that income from interest payments on mortgages William Pumpelly held was declining because people were unable to make their payments. In November, William wrote to John that expenses in Europe had now amounted to $5,400. "How we have gathered so much together seems remarkable from our crippled means. . . . [Raphael] said if he does not stay 2½ years he will come out at the little end. . . . Write and give me your opinion."[50] Mrs. Pumpelly returned home the following year, but Raffy stayed on. By November 1856 he had enrolled at the academy of mines at Freiberg, Saxony.

The professional geologist who perhaps influenced Pumpelly most of all during these wandering years was the man who was responsible for his decision to attend Freiberg. While in Vienna with his mother, Raphael attended a session of the Gesellschaft Deutscher Naturforscher und Ärzte, the general science society that had been a model for the British Association for the Advancement of Science, and there he struck up a conversation with a "kindly old gentleman" who proved to be Jacob Nöggerath, a distinguished professor of geology at the University of Bonn. Nöggerath was impressed with Pumpelly's sketches of the intrusive rocks of Corsica and recommended that he go to the mining school at Freiberg, where "instruction in Geology, Mineralogy, and Chemistry

Raphael Pumpelly at Freiberg, age nineteen (From *My Reminiscences* by Raphael Pumpelly. Copyright 1918 by Raphael Pumpelly. Henry Holt and Company, Inc., Publisher)

was of the best."[51] It was at this school that he was to learn to apply himself in a more disciplined way to the systematic studies he needed to prepare for a practical profession.

Freiberg Mining Academy: A Practical Education

If Pumpelly had known from the beginning that he wanted to prepare for a career as a mining geologist, he probably could not have found a better school than the Freiberg Mining Academy. It was considered the best practical school of mining in existence at the time and attracted many foreign students. The Freiberg professors taught the sciences as they applied to mining and the treatment of ores, although a few of them were interested in more basic research. Pumpelly thought that if chance had not landed him at Freiberg he might well have gone to a university, Berlin for example, where the emphasis on the pure rather than the applied sciences might have given a different direction to his future career. Or his interests could have led him earlier than they did into the sciences of man. But after two years in which he had enjoyed the freedom to explore various fields, he knew it was time to prepare for a practical profession, as his brother had urged.06.5[52]

Europe, with a longer history in mining than the United States, had many mining schools. Of the four European schools thought to be the best, Freiberg was the only one located at working mines. The École des Mines at Paris, far from any working mines, placed greater emphasis on mathematics and scientific theory than did the Freiberg academy. The same was true of the Russian Royal Academy of Mines in Saint Petersburg, although it had for purposes of instruction a model of a mine furnished with shafts, a ventilating system, and other features of an operating mine. A school of mines at Clausthal was near the mines of the Harz Mountains, but its best professors were transferred to the excellent Bergakademie at Berlin. The Berlin mining school, which was attended by some Americans who were attracted by life in that cosmopolitan city, had no nearby mines to provide hands-on experience for the students. The United States had no mining school at the time Pumpelly entered Freiberg, although mining-related courses were offered at some colleges. The Columbia School of Mines was not established until 1864.[53]

The Freiberg school had been established in 1765 near the mines in order to provide a practical education for those who worked them. Silver, copper, lead, and other ores had been mined at Freiberg since the twelfth century, although by Pumpelly's time they were yielding little profit. In the nineteenth century, Freiberg's fame was due less to the mines than to its school and its professors.[54]

The professor who had contributed most to the school's international reputation was Abraham Gottlob Werner, who had been a student at the school and professor of mining and mineralogy from 1775 until his death in 1817. Werner is perhaps best known for his "Neptunist" theory that the earth's crust had been formed in stages by precipitation from primeval oceans, a theory enthusiastically adopted for a time by his students. Werner had also attempted to bring order to mineralogy, as Carolus

Linnaeus had done for the plant kingdom, by devising a system of classification based on external characteristics of minerals. Most geologists, including Werner's own students, later rejected his Neptunist theory but retained other aspects of his teaching, and Werner remains one of the most important figures in the establishment of geology as a scientific discipline.[55]

Especially relevant to Pumpelly's later work in economic geology were Werner's studies on the origin of ores. Werner's *Neue Theorie von der Entstehung der Gänge,* published in 1791, initiated the scientific study of vein formation.[56] In this work Werner argued that ore beds were formed at the same time as the sedimentary strata in which they occurred but that veins "are really rents which . . . were originally open and were only later filled from above." Werner analyzed the vein material and developed criteria for determining the relative age of veins: "(1) A vein is always newer than another which it traverses; (2) the materials in the center of a vein are newer than those near its walls . . . ; (3) a mineral which occurs above others in a specimen is newer than the others, and one that appears to be grown into others is older than they."[57] The science of ore deposits was further developed and revised by the Freiberg professors with whom Pumpelly worked. Pumpelly and other Americans who studied at Freiberg were to continue the Wernerian tradition in their later research in the United States on ore deposits and vein formation.

One of Freiberg's most famous graduates was Alexander von Humboldt, who studied with Werner and worked as a mining engineer before setting out on the scientific travels to Central and South America that contributed to his reputation as a founder of geography.[58]

In 1819 William Keating, geologist with the 1823 expedition to the Rocky Mountains under Major Stephen H. Long, became the first American to enroll at the Freiberg academy; until 1856, when Pumpelly entered, only twelve Americans had attended the school. After the Civil War, an ever increasing number of Americans went there, and by the end of the 1860s one-fourth to one-half of the total enrollment was American. American graduates of Freiberg went home to take positions on state and national geological surveys, in mining engineering, and on the faculties of Lehigh University, Sheffield Scientific School, Massachusetts Institute of Technology, and other universities and technical colleges, making an important contribution to the professionalization of mining engineering and mining geology in the United States.[59]

American students at Freiberg at the time Pumpelly was there were James D. Hague, James P. Kimball, and the brothers Henry and Louis Janin, all of whom became his good friends for life. Hague had studied at

Harvard's Lawrence Scientific School and the University of Göttingen before coming to Freiberg, Kimball at Yale Scientific School (later Sheffield), the University of Berlin, and Göttingen. The Janin brothers, from New Orleans, had also studied at Yale Scientific.[60]

The Janins' father was a lawyer who had been involved in litigation over claims to the New Almaden quicksilver mines in California and, foreseeing a great expansion in mining operations in the United States, wanted his sons to prepare for a career as mining engineers. He had instructed them to report regularly on the progress of their studies. Their letters from Freiberg provide a better source of information about the school than those of Pumpelly, who hated writing letters and wrote few of them.

The Janins met Pumpelly on one of their first visits to Freiberg, before they had enrolled in any courses. They were having dinner at their hotel, the Black Horse, when Pumpelly and James Hague entered the room and were soon introduced to them. Henry was amused to find his new acquaintances were "real Yankees, with the nasal twang in perfection." He thought Pumpelly and Hague were "very agreeable young men, and seemingly studious, for in their rooms they had collections of minerals and moreover seemed to understand them. Mr. Pumpelly, who had first studied geology in Paris under Prof. D'Orbigny, has the most valuable collection in Freiberg—that is among the students."[61]

Entrance requirements for Americans, who paid to attend Freiberg, were more lenient than for German applicants, who studied at the expense of the state. The German students had to take a four-month preparatory course in the practical aspects of mining before they entered and were required to take an entrance examination. Foreigners did not have to take an examination. "They don't seem to care how much the others learn," Henry Janin wrote his father. He and Louis asked their father's approval to take the practical course before formally entering the school. The course included spending five hours a day in the mines to learn from the miners themselves how everything was done, even as simple a thing as holding a hammer and how to bore holes in the rock. "Those who take the course have to work themselves with hammer and chisels, load the cars with ore, in fact everything the common laborer does," Henry wrote. It appears the Janins did not take the practical course before entering, but did, on that visit, descend on ladders more than a thousand feet into one of the mines with Hague and a guide. "We kept the guide talking the whole four hours we were in the mine," Henry wrote. "He described everything for us, mostly for the benefit of Mr. Hague, but I understood a great deal."[62]

Even though they did not have to take an entrance examination, the American students with some background in the sciences profited more from the school's courses than those without. Hague, Kimball, and the Janins may have had more systematic preparation than Pumpelly, but he probably had a better knowledge of the rudiments of geology and paleontology than they did, thanks to his two years of independent study. Louis Janin felt that he had already had at Yale most of the math needed for Freiberg. Pumpelly, however, was sadly deficient in mathematics. Although he hired a servant to get him out of bed at 4:00 A.M. and a German student to tutor him before breakfast, he never acquired the proficiency he needed for courses such as crystallography, and he felt that he never overcame the disadvantage. In later life he wrote, "when interesting problems suggested themselves in research, requiring mathematics . . . of an advanced order, I would have to either abandon the further research, or call in expert aid." Other American geologists suffered from a similar handicap. Joseph LeConte, for example, who had been trained as a physician, had a minimal background in mathematics, and even Grove Karl Gilbert, who knew enough algebra, geometry, and calculus for most of his research in physical geology, had to ask for help from mathematical physicist Robert Woodward when he needed higher mathematics.[63]

For Pumpelly, the Janins, and others who were not well prepared in the basics of chemistry, mineralogy, or geology, the first year at Freiberg was spent in laying the groundwork for later courses. In their first term, Henry and Louis Janin took chemistry and mineralogy (including crystallography) because, as Henry said, "geology is the most difficult of all the scientific studies, requiring a knowledge of botany, zoology, conchology (to some extent) and of chemistry and mineralogy." The second term they had assaying and laboratory chemistry and attended lectures on geology, paleontology, the mining arts, metallurgy, and drawing. In the second year, there were more advanced courses in analytical chemistry, geology, mineral paragenesis, physics, surveying, the science of ore deposits, and lectures were more directly related to mining. In the last year the practice of working in the mines began. The students paid a guide to conduct them about the mines and introduce them to miners who would teach them methods of blasting, masonry, boring, and timbering. How to work the veins, what shafts to sink, how to predict the richness of a vein were "only to be learned by practice," Henry wrote, because "no rules for this are to be found in books which will apply equally in all cases."[64]

Henry Janin complained that chemical analysis was not as well taught at Freiberg, where it was treated in its relation to metallurgy, as it would have been where it was studied more scientifically. Because they felt that the laboratory facilities for chemistry were inadequate, Pumpelly and the Janins, along with some of the other more proficient chemistry students who were unhappy with the crowded and poorly arranged lab space, pooled their money to set up a private laboratory, purchasing their own supplies and equipment. One of the advanced German students acted as teacher.[65]

Many of the Freiberg professors were leaders and innovators in their fields. From Theodore Richter, successor to Karl Friedrich Plattner, Pumpelly learned blowpipe analysis, a technique long used by chemists and mineralogists for qualitative analysis. Plattner, however, had perfected its use for quantitative analysis, or assaying, giving Freiberg the reputation of being the best place to learn the art. The blowpipe, which had become an indispensable tool for geologists in the field, enabled the user to force a jet of air through a tube into a flame, intensifying the heat and causing a characteristic reaction in the mineral being analyzed.[66]

Pumpelly studied surveying with Julius Weisbach, who had been at the Bergakademie since 1832, teaching mathematics and mechanics as well as surveying and doing experimental work in hydraulics. Weisbach introduced the use of the theodolite and made other contributions to methods for the surveying of mines. Pumpelly found it difficult to keep up with Weisbach's lightning blackboard calculations during lectures, and he envied students who could follow them.[67]

By far the greatest influence on Pumpelly were his courses and fieldwork with mineralogist Johann Friedrich Breithaupt and geologist Carl Bernhard von Cotta. A student of Werner early in the century when Werner was an old man nearing the end of his career, Breithaupt had succeeded to Werner's place at Freiberg as professor of mineralogy in 1826. Although nearing retirement and wearing a "scandalously evident" brown wig, the old man was still an inspiring teacher and he whetted Pumpelly's enthusiasm for the study of crystal forms and systems. Fortunately for Pumpelly, Breithaupt ignored the mathematical aspects of his subject, describing each type of crystal by using wooden models that were visible to the whole class.[68]

Breithaupt's lectures helped Pumpelly understand better the "hidden story," as he called it, behind the surface appearance of minerals. Earlier, when examining the mineral specimens he had collected on Vesuvius, Pumpelly had realized that "their stories were in process of forming before my eyes, though to me still unreadable." Now, from Breithaupt he was learning the alphabet of crystal chemistry that enabled him to follow the sequence of crystallization processes that had formed the various minerals. In his *Die Paragenesis der Mineralien* (1849), Breithaupt had introduced the term "paragenesis" to refer to the relationships that exist between associated minerals, and his work was already stimulating other research that was especially important for understanding the relative age of minerals and the genesis of ore deposits. Through Breithaupt's lectures on paragenesis, Pumpelly began to realize that the kind of mineral arrangements found in different rocks could indicate the geological history of a formation, that the "structure and composition of mountain masses and ore deposits could often be found repeated on a small scale in small specimens."[69]

An experience with Breithaupt shows how seriously Pumpelly was taking his studies and illustrates a lesson he learned about rivalry among scientists. On a field trip he discovered some unusual crystallized specimens of feldspar, which he was convinced demonstrated a new law of twinning.[70] He showed the specimens to Professor Breithaupt, who was skeptical but asked to keep them for a day or two. As Pumpelly angrily reported to his brother-in-law,

The next day he opened the lecture saying that I had brought him some krystals on which *he had that morning discovered a new law of rotation until then unknown,* and then took up an hour explaining the thing exactly as I had described it to him, thus in scientifically villainous manner expropriating my discovery to himself. This vexed me very much, especially as it is considered next to impossible to make any new discovery in this particular and most important field of natural science in Germany.[71]

Many years later, with a long-established reputation as a scientist, Pumpelly was more tolerant about this incident than he had been when he was young and eager to make a name for himself. In his *Reminiscences* he said only that he had shown the crystals to Breithaupt, who had published the results, giving him credit. "I imagine that this was the first time my name had appeared in print, except perhaps when I was lost in Corsica and being looked for through Europe."[72]

One of the school's best-known professors in Pumpelly's day was Carl Bernhard von Cotta, whose many books, both popular and technical, had made him as well known in Germany as Charles Lyell was in England. Cotta had attended Freiberg from 1827 to 1831, had studied with Breithaupt, and now taught geology, paleontology, and the science of ore deposits. The Americans especially liked his course on petrology, because, as Henry Janin said, the study of rocks is "a subject which though less studied in America and England than in Germany is becoming every day more important for the science of geology."[73]

In his textbook, *Die Gesteinslehre,* Cotta classified the various sedimentary, igneous, and metamorphic rocks and discussed their formation from component minerals.[74] Cotta did not accept Charles Lyell's strict uniformitarianism or his belief that there had been no progressive development of species. Although he agreed with Lyell that current geological processes are the key to past activity, he thought past processes must have operated with greater force. And, while accepting the argument that presently existing rock formations were formed from the remnants of former ones, Cotta rejected Lyell's endless cycle of redistributed materials. Cotta's field observations and close studies of rocks had convinced him that recombinations of rock materials result in the production of new kinds of formations that had not existed in the past. Furthermore, Cotta thought that the forms of life in the organic world "have multiplied in an ever ascending ratio (partly in consequence of the change and increase of the conditions of existence from geological causes)."[75]

In other works, Cotta discussed, as he probably did in his classes, the effect of soil and geological structure on human populations and later tried to form a general law of terrestrial development based on Darwinian principles. Pumpelly must have absorbed Cotta's belief in the influence of the geographic environment on human development, for the subject was to continue to fascinate him throughout his life.[76]

While geologists in Germany and elsewhere had a high regard for Cotta, Lyell evidently did not admire him, as Pumpelly found out during a painful meeting with Lyell in 1865. In 1857–58, Cotta revised and wrote a preface for a German translation of the fifth edition of Lyell's *Principles of Geology,* and perhaps Cotta's points of disagreement with Lyell had worked their way into his edition of Lyell's book. Hoping to discuss the results of his recent explorations in China, Pumpelly called on Lyell, bringing a letter of introduction from Cotta. Lyell was curt to the point of rudeness; Cotta's letter was not welcome. "He made a miserable translation of my book," Lyell said, sitting down to his desk in dismissal. Pumpelly felt the rebuff deeply. It was a humiliating experience that made it impossible for him ever again to present a letter of introduction to anyone. In later life Pumpelly always made an effort to "take helpful interest in the many who have come to me for advice, and especially in the young."[77]

Cotta's *Die Lehre von den Erzlagerstätten,* translated into English in 1870, was an important influence on American mining geologists for it established the study of ore deposits as a specialized field of science within mining geology.[78] Cotta's course on ore deposits, which he had been teaching at Freiberg since 1851, was probably the first anywhere.

Pumpelly found the study fascinating. It was a "new department of science opening a wide range of problems to be solved." Building on Werner's work, but departing from the Neptunistic explanation that veins were filled from above by deposition from surface waters, Cotta adopted Élie de Beaumont's magmatic infiltration theory, which proposed that in most cases veins were filled by ascending hot solutions that originated from within the earth. As Mott T. Greene has pointed out, it was Werner's own students and French geologists, rather than the Scottish Vulcanists, who refuted Werner's strict Neptunism, although they retained his methodology. Cotta concluded that no one theory was applicable to all deposits, however. In later years, Pumpelly and other American geologists would continue to investigate and debate the role of meteoric (atmospheric) waters versus magmatic solutions in ore genesis.[79]

Cotta's weakest subject seems to have been paleontology. Apart from early work on fossil plants, Cotta was not a paleontologist, but he was responsible for teaching the course. Henry Janin regretted that there was no professor of paleontology, "as of course there is no possibility of geology without paleontology. As a substitute Professor Cotta . . . reads aloud from Quenstedt's work . . . and at the same time explains specimens from the collection."[80] The school's collection was a good one and Pumpelly learned enough to be able to identify strata from fossil content. However, much of his later work in stratigraphy involved identification of rocks through the use of the petrographic microscope and when he needed fossils identified he usually sent them to an expert paleontologist.

Even though Freiberg enjoyed a reputation as the best place to study the practical aspects of mining engineering, its professors were conducting a considerable amount of advanced research by the time Pumpelly was there, especially in geology, geophysics, and mineralogy. While their research was of importance to the mining industry, related as it was to a better understanding of ore deposits and to improvements in mining methods, it also contributed to the development of new geological disciplines. For example, the magnetic, electrical, and geothermal investigations of Ferdinand Reich, who taught physics at Freiberg from 1826 to 1865, were early contributions to the field of geophysics. The research of Breithaupt and Cotta in mineralogy, petrology, and the science of ore deposits helped lay the groundwork for modern geochemistry.[81]

The professors also encouraged their students to do research. Pumpelly had developed a tentative hypothesis to explain the traces of glacial activity he had found on Corsica, and Reich and Cotta suggested to him during his last year at Freiberg that he continue his work on the subject as a doctoral dissertation for the University of Heidelberg. Pumpelly thought that perhaps the Corsican glaciers had been formed during a period of increased precipitation when the climate was much colder than today, the source of the moisture being an inland sea where the Sahara Desert now lies. A warming climate had dried up the sea, he thought, and brought about the recession of the glaciers. He tried to join a French expedition to the Sahara in order to have a chance to test his hypothesis, but his efforts were unsuccessful, and he was unwilling to proceed without evidence confirming the existence of the sea. When he heard that later discoveries proved there could not have been a Saharan sea, he was glad he had not worked further on the project.[82]

The students who belonged to the private chemistry laboratory held a colloquium on Sunday evenings, when they met to drink tea and hear a paper read by various members. "The articles give rise to discussions which in fact constitute the most pleasant feature of the meetings, inasmuch as we thus see if what we have learnt has been well learnt," Louis Janin reported. Pumpelly read his paper on the glaciers of Corsica while other members of the group presented theirs on such subjects as the "State of the Science of Geology since the Time of Werner," "The Origin of the North American Indian," "The Distribution of Plants over the Face of the Earth," and "Origin and Formation of Veins."[83]

Pumpelly and the Janins profited from the practical experience of working in the mines and smelting works, but the lectures dealing with the details of mine construction were often very tiresome. The Americans wanted to learn the practical aspects of mining that would help them when they returned home to work, but Pumpelly thought that the attention to detail in the two-year series of lectures on mining methods swamped whatever may have been of use regarding the essentials of mine exploitation. Henry Janin reported that "in Bergbau-Kunst . . . we have the prosiest, most tiresome slow professor imaginable. He discusses every question and every instrument, all the shovels, pickaxes, spades, hooks, etc. that have been in use in Germany since the mines were first opened by the Romans. . . . In one lecture I made drawings of about fifteen species of Schaufel, viewed, each one in all possible perspectives."[84]

Field trips with Cotta, sometimes lasting a week or longer, were an important aspect of Pumpelly's education. Occasionally other professors joined the outings, which then became a "jovial picnic." Cotta gave his students instruction in field geology, took them to mines and smelting works in other cities, and used students as assistants in his research. On one excursion, Pumpelly and a friend went with Cotta to Thuringia, which Cotta had mapped ten years earlier. Cotta's geological survey maps were regarded as the best in Europe at the time, so the students must have gained valuable experience in map making.[85]

Some of the professors also arranged summer trips into neighboring regions to introduce their students to methods other than those at Freiberg. Louis and Henry Janin went on an extended trip with Cotta during the summer of 1860 to see the mines and smelting works at Chemnitz, then went on into Hungary. "All the professors have been vying with each other in showing us attention. I have never learned so much in so short a time," Louis wrote his father. "They are especially nice to us when they found we were Americans." During his last summer at Freiberg, Pumpelly and a fellow student traveled on their own into Hungary, combining visits to mines, to sooth their consciences, with less edifying adventures.[86]

Because Freiberg was isolated from the large cities with their cultural attractions, some students found it a dull place, but Pumpelly enjoyed it and seemed to have an active social life. His outgoing nature made him popular with both the Americans and the German students, and he was invited to many balls and parties, some of which included both townspeople and faculty and students of the mining school, while others included only the nobility of Freiberg and the surrounding region. Louis Janin, on the other hand, although conceding that its isolation made it a good place for study, wanted to finish the courses he needed and then "leave forever this horrid place." Henry seemed to share his brother's feelings, occasionally expressing his desire to give up the study of mining altogether and go to Berlin to study music and literature.[87]

Pumpelly especially appreciated the way in which the Freiberg professors mingled with the students, some of whom often joined students outside of classes to drink beer, smoke, talk, and tell stories. Pumpelly later claimed that this informal contact with the professors was an important element in his education, and he deplored the lack of it in American universities. The only exception he knew of was Nathaniel Shaler, whose popular geology courses at Harvard attracted large numbers of students.[88]

Like most college students at home or abroad, Pumpelly indulged in his share of student pranks. He was impulsive, reckless, extravagant, and often thoughtless but always good-hearted, fair, and kind to others from all levels of society, the very model of a democratic American young man. On his second summer in Corsica he acquired a tame mountain goat that had been raised as a pet, and he planned to parade it on a leash before his friends at school. Checking in at the best Vienna hotel, he tied the mouflon to a lamp post in the courtyard, but the animal broke loose and bounded into the hotel, butting his image in mirrors and generally wreaking havoc. The incident made a good story, to be repeated often for the rest of his life.[89]

In the fall of 1859, Pumpelly returned to the United States, realizing that after years of support from his parents he must begin working at his profession. Although he felt there was "a very widely neglected gap in the way of broader culture" and, like Henry Janin, would have liked to spend more years at a university studying history and archaeology, he had acquired the professional training that qualified him for a career as a mining geologist. The knowledge and experience he had gained through his education, both formal and informal, were to shape his future career and the way he was to work. His Freiberg professors had taught him the value of systematic and disciplined work, even though he did not entirely take to systematic methods himself. They had also given him an enthusiasm for research that led him beyond mining questions to problems in other fields of geology. From his travels with his mother and his independent investigations he had gained a confidence that through his own efforts he could learn a great deal about the world and at the same time indulge his taste for exploration and adventure. America at midcentury was in need of young men like him.

# Geology in America, 1835–1860

In 1860, when Pumpelly returned home, geology was already a well-established profession in the United States, offering a variety of opportunities for employment, most of them directly related to the country's economic expansion. Mining fever was sweeping the country and the search for scientifically trained mining personnel gave geologists a better chance than most other scientists to find work in private enterprise. The federal government had been sending out exploring expeditions, on which geologists were included, to survey for mineral resources and new railroad routes to the Pacific. Also, since the 1830s state geological surveys had been proliferating, providing opportunities for young men just out of school to acquire valuable field experience. Pumpelly and his Freiberg friends would not have trouble finding jobs.[1]

A number of talented men had contributed to this growth of geology in the United States, some of whom became involved with Pumpelly's subsequent career. Josiah Dwight Whitney, for example, who became Pumpelly's mentor, had already achieved a strong reputation as an expert on mineral resources by the time he was named head of California's first geological survey in 1860. William Phipps Blake, who was to go with Pumpelly to Japan, and John Strong Newberry, later to analyze fossils Pumpelly collected in China, were among the geologists of the Pacific Railroad surveys who had accompanied army engineers through the little-known western territories, giving geological exploration a reputation for combining scientific work with romantic adventure. The experience of James Hall, Jr., and the other geologists of New York's natural history survey shows that state governments, which expected practical results from their geologists, also provided the patronage that had stimulated the advance of geology as a science.

In these early days most geologists were generalists. They were interested in all facets of the science and did various kinds of work involving both practice and theory; it was not yet the day of the specialist. They might attend to the practical problems of determining sources of ore and evaluating its quality, but their search for a more scientific approach to mining was intimately connected to advances in the study of the geological formations in which ores were found. Investigation of economic resources often led, therefore, to more general studies in stratigraphy and structural geology.

Many of the problems that geologists of Pumpelly's generation would take up in the postwar years were already being investigated by professionals before the Civil War. As the work of the New York survey indicates, one of the principal interests of American geologists was stratigraphy: determining the extent and relative age of strata and making correlations with formations in other parts of the country and the world. Americans also debated how mountains were formed, whether rivers shaped their own courses, where former seas and continents had been, whether geological processes had acted uniformly or "catastrophically," and whether Agassiz's glacial theory was valid.

These were problems they shared with English and European geologists, for Americans were by no means provincial in these years. They kept pace with British and Continental developments through correspondence, exchange of journals, and travel. At the same time, foreign geologists were deeply interested in the geology of the North American continent and in what the Americans were finding out about it. Louis Agassiz and Charles Lyell, both of whom came to the United States in the 1840s to deliver lectures at Boston's Lowell Institute, met with their American counterparts and traveled with them to investigate geologically interesting parts of this country. Agassiz stayed on, becoming an influential professor at Harvard University's Lawrence Scientific School.

The proliferation of state geological surveys played an important part in professionalizing geology at an earlier date than most of the other sciences. The growth of state surveys that began in the 1830s and the resulting demand for trained geologists stimulated the addition of geology courses at many colleges and technical schools, the writing of textbooks, the organization of a professional society, and an increase in the number of papers on geological subjects published in science journals. By the end of the Civil War, professional geologists, Pumpelly among them, were ready to contribute to the country's tremendous economic growth.

Geologists as Mining Experts

The American economy had already been rapidly expanding in the 1840s and 1850s; the growth rate for the decade 1844–54 was higher than during almost any other period of the nineteenth century. The production of bituminous coal grew from about one million tons in 1835 to more than nine million by 1860 and anthracite from less than a million to over ten million. The discovery of copper in Michigan's Upper Peninsula in the 1840s and of gold in California in 1848 stimulated the development of mining elsewhere. The acquisition of new lands, the building of railroads, and increased manufacturing all meant an increased demand for minerals and a recognition that scientific knowledge must be put to use in the service of industry.[2]

Mining geology was an important aspect of state geological surveys, especially in states having large deposits of minerals; state geologists frequently examined mines and mineral deposits in order to provide knowledge about the occurrence of ores that would be of use to all mine owners. In Pennsylvania, for example, where coal deposits were vital to the state's economy, geologists spent a large proportion of their time on mining subjects. During the 1850s, Henry Darwin Rogers, head of the Pennsylvania geological survey and known to historians primarily for his studies of the structure of the Appalachians, published several papers on the state's bituminous and anthracite coalfields. His final report for the survey, *The Geology of Pennsylvania,* published in 1858, included a lengthy summary of the extent and geological structure of the coalfields that was very useful to the coal mining industry.[3]

The federal government also sponsored examinations of mineral lands by prominent geologists, among them a survey of parts of Iowa, Wisconsin, and Minnesota by David Dale Owen and one of the Lake Superior iron and copper region by Josiah Dwight Whitney and John W. Foster. The two-volume report by Foster and Whitney on the Lake Superior district, for example, provided valuable, practical information on the mines, although it also included much detail about climate and general geology.[4] It proved very useful to Pumpelly when he went to work in the same region in the late 1860s. The report contained tables of weather data and a comparison of mean temperatures with those of corresponding latitudes in Europe along isothermal lines. Three chapters provided descriptions of the extent, age, lithological character, and mineral associations of the igneous and sedimentary rock systems, including speculation about the forces that could have been responsible for their origin. In addition, James Hall of New York contributed a chapter on the paleontology of the district, and Edouard Desor, an associate of Louis Agassiz, discussed glacial drift.

The examination of nineteen mines provided practical information for the mining industry, contributing to a better general knowledge of the region than had previously been available. The observations, presented in tabular form, included each mine's location, the characteristics of the lode, the nature of the surrounding rock (the gangue), the depth of the shafts and length of the tunnels, the drainage, the percentage of copper, the number of men employed, and the number of shares of stock issued.[5]

The Foster-Whitney report made Whitney well known as a mining expert and enabled him to make a comfortable living as a consultant. In his consulting work he began to collect material for a survey of the mining industry of the United States and his *The Metallic Wealth of the United States* remained for several years the best source for statistics on gold, silver, copper, tin, mercury, iron, and other ore deposits and mines throughout the world. After becoming head of the Geological Survey of California in 1860, Whitney's activities ranged widely, from studies of the geology of gold formations to writings on climatic change in the glacial period.[6]

Pumpelly and his friends at Freiberg were well aware of the boom in mining in the United States, having kept up with developments in the industry by reading *Mining Magazine,* which the Janins' father may have been sending. The journal, edited by mineralogist and geologist William P. Blake, included statistics, news of the industry, and reports on specific mines. Articles in *Mining Magazine* indicate that during the 1850s several geologists were acting as consultants to mining proprietors. The 1854 volume, for example, contains reports by the former state geologist of Maine and New Hampshire, Charles T. Jackson, on "Moore's Gold Mines, Dahlonega, Georgia" and on the coal lands of five plantations along Deep River in North Carolina. William Barton Rogers, state geologist of Virginia, reported on "The Property of the Pridevale Iron Co." The magazine also included segments relevant to mining from the annual reports of state geological surveys. Other geologists who wrote for the journal were Whitney, Newberry, and J. Peter Lesley of the Pennsylvania geological survey. Under the direction of Blake, *Mining Magazine* promised to be an important and influential journal but unfortunately the approach of war caused its suspension in 1860 and it was never reinstated.[7]

Louis and Henry Janin were especially interested in Blake's article on silver mining in Arizona.[8] The region, which had recently become part of the United States through the Gadsden Purchase, was thought to be as rich in silver as Mexico, and the Janins' father was suggesting that they go there to work. His sons knew, however, that it would be difficult to bring modern methods to such a remote region. Blake's article, which outlined many of the difficulties, convinced them that although they knew something of silver mining at Freiberg, mining in Arizona under drastically different conditions would be another matter. Louis wanted his father to send him more information about transportation and the water and fuel supply, and he asked whether any American company had set up works and if the Indians were troublesome. He understood from what he had read that the "richness of the veins is counterbalanced . . . by the difficulty of carriage, the want of fuel and the bad supply of water." His brother Henry thought he would like to work in Arizona rather than in the East but would prefer to wait until things were more settled there. He knew that Arizona silver would "not attract adventurers as gold does because a single person can't work the mines."[9]

The American students who attended Freiberg played an important part in the growth of the mining industry in the United States. Many of them found places not only in mining-related work but also on state and federal geological surveys and on the faculty of colleges and technical schools. Of Pumpelly's friends, James D. Hague first went to work for a company that mined guano on remote Baker and Jarvis islands in the South Pacific. During the 1860s he was a member of Clarence King's Geological Exploration of the Fortieth Parallel, for which he produced a major report on the mining industry. Hague later had a highly successful career as mining consultant and as president of the prosperous North Star Mining Company in Grass Valley, California. James P. Kimball opened a mining bureau in New York City after leaving Freiberg and later worked on the Wisconsin and Illinois state geological surveys and taught at Lehigh University. In 1885 he became director of the U.S. Mint.[10]

Louis Janin's career was more exclusively in mining engineering and metallurgy than geology. He briefly superintended the Enriquita quicksilver mine in California and then worked for a company with mines on the Comstock Lode, where he developed improved methods for the reduction of silver. He also served as a mining engineer in Japan and Mexico and in later years was in great demand as an expert in mining litigation cases. Henry Janin worked for a time with Louis in a company they formed to recover silver from tailings in Nevada and as an independent mining consultant. His reputation as a highly regarded mining expert was damaged, however, by what came to be known as the "Great Diamond Hoax," when he gave an opinion on what he honestly thought was a rich diamond mine but which was discovered by Clarence King to be a fraud.[11]

Geologists and the Western Exploring Expeditions

New opportunities for professional geologists opened up in the 1850s when several civilian scientists accompanied federally sponsored exploring and mapping expeditions of the Army Corps of Topographical Engineers into the far West in a search for the best route for a transcontinental railroad. Although earlier expeditions had sometimes included civilian naturalists, the Pacific Railroad surveys of 1853–55 were the first major surveys of the West that specifically provided for the inclusion of geologists, the intention being that geologists, botanists, and zoologists could help to resolve the conflict between competing regions by providing solid data on the resources along the various routes under consideration. These and other surveys of the 1850s were the precursors to the federal surveys of the West during the next two decades that were more detailed and devoted more strictly to geology.[12]

The Pacific Railroad surveys must have seemed an exciting prospect for an adventurous young man like Pumpelly. He probably saw the survey reports, as the Janin brothers did, in the library at Freiberg, where, thanks to the Smithsonian's exchange program, eight volumes were received in 1858. Louis and Henry Janin wrote their father that they had been reading the volumes, which were beautifully illustrated with maps and plates of fossils, plants, and animals. Louis admired the accounts of Indian tribes and the descriptions of the natural history of the lands over which the exploring parties passed. Henry was fascinated by the reports and told his father he had heard that another such expedition might be sent out soon and hoped he would be able to get on one for five or six months before going to work at a mine.[13]

As it turned out, neither the Janins nor Pumpelly joined any of the western federal surveys, but they were right to think that it would be a good opportunity. Two of the six geologists who explored the West with the railroad surveys were young men at the start of their careers whose reputations were established by the experience, just as Pumpelly's would be by his explorations in China. Shortly after graduating with the first class of Yale Scientific School in 1852, William P. Blake accompanied the parties that explored the California coast and the Southwest, and his reports and articles resulting from the Pacific Railroad survey work made him well known to the geological community. In 1860 he was chosen, along with Pumpelly, to be a consultant on mining and geology for the Japanese government. John S. Newberry had a medical degree and had done paleontological work with James Hall of the New York State Natural History Survey when, on Hall's recommendation, he was appointed geologist with Lt. R. S. Williamson's survey of the northern Pacific coast. Newberry went on to a distinguished career as a professor of geology at the Columbia School of Mines and head of the Ohio geological survey.[14]

Even though the geologists who accompanied the Pacific Railroad surveys could do little more than a fast reconnaissance, their work contributed significantly to the store of geological knowledge about the West. Given the vastness of the region and the short time they had to explore it, the geologists were unable to do much more than describe features of geological interest and point out problems for further study. The next decades would see the more detailed investigations by geological teams that knew in advance the broad outlines of western geology and had more time to study it. These first geologists to see the West nevertheless made important contributions to paleontology, stratigraphy, and physical geography, to the growth of eastern institutional collections, and to the organization of geological data by the preparation of geological maps.

Eastern scientists saw the surveys as an excellent opportunity to build up their collections and, by recommending civilian personnel for the coveted scientific appointments, had an important part in shaping the scientific aims of the expeditions.[15] James Hall of New York, who recommended Newberry, had one of the best fossil collections in the country and was ever eager to add to it. Louis Agassiz, whose personal collection would become the basis for the Museum of Comparative Zoology at Harvard, saw his young French protégé, Jules Marcou, appointed geologist to the thirty-fifth parallel survey led by Lt. Amiel W. Whipple.

Joseph Henry of the Smithsonian and his young assistant secretary, Spencer F. Baird, played the most important part of all eastern scientists in promoting the scientific work of the Pacific Railroad surveys by advising on the appointment of the scientists and providing instructions to the exploring parties on what specimens were needed and how to obtain them. Both Henry and Baird were aware of the importance of western discoveries to the natural sciences and wanted to add to the Smithsonian's collections. By the end of the decade, Henry was able to say that the Smithsonian's collection of North American natural history specimens "far excels any other collection ever made." Baird was instrumental in placing Blake with Lt. R. S. Williamson's party.[16]

The routes taken by the various parties of the army engineers and their civilian scientists gave the geologists a chance to see collectively a wide spectrum of western geology. Their reports show that they looked for resources of economic value and also tried to identify geological formations and to place them in the expanding geological time scale. They were fascinated by the unfamiliar western land forms—the Great Basin, the rugged mountain ranges, the strange formations of the desert and plateau regions—and tried to find explanations of how wind, water, volcanoes, and earthquakes had shaped the land. Dr. James Schiel, surgeon and geologist with Lt. E. H. Beckwith's forty-first parallel expedition, was amazed to find that "in the character of the country between the Rocky Mountains and the Sierra Nevada, that whole formations disappear, as it were, before our eyes. The wearing and washing away of mountains takes place here on an immense scale. . . . Nature here seems only to demolish, without showing any compensating creative activity."[17]

Newberry, who accompanied parties northward from San Francisco to Oregon, observed traces of glacial action in the Cascades and suggested that the great volcanic peaks of the Cascade Range mark a line of fracture in the earth's surface, affording a clue to the way the range had been formed.[18]

One of the longest and most detailed of all the geological reports was that of Blake, whose reconnaissance work in California, from San Francisco to the southern deserts, covered much of the route of the later Southern Pacific Railroad and provided one of the earliest descriptions of the varied geology of the state. Blake identified some of the coastal strata as Tertiary and described the complex metamorphic and eruptive rocks of the San Francisco region, now known as the Franciscan formation. He also devoted a long chapter to the Colorado Desert of southern California that included a discussion of mineral deposits, wells, agricultural capabilities, and an analysis of sand hill movement and its possible effect on railroad lines. Blake's experiences in California supplied him with material for several articles in scientific journals and no doubt had much to do with his 1864 appointment as professor at the College of California (later the University of California at Berkeley).[19]

One of the aims of some of the railroad survey geologists was to prepare a geological map of the United States west of the Mississippi River. A map is one of the principal ways geologists organize and present their data, but making a large-scale map at that early date was almost impossible to do well considering the great area covered and the preliminary nature of their reconnaissance. Pumpelly was to encounter the same difficulty in attempting a first geological map of China. Jules Marcou used the data he gathered on the thirty-fifth parallel survey to complete a geological map of the United States, published after his return to France, that was severely criticized by Blake, James Hall, and James Dwight Dana for its excessive generalizations and extrapolations. The controversy that ensued over Marcou's map, stemming partly from the fact that Hall and Blake were working on their own maps and partly that Marcou's was first published in Europe, was an indication not only of the jealous nationalism with which Americans were defending their work but also of the difficulty involved in attempting an accurate geological map with insufficient data.[20]

The Pacific Railroad surveys and other exploring expeditions of the forties and fifties were a sign of increasing government involvement in science. A. Hunter Dupree believes that the results of such expeditions made the government aware that its participation in large-scale scientific exploration was indispensable and largely determined which sciences would be supported. These "exploring sciences" included astronomy, hydrography, terrestrial magnetism, meteorology, topographical mapping, botany, zoology, and anthropology as well as geology.[21]

The work of these surveys also indicates the increasing importance of "Humboldtian science" to the growth of science in the United States. William H. Goetzmann thinks that the western explorations of the 1850s such as the Pacific Railroad surveys are in the tradition of scientific exploration conducted by the great geographer and explorer Alexander von Humboldt, who emphasized the same "exploring sciences" mentioned by Dupree. By gathering all kinds of data about a region—geological, geophysical, botanical, and zoological—and showing their interrelatedness, Humboldt presented a cosmic picture of nature, which Goetzmann thinks is romantic in outlook.[22]

Susan Faye Cannon agrees that the kind of science Humboldt stood for is much more characteristic of American science at midcentury than a vague fact-gathering Baconianism, but she criticizes Goetzmann's interpretation of Humboldtian science for emphasizing its romanticism. According to Cannon, Humboldtian science was the rigorous study of nature that involved accurate measurements with the best instruments possible, a search for new and more sophisticated laws of nature, a new set of conceptual tools such as graphs and maps of isothermal lines, and application of these new methods not to isolated laboratory situations but to nature itself where complex interrelationships exist.[23]

The concept of Humboldtian science as holistic and romantic may apply to earlier expeditions of the army engineers, and to the Pacific Railroad reports taken as a whole, because they include all aspects of nature—the land itself with all its geomorphic features, the plants and animals, and even the Indians, who were seen as having adapted their way of life to natural conditions. By the end of the 1850s, however, the work of these earlier expeditions, plus that of the state geological and natural history surveys, had contributed so much new knowledge that specialization was now necessary. The employment of geologists, paleontologists, zoologists, and botanists on the Pacific Railroad surveys, equipped with directions and instruments supplied by the nation's most eminent scientists, helped to bring an end to the cosmic approach; each scientist was interested in expanding knowledge about his own subject. What Goetzmann says about the work later in the decade of Ferdinand V. Hayden and Fielding B. Meek could be applied to the geologists like Blake who accompanied the Pacific Railroad surveys: "They frankly concentrated on observation for its own sake, and for the achievement of a limited kind of truth."[24]

Humboldt's explorations must have been an inspiration to Pumpelly and his friends at Freiberg because Humboldt was their school's most famous graduate. Pumpelly's new dedication to science, together with his love of adventure and his romantic impulse to explore unknown places, would have made scientific expeditions such as the Pacific Railroad surveys very attractive to him as a possible source of employment. By 1859, when he returned to the United States, these surveys had come to an end, but his later travels—in China in the sixties, for example—gave him a reputation as a scientific explorer for which his Freiberg classmates dubbed him "the American Humboldt."[25]

State Geologists: The New York Natural History Survey

In the pre–Civil War years, the growth of geology as a profession owed much to the establishment of state geological and natural history surveys, which provided many job opportunities for geologists, probably more than mining and exploration put together. State surveys continued to flourish after the war, even though an increasing number of geologists were working on the federally sponsored geological surveys of the western territories or, after 1879, for the United States Geological Survey.

During the last half of the century, several American students who had attended Freiberg, Pumpelly included, occupied professional positions on various state surveys.

State surveys had their beginning in the 1820s when college science professors in North and South Carolina were asked to investigate their states' mineral resources. The first comprehensive survey was that of Massachusetts, established in 1830 by Edward Hitchcock and continued with state support until 1833, culminating with the publication of a 700-page final report. Others followed and soon almost every state had either completed or was in the process of conducting a geological survey. By 1860, twenty-eight states had passed bills establishing geological and natural history surveys.[26]

During the Jacksonian era the federal government had not been involved in the geological surveying of the states. Thus, state geologists bore the burden of discovering and making available to the people information about mineral resources, road, canal, and railroad routes, and other data needed for the growth of transportation, industry, and agriculture. The quality of work varied from state to state and many surveys were never completed or the reports never finished because the money ran out. Nevertheless, state geologists obtained a great deal of basic information about the geology and economic resources of their states and made important scientific contributions as well. They improved geological education by providing on-the-job training for survey assistants and by supplying specimens for state museums and colleges, and they often doubled as professors of geology. Among other things, their work helped to fill in the geological time scale, draw attention to the glacial theory, and advance the science of paleontology. Publication of the results of state work in official reports and in the scientific journals of the day greatly improved communication among scientists, and a meeting of state geologists called to share common problems resulted in the formation of the first professional scientific society in the country, the short-lived Association of American Geologists.

The problems that antebellum geologists faced are evident in the work of the New York Natural History Survey. Leonard G. Wilson has suggested that the publication of the four volumes of *Geology of New York* "may well be taken to mark the coming of age of geology" in America. Although several other states established geological surveys during the 1830s, New York's had the largest staff of well-trained professionals and its final reports were the most elaborate—admired and used in later years as a model for other states.[27]

Contributing to the success of the New York survey was the strong support of the state's governor and legislature. Many legislatures resented the time "wasted" on what they considered to be nonuseful activities, such as paleontology, but the legislature and Governor William Marcy had considerable sympathy for the scientific as well as the economic aims of New York's survey. Several legislators in Albany were members of scientific societies, and Marcy read Francis Bacon's *Advancement of Learning* and Charles Lyell's *Principles of Geology* to prepare himself for the task of selecting the best men from the many who applied for positions.[28]

Instead of appointing an overall director, Marcy selected four well-qualified geologists, professionals by the standards of their day, to head each of four geological districts. Most of these men had had some formal scientific training and had taught geology, mineralogy, or natural history, and some had already worked on other state surveys. All had contributed to their field through research and publication. Each was to receive a yearly salary of $1,500. Completing the natural history staff were a botanist, a zoologist, and a mineralogist.

The training and previous experience of the geologists appointed to the New York survey further illustrate the varied paths that led to geology as a career in the prewar years. William W. Mather, head of the first district, which included the lower part of the state and Long Island, had studied the applied physical sciences at the U.S. Military Academy and taught mineralogy, chemistry, and geology there. He had been a member of a federal topographic survey team in the Green Bay, Wisconsin, area before joining the New York survey in 1836. Ebenezer Emmons of the second district, covering the Hudson, Adirondack, and Saint Lawrence regions, was a graduate of Williams College in western Massachusetts and the Berkshire Medical College. Like many early geologists, Emmons combined the practice of medicine with an interest in geology. At Williams he had assisted on local surveys and then studied geology with Amos Eaton at the Rensselaer School. He taught mineralogy and chemistry and published a *Manual of Mineralogy and Geology* in 1826. In 1828 he became professor of natural history at Williams.[29]

Heading the third district west of the Hudson was Lardner Vanuxem, a graduate of the École des Mines in Paris where he had studied with France's distinguished paleontologist and stratigrapher Alexandre Brongniart. Vanuxem had taught geology, mineralogy, and chemistry at South Carolina College in Columbia, conducted a geological survey for South Carolina, and acquired considerable familiarity with the geology of other eastern states.[30]

Timothy Conrad, head of the fourth district during the first year, was primarily self-taught. He apparently had no formal education beyond high school but acquired a thorough knowledge of paleontology and natural history through his father, a professor of botany at the University of Pennsylvania, and as a member of the Academy of Natural Sciences of Philadelphia. Before joining the New York survey, he had published several papers on paleontology in the *American Journal of Science* and the *Journal of the Academy of Natural Sciences of Philadelphia*.[31] After the first year Conrad was appointed paleontologist for the whole state.

James Hall, who took over the fourth district from Conrad and eventually all of the paleontology, got his start in science as a laboratory assistant for the Boston Society of Natural History. At the age of nineteen, he heard about Amos Eaton's progressive way of teaching science by encouraging student participation, and he walked 220 miles to Troy, near Albany, to enter the Rensselaer School. He studied there with Eaton and Ebenezer Emmons, graduating with the master of arts degree in 1833.[32]

Paleontology soon became as important to the New York survey's work as it was to geology everywhere. Vanuxem's background in paleontology proved invaluable and provided a continuity with continental geology. From Brongniart, Vanuxem had learned to use fossils to determine the relative age of strata at a time when the method was still controversial. Such eminent geologists as Amos Eaton in the United States and Adam Sedgwick in England were suspicious of the fossil method and were still relying, as late as 1832, on relative position and rock characteristics to identify strata. At the time of the New York survey, Vanuxem and Conrad were among the few Americans who were well enough prepared to be able to identify the fossils of a particular layer of strata and to use them to correlate a section of strata with similar beds elsewhere in the United States or Europe. They had earlier collected the fossil evidence that made it possible to identify Cretaceous beds of the mid-Atlantic coast and to equate them with European Cretaceous formations. This was the first recognition of this system in America and one of the earliest of intercontinental correlations.[33]

The appointment of Conrad as state paleontologist is an indication that paleontology was already becoming a discipline separate from geology. Eventually, every state survey wanted its own paleontologist; as collections of fossils grew and knowledge of them increased, which was the case in New York, it was necessary that one person specialize in fossil identification and classification. The field geologist no longer had time to keep up. The rapidly growing fossil collections soon overwhelmed even Conrad, and in 1843 Hall succeeded him and worked for the rest of his life to complete the influential thirteen-volume *Paleontology of New York*, becoming in the process one of the country's foremost paleontologists. By 1850, when Hall worked as paleontologist for Foster and Whitney on the Michigan survey, Whitney wrote that "I shall learn a good deal from him in the way of Paleontology, a branch which I never expect to be a proficient in, in these days of specialties."[34] Pumpelly never became proficient at it either and had to rely on specialists when need arose.

Mineralogy was another subject requiring the work of a specialist, because it was now a science that needed laboratory analysis to identify the mineral composition of specimens. To prevent duplication of effort, Governor Marcy appointed Lewis Caleb Beck as mineralogist to analyze the specimens from all four districts. Beck had studied medicine at the Rensselaer School and at Union College, was an expert in botany and mineralogy, and had developed his own system of mineral classification; he was also able to do chemical analysis of minerals.[35]

The New York survey was unusual in that it did not have one overall director as other states did, but the four heads with their varied experience brought to the survey a body of expertise that one person alone might not have had. Their backgrounds indicate that even though no standardized requirements for a geological career as yet existed, well-qualified people were available for professional work. They coordinated their fieldwork in their separate districts and shared their findings at yearly meetings. Their cooperation within New York State was representative of the way American geologists from different states were sharing and coordinating new knowledge about the country as a whole.

Like all of the state geological surveys, including those of Michigan and Missouri on which Pumpelly worked in the 1870s, the main purpose of New York's was economic—to provide information that would be useful to the development of industry and agriculture. But at the same time, New York's geologists contributed to the growth of their science by gathering data about geological formations and proposing theories about their origins.

The New York geologists paid dutiful attention to economic geology. They looked for sources of building stone, limestone, clay for bricks, salt, mineral springs, natural gas, iron, and other useful materials, and they noted the presence of petroleum in western New York, although they did not yet appreciate its usefulness. The principal economic benefit of their work may have been the determination that it was useless to look for coal in New York State because they found that, unlike Pennsylvania, most of New York's strata lie below the Carboniferous. This discovery would save the state thousands of dollars, for in the fifty years prior to 1840 a quarter of a million dollars had been spent in fruitlessly exploring for coal in the black slates of the Hudson Valley alone.[36]

The geologists' scientific activity, which they justified in their reports by trying to show its relation to their practical work, was a mix of fact gathering and theory making. George H. Daniels has suggested that Americans were backward in science in the Jacksonian period when compared to Europeans because their approach to science was too Baconian. They avoided theory because they were absorbed with gathering data about the North American continent.[37] But the New York geologists were not only good observers and fact gatherers in the field, they were systematizers and theorists as well. They collected rock and fossil specimens from New York's strata and, working closely with each other and with their contemporaries in Europe, organized their data into a stratigraphic system that they hoped to see adopted for the whole country. They observed the widespread alluvial "drift," now known to be evidence of the glaciers that once covered New York, and debated Agassiz's glacial hypothesis, then still rejected by most geologists in the United States and abroad. Their stratigraphic work and their attitudes toward the glacial hypothesis can be used as examples of how geologists in this period worked together, shared ideas, organized and classified their data, and proposed theories to explain what they found.

Stratigraphy

As an active outdoor child, Pumpelly would have been familiar with the strata of western New York State, which are well exposed in many locations in deep ravines and river valleys, are full of fossils, and are relatively undisturbed compared to the mountainous regions to the east. Before Vanuxem and Conrad began work in their western districts, the rocks had been classed as "Transition" (a vague Wernerian term for rocks lying below the Secondary and above the oldest or Primitive rocks) and roughly equated with similar French and English formations. In England, just before and during the years of the New York survey, Adam Sedgwick and Roderick Murchison divided the Transition, not without controversy, into the Cambrian and Silurian systems. The Old Red Sandstone lying just above the Silurian and below the Carboniferous became the Devonian. Each of the new systems contained a number of separate formations characterized by distinct species of fossils.[38]

The New York geologists were just as energetic as their English colleagues in attempting to bring order to the stratigraphic formations they encountered. Conrad and Vanuxem led the way in identifying new species of trilobites and other fossils of the New York strata that corresponded in age to those of the Cambrian, Silurian, and Devonian periods, helping to establish the fact that these systems occur in the same relative position worldwide. The geologists of all four districts discovered, however, far more beds of sedimentary rocks than could be matched with those of England, and instead of trying to force their rocks to conform to the English ones, they developed their own, more comprehensive New York system, which they hoped would become the standard for the whole country to the west. Basing their names for each formation on the location where it was best represented, from the lowest Potsdam sandstone, a familiar building stone quarried near Potsdam, New York, to the Chemung or Catskill group, of Devonian age, at the top, the geologists of the different districts managed to agree on names for the four major groups or divisions that were found in all four districts, which enabled them to prepare a geological map of the state. Specimens displayed in Albany's new natural history museum illustrated the New York system for the general public. Hall actively promoted the New York nomenclature, but American geologists did not permanently adopt the system as a whole and eventually English names prevailed for the major groupings.[39]

The effort to promote American names for American formations over the whole country led to a better understanding of the processes by which the strata had been formed, however. Hall and the other geologists realized that the strata were much thicker in the eastern, mountainous part of the state, thinning toward the west but not disappearing completely, and that limestone formations became thicker toward the west. This fact, plus the presence of marine fossils, indicated to them that the strata had been laid down during the existence of a former great inland sea. Hall made several trips to the Midwest during the next several years and found that the Potsdam sandstone, the Hudson River group, and other New York strata extended throughout the Midwest, although greatly decreased in thickness. Hall's work was an important contribution to the understanding of what is now known as the craton—the oldest part of the continent undisturbed by tectonic activity. From his later studies of the greatly thickened strata in the East along the Appalachians, Hall developed a uniformitarian theory of erosion and uplift that was an important contribution to theories of mountain formation and challenged the catastrophic explanation of William and Henry Rogers.[40]

One of American geology's greatest controversies, in which Pumpelly became involved in the 1880s when working for the United States Geological Survey, arose out of Emmons's work in the second district. It became known as the "Taconic controversy" and paralleled the Silurian-Cambrian controversy in England. East of the Hudson are the Taconic

Mountains where folding and metamorphic distortion of the strata make age determination difficult and where conventional stratigraphic methods are now known to be inadequate. After detailed study of the area, Emmons became convinced that a formation lay below the Potsdam sandstone that was older than the Potsdam but younger than the oldest Primary or Precambrian rocks. He found primitive fossils that seemed to corroborate this theory and named the formation the Taconic. Most other geologists challenged his assessment. Mather, for example, thought the rocks in question were younger than the Potsdam but had been distorted through metamorphism. American geologists debated the Taconic question throughout the century, without conclusive resolution. Today the region is still being studied, under a different paradigm, as an area of complex tectonic activity.[41]

The Glacial Hypothesis

The reaction of the New York geologists to the glacial hypothesis, which was born while the New York survey was under way, indicates that Americans were as ready as geologists of any other country to theorize about the phenomena they observed. Louis Agassiz's *Études sur les Glaciers,* which Pumpelly read in connection with his study of the glaciers of Corsica, proposed that former continental glaciers had produced the grooved and polished rock surfaces and the erratic boulders and layers of loose sand and gravel called the "drift" that were widespread in the northern landscape. The New York geologists were familiar with the scratched rocks and the surface deposits in their state, but most of them were not ready to accept such a radical explanation for a whole class of phenomena. The theory suggested a "catastrophic" event in recent geological time that conflicted with their generally uniformitarian views.

Earlier, these phenomena had been attributed to Noah's Flood or to a series of widespread deluges. In the 1820s, Oxford's leading geologist and Canon of Christ Church, William Buckland, had traced the enormous deposits of rounded stones in the Midlands region and examined the bones of extinct animals found in underground caves. His *Reliquiae Diluvianae* attributed these findings to a last great deluge that had swept over the earth.[42] In 1832 clergyman geologist Edward Hitchcock, of Amherst and the Massachusetts survey, thought that the drift of Cape Ann was due to a "deluge of tremendous power" that must have swept over the cape with "devastating energy." Although the geologists who were clergymen did hope to reconcile Genesis with geology, this "diluvial theory" was not just a faithful adherence to Scripture; waters of an enormous flood seemed to them to be the only agency powerful enough to explain the drift. As Martin J. S. Rudwick has said: "Early nineteenth century naturalists were right to conclude that there had been an extremely peculiar episode in the recent history of the earth. . . . It is impossible to understand the scientific power of the diluvial theory without recognizing the strength of the evidence that seemed to demand some such drastic explanation."[43]

When Buckland first heard about the glacial hypothesis from his friend Agassiz, he immediately accepted it as an explanation of the "diluvial drift," becoming one of the first of the British geologists to do so. In 1842 Hitchcock made a similar although qualified turnaround in his presidential address to the Association of American Geologists when he indicated that he was ready to accept an "aqueo-glacial" explanation.[44]

In their final reports, the New York geologists made no connection between Noah and the drift, but neither were they ready to accept the idea of continental glaciers. Mather, whose Long Island district was covered with surficial deposits, had long been fascinated and puzzled by them and had collected much information on his travels through the Midwest. His final report for the New York survey devoted seventy pages to the subject, including an eight-page table of data on scratched and furrowed rocks. Mather did not accept the existence of continental glaciers because, like most American geologists at the time, he did not see how glaciers could have moved over land that was mostly level and without the slope necessary to cause motion in an ice sheet. Instead, Mather suggested that rocks embedded on the undersides of icebergs, which had been carried over submerged land by ocean currents, had scratched the surfaces over which they passed and had been deposited when the icebergs melted. His explanation was similar to that of Roderick Murchison and Charles Lyell, who were also reluctant to accept Agassiz's theory because they thought it too catastrophic.[45]

Emmons maintained that several factors might account for the rock scorings and drift deposits. He was a uniformitarian and rejected explanations that made use of sudden, unfamiliar causes; he wanted to explain phenomena in the "most quiet way possible—I care not how long it takes." There could not have been a continental ice sheet because it would have destroyed all life, and no such drastic break in the fossil record occurs. The floating iceberg theory might explain the drift but not the scratches, he concluded, for he had observed that scratches of rocks in the Champlain Valley were in a north-south direction and northeast-southwest in the valley of the Saint Lawrence. Because icebergs do not move in straight lines, he attributed the scratches to ice forming in wide shallow rivers.[46]

Hall, too, was uniformitarian in outlook, believing that nature's laws are always the same. He refused to accept sudden destructions or new creations as explanations of geological change and insisted that living things had changed only gradually, from earliest times to the present. He was aware of the many scratches on rocks in a northeast-southwest direction, but he was not ready to attribute the phenomena to glaciers, nor could he accept the floating iceberg explanation. He thought the drift in his district might have been moved by ice, although not over any great extent of country.[47]

Vanuxem accepted more of the glacial hypothesis than the others did. Icebergs with rocks embedded on their lower surface could not have caused long straight grooves, he argued, because the motion of icebergs is oscillatory and rotatory and because, in fact, no scratches by icebergs had been observed. Glaciers on the other hand have the necessary weight and are known to have stones embedded in them, and their movement is continuous from the perpetual snow line to the bottom of their valleys. The lowered temperature necessary to assume in order to explain the presence of so much ice at the time would also account for the destruction of the mammoth and other extinct animals whose bones are found in the alluvial debris of Europe. Vanuxem rejected the idea of a continental ice cap, however, favoring the term "local ice" rather than glacier.[48]

Glacial studies in the United States began in earnest in the 1860s when geologist Charles Whittlesey published the results of his studies of moraines and the effects of glacial erosion in the Great Lakes area. The delay in the acceptance of Agassiz's theory may have been due to an agreement that was reached by a special committee of the Association of American Geologists in 1843 favoring the theory that icebergs were responsible for erratic boulders and the drift.[49]

The data that the New York geologists accumulated eventually led to a general acceptance of the glacial theory, however, and their work in paleontology and stratigraphy set standards of excellence that the geologists of many state surveys tried to emulate. Like other state geologists, they were developing the content of areas of geology that would become distinct specialties later in the century when Pumpelly became an active member of the profession.

Professionalism

Nathan Reingold has suggested that it may be premature to speak of geology as a profession in the period before 1860. As he has pointed out, twentieth-century definitions of professionalism in science do not apply to this period when there were no set standards for education or employment. He divides the scientific community into three groups: (1) the cultivators, who collected specimens, participated in observation networks, and organized local scientific societies; (2) the practitioners, who were employed in scientific occupations, usually in government or college positions; and (3) the researchers, who advanced scientific knowledge through their devotion to original research. Some of the practitioners also did research.[50]

The geologists of the New York survey seemed to be proud of their professional status, however. Although they were doing the same work as the British "gentlemen geologists" of the same period, they differed in significant ways. The elite members of the Geological Society of London, as Roy Porter has suggested, advanced the science in Britain and developed it as a recognized discipline, but they separated themselves from the engineer/surveyors who hoped to become a professional body of scientific experts with an important part to play in the industrial development of the empire. William Smith, the surveyor who made the first geological map of England and recognized the value of fossils as a means of identifying strata, was never invited to become a member of the geological society. When society member Henry de la Beche became paid head of the Geological Survey of Great Britain in 1835, he was accused of "jobbery."[51]

As Robert V. Bruce has pointed out, practical work was less stigmatized in the United States than in Europe and the lines between it and theoretical science were less clearly drawn. The status of the paid geological surveyors who worked professionally for New York and other states confirms this view, because the state geologists were often the movers and shakers of their field. It may be as Alexis de Tocqueville said, that "the more a nation is democratic . . . the more will discoveries immediately applicable to productive industry confer gain, fame and even power."[52] Men like James Hall of New York, Henry Darwin Rogers of Pennsylvania, and William Barton Rogers of Virginia, whose work on state surveys was intended to have practical applications, corresponded and visited on what seems to have been an equal footing with Roderick Murchison, Charles Lyell, and other British "gentlemen" who held themselves above the professional surveyors of their own country.

Evidence of professionalism in American geology at this early date can be found not only in the contributions geologists like those of New York State were making to the growth of geological knowledge through research and publication but also through the formation of professional societies. The working New York geologists were instrumental in the establishment of the first national professional scientific society in the country, modeled in part on the Geological Society of London and the British Association for the Advancement of Science. They felt a practical need to coordinate the work of the various state geologists, not only because geological formations do not stop at state lines, but also because they wanted to establish a uniform nomenclature for North American strata based on their New York system. When the Rogers brothers proposed a numerical system for the Paleozoic rocks of Pennsylvania and Virginia, Vanuxem suggested that all state geologists meet to discuss a uniform nomenclature.[53]

The first meeting of the Association of American Geologists was held at the Franklin Institute in Philadelphia in April 1840 and was well attended by geologists from several state surveys. According to a "Resolve" written by Vanuxem, Mather, and Henry Rogers, the original intention of those who organized the AAG was that it be an organization of working geologists or "those devoted to Geological research with scientific views and objects." New members were to be limited to no more than ten per year.[54] This resolution, written by three of the best-trained geologists of the day, is a sign of the strong feeling these men had about preserving the standards of their profession, a concern usually attributed to professional societies organized later in the century.

This original exclusivity did not last. As Sally Gregory Kohlstedt has shown, the Association of American Geologists proved so successful that it became in 1848 the nucleus around which the American Association for the Advancement of Science was formed. For a few years geologists dominated the new society; in the first year, ten of the fourteen officers of the AAAS were geologists, although in the 1850s the leadership swung to physical scientists. Geologists did not again organize a national society until the founding of the Geological Society of America in 1888, with the venerable James Hall as president and Pumpelly as one of ninety-eight original fellows limited to "working Geologists and Teachers of Geology."[55]

As we have seen, by the time Pumpelly returned from Freiberg at the end of 1859, geology was a thriving profession, offering a choice of opportunities for an adventurous young man. Geologists had had a part in the exploration of the West, in the early growth of the mining industry, and in the development of the country's economic resources. Because of its demonstrated usefulness, both the states and the federal government supported geology and with this support geologists were able, paradoxically, to study problems not directly related to economic benefit, thus contributing to a great increase in knowledge about American geology. Although some of this activity was to be interrupted by war, it would resume with increased intensity in the postwar years. By then Pumpelly would be ready to contribute to the even more rapid expansion of the science that took place in the last part of the century.

3

Exploring "Across America and Asia"

In the 1860s, as the frontier moved westward to the Pacific, geologists and mining engineers like Pumpelly were moving with it, helping the nation to fulfill its "manifest destiny" to settle the continent. Entrepreneurs, investors, and federal officials were casting their eyes on newly acquired territories, looking for ways to develop them. Across the Pacific, Japan and China were opening their doors just enough to let Americans see the possibilities of those countries as new markets for American goods. The scientist who had an opportunity to obtain some solid information about these unfamiliar places at this early date was in a position to make a considerable contribution to knowledge and to make a name for himself as well.

Pumpelly's travels during the years 1860–65 gave him just such an opportunity. They took him initially to the part of southern Arizona and New Mexico that the United States had acquired in 1853 through the Gadsden Purchase. There, as one of the earliest scientifically trained geologists to be employed in silver mining, he was able to give an accurate assessment of the value of the mines and to study the general geology of the desolate and little-known region. His next job, as mining consultant to the Japanese government only five years after Commodore Matthew Perry had persuaded the Japanese to sign a trade agreement, gave him a unique inside view of a country that had long intrigued Americans. His exploring instinct then took him on to China where, as the first American geologist to visit China, he investigated that country's geology, prepared a geological map, and examined coal mines, a subject of great interest to American and British empire builders.

Like the expeditions of the Pacific Railroad surveys, Pumpelly's explorations were a preliminary reconnaissance of new regions about which very little was then known. His contributions to the knowledge of the mines and geology of Arizona, Japan, and China were partly superseded by later investigators, but his work was a beginning and provided a base of information upon which others would build.

Silver Mining in Arizona

When Pumpelly went to work for the Santa Rita Mining Company in late 1860, the mining industry in the West was in a period of transition. The day when the individual prospector could pan for gold or stumble upon rich silver ore was passing, and trained mining engineers and geologists were beginning to apply scientific knowledge from various disciplines to improve the efficient extraction of ores. By the end of the century, members of these professions—many of them educated in American schools of mines—would be playing a vital role in the expansion of the industry, but in 1860 the United States still had no mining schools as such and German-trained geologists like Pumpelly were in demand.[1]

The owners of the Santa Rita mines understood the importance of expert assistance in evaluating and extracting silver ores. A German-trained mineralogist and topographer, Herman Ehrenberg, had accompanied one of the founders of the company, Arizona pioneer Charles D. Poston, in exploring the area south of the Gila River, soon after the land was acquired by the United States, in order to locate abandoned Mexican mines. In 1856 Poston joined forces with Samuel Peter Heintzelman, a career army officer and promoter of the Southwest, and with a group of Cincinnati businessmen they formed the Sonora Exploring and Mining Company with headquarters at Tubac, thirty miles south of Tucson. The following year the company hired a German mining engineer, Frederick Brunckow, who discovered an extremely rich vein at the company's Heintzelman Mine. Promoting this mine as one of the richest silver mines in the world, the owners made ambitious plans to introduce the new Freiberg barrel amalgamation process for the extraction of the silver. They ordered machinery and hired a metallurgist, an Austrian graduate of Freiberg, to oversee the operation.[2]

Southern Arizona at that time was, as one writer described it, "a delightful country in every respect, except in climate, soil, production and inhabitants." Apache attacks and resentful Mexican laborers made mining a hazardous occupation for Americans. In 1859 Brunckow was murdered, and the next year, when the Sonora company formed the subsidiary Santa Rita Mining Company to develop abandoned mines east of Tubac, the directors initiated a search for another "scientific engineer" who combined "knowledge of mining with the science of his profession."[3]

Pumpelly was staying for a few weeks in Albany with his uncle Harmon and learned of the position by chance from Col. Ezekiel Jewett, curator of the New York State Museum and a man well known to museum visitors as a communicator of the latest developments in geology. Pumpelly went to Cincinnati to meet with the Santa Rita mine director, William Wrightson, who offered him the job. Wrightson warned Pumpelly of the dangers involved, but the prospect of danger "only strengthened my wish to go," Pumpelly later wrote. Leaving home in the fall of 1860, Pumpelly traveled by railroad to Jefferson City, Missouri, then the westernmost end of the railroad, and reached Tubac after a harrowing three-week journey by the Butterfield Overland Stage.[4]

On this, his first job, Pumpelly did not have the benefit of working with other professionals that he would have had if he had joined an organization like a state survey. At the Santa Rita he worked with the mine superintendent, Horace C. Grosvenor, but was responsible for the whole process of operating the mines, from selecting the ores to producing the refined silver. With the help of the company's carpenter and a few Mexican laborers he made charcoal from mesquite and built furnaces from sun-dried mud bricks (a wagon load of fired bricks from the East had been lost in an Indian attack in Texas). The Santa Rita had no machinery, the Mexican laborers were unskilled and resentful of Americans, and Indians often stole the horses and other animals.[5]

In a sense, the Santa Rita was Pumpelly's graduate school. His work at the mines was a test of the mineralogy, geology, engineering, and metallurgy he had learned at Freiberg. His mineralogical training served him well in helping him identify the principal rock formations in the foothills of the Santa Rita Mountains that contained various kinds of silver ore, some associated with lead and some with copper. Using the blowpipe, he assayed the ores from different veins and different parts of the same vein and then determined the proper proportion of the ores that should make up the charges for the furnace, separating the ores by hand.[6]

The practical metallurgy he had learned at Freiberg was little help to him. He wished he had been taught the simple methods of the ancients, those of Pliny or Agricola, for example. "In vain I studied carefully Kerl's *Metallurgie* for methods used in out-of-the-way places," he wrote later. "All were planned for elaborate methods of getting the greatest possible yield, and all demanded materials and machinery not open to us."[7]

The Sonora company had introduced the Freiberg barrel amalgamation method at its Heintzelman Mine, but Pumpelly thought the method as it was conducted there was inefficient and unsuitable for conditions in Arizona. The Freiberg method used a steam engine to revolve the barrels, in which ground ore that had been roasted with salt to form chlorides was mixed for a day with copper balls, water, and quicksilver. In the presence of the copper, metallic silver is formed, which then combines with the quicksilver to form an amalgam. The silver was separated from the quicksilver in a retort and as much as possible of the mercury was recovered to be used again. Pumpelly thought that the system had proved to be uneconomical for the Sonora company, partly because of the untrained and unpredictable labor supply and partly because of the cost. Salt was expensive because it had to be imported from the coast, wood for the furnace cost $4 to $6 a cord, much of the mercury was unrecoverable, and an estimated 20 to 30 percent of the silver was lost in the process. Pumpelly's opinion was that the Heintzelman Mine, which had yielded an estimated $100,000, might have produced silver worth more than $1 million if it had been properly worked.[8]

Because the Santa Rita company had no machinery and the ores in any case were too high in lead to be suitable for the barrel amalgamation process, Pumpelly devised a cheaper way to reduce the ores. William Wrightson had advised him, before he had left Cincinnati, to be as economical as he could because, as Wrightson told Pumpelly's mother, some companies had "spent large sums of money in erecting expensive works and then found them unadapted to their wants. . . . The great fault of Arizona mining had been its extravagance. Had the Sonora Mining Company practiced even moderate extravagance in its operations, with its magnificent mine it would have been paying large dividends at the present time."[9]

Pumpelly's reduction methods were based partly on primitive Mexican processes and partly on the metallurgical chemistry he had learned at Freiberg. He found that the Mexicans used amalgamation for some ores and smelting for others. The Santa Rita ores seemed to him most suitable for smelting in a very hot furnace. The company's carpenter helped him to devise a method of increasing the furnace heat by using a large blacksmith's bellows operated by horsepower. Each 350-pound charge was made up of definite proportions of the silver-lead and silver-copper ores together with cupel bottom, ironstone, and litharge (lead oxide). The silver became concentrated with the lead in *planchas* or pigs, from which it was then separated by cupelling. In looking back, Pumpelly thought that his efforts to find a suitable way to reduce the ores from the Santa Rita mines "symbolized the end of a struggle to use European methods in metallurgy in Arizona."[10]

Pumpelly became better known for his encounters with Apaches, about which he wrote vividly in *Across America and Asia*, than he was for his mining methods. In April 1861, with the firing on Fort Sumter, the government began to withdraw federal troops that had been stationed in Arizona, leaving the settlers more open to Indian attack. Grosvenor, the Santa Rita mine superintendent, was ambushed and murdered by a party of Apaches. By working day and night Pumpelly finished refining the last batch of ore and on June 15 he abandoned the camp, taking the silver to Tubac, where many of the people of the area were gathering for safety. In July the army destroyed and abandoned both Fort Buchanan and Fort Breckenridge, and many Arizonians, who felt betrayed by the Union, joined the Confederacy.[11]

Reports of the situation in Arizona reached Pumpelly's family in Owego. His worried mother had written to Wrightson for news, and Wrightson replied that his brother was in Washington trying to persuade the government to accept a regiment of mounted men from Cincinnati for service in Arizona. He suggested that Mrs. Pumpelly should ask Harmon Pumpelly to intercede with the secretary of war for protection of the American citizens of Arizona from both the Indians and the secessionists. Wrightson had written to Pumpelly on June 12 urging him not to give it all up when things had progressed so far, as "it would be like the immolation of an only child" to abandon the mines, but by then it was too late. After reaching Tubac safely, Pumpelly left to make a short excursion into Papago country with Charles Poston "to look up some mines there," and by August 18, 1861, he and Poston had arrived at Fort Yuma en route to San Francisco.[12]

When Pumpelly reached San Francisco he found a congenial group of geologists and naturalists who were eager to hear about his experiences in southern Arizona. He had a reunion with the Janins, who were then working at the Enriquita quicksilver mine in the coast range, and he toured some of the mines with James D. Hague. He met Josiah Dwight Whitney, the head of the newly established California geological survey, and survey members William H. Brewer and William Ashburner. Brewer, who had already heard much about Pumpelly, was appalled by his accounts of conditions in Arizona and described in his journal how Pumpelly had "escaped, as if by miracle, traveling six hundred miles across deserts with only *panoli* . . . to eat, and is now safely here." Brewer thought that Pumpelly would probably be employed by the California survey as an assistant.[13] Whitney, an active member of the California Academy of Natural Sciences and a central figure in the San Francisco scientific community, became interested in Pumpelly's career. It was probably Whitney who arranged for Pumpelly to share his knowledge of the mines and geology of southern Arizona with the members of the academy.

The paper Pumpelly read to the California Academy of Natural Sciences, his first to an American scientific organization, is a sign of his unfailing interest in geology and the scientific aspects of mining even in the face of the dangerous and difficult conditions he had endured. His audience must have listened attentively, because the subject of Pumpelly's paper was an arid and desolate region that few if any geologists had studied. The only previous survey of southern Arizona had been that of the Mexican Boundary Survey, begun in 1854 under topographical engineer William H. Emory.[14] Pumpelly described the Santa Rita, Heintzelman, and other mines he had visited, giving details on the ores, the actual and potential output, and the mining methods as well as a calm evaluation of the Indian threat. His paper also covered the general geology of the territory through which he and Poston had passed along the trail to Yuma—mountain structure, strata, petrologic formations, evidence of former volcanic action, and indications that the region had once been a sea.[15]

The Arizona experience provided Pumpelly with a chance to learn on the job and had shown that he could carry out mining operations independently under difficult conditions. His academy paper demonstrated parallel interests in mining and general geology that continued throughout his career. Whitney, evidently impressed by Pumpelly's work, recommended him to fill a position as mining consultant to the Japanese government, an experience that turned out to be a valuable opportunity for further travel, exploration, adventure, and the geological reconnaissance of unfamiliar lands.

Mining Consultant to Japan

Technical experts invited to an undeveloped country can fulfill two missions. They participate in introducing modern technological and scientific methods there, and they have an unusual opportunity to observe and report on the country's culture and natural resources for those at home who are eager to know more about them. Pumpelly was the first of a wave of American mining experts who would be working for Japan and other countries in increasing numbers in the years to come, especially after the Meiji restoration, and he used the experience to observe not only the country's mines and geology but also its arts and customs. On his return, he wrote a full account of his Japanese experiences for general readers in *Across America and Asia* as well as a report for his fellow scientists, which was published by the Smithsonian.[16]

Pumpelly's work in Japan in 1862 came at a time of great turmoil in that country's internal affairs and in its relations with other countries. In 1854 Commodore Matthew Perry had negotiated the first Japanese-American treaty with the Tokugawa shogun government, opening certain ports to trade, but in the intervening years factions allied with the imperial court had increasingly opposed any contact with foreigners. The Townsend Harris treaty, even more favorable to trade with the West, was signed in 1858, and in 1860 the first Japanese diplomatic mission was sent to the United States. Its purpose was to formalize the Harris treaty and to learn more about American ways. This first official visit to the United States must have stimulated the desire of the shogunate to import Western science and technology into Japan and was probably indirectly responsible for Pumpelly's employment.[17]

The Japanese mission to the United States, which consisted of a delegation of more than eighty people (including various ambassadors, monetary experts, interpreters, and military attachés), arrived in Washington, D.C., in June. They were received with great enthusiasm and were given tours of the Naval Observatory, the Treasury Department, and the Patent Office. They looked with wonder through telescopes, observed steam engines at work, and admired map-making equipment and all sorts of scientific instruments. At the Smithsonian they were greeted by the institution's secretary, Joseph Henry, and were shown "striking" electrical experiments. They were themselves the object of great curiosity, sometimes prevented by the crowds from seeing all the exhibits and from asking as many questions as they would have liked.[18]

One object of the embassy was to establish closer monetary relations between the countries. In Philadelphia some of the party visited the U.S. Mint where a few of their gold and silver coins—cobangs and itzebus—were assayed. Later they held a conference with mint officers to compare the coinage of the two nations and to discuss means of exchange. The embassy's visit to the mint was a first step in the reform of Japanese coinage that followed the Meiji restoration of 1868, improving the Japanese economy and international trade relations. As one Japanese historian has observed, the 1860 embassy as a whole enlightened government officials at the time and the knowledge gained "greatly influenced the foreign policy of Japan after that."[19]

The mission undoubtedly emphasized Japan's need to improve its mining efficiency. In the fall of 1861, the government instituted a search for two American mineralogists and mining engineers to come to Japan as consultants and teachers. The two who were appointed were Pumpelly and William P. Blake. Whitney recommended Pumpelly in California and Harmon Pumpelly apparently used his influence in Washington, for after "a conversation with Judge Harris, our U.S. Senator," his uncle wired Pumpelly that the appointment would be confirmed. Harmon was delighted at Pumpelly's good fortune. Not only was considerable prestige attached to the position, but the salary was to be $5,000 a year in gold, plus expenses. "The field is certainly a brilliant one," Harmon wrote his sister-in-law, "and I have no doubt if his life is spared and no misfortune happens to him that he will fill the station with honor to himself and credit to the government and last but not least a handsome salary."[20]

Blake's appointment was probably due to his reputation as a Pacific Railroad survey geologist and to his extensive experience as a mining consultant. Blake may have had mixed feelings about going to Japan. On one hand he must have been grateful for the work. The publication of his *Mining Magazine* had been suspended and, to his great disappointment, he had been passed over in favor of Whitney as California's state geologist. On the other hand, he was on a committee to plan California's contribution to a world's fair, to be held the following year in London, and he had hoped to be appointed to go to it in an official capacity. He was also married, and the thought of being away for an indefinite time may have made him hesitate. Pumpelly had hoped that his Freiberg classmate, James P. Kimball, would be appointed as the second geologist, but Charles W. Brooks, the Japanese commercial agent in San Francisco, was very much in favor of Blake. He wrote to Blake to remind him of the ship's November 23 sailing date: "Do try and be ready as I am anxious you should go."[21] Brooks may have wanted Blake because he was older and more experienced than Pumpelly and could perhaps advise the younger man.

The Japanese wanted the best possible Western technology and had provided liberally for instruments as well as for salaries. Members of the California geological survey and the Janins assisted Pumpelly in purchasing new instruments and a scientific library to take to Japan that included apparatus for a chemical and assaying laboratory; a transit-theodolite and a level made by Richard Patten, a well-known Baltimore instrument maker; a theodolite candle-bearer for use in mines; a pocket chronometer; a Gambey's sextant; and a number of books on mining, metallurgy, and general science. After they reached Japan, Pumpelly and Blake were asked to display the instruments for government officials, who wanted to know how the money had been spent. The governor of Hakodate spent a morning examining the instruments and asking questions about them, while others took notes and made sketches. One of the officers in the governor's party had been with the 1860 embassy to the United States and proudly displayed his Waltham watch acquired on the mission.[22]

The two geologists arrived in Yokohama in February 1862, and for three months they waited while the Japanese determined what their rank and duties should be. The presence of foreign technical experts confused protocol officials in a country where social status was ranked "from the god-Mikado to the lowest tidewater. . . . Were mining engineers and geologists mechanics, or were they officials? and if so, what position did they hold in the civil or military scale in the United States?" Townsend Harris, the U.S. minister to Japan, settled the question diplomatically by telling the Japanese that if they were at his house he would treat Pumpelly and Blake with the same consideration he would give Commodore Perry.[23]

Because of antiforeign demonstrations and political troubles that limited their field of activity and cut short their stay in Japan, Pumpelly and Blake were unable to accomplish much of scientific significance. Although they had originally been engaged to introduce modern methods at the important gold and copper mines of Japan, the plans had to be changed and they were sent instead to southern Yesso (now Hokkaido), a relatively undeveloped island, to examine mines and teach geology and mining engineering. While waiting for their transport to Yesso, Pumpelly studied Japanese, and he and Blake were allowed to take a few escorted sight-seeing trips in the vicinity of Yokohama and Yedo (Tokyo), although they were often followed by crowds and exposed to antiforeign demonstrations and name calling. Everywhere he went, Pumpelly observed with great interest the architecture, the effect of earthquakes, methods of agriculture and road building, medical and religious practices, and other customs.[24]

The work on Yesso, where the two were taken at the end of April 1862, involved teaching and the inspection of mining districts. In a letter to the governor of Hakodate, under whose authority they would be working, Pumpelly outlined his plans for conducting the work, suggesting first a "hasty examination" of already opened mines in order to determine which localities had the best facilities for conducting mining and metallurgical works with profit to the government. He could then tell which districts should be examined in more detail and which should be developed further.[25]

The students assigned to Pumpelly and Blake were five young samurai officers who accompanied them on their journeys on Yesso as "assistants, escorts and pupils." Two had distinguished themselves in science and two were with the government mining department. They had learned their science, mining theory, and methods primarily through the study of Dutch texts, available to them because the Dutch were the principal traders with Japan before the Americans arrived. Pumpelly admired the intelligence and ingenuity of one of the men, who had constructed a working furnace for smelting iron ore from a model in a textbook and had studied mathematics with the help of Nathaniel Bowditch's *Practical Navigator* and an English-Dutch and Dutch-Japanese dictionary. Teaching seems to have taken place mostly in the field, although for two months, while Pumpelly and Blake were stationed in Hakodate during an outbreak of measles, they were able to give more regular instruction in basic subjects, their greatest difficulty being the lack of Japanese equivalents for technical terms. Plans to establish a school were cut short by the political unrest.[26]

Pumpelly and Blake made two exploratory journeys on Yesso by horseback and boat to examine gold, lead, and sulfur mines and mining methods. Usually they traveled together, although on some occasions they separated, one going by boat and the other by land, on horseback. Pumpelly's descriptions of production methods at gold-washing operations and at lead and sulfur mines indicate his maturing expertise. He took notes on mining and metallurgical processes as well as on production efficiency, including costs of fuel and labor, estimates of daily expenses, and the amount of ore excavated per person per day. In general, he found that by American or European standards the mines they visited were inefficiently worked, but at a lead mine in the mountains he was "not a little surprised" to discover that the stamps that crushed the ore were "constructed on the same principle as those of Cornwall and Germany" and that extraction of the lead was based on a simple form of a German precipitation process.[27]

The principal contributions Pumpelly and Blake made to the improvement of Japanese mining were to introduce the use of gunpowder for blasting and to make recommendations for pumping water out of the mines. Neither procedure had been used previously, even though gunpowder had been used for centuries for other purposes. At the Yurup lead mines, which had been worked for some time but with low productivity, they taught the miners how to drill a hole, prepare the charge, tamp and light it. At first the miners ran off, "fully expecting to find the works fallen in, and the rash foreigners buried in the ruins. Their delight was indescribable when they saw the result of the blast, which, at the cost of an hour's labor, had accomplished more than they were able to do by their own process in a day."[28]

Blake discovered excellent seams of coal on the west coast, calling them the most valuable mineral resource he had seen on Yesso, and in 1872 he recommended that the bed be opened and developed on a large scale.[29]

In his scientific report on Japan, presented in the form of an itinerary, Pumpelly interspersed geological observations with descriptions of the mines. He was particularly fascinated by the volcanoes ringing Volcano Bay, which must have reminded him of his early independent study of Vesuvius. Because of his chemical studies at Freiberg he now better understood the geochemical processes at work, and he was able to provide good scientific descriptions of Japanese volcanoes. His party explored the sides and descended into the crater of Sawaradake, on the southeastern tip of the island, which had erupted in 1854 and was still emitting gases. He observed streams of pumice several hundred yards wide and the strata of the crater walls, and he tried to reconstruct the sequence of events that had resulted in repeated buildup and destruction of the cone. At Esan, on the north side of Volcano Bay, the decomposing action of sulfurous acid and steam was as amazing to him as it had been when he had observed it on Vesuvius. "Everywhere the scene is one of ruin. . . . Nowhere have I seen so well exhibited the levelling power of nature when she brings into action her more active agents."[30]

By January 1863, dissatisfaction with shogun rule and resentment of foreigners had created a state of crisis, and the emperor ordered the shogun to "drive out the barbarians." The shogunate could no longer control the rebellious feudal nobility that supported the emperor or prevent an attack on the British legation in which British citizens were killed. The feudal lords, perhaps afraid they would lose control of the mineral resources that were being investigated at the order of the shogun, accused Pumpelly and Blake of being spies, and in February the two geologists were advised that they must leave the country. All their ideas for carrying out the implementation of mining improvements and plans for a school had to be abandoned. The governor of Hakodate, who had been their sponsor, wrote: "You have been industrious, explored mines . . . the way of washing gold . . . and method of blasting hard rocks. . . . I wrote my government it is in the satisfaction. . . . Instruction will be closed temporarily and students will be sent to your country."[31]

Learning that foreigners were being allowed for the first time to travel into the interior of China, Pumpelly followed the urge to travel there, leaving in March for Shanghai. Blake returned to the United States by way of Alaska, where he spent some time exploring glaciers.

Pumpelly and Blake were only the first of a number of American experts to be engaged by the Japanese. Following the Meiji restoration in 1868, Japan, under its young emperor and his military advisers, came to realize the unavoidable necessity of keeping up with the West and embarked on a more ambitious program of bringing in foreign experts than had been done under the shogun government. Louis Janin and James D. Hague both served the Japanese government as advisers in the early 1870s. Benjamin Smith Lyman, also a Freiberg graduate, lived in Japan from 1872 to 1881, thoroughly surveying the mineral resources of Hokkaido and teaching Japanese students. In the seventies, as the governor had predicted, the Japanese began to send students out of the country to schools in the United States and Europe.[32] Just as German experts were used in the United States until Americans acquired their own professionalism, so Japan relied heavily upon Americans until, before the end of the century, it could supply its own needs.

Exploring in China

No professional assignment brought Pumpelly to China as it had to Japan; he was attracted solely by the prospect of exploring a little-known country that was just beginning to allow westerners to travel into the interior. He was there at a crucial time in China's history, for China, like Japan, was faced with the difficult problem of dealing with Western attempts to establish a foothold on the mainland and open the country to trade. Should it resist the "barbarians" or adopt their ways? Unlike Japan, which would adopt Western technology and become an important world power by the end of the century, China refused to change and remained weak and undeveloped, an "ever more helpless hulk on the way to disintegration."[33] Pumpelly's explorations enabled him to do the first survey of China's geology by a Western geologist, and his examination of coal mines convinced him that the development of the country's coal resources could support an industrial expansion that would greatly benefit the Chinese people, an expansion that was not to take place for many decades, however.

The influx of foreigners into China was becoming a fact of life when Pumpelly arrived at Shanghai in the spring of 1863. The second Opium War with Britain had been concluded by treaty in 1860 and the devastating Taiping rebellion had been mostly suppressed, allowing foreign diplomats, including ambassadors Anson Burlingame of the United States and Sir Frederick Bruce of Great Britain, to take up residence in Peking. Pumpelly believed that his understanding of China and its people began with his first meeting with Anson Burlingame, who invited Pumpelly to stay with him. From inside the legation Pumpelly was able to observe the political situation and soon came to share Burlingame's sympathy for the Chinese as an industrious, civilized people.[34]

Pumpelly made four exploratory trips in China and Mongolia, inspired perhaps by the memory of one of his favorite boyhood books, an account of the travels in China and Tibet of the French Catholic missionary, Abbé Évariste Régis Huc. Pumpelly's first journey was by chartered boat up the Yangtze, from Shanghai to the eastern border of Szechwan Province, passing through the great limestone gorges of the upper river. Two years earlier, a British explorer-ornithologist, Capt. Thomas Wright Blakiston, had led an expedition up the Yangtze, and Pumpelly may have felt challenged to make the same trip. Later in 1863 he inspected coal mines north of Peking at the request of the Chinese government, and in 1864 he spent six weeks traveling through the provinces of Chihli (Hopeh) and Shansi, along the Great Wall and onto the Mongolian plateau. At the end of the year he left China for home, traveling overland in winter through the Gobi Desert and Siberia to Moscow and thence to Paris and New York.[35]

Pumpelly's explorations were never just for the adventure, even though adventure was certainly a part of it; the notes he kept about the geology he observed formed the basis for much of his later Smithsonian report. Geological research was difficult under the conditions he experienced. He was not part of a team, he had almost no information about the geology of the interior, he had very few instruments, he did not know the language, and the Taiping rebels were still in control of parts of the country, preventing him from going as far as he would have liked. In spite of these handicaps Pumpelly did attempt some tentative generalizations, and his report on China's geology reveals themes that were to interest him in the years ahead. His work falls into four main categories: (1) stratigraphic and petrological observations, which he applied to the preparation of a geological map; (2) physical-geographic studies; (3) observations on loess, and (4) examinations of coal mines.[36]

Geological Map

Geological maps and cross sections are an essential mode of communication for geologists. They are the means by which geologists represent their three-dimensional discoveries visually in a way that cannot be achieved by text alone. The production of national geological maps was accelerating in the 1860s, even though mapping conventions were not yet standardized, and it was common practice to include some kind of geological map with the results of a survey. With considerable ingenuity and "much misgiving," Pumpelly constructed a "Hypothetical Map of the Structure of China" with color keys indicating six types of formation. He emphasized the map's hypothetical nature because of the limited area personally examined and the generalized nature of his own observations, calling it a "sketch-map" on which to provide a spatial representation of his ideas about China's geology at a time when Americans knew little about it. His map was no different from any other geological map in that it was based on his subjective interpretation of what he saw in the field. Later geologists, who read the data somewhat differently, disagreed with some of his interpretations and produced different maps.[37]

Pumpelly's personal observations were primarily lithological, an approach that is consistent with his education at Freiberg where mineralogy and petrology were emphasized. Along the southern edge of the Mongolian plateau he observed immense trachytic and basaltic lava beds, which he colored orange on the map. At Kalgan he examined a distinctive trachytic porphyry, colored deep blue. In the Yangtze gorges he was impressed with the great thickness of the yellow limestone cliffs, over 2,000 feet high. Here and in northern China he estimated that the limestone composing the highest ridges was more than 10,000 feet thick. The fact that the limestone overlay older schists and granites and was covered by coal-bearing formations led him to conclude from the stratigraphic evidence that the limestone, which he indicated with light blue on his map, must be Devonian. The coal measures, which lay in basins between the limestone ridges, he colored green.

What little fossil evidence Pumpelly found seemed to confirm that most of China's limestone was Devonian. The limestone that he examined personally had been subjected to metamorphism and was without fossils, but he obtained from curio shops a few Devonian brachiopods, which were said to have come from the limestone, and he found described in British and French scientific journals several species of shells from China, which he assumed must have come from the limestone formations. He personally collected a few specimens of fossil ferns from the coalfields and sent them for analysis to John S. Newberry at Yale, who found them to be of Mesozoic age. Pumpelly, probably relying too much on Newberry's study, assumed that most of the coals throughout the empire were of the same age.[38]

Pumpelly supplemented his own necessarily limited observations with those of previous travelers and the works of Chinese geographers. He haunted lapidary shops to learn the Chinese names of the minerals whose source he wanted to identify and then recruited Chinese assistants to compile a table, based on Chinese geographic works, containing data on the location of various minerals, coal, fossils, salt wells, limestone caves, and the like. This information helped him plat the different formations on the map.[39]

Pumpelly's map reflects his belief that there was a "general simplicity in the geological structure of the country." It became evident that this was an oversimplification as soon as other geologists began the study of China's geology and discovered new formations he had not seen. However, considering his brief reconnaissance, it was a reasonable first effort, probably comparable to Marcou's first map of the United States. Ferdinand von Richthofen, the next geologist to take up the study, praised the map, Pumpelly reported, "as a general expression of the structure and broad outline" of China's geology.[40]

Physical Geography

The varied features of China's geography were as new and fascinating to Pumpelly as the mountains, deserts, plateaus, and canyons of the western United States had been to the Pacific Railroad explorers and would be to John Wesley Powell, Clarence King, and the other geologists of the western surveys that would soon be under way in the United States. This interest in how past structural changes had created present surface features was to continue throughout Pumpelly's life and would play an especially prominent part in his studies in Turkestan. Although Pumpelly usually did not speculate about underlying causes, he did look for general laws that seemed to affect similar formations worldwide. He also had a considerable talent for visualizing and reconstructing a sequence of events in the evolution of landforms. Three areas that particularly interested him in China were the delta of the Yellow River, the major mountain systems, and the regions bordering the Mongolian plateau.

The changing course of rivers and the growth of river deltas were subjects that greatly interested Pumpelly and were also beginning to attract the attention of American geologists. During the 1860s, Eugene W. Hilgard, for example, as state geologist of Mississippi, made studies of sedimentation rates and changes in the Mississippi Delta that brought him membership in the National Academy of Sciences. Pumpelly's report on the changing course of the Yellow River across its delta, which was based more on historical sources than on personal observation, included a striking series of maps showing the different channels the river had followed over the past two thousand years, sometimes north and sometimes south of the mountainous Shantung Peninsula. "Nowhere can the rate of growth of deltas be better studied than in China," Pumpelly thought, because the records of Yellow River changes that had been kept by Chinese geographers were probably unparalleled.[41]

Pumpelly identified two major mountain systems of China, one having a northeast-to-southwest trend and the other running east to west. The northeast-southwest system determines the main continental features of eastern China while the east-west system determines the courses of the Yangtze and other great rivers. Pumpelly suggested that a mountain-creating "revolution" following the deposition of the limestone and the coal measures had uplifted and folded the coal strata just as in the Appalachians. He thought that the two orogenic events were contemporaneous because both mountain ranges had the same northeast-southwest trend and the same immense areas of folded coal-bearing strata. Pumpelly did not propose theories about the physical processes involved in mountain formation—whether mountain building was due to the earth's contraction, as James Dwight Dana believed, or to uplift and subsidence caused by an accumulation of sediment, as James Hall proposed. The debate between Dana and Hall over the origin of mountain ranges was still in its early stage, and Pumpelly may not have been aware of it. He did feel, however, that the northeast-southwest system, or "Sinian" system as he called it, illustrated a general law, because he knew that Dana, among others, had pointed out that other mountain ranges of the world had the same trend. The Sinian system was thus "one more link in the chain of evidence toward proving the subordination to harmonious laws of the causes that have produced all the varied features in the configuration of our planet."[42]

The two journeys that took Pumpelly onto the high plateau region of southern Mongolia prompted thoughts about the cause of the uplift of the plateau and the erosion that was wearing it away that were similar to those of Powell and the other geologists who later studied the forces that had shaped the Colorado plateau and the Grand Canyon of Arizona. Pumpelly speculated that the uplift of the Mongolian tableland had followed a period of intense volcanic activity when great flows of lava had poured out through the fault line marking the edge of the escarpment. Erosion patterns in the soft "lake loam" that covered the hills and valleys south of the plateau provided a vivid example of erosion patterns in general, he thought. With each succeeding rain, the ravine channels work themselves backward to the mountains and new tributary ravines start along the sides. "We have here in the softest material that can support such action," he wrote, "a repetition of the process which is causing the retrogression of Niagara Falls, and which probably plays an important part in all valley erosion."[43]

When Pumpelly left China to return home in December 1864, his route overland across the Mongolian tableland and the Gobi Desert, described in vivid detail in *Across America and Asia* and in his *Reminiscences,* enabled him to make a more extensive reconnaissance of the geology of Mongolia. Travel was perilous and the cold was intense, but even under the most adverse conditions he continued to make sketches and record his geological observations. The section that he drew of his route through Mongolia, reproduced in *Geological Researches,* was later hailed as the dawn of "a new era in the exploration of this region" by the geologists accompanying Roy Chapman Andrews on the Central Asian expedition of 1922–23, sponsored by the American Museum of Natural History. Pumpelly's "sane and simple analysis" of the physiography of Mongolia had been the first great step in unraveling that region's complex structure, they thought.[44]

Pumpelly predicted that the geology and physical geography of this vast region would be an important field for future exploration. He was sure that past changes must have had "an important influence on the recent history of our planet."[45] He thought he saw evidence, as had Humboldt and other geographers, that a sea had once covered a large part of northern Asia, from the Arctic to the Caspian Sea and from the Urals to near the Great Wall, but he had no time then to explore further. He was at last able to pursue his fascination with Central Asia's physiography and its influence on human history during his explorations in Turkestan in 1903–04.

Loess

Pumpelly's discussion of the extent and possible origin of China's loess deposits was one of the earliest technical treatments of the subject by an American geologist. The study of loess was to occupy Pumpelly in one form or another throughout much of his career. He referred to the deposits of this fine soil as "terrace deposits" or "calcareous loam" or "lake loam" in his published reports, although he used the German word "loess" at least once in his field notebook. David Dale Owen had briefly described the extensive loess deposits of the Mississippi Valley in 1840 and 1844, calling them a "silicious marl," but they were not treated in any detail by Americans until the 1870s when they were recognized to be the same as the "loess" deposits of the Rhine Valley.[46]

Pumpelly realized that this "loam," which constituted the fertile soil of northern China, was a recent deposit, because it covered the older formations of the northern provinces for thousands of square miles in present and former river valleys, rose in terraces far up the sides of mountains, and filled ravines to a depth of several hundred feet. In many places, as earlier travelers had noted, it formed vertical cliffs 200 to 300 feet high in which the inhabitants had carved out elaborate dwellings with plastered walls. Pumpelly's description of the loam could stand as a present-day textbook definition of loess. It was formed of "an almost impalpable powder," firm enough to be excavated yet easily crushed. "When breaks occur," he wrote, "the loam falls in immense plates . . . leaving a new vertical face. . . . A characteristic feature . . . is its tendency to cleave according to two vertical planes at right angles to each other, causing it to assume the form of needles under certain conditions of erosion."[47]

Pumpelly thought the loess had originated as sediments in a series of large freshwater lakes that had once been fed by the Yellow River and its tributaries. One of these lakes would have been in what is now the desert region enclosed by the northern bend of the Yellow River, between the Great Wall and the Mongolian plateau. When the river changed its course, which it had done many times in historical periods, the lakes receded, Pumpelly thought. The presence of freshwater shells in the loess deposits seemed to him to confirm his lacustrine hypothesis. He also thought it "remarkable" that, according to Chinese allegorical and historical accounts, two great floods were supposed to have occurred in that region around 3100 B.C., which some Western writers had once cited as proof of a universal deluge.[48]

The German geographer Ferdinand von Richthofen later challenged the lacustrine origin of loess. In his more extensive China explorations, Richthofen found the shells of land snails in loess deposits at levels that could not have been reached by lakes. Richthofen believed that the deposits were due to the action of wind, a hypothesis that Pumpelly himself soon accepted, probably realizing that the dust storms he had experienced in China were the means by which the fine particles were distributed.

Coal

Pumpelly was convinced that China had the potential to become a great nation. His belief was reinforced when he made a professional examination of coal mines west of Peking for the Chinese government. Coal mines had been in operation in northern China since the twelfth century, when a timber shortage had greatly increased the need for alternative sources of fuel. By the early 1860s, coal mines in many parts of the country were supplying a variety of industrial and household needs, but primitive methods and poor transportation kept the coal industry from growing, even though steam-powered shipping was creating greater demand. At that time the government was not allowing any foreign development of its mineral resources, even though many countries were interested in doing so, the English perhaps most of all.[49]

The idea of having Pumpelly inspect and evaluate coal mines for the Chinese originated with the British minister in Peking, Sir Frederick Bruce. The Chinese had decided to purchase a fleet of gunboats from the British for the suppression of smuggling and piracy, and they wanted to find an adequate source of coal locally rather than pay the high price of imported coal. With the approval of U.S. Secretary of State William H. Seward, the Chinese government hired Pumpelly to examine the coal resources in the province of Chihli (now Hopeh), northwest of Peking.[50] As Burlingame wrote to Seward,

Mr. Pumpelly has the singular satisfaction of being the first man employed by the Chinese government to carry the light of his branch of science into the hitherto unexplored mines of China. He is well fitted for the enterprise. He is young, modest and capable. He was most thoroughly educated in Germany, after which he explored the silver mines of Arizona and then upon the recommendation of the eminent geologist Mr. Whitney of California, was appointed to make a survey of Yesso.[51]

Pumpelly's investigation was limited to only a few mines, but it made him realize that their output could be enormous if methods were brought up to Western standards. He inspected each mine personally and thoroughly, crawling in one for hundreds of feet on hands and knees and observing methods of timbering, ventilating, and excavating. Mechanical fans at the mouths of shafts provided ventilation but no pumping machinery was used, so the coal that was below the water line was inaccessible. Pumpelly tested and evaluated the quality of various types of coal and their suitability for supplying steamers, and he sent samples to Yale's Sheffield Laboratory for analysis. The Fuh-Tau mine, with some of the best bituminous coal of the region, had a potential yield of $4\frac{1}{2}$ to 6 million tons of salable coal, according to his estimate, but because transportation of the coal from the mines to Peking was by mule and camel, one mine owner told him that the most he could deliver would be about 850 tons per year, or about one-third the amount needed for a medium-sized steamer.[52]

With proper drainage and other improvements in mining methods, and with the building of a railroad to reduce the cost of transport, the government could develop the mines with great profit to itself, Pumpelly suggested, or, if it preferred, it could put the trade in the hands of Chinese or foreign capitalists. Pumpelly had hoped to study other coalfields of the empire, but after his return to Peking he learned that the government had abandoned the idea of organizing a navy and would sell the boats back to England.[53]

People in the United States, France, and England who were interested in developing the Chinese coal deposits could have read Pumpelly's report to the Chinese government on the "Coal District of the Se-Shan." Burlingame sent it to Seward and Pumpelly used part of it in his *Geological Researches*. The *Annales des Mines* published it as did the British *Friend of China* in 1867. The British paper's correspondent wrote: "This Report is the only one that has been made by a professional man on the Si Shan coals." In spite of the great interest of foreign capitalists, internal resistance to Western technology kept the Chinese government from allowing the development of a system of railroads for many years. As late as 1895, the Chinese government had built only a few hundred miles of railroads in the whole country.[54] Pumpelly's vision of the development of China's enormous coal resources was thus prevented by political and economic realities from being realized until the twentieth century.

Joining the Scientific Community

When Pumpelly returned home in 1865 he found that his travels, which had taken him to some of the most remote parts of the world and had fulfilled an urge to explore that had been with him since childhood, now opened doors to scientific recognition. Pumpelly's friend and mentor, Josiah Dwight Whitney, a member of the newly established National Academy of Sciences, invited Pumpelly to give a paper on his explorations at the academy's August meeting in Northampton. Contrary to the usual practice of having members read papers of their guests, Pumpelly gave his paper in person to a distinguished group of scientists that included Benjamin Peirce of the U.S. Coast and Geodetic Survey, who chaired the meeting, and geologists Whitney, John S. Newberry, J. Peter Lesley of the Pennsylvania survey, and Thomas Sterry Hunt of Canada. The president of the academy, Joseph Henry, was not present. The papers read were followed by "considerable discussion," and Whitney moved that Pumpelly's paper be published in the academy's *Memoirs*.[55]

After the professional isolation in which Pumpelly had conducted his geological work in China, he now found himself encouraged and supported by some of America's most prominent scientists. Although his paper did not find its way into the academy's *Memoirs*, James Dwight Dana published it in his *American Journal of Science*.[56] At the urging of Whitney and probably of his mother and of Harmon Pumpelly as well, he began to write a fuller report on the geological aspects of his explorations. Whitney, an avid book collector, offered the use of his fine scientific library, and Pumpelly settled down for the summer of 1865 in Northampton near Whitney's home to write.[57] Although he had considerable literary talent, which he attributed to heredity and his mother's influence, Pumpelly found writing difficult. In a letter to Louis Janin, asking if there was "any room for me on the Pacific," he complained:

I find that everybody who knows of me is expecting great results and any number of books from my wanderings. So that instead of being allowed to jump again into active work and leave bookmaking to those who are much better fitted for that work than I am, I must needs settle down to try to bring order out of the confusion of a pile of illegible notebooks and manuscripts that contain about as much system as there is in madness. And all this with the fear before me of my work being much too near the little end of the horn to permit of its successful delivery.[58]

In spite of his fears, Pumpelly completed his memoir and with the national academy's support he submitted it to Joseph Henry of the Smithsonian Institution, who accepted it for publication in the Smithsonian's Contributions to Knowledge series.

Pumpelly was fortunate to have his report accepted by Henry. Contributions to Knowledge was a prestigious series and Henry had very high editorial standards for it. As he explained in the preface to the volumes in the series, Henry accepted no "unphilosophical" papers, only "original memoirs" examined by "a commission of persons of reputation in the branch to which the memoir pertains," a referee system that was unusual at the time. In Pumpelly's case the approval of the National Academy of Sciences took the place of referees. The Smithsonian paid for printing, which Henry considered a form of government patronage such as other countries dispensed to their scientists. He believed that this procedure enabled "true genius to place its productions before the world free of cost." The quarto volumes were exchanged for the publications of literary and scientific societies, copies were given to colleges and principal libraries, and abstracts were included in the Smithsonian's *Annual Report*.[59]

Henry was an active editor, personally involved with the publication of research papers. He and Pumpelly exchanged a number of letters involved with manuscript changes, the preparation of plates, and the spelling of Chinese names. Henry edited out a number of acknowledgments for hospitality received and a few inaccuracies but apparently did not attempt to make changes in the main body of the report.[60] The *Geological Researches,* included in the Contributions to Knowledge in 1867, was a handsomely printed work containing eighteen diagrams and nine plates, two of which were maps in six colors. Pumpelly's report was in good company; in the same volume were reports by Simon Newcomb on the orbit of Neptune, by Charles Whittlesey on the glacial period in the Midwest, and by Isaac I. Hayes on physical observations made on his 1860–61 exploring expedition of the Arctic.

Because of an "almost total absence of observations of a geological character throughout this wide field," as Henry remarked in his annual report to Congress, Pumpelly's research on the geology of Japan and China aroused considerable interest among geologists and geographers, in both the United States and England. The *American Journal of Science* published excerpts from the report and a reviewer of the complete work, probably Dana himself, expressed special interest in Pumpelly's observation of the similarity of the Sinian mountain system to the Appalachians. The journal printed Newberry's report on the fossil plants of the coal as well as Pumpelly's chapter on the delta of the Yellow River. Daniel Coit Gilman, then professor of geography at Yale's Sheffield Scientific School, in reviewing another article on China's geography, made a point of referring the reader to Pumpelly's "very instructive" series of diagrams on the changes in the Yellow River's course. He agreed that the historical records of the river's changes "are probably without a parallel in the history of physical geography." British geologists were especially interested in Pumpelly's estimates of the extent and age of China's coal, although one reviewer noted the small number of fossil plants on which Pumpelly had based his conclusions.[61]

At first, few reviewers had any serious criticisms of Pumpelly's scientific findings, for so little had been written to provide a basis for comparison. It was not until Ferdinand von Richthofen began his more thorough investigations of China's geology at the end of the decade that some of Pumpelly's conclusions were questioned. Richthofen, one of the major figures in the development of geography as a science, had studied geology at the Universities of Breslau and Berlin and in 1860 had visited the Far East as geologist with a German diplomatic mission but had been prevented by the Taiping rebellion from traveling into China's interior. He spent the next few years in California reporting on the mining situation for German newspapers and while there he became friendly with Pumpelly's mentor, Josiah Dwight Whitney. Whitney supported Richthofen in his plans to return to China for extensive geological study, helping him to get financing from the Bank of California and encouraging him to write letters about his discoveries, some of which Whitney sent to the *American Journal of Science* for publication.[62]

Although he admired Pumpelly's pioneering work, Richthofen believed that Pumpelly had reached some erroneous conclusions. Richthofen was in China from 1869 to 1872 and covered much more of the country than Pumpelly had been able to do. On one of his first excursions west of Shanghai to investigate a fossiliferous locality mentioned but not personally visited by Pumpelly, Richthofen found "almost at first sight" a limestone formation containing several species of nummulites characteristic of a distinct part of the Eocene. He found no brachiopods on which Pumpelly had based his opinion that all Chinese limestone was Devonian. Richthofen did not deny that true Devonian limestone might occur in the neighborhood indicated by Pumpelly's chart, but his discovery of nummulites showed that some parts of China might contain limestones of other periods as well. "The subject is not without practical interest," Richthofen believed, "where all limestone was assumed to underlie the coal and iron-bearing formations."[63]

Richthofen's discovery of Silurian and Carboniferous fossils in the coal controverted Pumpelly's opinion, based on Newberry's analysis, that China's coal measures were probably all of Mesozoic age. Whitney thought that the publication of Richthofen's work on China would show "a complete revolution in the topography of China. Newberry's and Pumpelly's discovery of the Triassic age of the coal is all set to o. R. found fossils in the greatest abundance. . . . It is strange that Pumpelly missed them so entirely."[64]

With *Geological Researches in China, Mongolia, and Japan,* Pumpelly achieved the "name" he had hoped for while he was still in school at Freiberg. Largely as a result of it he was invited in 1872 to become a member of the National Academy of Sciences. Pumpelly's report remained the pioneering work, the foundation on which later geologists built. Richthofen spent much of his later career writing his monumental multivolume work on China, and in it he acknowledged Pumpelly's contributions even as he modified them.

Soon after completing his scientific report for the Smithsonian, Pumpelly began to write a narrative of his travels for the general reader. This was not at all unusual; many explorers, including Humboldt and Darwin, wrote both scientific and popular accounts of their explorations. Nineteenth-century readers were avid consumers of travel works, and several geologists and mining engineers who worked professionally in parts of countries that were inaccessible to the average tourist were inspired to write for general audiences. Among Pumpelly's contemporaries, Clarence King wrote vividly about his experiences in the Sierras and John Wesley Powell published a popular version of his daring exploration of the Colorado River.[65]

Pumpelly's *Across America and Asia* popularized the science of geology while entertaining the reader with his exciting adventures and tales of his encounters with unfamiliar peoples. One of the most romantic of his stories was the one about his journey across Siberia on his return home, when he had to share his small sleigh for several days and nights with an attractive, fur-swathed young Polish woman returning from visiting her brother in a Siberian work camp. The science in Pumpelly's book, while not as technical as that of the Smithsonian report, was a substantial part of it. Pumpelly provided informed geographic sketches of Arizona, Japan, and China and wrote of the volcanoes, rivers, and the varied geological formations he observed along the route of his travels. His book was apparently widely read and went into several editions; people were still telling him as late as 1913 how much they had enjoyed it. The *North American Review* found it fresh and exciting, "at once sensible and racy." Pumpelly has had opportunities "rarely if ever enjoyed by a modern scientific observer," said the reviewer. While "keen in his observations, guarded in his statements, alive to all the phenomena of nature," as a scientist should be, his book is still a "popular narrative of travel in paths rarely trod by Americans." It is rare, the reviewer said, for "a young man to have so good a tale to tell, it is rarer still for a young man to tell his tale so well."[66]

Much of the interest in Pumpelly's "tale" was due to his sympathetic understanding of the people of the countries he visited. The opinions he formed about the nonwhite races with which he came into contact were much more tolerant than those of many scientists of his time. As John S. Haller has pointed out, some American scientists, geologists among them, adopted a neo-Lamarckian form of evolutionary theory which held that the colored races were arrested at a primitive stage of evolution; only the Caucasians had continued to evolve through adaptation to a favorable environment and inheritance of civilizing habits. Geologists Nathaniel Shaler and Joseph LeConte were among this group, which combined Herbert Spencer's form of Social Darwinism with techniques from the social and biological sciences—anthropometric measurement, phrenology, and statistics—to prove racial inferiority.[67]

Pumpelly, who came into contact with Native Americans and Asians on their home ground, formed a more liberal perception of these cultures that was based more on economic than biological factors. He saw firsthand the intensity with which the Apaches defended their lands, the high culture attained by the Japanese, and the ability of the hard-working Chinese to survive overpopulation, drought, and famine. He thought that if the Indians should gradually disappear simply from mere contact with whites, that would prove them to be "lacking in ability to do their share in the world's work," but the inhumane and dishonest treatment of the Indians by white Americans had not allowed them to prove whether they were capable of coexisting or advancing to a higher stage of development.[68]

In spite of his personal experience of Apache violence, Pumpelly wrote a passionate condemnation of the treatment of Indians, calling it "a sad commentary on the Protestant civilization of the past two centuries. In the history of no other conquest, heathen or Romish, do we find such a record of long-continued atrocity and treachery on the part of the conquerors." He admitted that no peaceful development of Arizona's mines could occur until the Indian question was settled, but he deplored the attitude of those who believed the Apaches must be exterminated by any means. Pumpelly urged the government to pay for confiscated lands and treat the Indian humanely, not to be swayed by the "interests of the frontiersman, who is restrained by no higher law than his own grossly selfish aim." Hubert Howe Bancroft praised Pumpelly's "philosophic view" of Indian affairs and social conditions in Arizona, but an offended Tucson reviewer of *Across America and Asia* attacked Pumpelly for his "hypocrisy" and for writing exaggerated accounts of Indian atrocities and then criticizing the "white inhabitants who would take vengeance for such outrages."[69]

Pumpelly believed the Chinese and Japanese had already demonstrated that they were capable of a high level of civilization but were only at a different stage technologically. Far from being a backward or simple people to be condescended to and exploited by westerners, they had much to offer the West. He greatly admired Oriental art, bought many prints and porcelains, and asked John La Farge to write a chapter for his book on the art of Japan, which was the first treatment of the subject by an American artist. At the request of Anson Burlingame and the British minister to China, Sir Frederick Bruce, Pumpelly wrote an article for the *North American Review* about American policy in China that promoted Burlingame's progressive attitude toward the Chinese and attempted to counteract the resistance of Americans to what they thought of as the "Yellow Peril."[70]

Pumpelly's interest in people and his knowledge of geology made him perhaps more aware than other travelers of the influence of geography on human development. In his later work on the prehistoric cultures of

Turkestan, Pumpelly placed more emphasis on environmental influences, particularly those of climate and soil, but he was especially conscious of these influences when he stood at the edge of the Mongolian plateau in 1864. Here, at "one of the sharpest boundary lines drawn by nature on our planet," he could plainly see the contrast between the dry and grassy plains of the plateau, inhabited only by nomads, and the varied and fertile region below. "On the plateau," he wrote, "the habits and status of these wanderers are fixed by nature; there can be no progress, no transition from the nomad life to a higher order of existence, since the very elements of such progress are excluded by the surrounding physical influences." South of the boundary the country is different. The nomads who were probably the first to settle there had found their habits revolutionized, he thought, by "the varied gifts of nature, and the necessity of using them." Out of the seeds "planted in a land wonderfully adapted to their growth" grew a civilization "which until recently towered above all others."[71]

Pumpelly's ideas about the influence of environment on society were probably not original with him, but it is hard to say where they originated. They were common enough in the nineteenth century. David N. Livingstone has discussed Nathaniel Shaler's environmentalism at considerable length and feels Shaler was influenced most by the writings of geographers Carl Ritter and Arnold Guyot, who were among the most important precursors of modern human geography. It is likely that Pumpelly was exposed to similar ideas at Freiberg from Carl Bernhard von Cotta, who himself wrote about the influence of physical geography on German society.[72] Pumpelly never adopted an extreme form of environmental determinism, for he was just as aware of the importance of heredity on human development, but he did believe that changing climate directly affected the lives of primitive peoples by causing migrations, the interaction of one culture on another, and the rise of more advanced societies.

During the American Civil War, most American geological surveys and government-supported scientific expeditions were suspended. Pumpelly was one of the few to continue to do scientific exploration during these years. His scientific travels "across America and Asia" were in the tradition of the earlier scientific explorations of the American West sponsored by the federal government. They were also a bridge to the later geological surveys of the West that were to be conducted during the next decade by King, Hayden, and other professional geologists. Like the earlier ones, his were primarily a reconnaissance. As a geologist working alone he did not attempt to do a comprehensive natural history survey along the route of his travels like that of the Pacific Railroad surveys, for example, and he could not do the detailed geological surveying that was characteristic of the western survey teams of the 1860s and 1870s. Nevertheless, his explorations were the work of a trained professional geologist and in this sense they were closer to the later western surveys than to the earlier ones.

4 Economic Geologist of the Gilded Age

E. J. Hobsbawm has identified as the "Age of Capital" the period from 1848 to 1875, when the growth of industry was accompanied by "iron pouring in millions of tons over the world, snaking in ribbons of railways across the continents."[1] Pumpelly was one of the geologists who played an important part in this growth during the 1870s and 1880s as he became more and more involved in the exploration for minerals and in research on the origins of ore deposits.

Although the specialty known as "economic geology" did not become formally identified as a subdiscipline until the twentieth century, geologists like Pumpelly who worked in mining-related fields were known as "economic geologists" as early as the 1870s. A description of what economic geologists do, published in the new journal *Economic Geology* in 1906, applies equally well to the geologists of Pumpelly's generation, who were doing the pioneer work in the field and establishing the methods and outlook that made it a science.[2]

In his inaugural editorial for the journal, Frederick L. Ransome, a geologist with the United States Geological Survey and later a professor of economic geology at California Institute of Technology, pointed out the differences between the economic or mining geologist and the mining engineer, whose work often overlapped. Both worked in an applied field, but mining geologists were "investigators of natural phenomena," while mining engineers were "primarily concerned with the most effective methods of forcing the rocks to give up their treasures." The economic geologist was more likely than the engineer to be concerned with the origin of ore deposits—the chemical and mineralogical relations of ores to the surrounding rock and their position relative to the geological structure of the whole mining region. The economic geologist needed to know physics, chemistry, mineralogy, petrology, and stratigraphy and like the general geologist was committed to scientific observation and interpretation. Economic geologists, according to Ransome, had a "spirit of system" and used their imagination to develop theories.[3]

Pumpelly, who has been called both a mining engineer and an economic geologist, belonged to the earlier generation when these differences were first becoming apparent. In Arizona he had functioned as both engineer and geologist, studying the occurrence of ores as well as methods of extraction. He was a founding member of the American Institute of Mining Engineers in 1871, but for much of his career he was more interested in investigating the natural phenomena related to the science of ore deposits. He clearly fits Ransome's definition of the economic geologist who is involved with theory and research.

In comparing the work of the economic geologist to that of the general geologist, Ransome acknowledged that economic geology in the United States and Britain had not had the prestige that the other earth sciences enjoyed. In these countries geologists were more interested in problems of stratigraphy, structure, volcanism, and erosion and looked upon the applied branch "with rather languid interest" not only because it seemed too commercial but also because it required "frequent descent into the gloom and grime of mines" rather than outdoor fieldwork in scenes of natural beauty. In Germany, however, some of the great names in geology—Werner and Cotta, for example—had acquired their fame from their association with mining and mining schools and there, where it had a greater foundation in theoretical research, the reputation of *praktische geologie* was as honorable as that of other branches of the science.[4] Freiberg, as we have seen, was a practical school of mines but with a faculty that emphasized the scientific study of ore deposits. American geologists like Pumpelly, who had studied in Germany and been influenced by German theories, held positions on state surveys and formed the nucleus of the United States Geological Survey when it was organized in 1879.

As the demand for gold and silver to finance the expanding world economy increased and as the U.S. consumption of copper, iron, and other metals grew, the need for and prestige of the economic geologist rose. Some legislators looked to economic geologists to bring order to an industry that had been built on wasteful exploitation and speculation. As a result, after the Civil War state surveys began to place more emphasis on economic geology and less on the broad type of natural history survey that had been conducted before the war.

From the time he returned from China in 1865, Pumpelly frequently worked as an economic geologist and held positions that, while not always directly related to mining, were of a practical nature, having to do with economic uses of the land and its resources. He investigated mining properties for private investors, worked for the state surveys of Michigan and Missouri, and directed a national survey of the coal and nonprecious metal resources for the Tenth Census in cooperation with the newly organized United States Geological Survey. From 1882 to 1884 Pumpelly directed the Northern Transcontinental Survey for Henry Villard, president of the Northern Pacific Railroad, in order to determine the nature and extent of the natural resources of that part of the Northwest through which the railroad would pass.

These phases of Pumpelly's career clearly indicate the close relationship that existed between economic and general geology, between practical and so-called pure science, for in his work for private industry as well as for state and federal surveys Pumpelly often found opportunities to pursue his own research interests while fulfilling the practical goals of his employers, who usually saw geology only as a means of economic gain.

Private Professional Work

After returning from China, Pumpelly became involved in a variety of activities that took him to regions of the country as remote—but not as dangerous—as Arizona. His first job, which he obtained on the recommendation of Josiah Dwight Whitney in 1865, was as an adviser on some geological problems encountered in the building of the Hoosac railroad tunnel in western Massachusetts. Pumpelly found the rock at the western end of the tunnel to be badly weathered and decomposed, threatening further excavation. The problem, he soon realized, was "as much one of geological structure as of engineering." By surveying across the mountain and by examining specimens from the problem area, he prepared a geological profile of that part of the mountain and was able to determine that the decomposed rock was due to a fold in the strata at that point and did not extend far into the mountain. His early structural studies of the mountains of Corsica were of help to him here, for he had learned then that a small specimen "might repeat in miniature that of the great rock masses from which the small piece had come." The Hoosac experience was itself useful to him nearly twenty years later when he analyzed the structure of the Green Mountains for the U.S. Geological Survey.[5]

Whitney, who had been asked to form a mining school at Harvard, invited Pumpelly to become professor of mining in the new school, an appointment Pumpelly accepted early in 1867, although he did not actually teach there until the winter of 1869–70. In accepting the appointment, Pumpelly wrote Harvard's president Thomas Hill that he saw in the position "the opening of a wide field for moulding our system of instruction in mining into a shape more in accordance with the peculiar conditions which affect this branch of industry in our country." He also had an offer from Yale's Sheffield Scientific School, apparently engineered by his cousin George Pumpelly, a Yale graduate. His mother and his cousin George were very disappointed when Pumpelly accepted the Harvard appointment. George had hoped that Pumpelly would become "one of the band of young men of science to build up the Scientific School at our Yale." George felt Sheffield had a more solid foundation than Harvard's Lawrence Scientific School, with which the school of mines would be affiliated. "All the hardest work has been done" at Yale, "the future is plain sailing," he wrote. "Your mother and father want you to consider it. . . . They might move to New Haven." Pumpelly was, however, by then committed to Whitney and Harvard. In the time before he started teaching, he had offers of jobs to examine mines in California, Nevada, Mexico, and Guatemala and was also asked to return to Arizona and China. Instead, he became associated with a mining bureau in New York organized by his Freiberg classmate, James P. Kimball, and soon accepted a request to evaluate a copper property in northern Michigan.[6]

When Pumpelly went to work in Michigan in 1866 it was boom time for the Upper Peninsula. Copper production had escalated and Michigan was now producing 69 percent of the nation's copper. By 1872 more than 65 percent of Michigan's copper was coming from the Calumet and Hecla mines, which were managed by Alexander Agassiz for his wealthy Boston brothers-in-law. Mining operations had already begun to alter some of the geological features of the mining regions, but Pumpelly was able to see geological conditions that no longer existed six years later when he served as geologist on the Michigan geological survey. He saw miners removing huge blocks of solid metallic copper from fissure veins, and his friend, James D. Hague, who was working at one of the mines, gave him a tour of the mines and mills, where he observed the methods used to recover copper from the different ores.[7]

Economic geology takes many forms, as Pumpelly's work in Michigan illustrates, and could be a lucrative form of employment. From 1867 to 1868 he worked for the Portage Lake and Lake Superior Ship Canal Company, at a salary of $12,000, to evaluate and select tracts of land set aside by the government to finance the company's canal across the Keweenaw Peninsula. When completed in 1873, the canal gave ships better access to mining establishments and shortened by many miles the passage to upper Lake Superior. Although the trustees wanted him to explore for gold and silver, Pumpelly convinced them that iron and pine would be more valuable. He organized a team that included experienced woodsmen to advise on selection of pine tracts, which, he reported, were rapidly disappearing due to the enormous demand, and he chose a Freiberg graduate, Hermann Credner, to help him in identifying lands containing iron ore.

In spite of the mining activity, much of northern Michigan was still a wilderness and working there was arduous. Using the maps of early geological surveys and the dip needle, a type of magnetometer, Pumpelly and Credner looked for outcrops of rock containing iron, and when they found what promised to be good ore deposits they studied the geological and structural conditions under which they occurred. In this way Pumpelly selected tracts in the Menominee iron region that by 1915, when he was writing his memoirs, had paid $10 million in royalties from its mines. The pine he selected was sold for nearly $6 million.[8]

Pumpelly was by no means oblivious to the possibilities of personal investment in northern Michigan land. The Morrill Act of 1862, making federal land available for the benefit of state colleges, had opened up enormous tracts of land for sale that private speculators and investors were buying for timber and hoped-for mineral resources. No doubt thinking of his own family's involvement with the lumber industry, Pumpelly invested some of his own money in pine. He also formed a partnership, which became a lifelong friendship, with Thomas Benton Brooks, a mining geologist of his own age whom he had met in Michigan, to invest in promising sources of iron ore. Brooks had studied engineering at Union College and geology at the University of Pennsylvania. He had worked for the New Jersey geological survey and for the U.S. Coast and Geodetic Survey in the South and had served as a military engineer in the Civil War before becoming superintendent of the Iron Cliff Mine in Michigan's Marquette iron district in 1865. Together, Pumpelly and Brooks formed the Spurr Iron Mining Company, which, in spite of producing a considerable amount of ore, failed in the Panic of 1873.[9]

Economic geologists were not infallible. Whitney, for example, had concluded in 1862, after having samples of oil analyzed, that California did not have petroleum in commercial quantities, and Henry Janin made a serious but honest mistake in the case of the "Great Diamond Hoax," when he pronounced a diamond mine genuine that later proved to be fraudulent. One of Pumpelly's less successful enterprises was his collaboration with Alexander Agassiz, a marine biologist, son of Louis Agassiz, and successor to his father as head of Harvard's Museum of Comparative Zoology. Agassiz was also the manager who had turned the Calumet and Hecla mines into a fabulously successful mining company for his wealthy Boston backers in his determination to make enough money to finance his scientific research. Based on his success with the Portage Lake canal company, Pumpelly proposed to Agassiz and his brother-in-law, Quincy Shaw, that they back him in purchasing iron and pine land in Michigan. They agreed that he should select the land for them and have the right to buy a quarter interest at cost on a joint account, although he was debarred from buying land independently.[10]

Proceeding as he had for the canal company, Pumpelly selected many acres of pine. He also recommended some land near Lake Gogebic where by chance he had seen yellow streaks of limonite in the rock. Because he had not seen this type of ore before in the Lake Superior region, his recommendation was apparently somewhat qualified. According to Pumpelly's account, Agassiz seemed to lose confidence in his recommendations and objected to further purchases of iron lands in the region, although Pumpelly did buy two miles of the land on the joint account. Pumpelly's discovery turned out to be the Gogebic iron range, which, by 1965 when the mines closed, had produced more than 255 million tons of high-quality iron oxide ore. A historic marker near Ironwood, Michigan, credits Pumpelly with the discovery of the Gogebic range on October 8, 1871.

Agassiz's version of the story is that he decided against investing in the property "on the advice of a distinguished consulting engineer of the day" (presumably Pumpelly), who reported that the region was not worth developing. If Pumpelly had gone ahead and bought all the available sections, in spite of Agassiz's objections, both he and his investors would have made a fortune. As it was, the two-mile purchase, in which he had a quarter interest, resulted in the establishment of two highly profitable mines that had produced 12 million tons of ore by 1915, when he was writing his memoirs. In his old age he had no regrets for the lost bonanza for he was sure that the wealth would have made his life very different and might have "led to disaster" instead of to a life of "usefulness and happiness." Pumpelly could conceivably have found a roundabout way to invest his own money in the iron land in spite of his agreement with his backers. Some of his friends were not above acting in this way. James D. Hague, for example, sent inside information on a copper mine he superintended to a friend in Boston, who bought shares in the mine for Hague. Pumpelly, however, always seems to have upheld the ethical standards that were increasingly demanded of professional mining geologists and engineers.[11]

Throughout much of his life Pumpelly continued to work occasionally for private clients and to investigate possible mining ventures of his own as a way of supporting a growing family and his own aristocratic tastes. However, the revival of state geological surveys in the postwar years, while not paying as well, must have seemed an opportunity for steady work and a chance for greater participation in the scientific community. In 1869 a new geological survey of Michigan was organized and both Brooks and Pumpelly, with their experience in the mineral region of the Upper Peninsula, were asked to join it.

Michigan Geological Survey

From the establishment of the first state survey, that of Massachusetts in 1830, the search for minerals of economic value was only part of a survey that was meant to evaluate all the natural resources of a state—soil, forests, plants, and animals as well as geology. The Civil War interrupted state survey activity almost everywhere, and after the war there was a need to update the geology of mineral-producing regions in light of the country's industrial expansion. As new surveys were organized in the late 1860s, the emphasis turned more and more to economic geology. This change was due not only to the genuine need for reliable information about ore deposits but also to the fact that a practically oriented economic survey was more likely to receive governmental support.[12]

Michigan had already had more than one survey by competent geologists. The first had been authorized in 1837, soon after Michigan's admission as a state. One of its major purposes was to locate sources of salt, but it soon became apparent that upper Michigan contained valuable copper and iron deposits. The state geologist, Douglass Houghton, found copper on the Keweenaw Peninsula and his rather cautious report of 1841, including his statement regarding important deposits of copper in its pure metallic form, set off the first big mining boom in the United States. When the boom collapsed in 1847, Congress authorized a federal survey of the Lake Superior mineral regions. The final report by Josiah Dwight Whitney and John W. Foster was one of the earliest comprehensive federal reports on western ore deposits.[13]

The Houghton and the Foster-Whitney reports of the 1840s and 1850s reflected the still strong influence of Alexander von Humboldt on geological exploration. They included not just mining and geological data but also general geographical information on climate, meteorology, and terrestrial magnetism. The director of the second Michigan geological survey in 1859–60 was Alexander Winchell, a professor of geology at the University of Michigan, who believed that his survey should include climate, hydrology, soils, forestry, botany, and zoology as well as geology.

But with the start of the third state survey in 1869, under Winchell's direction, the legislature began to question the usefulness of including subjects "not belonging strictly to a geological survey." When the legislature refused to accept Winchell's comprehensive plan and denied his request for an appropriation of more than $60,000, Winchell resigned in protest and the survey continued under a geological board. The state reduced the survey's appropriation, eliminated all investigations in paleontology, topography, physical geography, and climate, and appointed three geologists to conduct economic surveys throughout the state: Pumpelly for the copper region of the Upper Peninsula, Brooks for the iron region, and Dr. Carl Rominger of Ann Arbor for the lower part of the state.[14]

The surveys by Pumpelly and Brooks of the Upper Peninsula were strictly economic and provided a solid basis for the orderly development of the region. The copper miners were hostile to Pumpelly at first, having expected that a Michigan geologist would be named. They may also have had a disdain for "them damned eddicated fellers," as one western miner expressed it, and perhaps preferred a more practical geologist. They had greatly admired Douglass Houghton, for example, feeling he was one of them, and they had deeply mourned his early death by drowning. The governor had appointed Pumpelly before this opposition was known, however, and as a result many copper companies refused to cooperate with the Pumpelly survey. Brooks, a mining man himself, was known to the mining community and took the assignment on condition that he would be able to accept all the assistance he could get from the mining companies of the region, inasmuch as the total appropriation of $8,000 per year was not large enough to conduct a thorough survey.[15]

State geologists had to strike a careful balance between the pure and applied aspects of geology, because not all legislators were pleased when the geologists placed too much emphasis on theoretical science. The reports of Brooks and Pumpelly provide interesting examples of the practical versus the scientific emphasis in government survey work. Brooks, who had less formal training in geology and more practical mining experience than Pumpelly, aimed his final report at instructing iron miners. He in fact considered it an "industrial report" and apologized for including in the appendix a scientific treatise on lithology by Alexis A. Julien, a professor at the Columbia School of Mines, that Brooks felt might better have been published in a scientific journal. Brooks's report included a history of mining development in the iron region, a description of the various mines, analyses of their ores, and an account of the machinery used. He gave extensive practical advice for miners on how and where to explore for ore and even provided information about the provisions, equipment, and instruments they would need. His discussion of the rocks in which iron ores occur is, as he said, "a popular presentation" of the subject to meet "the practical needs of the explorer and miner."[16]

Pumpelly's report achieved a nice balance between the practical and scientific subjects relating to the copper region. With his limited appropriation, he could not undertake a thorough survey of the whole copper region, and without the full cooperation of the mine owners he could not compile data on individual mines as Brooks did. Instead, with the help of two geological assistants, one of whom was his former student, Archibald Marvine, he constructed a series of stratigraphic cross sections in three key districts on the Keweenaw Peninsula and studied those thoroughly, mapping and correlating each with the others. The cross sections served a practical need, he thought, by providing owners of mining properties with "a number of accurately determined geological landmarks as guides in exploring for any given bed" and by establishing a base from which to continue the survey into neighboring counties. Two chapters of Pumpelly's report on the copper region were pioneering contributions to the science of ore deposits, helping to establish a tradition of research among economic geologists. One was "On the Age of the Copper-bearing Rocks" and the other "On the Paragenesis and Derivation of Copper and its associates on Keweenaw Point." These were not likely to be subjects of great interest to the copper miners but at least they were related, as Pumpelly pointed out in the preface to his report, to the "distribution and manner of occurrence of the copper."[17]

It was a common practice among state geologists to report interesting discoveries or results of research at scientific meetings or in scientific journals before writing their official reports for the state. This practice became common because publication of state reports was often delayed or, in cases where funding ceased, the reports were never published at all. Sometimes the more purely scientific findings appeared in the journals while the practical parts were reserved for the state reports. In Pumpelly's case, both of his scientific chapters had already been published in slightly longer form in the *American Journal of Science* before his state report appeared.[18]

Because so much of his Michigan report was in the form of plates and diagrams, Pumpelly thought it proper that the previously published scientific chapters be added to the text of the state report. He omitted, however, a passage in which he had expressed his belief that we can "arrive at a knowledge of the laws which govern the distribution of ore deposits" by studying the conditions under which they occur. He was most likely sensitive to the possibility that a search for general laws at state expense might not please the cost-conscious legislators.

Pumpelly's interest in paragenesis and in finding laws that govern the changes rocks undergo and the conditions under which ores are formed dated from his studies at Freiberg with Breithaupt and Cotta. Paragenetic studies reveal the way certain minerals become associated with others, the chemical effect of one on another, the relative order in which they crystallize, and the sequence in which one may succeed another. They help to determine the relative age of the associated minerals that make up ore deposits. Among other studies, Pumpelly investigated the amygdaloid rock formations of Keweenaw Point, where much of the copper ore was found Amygdaloids, or "trap" as the miners called them, are volcanic rocks containing small vesicles that have become filled with various combinations of native copper and copper-containing minerals. Pumpelly collected several thousand rock specimens representative of various sequences of minerals, and by detailed examination he was able to identify the relative order in which some of the minerals had been replaced by others or by native copper in different types of ore deposits.

His paper on paragenesis was one of the earliest in this field in the United States. It has become one of the classics of American geology, and his research in the copper region has become a model for later geological work there. A 1915 report on the Keweenaw rocks, for example, frequently cities Pumpelly's "minute" studies of the copper-bearing rocks and quotes several passages from his report. In 1925 a green copper mineral from the Keweenaw Peninsula, probably one he had called a "green earth," was named Pumpellyite in honor of his pioneer work on the paragenesis of copper.[19]

In October 1869, Pumpelly married Eliza Shepard, one of four beautiful daughters of Otis Shepard of Dorchester, Massachusetts. They met at the home of mutual friends and soon discovered on an evening walk in the hills that they had both felt moments of spiritual exaltation when "on the heights." Eliza missed her husband badly when his work took him

Eliza Shepard Pumpelly, age twenty; Raphael Pumpelly, age thirty (From *My Reminiscences* by Raphael Pumpelly. Copyright 1918 by Raphael Pumpelly. Henry Holt and Company, Inc., Publisher)

away from home for long periods. In the early years of their marriage she went with him as often as she could. Although not in the best of health, she camped with him on Lake Superior in the summers of 1870 and 1871, sometimes staying behind in camp with only a guide and his Indian wife as company. She often longed for home but loved the hemlock and spruce forests and enjoyed evenings by the campfire when her companion Priscilla told Indian tales. In October 1871, while Pumpelly was investigating the iron formations in northern Michigan, Eliza was at a base camp on the Montreal River in Ontario and demonstrated her newfound hardiness by walking twenty miles through an early snow to meet her husband at the mouth of the river on Lake Superior.[20]

During the winters of 1869–70 and 1870–71, Pumpelly lectured on mining deposits at Harvard's new School of Mining and Practical Geology. The school of mining had been organized in a decade that also saw the opening of the Columbia School of Mines (in 1864). The Columbia school flourished but for some reason the Harvard school was not successful; it never attracted many students and was discontinued in 1875. Its failure may have been due to the frequent absences of Whitney, who spent much of his time in California, and to Pumpelly's resignation in 1871. In addition to Pumpelly as professor of mining, the faculty in the 1869–70 academic year included Thomas Messenger Drown, instructor in metallurgy, who went on to become professor at MIT and president of Lehigh University, and William H. Pettee, instructor in mining, who later taught at the University of Michigan. Pumpelly lectured on ore deposits to three students: William Morris Davis, Henry Gannett, and Archibald Marvine. Although none of his lecture notes survive, Pumpelly would almost certainly have based his lectures on those given by Cotta at Freiberg. He may even have used Cotta's textbook, *Die Lehre von den Erzlagerstätten,* an English translation of which appeared in 1870, and no doubt would also have drawn upon his own research on Michigan's copper deposits. Like Cotta, Pumpelly would have emphasized the genesis of ores, their mineral associations, and the influence of the surrounding rock as well as current theories about the possible role of ascending, descending, or lateral secretion of mineral waters on the formation of veins.[21]

Pumpelly decided to give up the Harvard professorship after a group of students who may have had a grudge against his landlady set off an explosion on the verandah of the house in Cambridge where he and Eliza were living. In anger he went immediately to the president, who got out of bed to investigate the matter. This prank, which Pumpelly believed had caused his wife to have a miscarriage, plus the fact that "the Boston climate disagreed with me," contributed to his accepting an offer that came in the fall of 1871 to direct a geological survey for the state of Missouri.[22] While working for Michigan, Pumpelly had managed to combine his own research interests with practical investigations, but he and Brooks had been hampered by budget restrictions. He may have hoped that as head of his own organization he would be able to attract more liberal funding and accomplish a thorough economic survey.

The Missouri Survey

Missouri, like Michigan, had valuable mineral deposits, and wartime demand had caused considerable expansion of its lead and iron mines. By the early 1870s, with the completion of railroad lines and increased immigration to supply labor, the iron, lead, and zinc mining industries were growing rapidly. As a result, mining interests had for some time been pressing for the establishment of a new geological survey.[23] Pumpelly became Missouri's state geologist in November 1871, a position he held until illness forced him to resign in May 1873. During that period he continued to work for Michigan, conducting fieldwork on the Keweenaw Peninsula in the summer of 1872. His reports for both surveys were published in 1873.

Now in his midthirties, Pumpelly had his first experience as a government administrator, learning at firsthand the necessity of cultivating government patronage. As in other states, each survey was established by an act of the legislature and was renewed year by year if it produced satisfactory work. Missouri's first geological survey, directed from 1853 to 1862 by George C. Swallow, had been suspended during the Civil War. The first postwar survey, established in 1870, had been directed by geologist Albert D. Hager of Vermont, who lasted only until August 1871, relieved of his position for unknown reasons but possibly because he had managed to produce only a twenty-one-page report of progress. Pumpelly was appointed director, under a new act creating a Bureau of Geology and Mines, to complete the previous geological surveys of the state. The act provided for inclusion of a paleontologist and analytical chemist among the survey personnel but it made no provisions for zoological or botanical work.

Pumpelly was able to establish a good personal relationship with Governor B. Gratz Brown, a liberal Republican and a man of considerable political awareness, soon to be vice-presidential running mate of Horace Greeley in the 1872 election. The governor accompanied Pumpelly and Eliza on a forty-mile trip through the Mississippi Valley, entertaining them with his conversation most of the way and charming Eliza, although she "did not like his face very much." Brown was one of a five-member board of managers that had overall responsibility for the survey. Pumpelly had been led to expect difficulty in dealing with Brown and the legislature but instead had "only cordial support." He evidently convinced the governor that he would need more to accomplish the goals set forth by the legislature than the $5,000 that had originally been appropriated. On Brown's recommendation, the legislature increased the survey's appropriation to $20,000, allotted an additional $12,000 for publication, and repealed a section of the act that had limited the survey's total yearly expenses to $10,000.[24]

A major problem Pumpelly had to face in Missouri was the neglect of the survey since the beginning of the Civil War. As in many other states, a great deal of fieldwork had been done that had never been published for lack of funding. The Swallow survey had classified rocks and geological formations, prepared a good state map, and issued a few county reports, but surveys of several counties had never been published and Missouri's mining industry had been growing haphazardly without a thorough study of the state's mineral resources.

Pumpelly proved to be a good organizer. He perceived the problems, selected a talented staff of specialists, and drew up an ambitious plan of action, concentrating on the study of economic resources. His first priority was to publish the old county reports. The resulting 323-page volume, covering work done between 1855 and 1871, included sections on the general or "scientific" geology and "economical geology" for twenty counties that had been prepared by three assistants working under Swallow before the war. In his haste to publish, Pumpelly was not able to have all of the reports updated, and he included maps that had been engraved before 1861 because he believed they were "better than none." As Stephen P. Turner has pointed out, in most states no county wanted to be without its own survey, no matter what its natural resources were; paying attention to all the counties was one way of broadening political support. This fact may explain Pumpelly's efforts to get the old county reports published, as his staff would not have had time to prepare new ones in the first year of his tenure.[25]

Pumpelly's plan for new work was to pay particular attention to the iron and other ores and to do a systematic survey of coal resources. As assistants, he picked young, well-trained professionals, three of whom were Freiberg graduates. He gave the job of surveying the iron ores to a former classmate, Adolph Schmidt, who had been the director of an ironworks and supervisor of the scientific department of a Bessemer steel plant in Europe. Regis Chauvenet, later president of Colorado School of Mines, and Andrew A. Blair, a graduate of the U.S. Naval Academy, were the survey's metallurgical chemists. Geologist Garland C. Broadhead, who had been with the Swallow survey and who was to succeed Pumpelly as the next director, reported on the coals and was the assistant for general geology. Most of the resulting volume of reports was the work of Pumpelly's assistants. The 441-page report on *The Iron Ores and Coal Fields from the Field Work of 1872* included lengthy reports by Schmidt and Broadhead, chemical analyses of coal and iron ore samples by Chauvenet and Blair, and surveys of eight more counties by Broadhead.

Although administering the survey left little time for any research of his own, Pumpelly included in the report the results of his own study of the geology of Pilot Knob and Iron Mountain, two remarkable mountains in eastern Missouri that contained unusually pure deposits of hematite. An atlas contained maps and geological sections of Pilot Knob and other parts of the state. A reviewer for the *American Journal of Science* praised the report, commenting that the maps are "well engraved, and very neatly and tastefully colored.... The volume throughout is an excellent commencement of the series of reports which may be expected from the survey now in progress." Thomas Sterry Hunt, writing in the *American Naturalist,* thought that the discussions of various points "show good and thorough work alike for science and for the material advancement of the state."[26]

The act establishing the survey had specified the inclusion of a paleontologist, but the report was very deficient in this area. This was one of Pumpelly's biggest worries, as he had tried very hard to obtain the services of Fielding B. Meek, one of the country's leading paleontologists and a former member of the Missouri survey. Missouri's coal and other formations contain a great variety of fossils, many of which had been collected by the Swallow survey but were still in boxes, unclassified and unreported. Pumpelly's correspondence with Meek about working on those fossils provides an interesting sidelight on the reduced role of paleontology in the state surveys at the time.

Although paleontology is indispensable to geology, it had on occasion been the cause of conflict between legislators and state geologists. The volumes of *Paleontology* by New York's James Hall were the envy of other state surveys, but state geologists who tried to produce a similar work often met with opposition from their legislatures. Josiah Dwight Whitney, as director of California's survey, had made the mistake of publishing a volume on paleontology before any practical results of the survey were made public. One legislator read long technical passages from it in the California legislature to demonstrate the impractical way state money was being spent, and cutbacks in the survey were not long in coming. In Ohio, John S. Newberry made the same tactical error in his battle over funding with the state legislature. In spite of his insistence that fossils were the alphabet of geology, Newberry was forced to resign as director of the Ohio survey in 1874 when his beautifully printed *Paleontology* appeared before the economic reports were finished.[27]

Fielding B. Meek had worked during the 1850s as assistant to James Hall in New York and with Ferdinand V. Hayden in Nebraska Territory, where he had identified Jurassic, Cretaceous, and Tertiary invertebrate fossils. Meek's skill in identifying, classifying, and drawing fossils was superb, and he had since been much in demand. His work was of major importance in establishing the geological age of much of the Midwest. Wanting the best, Pumpelly tried to persuade Meek to come back to Missouri from Washington where he had rooms in a tower of the Smithsonian building. He asked Meek for an estimate of the time and expense required to "describe and illustrate, in as thorough a manner as may be desirable the paleontology of the State," including not only fossils found as a result of new work but also the large collection that was housed in considerable confusion at the University of Missouri at Columbia. Pumpelly was worried that the university, which was "not friendly" to the survey and wanted to dispose of the old fossils, would invoke an old law requiring the distribution of the collection to state institutions before they could be identified; such an action "would embarrass matters somewhat." He was particularly anxious that the work be done by Meek and not someone else.[28]

Meek at first was interested in working for Pumpelly, as the possibility of finding new species or unusually fine specimens of old ones was very appealing to him, but he also had reservations about undertaking the work and in the end was not able to do it. Not only was his health deteriorating, but he was also working on the fossils collected by the Ohio survey as well as those of the four federal surveys of the territories, and all of the directors wanted to go to press at the same time. He thought he could do it within a year, but he wanted selected fossils shipped to him in Washington, where he had access to all the necessary books, scientific periodicals, and transactions of societies in various languages. Apparently Pumpelly did not find it possible to ship the fossils.

Meek's realistic advice to Pumpelly was that the best approach would be *not* to attempt a comprehensive paleontological report as some states had done but to illustrate a series of the characteristic forms of the various groups of rocks; the illustrations would aid in identifying the different formations and their relative age. He was especially adamant that the collections should not be dispersed before they were analyzed, because it would be impossible to know which ones would be important for the preparation of the report. As for the educational value of distributing collections of fossils that had not been named and classified, Meek thought they would be "of little more use than so many toys, or mere curiosities of any other kind. They cannot be used in teaching or in any other way."[29]

Perhaps one reason for Meek's reluctance to go to Missouri was that his long experience with government surveys had made him skeptical about the reliability of continued support for the Missouri survey and for paleontology. He knew that, due to political pressures, three different survey heads had served since 1870, and he had heard that "some such influences are at work again." This was a situation Meek deplored. "It is much to be regretted," he wrote Pumpelly,

that it is not generally understood, how great a loss to the state such changes cause. When a survey has been in progress for a few years, under the direction of one party, and he is then removed and the work given to another, the money expended by the first one, is, to a great extent lost, and this loss is repeated with every new change. It is a shame that all such surveys should not be so established by the organic law ordering them, as to be entirely beyond the whims of party politics.[30]

Because Meek was unable to do the work and was so late in saying so, paleontology in Pumpelly's report on the fieldwork of 1872 was limited to a list of fossils from the coal measures, compiled by C. J. Norwood.

In May 1873 Pumpelly became ill with meningitis and resigned from the Missouri survey. Eliza was pregnant and wanted to be closer to her family when the baby was born. They moved to an old farm near Newburgh, New York, and Pumpelly did not become involved in any other government survey work until 1879. If politics had played a part in his resignation, he did not say anything about it in his memoirs. Perhaps the expense of the 1872 survey had worked against him; the new governor elected in 1872 may not have been as supportive, which might explain the rumors Meek had heard. The Panic of 1873 and the resulting depression must also have affected Missouri's survey as well as those of other states. Pumpelly's assistant, Garland Broadhead, succeeded him, and he too resigned within two years, after completing a commendable report based on work that Pumpelly had begun. It was not until well into the twentieth century that the Missouri survey was removed from the control of a board of managers and made a department of the state, finally more or less "beyond the whims of party politics," as Meek had hoped.

Tenth Census Survey of the Mining Industries

Economic geology took a more important place in the federal government on March 3, 1879, when Congress passed an act establishing both the United States Geological Survey and the Tenth Census. The new geological survey director, Clarence King, and the census superintendent, Francis Amasa Walker, who had backed King as the head of the new survey, came to an agreement to use survey geologists as technical experts to gather mining data for the census. King picked Pumpelly to direct the Division of Mining Geology of the newly organized survey and simultaneously named him as special agent of the census in charge of compiling statistics on the mineral industries of the United States, exclusive of the precious metals.

Under Walker's direction, the Tenth Census became a large-scale, comprehensive statistical study of the nation's natural resources. An experienced economist and statistician, Walker had been head of the U.S. Bureau of Statistics from 1869 to 1871, had conducted the census of 1870, and had since been teaching political economy at Sheffield Scientific School. Although he resigned from the census in 1881 to become president of MIT, it was his influence that gave the 1880 census its wide scope.[31]

Pumpelly was only one of several experts in various fields who acted as special agents to supervise the collection of data in industries of economic importance; some of the experts, like Pumpelly and King, were Walker's fellow members of the National Academy of Sciences. Other academy members who acted as census experts, producing reports of major significance, were John S. Newberry, reporting on quarries and building stone, Eugene W. Hilgard on cotton production, Charles Sprague Sargent of Harvard on forests, engineer William P. Trowbridge on power and machinery, and John Shaw Billings on mortality and vital statistics. A young engineer, Herman Hollerith, who reported on power used in manufacturing for the 1880 census, was soon to invent the punched card tabulating system, first used in the 1890 census, that revolutionized the processing of large amounts of data.[32]

The collaboration between the census and the United States Geological

Survey (USGS) was mutually beneficial to both organizations. As various observers have pointed out, King believed that the geological survey should concentrate primarily on mining geology, although he wanted the survey to make contributions to general geology as well. In his first and only annual report, King wrote that the major role of the USGS should be to bring order to the mining industry through the dissemination of information about the quality, size, and location of the various ore deposits necessary for the economic development of the country. Except for the Foster and Whitney report, he said, little information of value had been provided by the federal government, which alone was in a position to provide an overall assessment. Like the state geologists, King was also quite aware that the size of future appropriations would depend on the usefulness of the survey's work.[33]

King already had a sound background in economic geology and geological exploration when he became head of the USGS at age thirty-seven. He had graduated in 1862 from the Sheffield Scientific School and had his first field experience under Whitney on the California geological survey, where he examined mines and mountains, named Mount Whitney, discovered glaciers, and learned how not to conduct a survey by observing Whitney's mistakes. King had become famous in 1872 as the exposer of the "Great Diamond Hoax" and from 1867 to 1878 had directed the U.S. Geological Exploration of the Fortieth Parallel (known as the Fortieth Parallel survey), one of the four geological surveys of the western territories that had led to the establishment of the USGS.[34]

In organizing the USGS, King had set requirements for new positions that indicate the high degree of professionalism he expected of his staff. Applicants for the Division of Mining Geology, for example, were required to submit evidence of "a working knowledge of mathematics, mechanics, mining geology, chemistry, metallurgy and the mineralogy of mineral products." This evidence could consist of "degrees of universities, or the testimony of experts in the required branches, or the result of a written examination." Pumpelly met these requirements easily. King in fact thought him the best geologist on his staff.[35]

King also hired other geologists who had been trained in German mining schools. George Ferdinand Becker had attended the University of Heidelberg and the Royal Academy of Mines at Berlin, worked for steelworks, made an early study of the Comstock Lode, and taught mining and metallurgy at the University of California. Samuel Franklin Emmons had graduated from Harvard in 1861 and had then gone on to study mining geology in Paris and with Cotta at Freiberg. Arnold Hague, the younger brother of Pumpelly's friend James D. Hague, had been at

Sheffield Scientific School at the same time as King and then followed his brother James to Germany where he studied at Heidelberg, Göttingen, and Freiberg. Both Emmons and Hague had worked on King's Fortieth Parallel survey. King thus seems to have chosen some of his geologists partly out of friendship or for their connections but principally for their training and experience in mining geology.[36]

The affiliation of USGS geologists with Walker's census organization suited King, not only because it coincided with his plan to make the national survey an economic one, but also because it made possible the opportunity for the federal geological survey to cover the eastern states, an area it was not otherwise authorized to cover. The original act that established the survey was interpreted to mean that the USGS was to conduct its work only in the public lands and not to enter states where state surveys already existed, but Pumpelly's appointment as special agent for the census meant that he could investigate iron, copper, lead, and other types of mining production in states east of the Rockies. The census of the precious metals industries, most of which were in California, Nevada, and other parts of the West, was carried out by Becker and Emmons under King's direction.[37]

Pumpelly's organization of his census work and the resulting report show him to have been an effective administrator with high expectations for quality performance and an ability to get things done. His *Report on the Mining Industries* was an impressive compendium of geological reports, tables of data, maps, charts, graphs, and statistical analyses of mining on a scale never before attempted by the federal government.

As always, he wanted the best men he could get and wanted to pay them well. "Can I employ leaders in field under Survey salaries?" he asked King. And "Can I count on $80,000 next year? If not, how much?" Because King's entire appropriation for the survey for the first year was only $150,000, Pumpelly's request was unrealistic, even though survey funds were augmented by the census. Pumpelly did, however, recruit an impressive group of census agents. He appointed twenty-seven men as special agents, including state geologists and college professors, who personally or through deputies visited mines in their region to collect samples, interview mine operators, and fill out the census schedules. He also employed four geologists full-time to concentrate on surveying iron-mining districts and collect samples of iron ores. A staff of seven chemists conducted chemical analyses of the iron ore samples collected.[38]

Recruiting people to serve as agents was relatively easy because there was an existing network of state survey personnel, college and university professors, and members of scientific societies who could be called upon. A more difficult problem was identifying the mining establishments to be canvassed, as none of the states kept complete lists of mines. A directory of the mines that Pumpelly's staff compiled was published in his report in order to give the next census a starting point that had not been available to him.[39]

An important aspect of the work was preparing the schedules and drawing up the questions to be asked of mine operators. Pumpelly was particularly concerned that the fundamental questions should be so worded as to provide a uniform result that could be expressed numerically in totals for the whole country. In consultation with census experts, he prepared a list of eighty-eight questions for the coal mines and drew up similar ones for the copper, iron, lead, and zinc mines relating to production, materials, power, labor, and capital, expressed in amount or value. The schedules also covered the social aspects of the industry with questions about mine safety, time lost in strikes, the number of boys employed, and company stores.[40]

Pumpelly focused on what he believed to be the primary object of the census—the economic information—rather than on any investigation of the technical aspects of the industries. King wanted to prepare a comprehensive report on all aspects of the precious metals industry and his twenty-four schedules included many technical questions about methods used in the mining and refining of gold and silver. Pumpelly, however, thought that if a technical report on the state of mining of the different metals was needed, experts should be sent to study only "well-developed and established mines" and the information obtained incorporated into a special report, separate from the census report.[41]

King, in fact, did hope that members of the survey would prepare technical reports on the mining industries as USGS monographs. In his first annual report, King announced the forthcoming publication of ten monographs on mining geology, including reports on the booming silver mining districts of Leadville, Eureka, and the Comstock Lode by Emmons, Hague, and Becker, respectively. Pumpelly was to write three monographs, one each on coal, iron, and the "Lesser Metals and General Mineral Resources." Another, under Pumpelly's direction, would be a report on the copper-bearing rocks of the Lake Superior region by Professor Roland Duer Irving of the University of Wisconsin. King himself would write on the precious metals.[42] Pumpelly never produced monographs on his assigned subjects, however, as he resigned from the survey in 1881 to organize the Northern Transcontinental Survey. His own work on the coal, iron, and "lesser metals" appeared only in relatively brief papers included in the 1,886-page census volume he edited. King's precious metals monograph did not get written either, except for the census volume, but reports by Becker, Emmons, and Hague did eventually appear as important USGS monographs after King had been succeeded as director by John Wesley Powell.

The major part of Pumpelly's Tenth Census work was an exhaustive study of the iron ores. Realizing that the time and resources available under the census were too limited for comprehensive coverage of the entire nonprecious mineral industry, he decided to focus on the iron ores because of the rapid growth of iron and steel manufacturing during the previous decade, growth that had "called into existence a vast number of mines producing ores of the most varied characters." The introduction of the Bessemer process of steel making had caused a "great revolution" in the industry, making possible the production of cheaper steel for railroads and creating a greatly increased demand for ores with a low phosphorus content. Pumpelly knew from personal experience in Michigan and Missouri that iron ores from different deposits can vary greatly in composition, and he planned to set up a system of classification for the various iron ores and to determine their distribution and manner of occurrence. He also wanted to assess the potential capacity of ore fields and to gather information to assist in getting ores of the right quality to the appropriate manufacturing centers. He realized that reliable information about the country's capacity for iron and steel production would have an important bearing on trade, foreign competition, and other aspects of political economy. To begin the gathering of this information he had his geologists collect samples from many sources for analysis in his own laboratory.[43]

It was an undertaking of enormous scope, but he "daringly hurdled the difficulties," Bailey Willis remembered, "with very inadequate resources in men and money." Pumpelly established his census headquarters in Newport, Rhode Island, where he and Eliza then lived, making it possible for him to work near home although he made frequent trips into the field. In the winter of 1880–81 he and Eliza built a large house on Gibbs Avenue for their growing family, which now consisted of three little daughters, Margarita, Elise, and Pauline. A baby boy, Raphael Welles Pumpelly, arrived the following year. Pumpelly's offices were in "the historical old Vernon house," which had served for a time as French headquarters during the American Revolution. There he set up a chemical laboratory staffed by six chemists who analyzed the samples that came by mail "in a steady stream . . . in groups of five-pound bags, each one accompanied by description and geological diagrams of the occur-

The house at Newport, Rhode Island, 1881 (From *My Reminiscences* by Raphael Pumpelly. Copyright 1918 by Raphael Pumpelly. Henry Holt and Company, Inc., Publisher)

rence." His chief chemist was Andrew Blair, who had been with Pumpelly on the Missouri survey and had been serving as chief chemist of the United States Board to Test Iron, Steel and other Metals. The assistant chemists included Frank A. Gooch, a Harvard graduate with a Ph.D. in chemistry who had studied in Vienna and who later became head of the chemistry department at Yale. Nearly 1,400 samples were collected for analysis, including those sent in by the agents for Becker and Emmons, west of the hundredth meridian. It may have been too ambitious a project; the appropriation ran out before the work was finished. Nevertheless, the chemists conducted 95 complete analyses of samples and 1,157 partial ones, and the special apparatus and methods for the determination of phosphorus, sulfur, silica, and other elements in iron ores that Blair, Gooch, and the other chemists devised were useful contributions to the field of metallurgical chemistry.[44]

The men who worked for Pumpelly found that he was sympathetic and kind but expected superior performance of them, often leaving them to work out problems for themselves. Willis, fresh from the Columbia School of Mines, was one of four young geologists Pumpelly sent into the field to visit mines, study the mode of occurrence of the ores, and collect samples in the states east of the hundredth meridian. The others were Bayard T. Putnam, Edward R. Benton, and William M. Chauvenet. Willis had degrees in mining and civil engineering but little experience. Only later did he appreciate the humor of being titled "special expert."[45]

As in any science, the newcomer to geology gains the necessary hands-on experience by working with those with more experience. Pumpelly took Willis "into the forest in Michigan and taught me the rudiments of exploratory surveying by pacing and compass," Willis remembered long after. Pumpelly then sent him to work with Bayard Putnam at the Michigamme Mine on Lake Superior with a note urging Willis "to learn thoroughly the art of taking samples of iron ore" and to "bear in mind the necessity of patience and judgment and conscientious accuracy in the work of sampling. Also the importance of using the opportunity offered, in this series of visits to important localities, to fill your mind and your notebook, and that your career depends essentially upon your efforts in this direction."[46] Willis must have learned his lessons well. The years he spent working under Pumpelly influenced him profoundly; it was the beginning of a long and productive career for him as government geologist and educator. Both Willis and Putnam worked with Pumpelly on the Northern Transcontinental Survey, and Putnam was later part of Pumpelly's team on his USGS study of the structure of the Green Mountains.

Dispatched to various parts of the country east of the Missouri River, Willis and the other geologists often faced difficult conditions of wilderness work. Willis recalled that Pumpelly "sent me to search for the 'ore banks' from which the Confederates made iron and I found many of them with the aid of the gray-bearded mountaineers and moonshiners whom I encountered in a solitary ride of 600 miles through the valleys and mountains of the South." In September and October 1880, Pumpelly sent Willis to "visit all the iron ore deposits of Minnesota," of which little was known, to collect samples at mines and potential iron ranges. Trekking by canoe and on snowshoes to an iron range near Lake Vermillion, Willis and his small group of woodsmen got caught in early snow. On returning to town he found a telegram waiting for him from Pumpelly, who was in Birmingham, Alabama, instructing him to go immediately to another site, in Wisconsin. It was rugged and demanding work, requiring physical fitness and a spirit of adventure as well as expertise. Pumpelly had these qualities and must have looked for them in his assistants, of whom he expected the same. There was a remarkable esprit de corps among the staff. Willis remembered the "thrill of it" even forty

DEPARTMENT OF THE INTERIOR
United States Geological Survey
DIVISION OF MINING GEOLOGY

Newport Oct 13. 1879

Mr. Bailey Willis.
My dear Sir.

For the present you
would wish to learn thoroughly
the art of taking samples of
iron ore and for that purpose
you will please to report to
Mr. Bayard Putnam at the
Michipammie mine, Lake Superior.
Bear in mind the necessity of patience
and judgment and conservatism in coming
to the result of sampling. Near the
importance of many the opportunity
offered, in their series of visits to important
localities, to fill your mind and your
note book, and that your career depends
essentially upon your efforts in this
direction.

Yours truly
Raphael Pumpelly

A letter of instruction from Raphael Pumpelly to his assistant, Bailey Willis, October 13, 1879 (Reproduced by permission of the Huntington Library, San Marino, California) years later, attributing it to Pumpelly's "own abounding enthusiasm and generous confidence in the loyalty and capacity of the young men whom he drew about him."[47]

Pumpelly's Tenth Census volume became a standard source of information on the iron ores, even though its statistics were soon outdated. Ralph S. Tarr's 1894 textbook *Economic Geology of the United States* referred students to it for "a very complete account of the iron industry of this country."[48]

In March 1881 Clarence King resigned as head of the USGS and was succeeded by John Wesley Powell, who had played an important role in the establishment of the survey in 1879. The major part of the work of gathering data for the Tenth Census was finished, but compilation of the report was just beginning when, in July, Pumpelly too resigned from the USGS to conduct a survey for Henry Villard of the Northern Pacific Railroad. Under Powell, the survey's emphasis on mining geology was reduced and after Pumpelly left, taking some of his Tenth Census staff with him, the USGS Division of Mining Geology was discontinued.[49]

The Northern Transcontinental Survey

Pumpelly may have hoped, as he began to organize the Northern Transcontinental Survey, that railroad money would be a more reliable source of support for a scientific survey than the governmental agencies for which he had worked, but this hope was not to be realized. The business of railroad financing in the Gilded Age was cutthroat and volatile. The most admirable of intentions could go awry, as is shown by the rise and fall of Henry Villard, financier and president of the Northern Pacific, who engaged Pumpelly to conduct perhaps the most ambitious geographical-geological survey ever undertaken by a private railroad.

Villard, who had gained control of the Northern Pacific in 1881, wanted a "thorough scientific exploration" of the region the railroad would serve—more than 400,000 square miles, from the Dakotas to Washington—which he knew contained enormous resources of timber, coal, and agricultural land. Pumpelly shared Villard's enthusiasm for the potential of this largely unexplored territory and organized a survey team that included experts on soil science, forestry, hydrology, mining, and geology, hoping to prepare a plan that would guide rational development of the Northwest. His survey resembled in some respects Powell's plan for development of the arid regions of the whole western United States. Like Powell's, Pumpelly's plan was never completely realized, although he had support for it as long as Villard was in control. When Villard's empire collapsed in 1883, Pumpelly had to disband his staff on short notice and, although much of the work was never published or put to use, the Northern Transcontinental Survey (NTS) made public valuable information on coal, produced some of the first accurate geological maps of the region, and gave to the scientists involved opportunities for research that they might not otherwise have had.

The Northwest had of course been explored many times before, for various purposes. Lewis and Clark had covered much of the region when they traveled up the Missouri and across the northern Rockies to the Columbia River and the Pacific in 1803, on a mission that was at least partly scientific, and trappers, traders, and missionaries explored in the 1830s and 1840s for the purpose of trade and settlement. The first major railroad survey took place during the 1850s, when Congress authorized the Pacific Railroad surveys to look for routes for the transcontinental railroad. The northern route from Lake Superior to Puget Sound was surveyed by parties under Isaac Stevens, a former member of the Army Corps of Topographical Engineers and first governor of Washington Territory, who was convinced of the rich potential of the region and was most anxious for a northern route to be chosen. Although the Central Pacific became the first transcontinental line, Stevens's highly praised report formed the basis for the later founding of the Northern Pacific Railroad Company.[50]

As discussed earlier, these explorations by the engineering corps included geologists and naturalists but only as subsidiaries to the engineers. Pumpelly's survey was organized for different reasons than those that had gone before. The route of the Northern Pacific had already been determined and building was well under way when his survey began in 1881. The object of the NTS was to gather data that would guide the construction of branch lines and the building of new industries and would direct immigration to the proper points.

Construction of the Northern Pacific had begun in July 1870 with financing arranged by Jay Cooke. Cooke's company had laid six hundred miles of track before declaring bankruptcy during the financial panic of 1873. The new president, Frederick Billings, reorganized the company and by 1880 construction was under way all along the line. At this point Henry Villard, president of the highly successful Oregon Railway and Navigation Company, which operated steamships and connecting railways along the Columbia River, began to feel threatened by the encroachments of the Northern Pacific. An imaginative financier, Villard managed to raise $20 million through his famous "Blind Pool" from investors who were not told the purpose of their investment, and with this money Villard bought controlling stock in the Northern Pacific.[51]

Villard had an exceptionally broad vision of the growth and development of the whole Northwest. Born Henry Hilgard in Germany in 1835, he changed his name to Villard when he immigrated to the United States in 1853. After a successful career as a journalist reporting on the Civil War, he went to the Northwest to represent the interests of Germans who had investments there, a move that led to his own involvement in transportation companies in Oregon. He was a cousin of University of California geologist and agriculture professor Eugene W. Hilgard, and in 1880 he had commissioned Hilgard to survey Oregon and Washington coalfields with the idea of including coal mining as part of his Oregon railway company's business. The idea of a more complete survey occurred to Villard soon after a trip he took eastward from Portland to inspect his new domain and the progress of the railroad. The rich soil and timber that he saw on the company's lands "gave rise in his mind to a desire to start a thorough scientific exploration of the entire unknown portion of the Northern Pacific land grant," and he engaged Pumpelly to organize it. "It is of vital importance" to learn about the distribution of the region's resources, he told Pumpelly, "to guide us in building feeding lines." Villard thus became the patron of a scientifically oriented economic survey and supported it liberally. He agreed to pay Pumpelly a salary of $10,000 a year, allotted $30,000 for other salaries and laboratory expenses, and allowed Pumpelly to keep his headquarters at Newport.[52]

The Northern Transcontinental Survey, as Pumpelly called it, became an economic survey of much broader proportions than anything he had done before. It was "a survey after my own heart," one that would have a practical purpose but would also involve exploration into new territory and employ leaders in various scientific fields using the latest scientific methods. That he thought of it as economic is shown by a letter he wrote to Powell recommending Thomas Nelson Dale, who had worked with him on the Tenth Census, for a position on the USGS. "I would use him on the NTS," Pumpelly wrote, "but I need only economic geologists and his training and tastes are in the direction of purely scientific enquiry." The letter is also an indication of the more scientific direction the national survey was taking under Powell. Dale later became a valuable member of Pumpelly's USGS team that investigated the structure of the Green Mountains.[53]

Pumpelly's plan for the NTS, the broad outlines of which he drafted in only "two or three days," was not only to conduct a survey of timber and mineral lands but also to investigate the agricultural potential of the semiarid regions, including studies of the soils, climate, rainfall, and stream flow. There were seven divisions: one each for mineral resources, climate and rivers, soils, forests, economic botany, chemistry, and topography. Pumpelly staffed these divisions with some of his Tenth Census people; others he chose for their recognized expertise in their fields. The directors of divisions were "men whose names vouch for their value," he reported proudly. All of his men, he recalled in his *Reminiscences*, were "able, energetic, efficient, and anxious to make a survey succeed. . . . Of those now living, at least four are now members of the National Academy of Sciences."[54]

The Division of Mineral Resources was to trace rock formations, search for coal and iron ore, and investigate underground water and artesian wells as sources of water supply. The geologists had the newest equipment in the form of a diamond drill with which to sink test cores to a greater depth than before possible. Pumpelly made three journeys to the Northwest to pick the locations for more detailed study. His young geological assistants, Bailey Willis, George Eldridge, and Bayard Putnam, who had come to the NTS from the Tenth Census, were given assignments to examine and measure known deposits of coal and to look for new sources. Willis worked in the Cascades and around Puget Sound while Putnam was assigned to western Montana. George Eldridge, a hardworking young former high school teacher who had studied with Nathaniel Shaler, explored central Montana in the Judith Basin between the Musselshell and Missouri rivers and in the Livingstone and Bozeman coalfields. Eldridge found excellent deposits of bituminous coal for the locomotives close to the Bozeman railroad tunnel.[55]

This was economic geology in the most practical, applied sense, directly related to the needs of the railroad, but some members of Pumpelly's team were managing to conduct scientific investigations at the same time. William Morris Davis, who had studied with Pumpelly, Whitney, and Shaler at Harvard, and Waldemar Lindgren, who came to Pumpelly with a letter of introduction from his Freiberg professors, were given jobs on the NTS in 1883 as assistants to Eldridge in central Montana. There Davis, who was to become one of the country's most influential geomorphologists, made the observations that later led to the formulation of his theory of the cycle of erosion. In his report for Pumpelly's Tenth Census volume, Davis described the denudation that he believed had taken place due to river erosion, not ice, as some had thought. "In order that these agents should produce a smooth surface," he wrote, "they must perseveringly act until their valleys widen and consume the intervening hills and reduce the surface nearly to the base-level of erosion."[56]

Although the concept of reduction to base level had been proposed by Powell in his 1875 *Exploration of the Colorado River of the West*, for Davis the perception that the smooth plains of eastern Montana were old, not young as he had thought, and that the study of the history of river erosion could help to explain the present shape of the land apparently came to him in Montana as something of a peak experience or flash of understanding. When he later returned to Harvard, he introduced the "natural history of rivers" into his course on physical geography and "enlivened what had been before a very dull topic."[57] Waldemar Lindgren's report for Pumpelly on "eruptive rocks" was a scientific study of the porphyries, basalts, and other igneous rocks in the mountains of central Montana that preceded the later research on ore formation for which he was to become well known.[58]

The chemical department laboratory at Newport analyzed the samples collected by the geologists and conducted experiments to determine the commercial value of materials discovered by the survey. Head chemist Frank A. Gooch reported on his work in developing a new process for converting the low-grade brown lignite coal of North Dakota into a more efficient locomotive fuel. Although Eldridge discovered the high-grade coal of the Bozeman field while these experiments were going on, Pumpelly recommended that enough of the new product should be prepared for locomotive tests in the hope that the plentiful brown Dakota coals found along the route could be better utilized. Tests conducted on a Pennsylvania Railroad locomotive were successful, but the product was apparently not manufactured for the Northern Pacific.[59]

Irrigation in the territory made accessible by the Northern Pacific was a question of great interest to Pumpelly, and he had ambitious plans for research on matters relating to it. His ideas, progressive for that time, owed much to John Wesley Powell's *Arid Region* report that had first been published in 1878. Powell's report was a reform document, advocating a radically new policy for development of public lands in the rain-poor regions west of the hundredth meridian. Having seen the failures of farmers who had tried to homestead in dry regions, Powell recommended that in place of a system that divided parcels on a rectangular grid plan, without taking into account the nature of the land, a new system of grants should be set up, based on type of terrain and access to water. Lands should be classified according to their suitability for irrigation agriculture or for pasturage, and different amounts of acreage should be granted for each type of use. Powell's proposal, which also included suggestions for social cooperation among farmers along lines used by the Mormons, was, as Wallace Stegner has said, "a blueprint . . . that would, if adopted, remake society and thought" in the arid region. It was also "bear language in a bull market" at a time when settlers were moving west by the thousands, encouraged by glowing reports of agricultural richness when in actuality there was a 66 percent chance of failure. Powell submitted his report to Congress but it was not acted upon, and the importance of his recommendations were not appreciated until the Dust Bowl years of the 1930s.[60]

Working for the railroad, Pumpelly did not make such far-reaching proposals as Powell, but he did do more than simply identify mineral lands and timberlands that would be of use to the railroad. He wanted to determine the areas where agriculture should be discouraged in order to protect land better suited for grazing and "for what areas the opposite policy should be adopted." The NTS should obtain all the relevant data about irrigation, he thought, because the region's capacity to support agriculture was just as important as its ability to produce raw materials. "It seems to me," he wrote, "that there is no direction in which the Survey can be of greater service both to the roads and the country than in that of determining the fundamental facts relating to the possibility of irrigation and artesian wells in this region."[61]

The "chief factors in the problem" as he outlined them were: "The determining of the maximum and minimum amounts of water in the streams; the periods of flood; the areas where the climate renders irrigation necessary and where unnecessary; the areas . . . adapted to irrigation, and the relation . . . between the area needing irrigation and the water supply and the times of different stages of water."[62]

Pumpelly set up three divisions that were involved in the irrigation question: the Division of Climate and Rivers, the Division of Soils, and the Division of Topography. To head the Division of Climate and Rivers he appointed Edward Singleton Holden, who may have been a personal friend inasmuch as Holden had studied astronomy under William Chauvenet at Washington University in Saint Louis and married Chauvenet's daughter, whose brothers Regis and William M. Chauvenet had served as Pumpelly's assistants on the Missouri and Tenth Census surveys. Holden had graduated from West Point and had taught mathematics and served as librarian at the Naval Observatory before becoming director of the Washburn Observatory at Madison, Wisconsin. Although he apparently had little experience in climatology, Holden had done a number of compilations and catalogs, both as librarian and astronomer, and one of his NTS functions was to compile previously recorded meteorological data for the Northwest. By September 1882 Holden had "collated all the information in existence bearing on climate" between the forty-third and sixtieth parallels and the data were in the process of being mapped.[63]

Holden's division was also to gauge streams as an aid in determining "the relation between the prospective demand and supply of water for irrigation in the different valleys." At a time when stream measurement was in its infancy, Holden prepared instructions for the gauging of streams and for making periodic measurements of the heights of water. The USGS did not develop stream-gauging methods until 1889, after Powell persuaded Congress to appropriate funds for the establishment of an irrigation survey.[64]

Pumpelly assigned the Division of Soils to Villard's cousin Eugene W. Hilgard, who like Villard had been born in Germany but who came to the United States with his family when he was two years old. He had studied chemistry with Robert Bunsen at Heidelberg and mining geology at Freiberg but became interested in the agricultural aspects of geology while head of the Mississippi geological survey. In 1875 Hilgard became professor of agriculture at the University of California, where he established its Agricultural Experiment Station, and as a recognized soil expert he had been in charge of the Tenth Census report on cotton production. Hilgard was probably the best person Pumpelly could have lined up to head the soils division, the aim of which was to classify the soils according to their irrigability and determine their areas for representation on a map. For the NTS, Hilgard prepared large folio maps of the Yakima and Colville regions, accompanied by a page of text discussing the alkali and basalt soils of eastern Washington. The maps indicated in six colors the areas that were irrigable, partially irrigable, suitable for grazing, or unsuitable for either irrigation or grazing.[65]

The goal of the Division of Forests, headed by Charles S. Sargent, was to identify and determine the distribution of the trees of economic value and to assess the need for tree planting. Sargent, undoubtedly the country's foremost authority on forestry, was director of Harvard's Arnold Arboretum and had been responsible for the Tenth Census volume on American forests. Pumpelly put botanist W. M. Canby in charge of the Division of Economic Botany to study forage plants, the basis of the sheep- and cattle-raising industry, and even included an economic entomologist on his roster of experts. Dr. H. A. Hagen of Harvard was to make annual visits to the Northwest to study the insects injurious to both vegetation and timber, "even though the value of the results might not be at present apparent." Hagen apparently made only one trip in 1882 to Washington, for which he was paid $500. He discovered that the larvae of a butterfly had injured immense numbers of yellow pine and recommended that the trees be utilized as soon as possible.[66]

Pumpelly's plans to have topographic maps prepared of the region paralleled those of Powell, who was embarking on what he considered the necessary project of having the USGS make topographic maps for the whole country. Good topographic maps are "as essential to the rapid progress of the geologic work as the rails for the locomotive," topographer Gilbert Thompson had written to Powell. A similar opinion was expressed by Pumpelly when he reported that "the information obtained concerning this great area can be expressed only in very general terms unless we have at least proximately accurate maps on which the facts obtained in each division of the work may be represented."[67]

No accurate maps existed for most of the Northwest, so Pumpelly realized that the NTS would have to make them. He apparently never intended to publish an elaborate written report: "All the physical facts that have an important bearing on the prosperity of that region" were to be shown on maps drawn two miles to the inch and with contour lines representing 200 feet of vertical distance. Different sets of maps would show water levels in the streams at various seasons; rainfall, temperature, and other factors affecting crops by month and crop seasons; and the distribution of soils, forests, grazing lands, and minerals. Allen D. Wilson, who had been topographer on the King and Hayden surveys in Oregon, Nevada, and Colorado, joined the NTS to undertake the mapping of the more important parts of the region covered by the survey. The maps produced by Wilson were of superior quality although probably unappreciated by the officials of the railroad. The maps of the Yakima and Colville regions in Washington Territory and of the Judith Basin and the Crazy Mountains in Montana were on a scale of 1:126,729, with contour lines drawn to represent 200 feet of elevation.[68]

Powell wrote Pumpelly on April 20, 1882, inquiring about the scope of Pumpelly's NTS work. In reply, Pumpelly told Powell of his plans for mapping the region and said he would be glad to consider any plans in regard to cooperation with the U.S. Geological Survey. It is possible that Pumpelly's maps were adopted by the USGS.[69]

Both Sargent and Hilgard saw the NTS as an opportunity to travel and do research at the expense of a railroad baron that they would not otherwise have been able to do. Hilgard surveyed the soils of various parts of Washington for his NTS soil map and Sargent traveled through Washington and parts of Montana with Pumpelly to study the timber resources, but both men had further uses for the data they obtained. Hilgard had often been frustrated at "the slow process of educating authority to loosen purse-strings." His survey of California's cotton-producing region, which had been of great benefit to the state, had been done with Tenth Census funds. He had been able to do research in southern California only because of a Northern Pacific assignment to investigate asphaltum deposits. Pumpelly's Northern Transcontinental Survey now gave him the chance to study the soils of the Northwest. "Without the wider experience given me by these explorations," he later wrote, "which I have taken advantage of extensively, too, for my book on 'Soils,' I should not have been able to give my series of publications the scope they have had."[70]

In the spring of 1882, Spencer Baird had asked Sargent if he could prepare a silva to be sponsored by the Smithsonian; thus, when Pumpelly asked him to join the NTS team, Sargent envisioned "an expense-paid collecting trip in the Northwest" that would greatly benefit the project. Sargent's fourteen-volume *Silva of North America,* with illustrations of every known tree specimen, was the most authoritative source ever published on North American trees.[71]

Pumpelly made three reconnaissance trips in the summers of 1881, 1882, and 1883 to locate important stands of timber and to identify places where his men should conduct explorations for coal. He also needed to determine which lands should be kept for the railroad, which ones should be sold for revenue, and which areas should be mapped in detail. In 1881 he traveled from Portland and Puget Sound up the Columbia River by steamboat and then on horseback through eastern Washington and Idaho to Missoula, returning to the East by railroad. He visited Bailey Willis, already at work in the Cascades, and inspected a number of coal and iron mines. The geological formations along his route never failed to fascinate him, and he regularly made notes on rock formations, old lava flows, and evidences of erosion and glaciation.[72]

In 1882 Pumpelly traveled westward by private railroad car from Saint Paul to the end of the line in eastern Montana, then by stagecoach to see Eldridge near Bozeman, followed by an expedition with pack train into the northern Rockies. He passed the railroad construction camps, soon to be towns, that had sprung up with their attendant camp followers and saw that the land was rapidly being settled. He was now paying special attention to lands suitable for grazing and for growing wheat and oats, occupations, just in the initial stages of growth, that were to make Montana one of the principal producers of grain and livestock. "The lands adjoining the Yellowstone are being rapidly occupied," he observed. "The bottoms have deep soil and the only question is that of the present annual rainfall representing the normal. Irrigation is practicable on an immense and doubtless successful scale and the silt of the Yellowstone freshets is probably a fertilizer." Farther north, in less-settled territory, he saw that the soils of the valleys of the Dearborn, Sun, and Teton rivers were of fine loam evidently rich in lime, and he realized that the "rapidly falling creeks and rivers could be made available to the extent of their water over large areas."[73]

On this expedition and again in 1883, Pumpelly entered what is now Glacier National Park and made the first sighting by a professional geologist of a glacier in the Rockies, for which a glacier in the park has been given his name. In 1882 he tried to cross the continental divide to the western side of the Rockies, but even though it was July, the snow and ice blocked the passes. That year he saw evidences of past glaciers in the form of "large amphitheaters opening into the valley at a height many 100 ft above the stream."[74]

The following year he tried again, entering the mountains from the west and crossing the divide at Cut Bank Pass. With him, in addition to his packer and Indian guide, were Charles Sargent, botanist Canby, and two young men perhaps along for the adventure. They were Paul Dana, son of Charles Anderson Dana, editor and part owner of the *New York Sun,* and William A. Stiles, editor of Sargent's *Garden and Forests* magazine. As Pumpelly's notes indicate, Sargent made observations on species of larch, pine, and spruce on this trip, which no doubt provided material for his *Silva.*[75]

Pumpelly first suspected the existence of a glacier when he noticed that the water of a creek along the route was milky. Climbing a nearby peak, he could see the glacier with his field glasses, and on the third of August he started to follow the milky stream to its source in a large amphitheater. There he saw "one of the most magnificent of cirques, immense, perfect in shape and clothed with verdure and rendered parklike by groups of the Engelmann spruce." At the top of a 2,000-foot cliff was the terminal face of the glacier, rising another 500 feet above the cliff, from which descended several beautiful waterfalls. A piece of the glacier had broken off and carved a swath through a forest of large Douglas firs far below.[76] Both Sargent and Bailey Willis were active in promoting the preservation of the land, which finally became Glacier National Park in 1910. The glacier Pumpelly discovered was named for him but, strangely enough, he never published anything about his discovery nor, apparently, did he campaign for the creation of a park, although he obviously appreciated its beauty. His failure to publish may have been due to the abrupt end of the NTS, which was a great personal disappointment to him.

As Willis remarked, the Northern Transcontinental Survey "was born too big to live long." Pumpelly's ambitions for the survey ended in December 1883 when Villard lost control of the railroad. The expenses of building the road had been far more than Villard had anticipated and this fact, combined with the high dividends that he had promised investors, resulted in a deficit of more than $9 million by October 1883. Although Villard knew he was in trouble, he went ahead with plans for an elaborate ceremony to celebrate the completion of the road, perhaps hoping to build faith in the railroad. Former President Ulysses S. Grant, governors of states and territories, and representatives of foreign governments were there when the last spike was driven at Gold Creek, Montana, on September 8, 1883, but the price of Northern Pacific stock began to decline even while Villard was arranging celebratory excursions. Deserted by his friends, abused by the press, and on the verge of bankruptcy, he resigned the presidency on December 17.[77]

Villard had given Pumpelly his support from the beginning, even though Pumpelly had warned him that "to execute the Survey in the manner planned requires the organized effort of a force working at considerable expense." The total expenditure after two years of work amounted to $398,940, of which "more than a third was spent in the special exploration of the coal fields, in digging and boring." Salaries alone for himself and the forty-one members of the survey amounted to more than $200,000 for the four years of its existence, through 1884, although some of this money may have come from Pumpelly's own pocket. Pumpelly felt the results of the survey were worth far more than it had cost. He had estimated in his 1883 report that the bituminous coal lands alone that were selected by Willis and Eldridge would have a market value of $2 million within ten years. Among other benefits of Pumpelly's survey was its exposure of officials of the railroad's land department who had been selling off the railroad lands for their private gain, an outcome Willis felt far more than offset the cost of the survey.[78]

The NTS was terminated at once. Pumpelly appealed to the new directors to support the survey at least long enough to have the results written up, but they rejected his appeal. The railroad officials had never been in favor of the survey and the new directors apparently had no idea what the NTS had been trying to accomplish. They understood neither the meaning of the contour lines on his maps nor the need to analyze samples of coal. "When we want maps our engineers will make them, and when we want coal we will send our men to look for it," a committee chairman told him.[79]

The collapse of the survey meant that what had been accomplished to date would be made known only in scattered publications, their origin not always even apparent. Willis, Eldridge, Gooch, and others of the staff worked at Newport through the winter of 1883–84 writing up reports that Pumpelly used in his Tenth Census volume as part of the section on "The Coals of the United States." Also included in that volume were fifty-two maps and geological sections of Washington and Montana coal regions, many of them in color. Pumpelly issued some maps as "Map Bulletins," in limited editions of 600, distributed to libraries and societies, and a few members of the survey published papers in various journals based on their work.[80] Between 1884 and 1887, Hilgard wrote papers on "The agricultural features of eastern Washington Territory," on alkali soils, and on "The processes of soil formation from the northwestern basalts." Bailey Willis continued to study the stratigraphy and structure of the Puget Sound region, publishing a paper on the subject as late as 1898 that was based in part on his NTS work.[81]

Pumpelly's experiences as an economic geologist illustrate some of the difficulties encountered by those trying to apply their science to the solution of practical problems. Like King, Powell, and other geologists in government service, Pumpelly believed that generously supported science could provide guidance for the rational development of natural resources and could prevent wasteful exploitation. His vision of what economic geologists could do by providing comprehensive information on the iron industry, for example, was farsighted in its scope, anticipating the needs of his day as well as those of the future.

He learned, however, that continuing support depended not only on how well geologists fulfilled the expectations of their employers or clients but also on factors beyond their control, such as economic depression or financial collapse of an enterprise. In his administration of various surveys, Pumpelly obtained the services of some of the top people in their fields, believing that by using people of proven ability he could best accomplish the objectives expected of him and that he set for himself. His problem was finding the money to keep the work going at the level of quality he wanted. As long as he had the support of men who shared his goals, like Villard and Governor Gratz Brown of Missouri, he was successful. But when he was unable to educate those who held the purse strings in the value of his work, as in the case of the men who succeeded Villard, he could do nothing further. In government work, his knowledge of mining geology gained him the respect and confidence of such people as Clarence King and Governor Brown, but he was not comfortable with the politics of getting support. Perhaps it was his dislike of politics as much as his illness that led to his resignation from the Missouri survey in 1873 to do research that was "more congenial" to him.[82]

5 Gentleman Geologist

For certain periods in his life Pumpelly lived in the style of what has been called the "gentleman geologist." Although he was professionally trained and had various kinds of paying jobs at different times, some of his most important work was done at his own expense, on his own time, and on subjects of his own choice. His geological explorations in China are one example of this way of working. Another period of independent creative activity occurred after his resignation from the Missouri survey in 1873 when, living as a gentleman farmer near Newburgh and Owego, New York, he spent five years in research and writing.

Throughout his career, Pumpelly's Gilded Age life-style allowed him to avoid some of the more restrictive aspects of professional life. He made several career changes, from economic geology to more general geological research to archaeological geology, and never had the demands on his time that would have come from a permanent professional teaching position. Through his extensive travels and explorations he became truly cosmopolitan in his experience of the world and in his wide-ranging interests. Among his friends were many artists and writers as well as scientists, and he enjoyed the cultural exchange that was made possible by membership in various clubs. Like other cultivated Victorian gentlemen, he did many things well but developed few in depth. For these and other reasons it seems fitting to describe Pumpelly as a "gentleman geologist."

Roy Porter has discussed the persistence in Britain of a "gentlemanly" attitude to geology that was a holdover from an earlier time when geology was practiced by amateurs. He found that traits of the "gentleman geologist" could still be detected in members of the Geological Survey of Great Britain after the survey had become professionalized.[1]

The association of gentlemen and geology in Britain dates from the seventeenth century, when a few gentlemen of leisure joined clergymen and medical practitioners to debate such questions as the meaning of fossils and the causes of the Deluge. The association continued into the nineteenth century with the establishment of the Geological Society of London, several of whose members were of the landed gentry, including Roderick Murchison, Charles Darwin, and Charles Lyell. Anglican clergymen-geologists like William Buckland and Adam Sedgwick also exhibited gentlemanly characteristics, combining, as Charles C. Gillispie has put it, "the bluff, outdoor spirit of the gentry with the Church's vague sponsorship of genteel learning." These gentlemen were no longer the amateurs of the earlier period, however; their devotion to research and their contributions to a more sophisticated knowledge of the structure and evolution of the earth gave them a career status that was professional in every way except for the fact that they did not hold degrees or paid positions in their field.[2]

These British gentlemen geologists, as Porter has pointed out, were often of the landed class, with an independent income that allowed them to pursue an avid, lifelong interest in geology. They were cosmopolitan—able to travel to Europe and, in Lyell's case, to the United States, where they explored, did fieldwork, collected specimens, attended meetings, and exchanged ideas with other scientists. Because of their financial independence the gentlemen geologists were free to devote time to research, buying their own equipment and hiring assistants when needed, and to "scorn posts" if they felt so inclined, preferring, like Lyell, to have the freedom to pursue their own interests rather than be tied to an academic teaching position. They enjoyed the society of their peers at meetings of the Geological Society of London, a place not only for scientific exchange but also for good fellowship, and they were prominent among the gentlemen of science who were responsible in 1836 for organizing the British Association for the Advancement of Science, whose meetings, held in different cities each year, became events of both social and scientific importance.[3]

Victorian geologists, both British and American, held a number of romantic notions about their work. Their closeness to and love for the land may have motivated many of the gentlemen to cultivate a scientific interest in it. Field trips and the challenges and dangers that accompanied geological exploration allowed them to indulge the country gentleman's propensity for rugged, outdoor, manly activity. Studying fossils, structure, and stratigraphy in the field stimulated imaginative interpretations of the earth's past as geologists pondered the questions of the causes of change over vast periods of time. The life in the outdoors, often in settings of great natural beauty, was also a source of spiritual uplift, for there, as Humphry Davy remarked, one could find "that part of Almighty God which resides in the rocks and woods."[4]

Pumpelly is a particularly good example of a late-Victorian, American gentleman geologist. He was dedicated to his scientific career, did theoretical and applied research, published scientific papers, and belonged to scientific organizations, but his independent income at times allowed him to pursue outside interests and avoid some of the irksome duties that had to be performed by those whose income came solely from their profession. The profitable investments he made in mines and timberland in northern Michigan, supplemented by lucrative consulting work and an inheritance from his father, who died in 1876, no doubt contributed to his ability to live the life of a country gentleman.

In 1873, when Pumpelly purchased a neglected farm near the Hudson in Balmville, New York, and later, when he tried his hand at dairy farming on a farm near Owego that had belonged to his father, he did so thinking that outdoor life would improve his health. His wife Eliza shared his love for the out-of-doors and, like him, wanted to bring up their children where they could have the benefits of fresh air and outdoor activities. He was also pursuing the pastoral ideal that inspired so many Americans, before and after him, to move to the country. Shaler, too, had "a feudal leaning toward a large estate," according to his wife. While a full-time professor at Harvard, Shaler bought several old farmsteads on the north shore of Martha's Vineyard until he had a sizable farm, which became more a retreat from the pressures of teaching and the fulfillment of a desire to be close to the earth than a serious attempt at farming, although he believed that farming was a duty of man and the farmer a naturalist who can gain "spiritual profit" from an "intimate relation with the forces which control the development of the world." Shaler bought one tract because he wanted to have a "moraine of his own," for he "coveted the rocks as much as he did the soil," his wife remembered.[5]

The characteristics of a group of American gentleman farmers can be found in Tamara Plakins Thornton's study of the elite Boston professionals and textile manufacturers who, earlier in the century, had bought rural estates to which they could retreat, planning to practice scientific agriculture as an antidote to what they perceived to be the decline of moral values associated with excessive commercialism.[6] Like those Boston "landed gentry," Pumpelly was interested in providing examples of improved methods that would benefit local farmers, a goal only partially realized on the large plantation in southwest Georgia near Bainbridge that his friend, Thomas Benton Brooks, persuaded him to buy in 1884.

Pumpelly seems to have achieved an ideal peaceful life in the country, especially at the Balmville farm where the couple's first two children, Margarita and Elise, were born. Every morning before breakfast he would ride around his "estate" with two-year-old Margarita on his lap, pausing on a hill to enjoy the view down the Hudson to the gap in the mountain at Storm King. On the Hudson Valley farm, and later in Dublin, New Hampshire, where he built a summer home near Mount Monadnock, he and Eliza socialized with a congenial group of artists and writers who had also retreated from the city. As the children grew older, they were out-of-doors a great deal of the time, riding their horses with their friends and exploring the countryside around Bainbridge or Dublin as their father had done as a child in Owego. In Georgia, the Brooks and Pumpelly families lived in a semicommunal style, achieving an almost utopian harmony with the land and with each other.[7]

But as an experiment in agriculture, the pastoral experience was a failure. Pumpelly had bought the Georgia plantation at the suggestion of Brooks as a place to "rest and to roam in," where he and his family would spend their winters. He soon found, however, that Brooks, who was full of "restless energy," had different ideas.

I listened to his alluring advice and we joined our plantations and bought neighboring ones till we had nearly 6,000 acres. We would stock them with cattle and do scientific farming. The Georgia planters were staggering under mortgages bearing 12% to 18% interest, and were therefore forced to plant cotton at a loss because it was a "money crop." We would show them the way to success.[8]

Pumpelly himself was apparently not a hands-on farmer, however. He seems to have had little practical business sense and did not devote full time to running the farms. The dairy farm near Owego and the plantation in Georgia became financial disasters when he took bad advice on the purchase of breeding animals or local caretakers took advantage of his trusting nature. Promising experiments in raising crops of Sumatra tobacco and experimental herds of Devon cattle in Georgia failed for lack of capital or a receptive market.

Pumpelly's lack of success as a farmer was probably due to the fact that he was more interested in continuing the geological research he had begun earlier, work that was more satisfying to him than that required by the state surveys. The leisurely country life at Balmville enabled him to take up some of the research he had been forced to neglect while director of the Missouri geological survey.[9]

One of the advantages of being an independent researcher was having the luxury of time in which to do detailed work and to reflect on its significance. Time had been in short supply on the state surveys, where yearly deadlines had to be met and administrative duties attended to. Pumpelly might well have sympathized with the conclusion of the English gentleman scientist, Henry Clifton Sorby, that two of the most essential requisites for the successful prosecution of original inquiry are "abundance of time for continuous and extended experiments, and freedom from all those disturbing cares and engagements" that interrupt or occupy the attention, so as to "prevent the mind from properly digesting the results." In a contribution to a collection of essays by a group of Oxford University scientists supporting the endowment of research, Sorby used his personal experience as a private investigator with inherited income to argue that original research was very difficult when combined with a business or profession, that scientific discovery came slowly, often with false starts and blind alleys, and that undisturbed time for work and reflection was absolutely necessary.[10]

In the period before the endowment of research enabled researchers to find this undisturbed time, it was principally people like Sorby and Pumpelly who could afford to do it. The years between 1873 and 1879, during which Pumpelly was able to work uninterruptedly on his own projects, were at least as productive for him as the years in which he received support from other sources. One memorialist called this "the really one creatively productive period of his busy life,"[11] although Pumpelly himself thought his explorations in Turkestan supported by his own and Carnegie funds were his greatest accomplishment.

Pumpelly did not find it possible to combine research with teaching, as some of his contemporaries did, although he taught briefly at Harvard's short-lived mining school. As university departments of geology became more common, some geologists apparently happily combined winter academic work with summer fieldwork for state and federal surveys and did research as well. Nathaniel Shaler, for example, had a long and successful career as a popular geology and geography professor at Harvard while acting as head of the Geological Survey of Kentucky and later as a division head for the USGS. Shaler also found time to write extensively on physical geography and his theories of Social Darwinism. Thomas Chrowder Chamberlin was another effective teacher who taught geology at his alma mater, Beloit College, while head of the Wisconsin geological survey. He later rose to the presidency of the University of Wisconsin, then founded the department of geology at the University of Chicago. Chamberlin did important research in the field of glaciology and at Chicago founded the *Journal of Geology* in order to publish departmental and outside research.[12]

Pumpelly, however, did not take to academic life. He probably shared Whitney's feelings about teaching. Whitney was not an effective teacher; he was better at presenting his ideas in written form than lecturing to a class of students, preferring research and working with a few advanced students. Most of the undergraduate teaching in geology at Harvard fell to Shaler.[13] Like Whitney, Pumpelly preferred research and the solving of new problems to the repeated lecturing on the basics of his subject. His fondness for and encouragement of young people was remarked on by Bailey Willis and others, but even so, Pumpelly may have found it difficult to organize and systematize his knowledge for classroom presentation; he would rather be in the field and at the cutting edge of new developments. "Inspiring as he was as an instructor in the presence of Nature," Willis wrote, "he was ill fitted for systematic teaching in an institution."[14] It is possible that two of Pumpelly's Harvard students who worked with him as survey assistants, Archibald Marvine on the Michigan survey and William Morris Davis on the Northern Transcontinental Survey, learned as much or more from him informally in the field as they did in the classroom.

Putting his ideas into textbook form was also difficult for Pumpelly. His friend, publisher Henry Holt, asked him to write a general geology textbook for an American Science Series. To work on it, Pumpelly spent part of the winter of 1875–76 in Cambridge, where Alexander Agassiz made a room available for him at the Museum of Comparative Zoology. "I was always full of what I wanted to say . . . but I could not make a logical statement of the subjects in my mind," he wrote later. He attributed his difficulty to the fact that he had resolved to stop the heavy smoking he had begun in Corsica. The geology text Holt wanted was finally written many years later—the classic three-volume *Geology* by Chamberlin and Rollin D. Salisbury.[15]

Although the immediate cause of Pumpelly's leaving Harvard was the explosion set off by some undergraduates on the porch of the house where he was living, it is more likely that he felt that the growing professionalization of geology, starting in the 1870s, was reducing academic geology to a dry, routine science that bored teachers and students alike. Even H. G. Wells, a student at Britain's Royal School of Mines, thought geology was far less exciting than biology or physics. Late Victorians like Pumpelly who had contributed to the foundations of geology must have disliked the routinization of the science that was still exciting to them. Pumpelly admired a born teacher like Shaler, who inspired his students with enthusiasm in the classroom and maintained warm informal relations with them outside of it, in the manner of Cotta and other German professors: "Bless them and him: for they are remembered with affection and gratitude." But Pumpelly was not a born teacher and he probably found that his own enthusiasm for his science could flourish not in an academic setting but through fieldwork and independent research.[16]

The research that Pumpelly took up during the six years after leaving the Missouri survey in 1873 and before joining the USGS in 1879 was a continuation of the work he had done in China, Michigan, and Missouri. He concentrated primarily on two subjects: petrologic studies using new microscopical techniques, and the development of a theory to account for the origin of loess.

Independent Research

The microscopic study of rocks in thin section was a new technique hardly known in the United States when Pumpelly began his work on the rocks of the Lake Superior region. Henry Clifton Sorby had pioneered this study in England, beginning about 1850, by painstakingly grinding small chips of rock to an almost transparent thinness and examining them under a microscope equipped with a Nicol prism to produce polarized light. Sorby used these studies to determine the structure and mineral composition of certain sedimentary and metamorphic rocks and to resolve long-standing questions of their origin.[17]

Microscopic petrography was slow to be adopted in England, where it was an unfashionable topic among geologists who were more interested in stratigraphy. Sorby published several papers on the results of his research but unfortunately did not describe his methods, so his publications did not have the impact they might have had in stimulating work by others in this field. It was two German geologists who fully developed the method. On a tour Sorby took in Germany in 1861, his companion and guide was Ferdinand Zirkel, who had just received his Ph.D. degree from the University of Bonn with a dissertation on the volcanic rocks of Iceland. Zirkel became enthusiastic about Sorby's work and decided to take it up himself. His first paper on microscopic petrography appeared in 1862 and soon others in Germany started using the method. Zirkel's *Die Mikroskopische Beschaffenheit der Mineralien und Gesteine*, published in Leipzig in 1873, was an influential work containing detailed descriptions, based on his microscopic studies, of many types of rocks and minerals.

Also in 1873 appeared *Mikroskopische Physiographie der petrographisch wichtigen Mineralien* by Harry Rosenbusch, professor of mineralogy and petrography at the University of Strasbourg, which further emphasized the importance of microscopical studies of rock-forming minerals and discussed the optical principles on which they were based. Rosenbusch's book went into four editions, each enlarged by his latest discoveries. The method was soon widely adopted and by the first part of the twentieth century was accepted practice.[18] As Arthur Holmes remarked in his 1921 textbook on petrographic methods, "No other laboratory method of investigating rocks has been more extensively cultivated; and from being a curious novelty apparently devoid of significance, the thin section has become a recognized means for attacking the manifold problems associated with rocks and ore-deposits."[19]

Pumpelly was one of the first American geologists to adopt the new method, although it was two years before he published anything about it. It is not clear how he learned the technique of preparing thin sections, but he must have obtained the German publications of Rosenbusch and Zirkel and studied them carefully, setting to work soon after leaving the Missouri survey in 1873. These investigations occupied him much of the time until 1878, when he published the results of his microscopic studies of the copper-bearing rocks of Lake Superior. There is no indication that Pumpelly had made use of this method for his paper on paragenesis, first published in 1871 and included in his Michigan geological survey report. He would have been aware of the technique before 1873, however, because the Michigan geological survey report on the iron ores by his friend Thomas Benton Brooks had included results of microscopic work by Alexis A. Julien of the Columbia School of Mines and Charles E. Wright, a student at Freiberg. Under the direction of Professor Cotta, Wright prepared thin sections from seventy-eight iron ore specimens that Brooks had sent to Freiberg, and for the Michigan report Wright briefly described and identified the minerals found in the specimens.[20]

Another path by which German methods were brought to the United States was through Clarence King's Fortieth Parallel survey. King wanted the most advanced investigative methods used for his reports so that they would be "on an equal footing with the best European productions." He hired Wright to study the microstructure of western rocks and sent Samuel Franklin Emmons to Europe in 1874 to study British and Continental methods, to buy books and German microscopes, and to confer with Zirkel in Leipzig. Emmons persuaded Zirkel to come to King's New York headquarters to oversee the microscopic work. The resulting report by Zirkel, *Microscopical Petrography,* with twelve plates, was a greatly admired volume and was of enormous importance in furthering the development of petrology in America.[21]

According to George P. Merrill, the first public announcement of the introduction of microscopic petrography to the United States was by Yale mineralogist Edward S. Dana at the August 1874 meeting of the American Association for the Advancement of Science. Dana gave a preliminary report of work in progress by himself and G. W. Dawes on the Triassic trap rocks of the Connecticut Valley. They had done microscopic examinations of specimens from many locations, observing texture, mineral components, and water content of the rocks.[22]

Pumpelly was not interested in using the microscope just to identify, describe, or classify rocks as others were doing. He wanted to study the way rocks had evolved through successive alterations of the rock-forming minerals, work that grew out of his earlier research on paragenesis. What he had investigated before with all the standard methods then known, he now undertook to study microscopically. These studies contributed to a better understanding of the processes by which some of the oldest metamorphic rocks of the continent had been formed.

As Willis pointed out, it is surprising to realize that the adventurous explorer of Arizona and Asia had the patience for this kind of work. "For most of the work I had to cut from rocks, for study under a microscope, sections thinner than the thinnest tissue paper—it was a method just introduced in Germany," Pumpelly later wrote. "This study occupied my time during the three years we lived at Balmville." There, in a room over the kitchen, distracted only by children, dogs, and the birth of kittens, he did the painstaking and tedious cutting and grinding of chips of stone and preparation of the slides he wanted to study. Later he had an assistant help him with the grinding, but one reason he wanted to prepare the slides himself was to make various tests on the thin sections before capping them.[23]

Pumpelly's first publication utilizing microscopic studies, which appeared in 1875 in the *American Journal of Science,* describes how he was able to determine certain successive changes that had taken place in the rocks over a long period of geologic time by taking optical measurements of crystals in the thin sections. He found that crystals from a bed of chloritic schist in the Michigamme iron range had retained the form of garnets but the mineral of the garnets had been replaced by chlorite. He cut several thin sections, about one inch in diameter, through the middle of the crystals and studied their optical characteristics as well as their appearance under various magnifications, using "one of Beck's first class binoculars, in which the polarizer is attached to a sub-stage, and the main stage is graduated." He described and at least partially identified the chloritic mineral that had attacked and in many cases completely replaced the garnet.[24]

In research for his best-known paper based on work with thin sections, Pumpelly turned again to the copper-bearing rocks of the Keweenaw Peninsula of upper Michigan to study alterations in Precambrian basaltic rocks of approximately Huronian age that had led to the deposition of copper. It was a pioneering study in metasomatism, the process by which elements in the host rock are dissolved and replaced by the metal ions of entering solutions.[25] Whereas his 1871 paper on paragenesis had been concerned with the alteration of minerals in veins, this study concentrated on changes in rocks surrounding the veins. His purpose, as he said, was not simply to describe the rocks but "to trace the changes that have taken place in the interior of the rock masses, in places where the only ingress and egress was through the capillary cracks formed by the cleavage and mutual boundary planes of the crystalline constituents."[26]

Pumpelly was interested in the metasomatic process itself and the order of the succeeding replacements that led to the deposit of copper. He did not develop a theory to explain the origin of the mineral solutions nor, as an *American Journal of Science* reviewer pointed out, did he discuss the chemistry of the metasomatic processes involved, but he did establish the order of succession for a number of minerals and his detailed microscopic studies helped to provide a firm basis of fact on which later theory rests. Waldemar Lindgren, head of the geology department and professor of economic geology at MIT from 1912 until 1933, who carried this kind of research much further, thought that Pumpelly was the first to apply the principles of metasomatism to the origin of ore deposits in this country and the first to use the microscope for its study.[27]

Lindgren became familiar with Pumpelly's petrographic work at Newport in 1883 or 1884 when doing microscopic studies, under Pumpelly's direction, of rocks from the Northern Transcontinental Survey. "As I began to dip into metasomatism later on," Lindgren told Bailey Willis, "I soon found that he was really a pioneer in the study of changes which minerals undergo. . . . Our geology of today certainly owes a great deal to his pioneering work."[28]

For a time, Pumpelly was the recognized authority on ore deposits, particularly the copper-bearing rocks of Michigan. He contributed, without compensation, a chapter on the "Lithology of the Keweenawan System" to Thomas C. Chamberlin's 1880 *Geology of Wisconsin,* in which he classified the rocks from various collections by microscopic examination of over one hundred thin sections, as an aid in comparing the rocks of the Keweenawan series of Michigan with those of Wisconsin. Chamberlin acknowledged that "the eminence of his authority on this series lends great value to this report." Pumpelly also contributed an authoritative chapter on "Ore Deposits" to *Johnson's New Universal Cyclopedia*, a popular encyclopedia that included technical articles by specialists. The encyclopedia went into many editions. Pumpelly's article was still being used in the edition of 1899, revised to include new theories of ore deposition by Charles Kirchhoff.[29]

But even though Pumpelly became known for his knowledge of this subject, he had the luxury as a gentleman geologist of avoiding narrow specialization. He branched out into other fields of geology during this period of retirement, most notably by investigating the source of the materials for loess.

Pumpelly's interest in loess was first aroused when he encountered the great loess deposits of northern China, which he believed had originated as sediments of former lakes. While he was working on the Missouri survey he had an opportunity to observe the extensive areas of the Midwest that were mantled with the fine-grained fertile soil. Then in 1877 appeared the first volume of Ferdinand von Richthofen's major study of the geology and geography of China. Reading it for review caused Pumpelly to abandon the idea of lacustrine origin and to give his support to Richthofen's theory that loess had been deposited by wind. He soon became one of Richthofen's principal promoters and a transmitter of the eolian theory to the American geologists who did not read German.[30]

The question of the origin of loess was one of the more controversial problems that divided geologists during the last quarter of the nineteenth century. Today the generally accepted definition of loess is that it is a yellowish, unstratified, porous deposit with high carbonate content that is formed by the "transportation of silt-sized particles by wind." The problems that concerned nineteenth-century geologists, and still concern many geologists today, are: (1) How were the silt-sized particles formed? (2) What is responsible for the carbonate content? (3) How were the particles transported? and (4) What events occurred after the initial deposit was formed?[31] By 1879 Pumpelly had formulated a comprehensive theory that provided answers to all of these questions, a theory that is much like the one accepted today. His interpretation, however, was not generally adopted by American geologists until the end of the century.

In 1878, when Pumpelly reviewed volume one of Richthofen's *China,* most geologists believed, as he had, that loess had been deposited in water. When Charles Lyell visited the United States in 1845 and 1846, he recognized that the bluff deposits along the Mississippi were similar to those along the Rhine known as *loess,* and he thought that in both cases the loess deposits were river sediments. American geologists, however, preferred the theory of lacustrine origin, which was well stated by the Iowa state geologist, Charles A. White, in an 1870 report on what he called the "Bluff Deposit." White argued that the deep, unstratified soil of the high bluffs along the Missouri River had been formed from rock material that had been finely ground by glaciers and deposited in the postglacial period as a sediment in the still waters of freshwater lakes. Only land and freshwater mollusks had been found, so marine deposition was ruled out.[32]

In his review of Richthofen's book for the *Nation* and in a paper he read before the National Academy of Sciences on April 10, 1878, Pumpelly revealed his conversion to the eolian hypothesis.[33] The fact that he was the only American geologist who had seen the great deposits of northern China and witnessed its "fearful dust-storms" no doubt contributed to his being the first to accept Richthofen's theory. He thought Richthofen's treatment of the question was "both masterly and remarkable for its completeness, and for the light that it throws upon some important problems in other parts of the world."[34] Richthofen had found loess deposits more than 18,000 feet above sea level containing only the shells of land snails, a finding that helped to convince Pumpelly that an aqueous origin was impossible. He admired Richthofen's comprehensive explanation of a progressively drying continental interior, where products of disintegration are no longer carried by rivers to the ocean but instead are sorted and blown by the wind. Where the dust comes to rest on grassy steppes, the vegetation holds it in place and "in this way, portions of the country become buried in their own and their neighbor's debris. Great thicknesses thus gradually accumulate, undergoing a transformation into loess by the rootlets and stems of the vegetation."[35]

Pumpelly thought, however, that Richthofen had not adequately explained how the fine material of which loess is composed had originated. Richthofen's explanation, according to Pumpelly, could not account for the tremendous amount of material that would have been required to build up the great thickness and immense area of some loess deposits, and he proposed that the material had come from two sources. One source, which Richthofen and many American geologists accepted, was silt produced by glacial grinding, which had first been brought by rivers to central regions and then when dried had been dispersed by wind, in dust storms. Because Pumpelly thought that glacial grinding alone could not have provided enough fine material, he suggested a second source, based on his own observations and knowledge of petrology. He was convinced that much of the material must have come from an ongoing (secular) process of rock decay over a long period of geological time. He believed that carbonic acid generated by overlying vegetation had partially decomposed granites and gneisses and left masses of fine insoluble clays and sands surrounding undisturbed rock cores. The decomposed mass extended to great depths over much of the country, in most places protected from the processes of erosion by abundant vegetation. Pumpelly had observed this kind of rock decay in railroad cuts in unglaciated areas of the eastern states, and he had noted its relation to the iron, lead, and zinc ores of Missouri. In the moist northern part of the country, the disintegration products had been removed by the continental glaciers, but where the climate had become progressively drier, the fine material had become the prey of the winds, eventually forming the fertile soil that sustained large populations.[36]

Few American geologists seconded Pumpelly's support of the eolian hypothesis. One reason for this lack of support may have been the difference between geographic conditions in China and the United States. The loess of the bluffs along the Missouri and Mississippi valleys seemed closely associated with the rivers, which most geologists believed must have had a role in its formation. Mississippi state geologist Eugene W. Hilgard, who was an expert on the sediments of the Mississippi Delta and believed strongly in river deposition, rejected the role of wind, saying in 1879 that "the sum total of anomalous conditions required to sustain the eolian hypothesis partakes strongly of the marvelous."[37]

Many of those who refused to accept the hypothesis were glaciologists, a group that included some of the country's most influential geologists, most notably Thomas C. Chamberlin. They tended to believe that the material of loess had been produced by glacial grinding, but they thought it had been deposited in lakes formed from glacial meltwaters, under special conditions that separated fine from coarser products. Chamberlin and Rollin D. Salisbury of the U.S. Geological Survey's glacial division gave the eolian theory a sympathetic hearing and even admitted in 1885 that it "presents many attractions," but they were reluctant to apply to American formations a theory that had been based mainly on observations in China. By 1897 Chamberlin still favored the lacustrine theory but seemed willing to accept the eolian hypothesis in certain cases: "A Janus-faced hypothesis is here offered in the hope that by a judicious reference of a part of the loess to one class of action and a part to the other, a joint explanation may be found to afford a true elucidation of the perplexing formation."[38]

Chamberlin's 1897 paper, "Supplementary Hypothesis Respecting the Origin of the Loess," appears in the same volume of his *Journal of Geology* that contains his famous methodology paper, "The Method of Multiple Working Hypotheses," and is a good example of the method he advocated. Chamberlin urged the reader to avoid holding a "ruling theory" that might blind the investigator to new possibilities and instead to "bring up into view every rational explanation of the phenomenon in hand and to develop every tenable hypothesis relative to its nature, cause or origin, and to give to all of these as impartially as possible a working form and a due place in the investigation."[39] He seemed to be applying his own method when he suggested that water had played the predominant role in forming some loess deposits while wind may have been the principal factor in others. His continuing insistence on giving water "a due place in the investigation" may have delayed, however, the general acceptance of the role of wind.

Pumpelly's method of investigation, Willis believed, was the use of "sequential hypotheses." Pumpelly quickly grasped the important facts and almost as quickly formed a hypothesis to explain them. If it did not hold up after more facts were presented, he either formulated another or adopted one suggested by someone else, if it provided a better explanation. He was apparently satisfied that his modification of Richthofen's theory, as presented in his 1879 paper on rock disintegration, was the correct one and did not take further part, at least in print, in the debate over the origin of loess. One of the papers that helped to persuade Americans to accept the theory of wind transport was that of paleontologist Bohumil Shimek, who wrote in 1899 of his detailed study of loess fossils and their living counterparts in Mississippi, Iowa, and Nebraska. He found that the fossils were almost entirely those of land snails, and that their most delicate parts were preserved intact, which would have been possible only if buried in place by dust and not if they had been transported any distance by water.[40]

Pumpelly's 1879 paper on "Secular Rock-Disintegration" has been credited with providing the correct interpretation of the Mississippi Valley loess deposits. As Herbert E. Gregory wrote in 1918, in summing up one hundred years of progress in geomorphology, "the evidence presented by Pumpelly for the Eolian origin of loess—structure, texture, composition, fossil content and topographic position—is complete, and to him belongs the credit for the correct interpretation."[41]

Pumpelly's vision enabled him to perceive that the eolian hypothesis explained a whole series of events in the evolution of a landform, but he did not have the patience or perhaps the interest to take up the detailed investigations that were necessary to convince others. Perhaps the slowness to accept his view may have been partly due to his gentlemanly reluctance to engage in controversy.

Pumpelly did not publish anything else on the subject until the appearance of his report on his explorations in Turkestan. By then his views had developed still further, becoming an integral part of his interpretation of the physiographic evolution of Central Asia. In his presidential address to the Geological Society of America in 1905 on the results of his expeditions to Turkestan, he discussed the relation between progressive desiccation, the formation of loess, and the development of agriculture. In that address, Pumpelly's dramatic descriptions of wind-blown dust that changed the face of the land probably helped to convince the last doubters of the truth of the eolian hypothesis. By that time his version of Richthofen's theory had been confirmed by others, and his view was soon "all but universal."[42]

Gentleman and Geologist

Like the gentlemen geologists of an earlier day, Pumpelly was by no means an isolated researcher but found intellectual stimulation through membership in both general and specialized scientific societies. As a member he attended meetings of the National Academy of Sciences, the American Association for the Advancement of Science, and the American Academy of Arts and Sciences in Boston. He was a founding member of the American Institute of Mining Engineers, established in 1871, and of the Geological Society of America, founded in 1888, and attended meetings at home and abroad of the International Geological Congress. Although he was not very active in any of these organizations, he presented papers at meetings and enjoyed the social contact with other scientists. He was a vice-president of the International Geological Congress at its Washington meeting in 1891, arranging a tour of the Lake Superior region for the heads of various foreign geological surveys, and he served as president of the Geological Society of America in 1905.[43]

His social clubs, too, were a source of stimulation and enjoyment. After the Civil War, these gentlemen's clubs, whose memberships had been made up primarily of artists, writers, civic leaders, and philanthropists, began to admit more scientists. Boston's elite Saturday Club, for example, where such "Olympians" as Emerson and Longfellow had gathered and where almost the only scientists were the gregarious Louis Agassiz and the physician-anatomist-poet Oliver Wendell Holmes, was now reflecting the changes in society at large by admitting a few more science professors: Asa Gray, Alexander Agassiz, Wolcott Gibbs, and Theodore Lyman of Harvard and geologist William Barton Rogers, founder and president of MIT. Pumpelly became a member in 1883.[44] In these clubs, exchanges of ideas took place that, although largely undocumented, must have helped to encourage interest in new scientific developments among members. The time had not yet come when science was so specialized that the educated laymen could no longer follow it.

Pumpelly enjoyed his clubs and the chance to meet and converse with people of different interests. His memberships were important to him, not necessarily as a means of making contacts useful to his career, although that did happen, but as a means of keeping in touch with wider aspects of the cultural life of the times. His own experiences as an explorer, his scientific knowledge, and his considerable talent for conversation and storytelling made him a desirable member of clubs where good talk was valued and the latest discoveries in science were discussed along with other current topics.

Perhaps Pumpelly's favorite club was New York's Century Club, already a recognized center in the social and literary life of New York when he joined it in 1867. During the winter of 1867–68 he was living in New York at the Oriental Hotel on Lafayette Place, writing *Across America and Asia* and working as a consultant in the mining bureau of his Freiberg classmate, James P. Kimball, who had become a member the year before. Pumpelly's sponsors for membership were the well-known scientists Wolcott Gibbs and Lewis Rutherfurd.[45] "I felt it to be a great honor to be elected at my age into the Century—into contact with the brains of the metropolis," Pumpelly wrote in his *Reminiscences*. "It was perhaps the most broadening phase of my education."

It would be hard to overestimate the value of the Century to a young man interested in everything and still in the formative period. Little groups gathered in the easy chairs to talk under the amiable accompaniment of cigars and moderate libations. These informal talks brought out the different points of view derived from individual thought and experience. . . . They covered a wide range of intellectual activity.[46]

Although he lived in New York only during the winters of 1867 and 1868, he returned to the Century Club on his later trips to the city, becoming well known to members: "You might find the fabulous Raphael Pumpelly—his very name was an invitation . . . a great blue-eyed giant with a long flowing beard, a vivacious tongue, and a courtly manner."[47]

The cultivation of art and literature were prominent among the aims of the club (planning for the Metropolitan Museum began there), but several scientists were now members, and conversation, as Allan Nevins wrote, ranged from "the Decalogue to the newest guesses in science . . . from Calvinism to Darwinism." Pumpelly met scientists from Columbia College and the new Columbia School of Mines, who invited him to their homes and laboratories: geologist John S. Newberry, chemist Charles F. Chandler, and physicist Ogden Nicholas Rood, as well as amateur astronomer and Columbia trustee Lewis Rutherfurd. At the club he might also have run into Clarence King, elected to membership in 1874, who charmed members with his wit and brilliant conversation. King "could take the most commonplace topic and blow it into a succession of many-colored bubbles," remembered one observer. The Century Club was useful to King, who was more involved politically than Pumpelly; it may well have been through the club that King became friendly with longtime member Abram S. Hewitt, newly elected to Congress. It was Hewitt who, at the instigation of King and John Wesley Powell, was to introduce the legislation establishing the United States Geological Survey.[48]

Outside the club, other scientists, perhaps under a greater pressure of work, were not sympathetic to King's or Pumpelly's fondness for the Century. Nathaniel Shaler, for example, once told Thomas C. Chamberlin that "he could not travel to Washington with Pumpelly because the latter would want to stop off in New York and spend the evening at the club and go on the next day. Time was a matter of less consequence to him than to Shaler."[49]

One of the things Pumpelly found so attractive about the club was the opportunity to associate with artists, writers, and publishers as well as with scientists. The artist John La Farge was one of the first friends he made there. La Farge had already become interested in Japanese art, collecting prints and incorporating Japanese effects into his painting as early as 1859, but his interest deepened when he saw the collection of prints and other works of art Pumpelly had bought on his travels in Japan and China, some of which were eventually given to the Metropolitan Museum. With a characteristic anticipation of new trends, Pumpelly persuaded La Farge to write a chapter on the art of Japan for *Across America and Asia* that was La Farge's first writing on the subject and the first by any Western painter. The article has been credited with contributing substantially to the nineteenth-century enthusiasm for Japanese art in the United States.[50]

Through the club Pumpelly also met Henry Holt, who published *Across America and Asia* and became a lifelong friend. Edwin L. Godkin, founder in 1865 of the *Nation,* was also a member of the Century. His literary editor, J. R. Dennett, according to Holt, did more than anyone else to raise the standards of literary criticism, sending books to specialists in the field for review at a time when few other editors did so.[51] Pumpelly's reviews of books on Asian exploration and geography for the *Nation* probably came about through a meeting with Godkin at their club.

The most notable among Pumpelly's friends in the literary world was Henry Adams, who, perhaps more than any other literary figure at the time, made use in his writing of ideas from geology and the other sciences. Adams's interest in geology had begun in 1868 when he reviewed the tenth edition of Charles Lyell's *Principles of Geology* in a long article for the *North American Review.* As a result, "Adams passed for a friend of geologists" and often picked their brains when he needed to clarify a problem or verify a fact in trying to formulate a scientific theory of history. Pumpelly and Adams were colleagues at Harvard for a brief time in the early seventies, when Adams was teaching history there. Adams came to admire Pumpelly for his "large experience of the world," and Adams's interest in science was stimulated by Pumpelly's friendship. Pumpelly, admiring in turn Adams's sincere and studious efforts to understand science, gave what help he could. In 1903, when Adams was struggling to understand the complexities of modern forces, physical and technological as well as social, Pumpelly introduced him to Karl Pearson's difficult but influential *Grammar of Science,* remarking that Wolcott Gibbs had found it helpful. Adams (who had at first confused Wolcott Gibbs, the chemist, with Josiah Willard Gibbs, the mathematical physicist) used Pearson's book as the basis for a chapter in *The Education.*[52]

On trips to Washington, D.C., Pumpelly sometimes visited the Adamses, charming Adams's wife, "Clover," with his courtly manner and tales of his explorations. Clover wrote her father about one such visit: "Mr. Pumpelly to tea and stayed on to dine, was charming as ever. His account of the Great Northwest on the line of the Northern Pacific is like a fairy tale. . . . I've no desire to go abroad again, but should like to go in a director's car over that line to the Pacific when the country is a little more settled."[53]

Clover Adams, an accomplished photographer, did a portrait of Pumpelly in 1884. The following year, suffering from severe depression after her father's death, she committed suicide by taking potassium cyanide from her photographic chemicals, an event that undoubtedly contributed to Adams's growing pessimism. Pumpelly had offered to assist with guides and travel arrangements for a western trip they had planned just

Raphael Pumpelly at age forty-seven. Photograph by Marian (Mrs. Henry) Adams (Courtesy of Massachusetts Historical Society)

before Clover's death, but her depression apparently made such a trip inadvisable.[54]

A geologist who was an even closer friend of Adams than Pumpelly was Clarence King, who, like Pumpelly, had many qualities of the gentleman geologist. In *The Education,* Adams tells of his meeting with King when he went west to visit a field party of King's Fortieth Parallel survey, on which Samuel Franklin Emmons, his childhood friend, was working. Adams admired King extravagantly and found in him a rare, close friend, for King "had everything to interest and delight Adams." King became part of the Adamses' intimate circle known as "the Five of Hearts," made up of themselves, King, and Mr. and Mrs. John Hay. To Adams, King was an avatar, the perfect ideal of an American. He knew art, poetry, women, the West; "he knew the professor by heart, and he knew the Congressman better than he did the professor." He also understood practical geology and "saw ahead at least one generation further than the textbooks." Adams believed that with ordinary luck King "would die at eighty the richest and most many-sided genius of his day."[55]

According to critic R. P. Blackmur, King symbolized for Adams both the potential and the failure of the American ideal. While King was indeed an attractive and widely admired man, the King "as Adams gives him, may never have existed." Adams used King's "failure" to illustrate the failure of American society, education, and science to cope with the changes of the Gilded Age. King's affairs went into decline after his brilliant successes with the Fortieth Parallel survey and the United States Geological Survey. He had hoped to build a fortune through mining investments, but, although he made large fees as a mining consultant, his investments were largely unsuccessful. Even his marriage was not a "success," Adams thought, in that it did not bring him added income or social status, for, as Adams knew, King married Ada Todd, a black woman whom he loved and with whom he had five children but whom he kept hidden in Brooklyn, afraid to let his family and friends know of her. King also failed financially, losing almost everything in the Panic of 1893. He had a nervous breakdown and died of tuberculosis in 1901.[56]

Pumpelly, in contrast, had the good fortune that King missed: good luck in his investments, the summer home in Dublin that King envied,[57] the wife who shared both his professional and his social life, and intellectual interests that he pursued enthusiastically into old age. His was, for the most part, a happy and successful life but not illustrative of Adams's gloomy theme.

Pumpelly stimulated Adams because of his travels to remote places and his ideas about the ancient past. They discussed the effect of geography on the development of the Aryan race, and Adams encouraged Pumpelly in his plan to go to Central Asia to search for evidence. But their philosophical outlook was different: Adams was a pessimist; Pumpelly was an optimist. In *The Education* Adams was obsessed with the idea of failure, and his other late writings illustrate what he believed to be the tendency of history toward decline and dissipation of energy. In "A Letter to American Teachers of History," intended to provoke thought and discussion among historians, Adams tried to show how Kelvin's Second Law of Thermodynamics could be applied to history. Darwinism falsely led people to think that society was progressing upward, but Kelvin's law pointed to a loss of energy and the resulting decline of all forms of human activity. Adams argued that if the sun and earth are losing heat, as Kelvin believed, all human energy that depends on heat, including even thought, must also eventually dissipate.[58]

"Kelvin was a great man," Adams told his friend Charles Milnes Gaskell, "and I am sorry I did not know enough mathematics to follow him instead of Darwin who led us all wrong. Our early Victorian epoch was vastly *naïf!*"[59] Adams's championship of Kelvin became one of the major statements of fin-de-siècle disillusionment but had little impact on his fellow historians. Adams's selective use of Kelvin and other physical scientists to support his pessimistic interpretation of history is similar to the uses to which the theories of Darwin and Herbert Spencer were put by Americans who had earlier promoted a progressive, competitive Social Darwinism.

As both a scientist and an optimist, Pumpelly disagreed with Adams. His reply to Adams on reading the "Letter to American Teachers" reflected the opinion of many geologists that Kelvin's estimates of the earth's age had already been made obsolete by recent discoveries in radioactivity. As an optimist, Pumpelly did not believe that signs of decline were already plentifully in evidence as Adams did. He jokingly said he was not worried, because the clockwork of nature was running down so slowly that "he and his" would escape the end. More seriously, he was hopeful that the new discoveries in the field of radiation would provide new, as yet unknown, sources of energy. It was more likely, Pumpelly thought, that the human race would "die out in world-wide congestion" due to man's prolific rate of reproduction.[60]

Pumpelly's letter prompted a long reply from Adams, expounding on Emile Blandet's theory of solar condensation and its relation to temperature change in the planets and complaining about the objections to the "Letter" his field-geologist friends had made. They had all "written to me at once, with an air of satisfaction as though they were easily disposing of the physicist theory, to tell me, what of course as an ignorant outsider I could not know, that there had been a number of glacial epochs in history." Pumpelly's letter, while not in full agreement with Adams's thesis, had nevertheless been "a God-send: It gave me a chance to talk with somebody, which I've not had for geological aeons." As an example of the depths to which society had sunk, Adams told Pumpelly how he had been made to "grovel" on the dock at the port of New York by a "dirty employee of a dirtier Jew cad" customs inspector who had evidently challenged his importation of a gift. It is hard to imagine what Pumpelly, who was by no means a racist, thought of this racial slur.[61]

Perhaps Pumpelly was able to be helpful to Adams because as a "gentleman of science" he was comfortable in the world of society and letters and was himself used to drawing upon the facts of science in order to bring them to bear upon larger questions.

When Eliza Pumpelly died in early February 1915, Adams wrote to express his sympathy. Adams's letter of condolence makes clear his admiration for his friend as well as for Eliza and reveals a little of Adams's feelings about his wife's suicide.

It is thirty years since I went through the same thing, and I never lifted my head again. There is nothing to say except perhaps that we are now thirty years older, and nothing matters much or long. You always had more life and vigor than I, and even now you can stand up under far heavier burdens. I have the right still to envy you from every point of view, even from this, and to wish I were in your place. For her there is nothing to wish. She has had all there is. . . . I know no one else whose life has been so rich and so long in its fulness. I hope you know how much this means to you, even more than to her.[62]

Like the geologists of an earlier time, Pumpelly found spiritual uplift and inspiration in nature. In his grief after his wife's death, Pumpelly returned to the desert of Arizona, feeling that "in the decadence of faith, in anxiety or grief, one may still seek counsel and strength in those silent realms of Nature." The few passages about religion in his *Reminiscences* indicate his religious skepticism and rejection of organized religion. He did not have much use for churches or the religious practices of any faith. The reassuring natural theology of the early Victorian geologists like William Buckland or Adam Sedgwick was not for him, although he may have been somewhat sympathetic to the post-Darwinian attempts to reconcile science and religion like that of his contemporary, Nathaniel Shaler. Shaler tried to formulate a new, more secular natural theology that would make Darwinism compatible with a liberal Christianity. Pumpelly probably cared less, if he read them, for the religious writings of glaciologist George Frederick Wright, a Congregationalist minister and an opponent of liberalized religion, who defended Darwinism but made it clear that God was the ultimate cause of variation.[63]

Pumpelly was really more of a mystic than a skeptic but he could easily have been the model for George Strong, the charming paleontologist and religious skeptic in Adams's 1884 novel *Esther*. It is Strong who tries to comfort his cousin Esther, a sensitive young woman engaged to the pastor of a fashionable New York parish, in her struggles with religious doubt. Strong "looked at churches very much as he would have looked at a layer of extinct oysters in a buried mud-bank" and assumed that they "probably served some necessary purpose in human economy," although he could not himself understand the good of them.[64]

Even as a child Pumpelly had detested the long church services and prayer meetings his mother and father had forced him to attend, preferring by far the mysterious tales and legends told him by a young Irishman who was studying with the local priest. As an adult he may have attended church with his wife, but when asked to teach a Sunday school class he remarked that the pupils would be more likely to remember the language he used to get them out of his cherry trees than any moral lessons he might teach them. He was even scornful of the Buddhist prayer machines he saw in Asia and of the lamas of Tibet, the "drones" who live off the population, "practicing all the arts of a crafty priesthood," and serving the "superstitions" of the people.[65]

Like a mystic or prophet, Pumpelly received religious inspiration on the mountain heights and in the deserts. "In the great solitudes" he had felt "some subtle influence lifting me to a medium beyond the bounds of self to a clearer perception of relations and values in life. . . . In the starlit heavens mind . . . is raised to a higher level of spiritual consciousness." His own experiences made him realize that the religious experiences of early man had begun in such wildernesses and that "it was among these aspects of Nature, and through their influence, that began all the spiritual and material changes from savagery to civilization."[66] His strongly felt affinity with the religions of early man may have contributed to his desire to search for the remains of prehistoric man in Central Asia.

Viewing Pumpelly as a gentleman geologist is not to suggest that he was not a thoroughly professional one. For much of his career he was in the employ of others. After the Northern Transcontinental Survey was abandoned, he returned to the United States Geological Survey, where he remained for nine years. As head of a division of the USGS he had a high reputation among his fellow geologists, and as a member of the National Academy of Sciences he was one of the elite members of the scientific community. But because of his income, and partly because of his indulgence in "gentlemanly" activities such as travel, art collecting, and maintaining membership in his clubs, he had something of a reputation for not finishing what he started. His fertile ideas stimulated others but, as in the case of his work on loess, he himself did not do the detailed research that might have made the eolian theory acceptable at an earlier date.

Chamberlin regarded Pumpelly as "a man of commanding ability, good judgment and clear insight, but one who habitually showed a reluctance to finish up and put out his results." This reluctance was partly due, Chamberlin thought, to his "high standards of accomplishment which made him feel that he was not quite ready" but also perhaps to "his having been molded in an atmosphere of rather easy circumstances."[67]

In writing his memorial to Pumpelly, Willis asked Charles K. Leith of the University of Wisconsin Department of Geology to assess Pumpelly's work in the Lake Superior region. Leith had not known Pumpelly personally but had known Charles Richard Van Hise, who had worked closely with Pumpelly on the USGS and had been inspired by Pumpelly's insight into Precambrian problems. Pumpelly, said Leith, asking not to be quoted,

saw something new in almost everything he touched, and he opened up fields in which brilliant results were to be expected. Unfortunately, after this promising start he did not follow through. Time and again we have had occasion to feel regret that he had not taken time to work out some of the problems he so clearly outlined. . . . My impression is that very great abilities were allowed in considerable part to go to waste in order that he might take advantage of his extraordinary opportunities for rich and varied experience in living.[68]

There is some truth in what Leith wrote, however, in that Pumpelly did have the imagination, insight, and opportunity to pursue a wide variety of activities, some of which went unfinished. But Leith was speaking only of the Lake Superior work, which was completed by Van Hise when Pumpelly was assigned to New England. Pumpelly did produce a thoroughly professional body of work in petrology, in his landmark study of the Green Mountains in Massachusetts, and in his geoarchaeological research in Central Asia. His list of publications is rather meager when compared to those of some of his contemporaries—Chamberlin, Gilbert, Shaler, and Hilgard, for example. Much of his influence was felt through discussion of problems and the proposal of ideas to others in the field and at scientific meetings. Like other gentleman scientists, even the great Humboldt, he was intrigued by too many subjects to be able to follow through on them all himself. Bailey

Willis concluded that Pumpelly belongs "outside the circle of specialists, in the group of great explorers of the physical and intellectual world."[69] Leith's statement may reflect a twentieth-century point of view on the part of professional geologists toward earlier generalists, for, in fact, by 1924 the day of the gentleman geologist was over.

6

With the United States Geological Survey

In the 1880s, geology became more professionalized and more centralized as the United States Geological Survey prospered under John Wesley Powell. State surveys were still strong, often devoted primarily to economic geology, but, while some had good cooperative arrangements with the USGS, others accused the federal bureau of becoming too powerful, usurping work better done by the states. Geology at the colleges and universities was expanding at the same time, and, although many teachers and students found summer employment on the federal survey, some friction arose over how much and what kinds of research ought to be undertaken by the federal government.

When Pumpelly returned to the USGS in 1884, it was not the same organization he had left in 1881 to conduct the Northern Transcontinental Survey for Henry Villard. Powell had replaced Clarence King as director in March 1881 and had begun to emphasize topographic mapping, general geology, and paleontology rather than economic geology. By 1885 Powell had demonstrated his power and influence as the government's most effective science administrator by getting an appropriation of $489,000, more than tripling the amount King had received in his last year.

Powell strongly supported research, and for ten years he had the power to encourage it. He appointed men at the top of the profession, experts in their fields, to head the geological divisions of the survey and gave them considerable autonomy in conducting their assignments. These division directors, of whom Pumpelly was one, employed some of the best-trained young geologists in the profession as assistants, many of whom were university graduate students or professors hired on a part-time or temporary basis. The survey teams of the various divisions functioned much like a graduate research school, with the assistants doing fieldwork and conducting independent research under the guidance of their director. During this period the USGS produced research of high quality, but in the 1890s, when Congress cut appropriations for the survey and demanded more practical results, research declined. In 1907 Thomas C. Chamberlin editorialized, in the journal he had founded to promote research, that during the decade just past "the larger and more far-reaching contributions to the science of geology have come from the universities."[1]

Pumpelly remained with the USGS for eight years, his career tied to Powell's rise and fall. As head of the Archean Division with a top salary, he spent most of these years working on the complex geology of the Green Mountains in western Massachusetts, scene of the "Taconic controversy," one of American geology's oldest unsolved problems. The year 1892 saw the beginning of Powell's decline; he lost favor with a Congress that was opposed to some of his programs and was looking for ways to reduce the costs of government. When Powell was forced to cut back the survey's operations, Pumpelly was one of the geologists who was let go. It was the end of Pumpelly's career as a professional government geologist.

Pumpelly and the Powell Survey

John Wesley Powell was a self-made man with a homemade education who had made his way to the highest position in government geology through his federally supported Geographical and Geological Survey of the Rocky Mountain Region. He had become a national hero for his daring 1869 exploration of the Colorado River and had played a role in the consolidation of the western surveys to form the United States Geological Survey. Powell knew congressmen even better than Clarence King had. He knew how to get bills through Congress, how to wangle appropriations, and how to organize an efficient and well-run bureau. He was, in fact, head of two bureaus. His great love was ethnology and while King was directing the new USGS, Powell had organized the Bureau of Ethnology under the Smithsonian, establishing procedures and directions of research that were to guide the study of Indian languages and cultures for many years to come. After 1881, as head of two bureaus, Powell was, according to Wallace Stegner, "perhaps the most powerfully placed scientist in the United States."[2]

The year Pumpelly returned to the USGS, Powell organized the geological work into six divisions, representing subjects he felt needed attention. Powell's highest priority was topographic mapping, for he considered accurate topographic maps to be a necessary base on which to chart geological formations and mineral resources. The geologic work emphasized paleontology, glaciology, and studies of metamorphic rocks, fields to which the USGS made important contributions. Chamberlin was named head of the Division of Glacial Geology. Clarence Dutton was responsible for volcanic geology; Grove Karl Gilbert for the areal, structural, and historical geology of the Appalachian region; and Arnold Hague for a topographic and geologic survey of Yellowstone Park. Relatively little was done in economic geology, although Powell learned to emphasize the fact that "all sound scientific research conduces to the welfare of the people, not only by increasing knowledge, but ultimately by affecting all the industries of the people."[3]

Powell set up two divisions to study the Archean and metamorphic rocks of the continent. He named Pumpelly head of the Archean Division, assigning him to the Appalachian region, and picked Roland Duer Irving, of the University of Wisconsin and the Wisconsin geological survey, to head the Lake Superior Division. As head of the Archean Division, Pumpelly was concerned with the oldest rocks of the continent—the granites, gneisses, and crystalline schists that make up the continental base, most of which are today referred to as belonging to the Precambrian.

Powell thought it was important to study these rocks, not only because they contained useful minerals, but also because such investigations would result in the "advancement of our knowledge of the principles involved in this branch of geologic science." The origin of the Archean rocks and their relation to other formations were little understood, and the absence of fossils, the folded and distorted condition of the beds, and the fact that they were generally covered by more recent rocks made their study extremely difficult. The Archean rocks represented, Powell thought, "one of the most interesting and at the same time obscure stages in the geologic development of the globe" and offered "one of the most promising subjects for geologic study in this and other countries." Powell realized that the Archean Division would have to develop improved methods of investigating these rocks and better criteria for their classification.[4]

Pumpelly's qualifications for this difficult work were excellent, which was probably why Powell wanted him to do research in this field rather than to work as an economic geologist as he had done under King.

Pumpelly was thoroughly familiar with the altered metamorphic rocks of the Lake Superior region through his work on the Michigan survey and his private petrographic studies of copper-bearing rocks. His only previous professional work in New England had been on the Hoosac Tunnel in 1865, but he knew the geology of the area near his summer residence at Dublin, New Hampshire, and he no doubt preferred to work near home.

Powell's position as the most powerful scientist in Washington and the involvement of his geologists in research did not go unchallenged. In 1884 Congress authorized a joint congressional commission, known as the Allison Commission, to investigate the efficiency and utility of the USGS and three other government scientific bureaus and to consider the possibility of combining some of the activities of these bureaus. During the hearings, which lasted from late 1884 to early 1886, Powell was criticized for spending too much money and for investigating questions that some thought should be the province of the states or universities.[5]

One of Powell's severest critics was Pumpelly's former employer, financier and zoologist Alexander Agassiz of Harvard's Museum of Comparative Zoology. Agassiz was a fiery opponent of government science. "Official science . . . has killed all individuality in Geology," he wrote his friend Thomas Henry Huxley in 1888, "the Professors of Geology in the United States being, with few exceptions, the satellites of the Director of the Geological Survey." Agassiz provided Representative Hilary A. Herbert, the survey's principal opponent on the commission, with ammunition against Powell in a letter, printed in the record of the hearings, in which Agassiz criticized the survey for its extravagant publications and for investigating subjects that he thought were better left to "private individuals and learned societies."[6]

Powell's eloquent testimony before the Allison Commission in defense of the survey had much to do with saving it and helps to understand why Powell encouraged the kind of research Pumpelly was conducting in the Green Mountains. The son of a farmer and itinerant preacher, Powell had great sympathy for supporting the research of those who could not afford to do it privately, and, in answer to Agassiz's criticism, he made a strong final statement regarding the need for federal support of scientific research. He agreed that government should not work in scientific fields that were well covered by others, but he gave several convincing reasons why geology was not one of them. No individuals or institutions would be willing to prepare topographic maps for the whole country, for example, nor could they afford the increasingly expensive research tools necessary for scientific research, such as observatories, laboratories, and libraries. Powell also pointed out that growing specialization in the sciences was causing a division of labor and that only a governmental scientific bureau could provide needed organization and integration.[7]

The geology of the continent is a unit, its parts interrelated, Powell argued; therefore a geological survey should be "organized upon the broadest territorial basis possible." What is learned in one locality can be applied to other places, thus illuminating the interrelationship of different districts. To emphasize his point, he cited Pumpelly's work in New England, explaining that Pumpelly had transferred his operations to northern Georgia during the winter because the same problems existed there as in New England and their study would provide additional information of direct interest to the New England area. Although Pumpelly had acquired his Bainbridge plantation for his family, he brought his survey assistants there during the winters, making that his winter headquarters. Pumpelly also spent a part of each year traveling to various areas in the Appalachians and to Lake Superior, to study other Archean formations and to confer with and advise geologists working in those regions.[8]

Powell's final point was an appeal for an understanding of the way government science "stimulates, promotes, and guides private research." Knowledge is not like private property, he said. It cannot be owned; its possession adds to the common knowledge of all. Far from hindering private research, the work of survey geologists stimulates it. Powell thought that research done by the federal survey had already proven to be of use to college professors and their students and to local governments and scientific societies. Government-sponsored science "everywhere inspires new research and informs it with sound principles and wise methods."[9] The work of Pumpelly's assistants in the Green Mountains was to prove the truth of this claim. Several of them applied their survey experience to further research at their respective universities.

The commission eventually approved and upheld Powell's work and granted the survey a permanent place as a scientific agency of the government, but during the hearings rumors circulated that Powell was to be replaced, either by Nathaniel Shaler or by Pumpelly. Although Pumpelly's *Reminiscences* tell us almost nothing about his work for the USGS and nothing at all about his relations with Powell, it is clear that he had no wish to become head of the survey. He publicly expressed his loyalty to Powell and admiration for his ability during this period when Powell and the survey were being attacked. In June 1885 both the *Boston Evening Record* and the *Engineering and Mining Journal* reported "that Powell will be superseded by Professor Raphael Pumpelly of Newport who is now a member of the Survey."[10] Pumpelly wrote letters at once to correct the rumor, saying that the report was "decidedly in error. . . . I am not in any sense and never was, a candidate for the position; and, in common with most geologists would exceedingly regret to see anybody supersede Major Powell, who has proved to be an extremely able and earnest chief of a great work, and, in my opinion, the very best man for the place."[11]

It is unlikely that Pumpelly, who was known for his extravagance, would have been able to manage the survey's affairs as well as Powell. Although Pumpelly was a commanding figure with the highest reputation as a scientist, he disliked politics and probably had no desire to become embroiled in the kind of controversy that surrounded the head of the USGS.

When Powell, in his testimony, expressed his belief that knowledge should be public property, he was revealing his personal feelings about the free exchange of ideas among geologists. Powell to a great extent guided the work of younger men by furnishing hypotheses and suggesting lines of research that he had neither the time nor inclination to carry out himself.[12] Gilbert was another who did not believe in "scientific preserves." As Powell's administrative right hand, Gilbert was often confined to office work and willingly shared his fertile thoughts about the mechanics of crustal movements with others. Bailey Willis, who inherited the problems of Appalachian structure from Gilbert, acknowledged that it was Gilbert who had provided his introduction to the subject.[13]

Willis also attributed to Pumpelly the capacity for freely sharing fruitful ideas with others.

It was his influence, joined to that of Chamberlin, Gilbert, and Powell, which introduced into American geology the habit of give and take in research. It has become so general that he who does not exchange ideas with his fellow or fails to give credit where credit is due achieves something of the unenviable reputation of a miser, as one who is to be condemned for his avariciousness of thought and to be pitied for what he loses.[14]

As Pumpelly began work on the problems of the Green Mountains, his willingness to "give and take" is evident. He selected well-trained and experienced men as assistants, outlined the broad approach, gave suggestions, and then allowed them considerable freedom to develop and present their own ideas. Later geologists who worked in the region called the joint work of Pumpelly, John Eliot Wolff, and T. Nelson Dale "a lasting monument" and a major contribution to the ongoing study of the "Taconic Question."[15]

The Taconic Controversy

The controversy over the age of the rocks of the Taconic range along the border between New York, Massachusetts, and Vermont has a long history going back to the days of the New York Natural History Survey. In 1842 Ebenezer Emmons, of the New York second district, claimed that he had discovered in the Taconic Mountains east of the Hudson River a group of rocks that were older than the Potsdam sandstone. At that time, most members of the survey believed the Potsdam (today part of the upper Cambrian) to be the oldest stratified formation, lying just above the crystalline bedrock known then as the Primary. Emmons became convinced that the Taconic rocks constituted a new system that extended the length of the Appalachians and into Canada. A few of the New York geologists disagreed with Emmons and the disagreement spread to other states. The controversy, as controversies often do, inspired intensive work on the Paleozoic rocks and eventually involved most of the country's leading geologists. Most of them thought Emmons was wrong. James Dwight Dana of Yale, for example, thought that the Taconic rocks were more recent formations that had been subjected to metamorphism.[16]

In many respects, the Taconic controversy resembles the one that started at about the same time in England between Roderick Murchison and Adam Sedgwick over Sedgwick's proposed Cambrian system, a distinct group of rocks with their own characteristic fossils that lay below Murchison's Silurian. The Taconic question also has features in common with the "great Devonian controversy," which ended with the recognition of the Devonian system, lying just above the Silurian. That controversy was resolved, Martin J. S. Rudwick believes, when the leading geologists who were involved agreed among themselves to recognize a new system. In the Taconic controversy, on the other hand, the leading geologists who opposed Emmons's theory had not resolved the problem. It was only after several decades that various parts of Emmons's Taconic rocks were found to belong to different systems, some to the Cambrian and some to the Ordovician.[17]

The Taconic controversy arose because the geology of the region could not be worked out by conventional stratigraphic methods then in use. The common assumptions held by geologists working in stratigraphy were: (1) that strata were laid down consecutively, the higher layers of strata being younger than the lower; (2) that each stratigraphic system is set apart from those above and below by a distinct boundary or unconformity; and (3) that each group of strata contains characteristic fossils. In

Emmons's Taconic rocks it was hard to find any fossils at all, and in some places early species of fossils were found in strata lying *above* rocks that contained more recent fossils. The altered and metamorphosed condition of the rocks, the same rock being altered in a somewhat different way from one locality to another, made it impossible for geologists to determine age on external lithologic features alone. The solution seemed to lie in a better understanding of structural geology and the conditions under which metamorphic rocks were formed. In the 1880s geologists were only beginning to develop new methods and theories to deal with these problems, as Powell had pointed out.

Powell's reasons for assigning Pumpelly to the Green Mountains may have been the challenge of seeing if government science could solve a geological problem that had been unsettled for more than forty years. Dana, who had been opposed to Emmons's system almost from the beginning, had been conducting his own investigations in western Massachusetts since the early 1870s, hoping to resolve the problem once and for all. Dana had no fondness for the national survey and resented its intrusion into Massachusetts, even though the state survey was cooperating with Powell in preparing topographic maps of the state. Powell, however, had told Dana at a meeting of the National Academy of Sciences in 1883 that geologists doubted his work and results, to which Dana replied that "doubt was to be expected from those who had not actually examined the rocks." Dana realized later that perhaps Powell was preparing him for the entrance of the USGS into New England, where he himself had been working for so long.[18]

Powell must have thought the USGS could bring a fresh approach to the problem. Pumpelly may have convinced him that the Taconic question could be better attacked by coordinating investigations there with related studies in other states the length of the Appalachians and with similar work being done in the Lake Superior region. In 1885 Powell reported that he expected the Taconic question would be solved "within four or five years."[19]

The Green Mountains in Massachusetts

In the summer of 1885 Pumpelly began a reconnaissance of northwestern Massachusetts in preparation for a detailed study of the region. On beginning his investigation in the Green Mountains, he decided to treat it as new work, to "keep wholly clear of the Taconic controversy," and to concentrate on "accurate study and interpretation of structure."[20] His emphasis on structure reflected the growing interest of many European and American geologists in problems related to the enormous amount of folding and faulting of solid rock strata that had taken place during the process of mountain building. Structural geology was becoming a separate branch of the science, and its methods were to add significantly to those used in the earlier attempts to fit the Taconic formations into the New York stratigraphic system.

One of the most important influences on the development of American structural geology was the work of the European geologists who, in the 1870s and 1880s, were investigating the structure of the Alps. Particularly relevant to Pumpelly's work in the Green Mountains were the studies of the Swiss geologist Albert Heim on Alpine tectonics and the mechanics of rock deformation. Heim's *Mechanismus der Gebirgsbildung* (Mechanics of mountain building), based on extensive fieldwork and microscopic investigations, identified some of the processes by which rock strata had been bent and folded without breaking during periods of mountain building. Heim determined that under conditions of sufficient pressure from the overlying load, solid rock strata could become plastic, flow, and recrystallize. Heim's *Mechanismus* became the standard work in the field and inspired similar investigations by Americans working in mountainous regions, including Pumpelly and his assistants.[21]

In the United States, earlier work on mountain structure had resulted in the rise of several theories to account for mountain building and the often extreme folding of the strata. William and Henry Rogers, James Hall, and James Dwight Dana had all proposed ways the folded structure of the Appalachians could have come about that involved various combinations of vertical, horizontal, or gravitational forces. The most generally accepted interpretation, until at least the end of the century, was Dana's theory of lateral pressure exerted by a cooling and contracting earth. To the extent that he discussed theory at all, Pumpelly seems to have agreed with Dana. In practice, however, Pumpelly belonged with the large group of American geologists who believed that agreement on theory was not necessary for the advancement of the science. As Mott Greene has pointed out, these geologists were content to concentrate on solving specific problems of regional structural geology, in "general and even cheerful agreement" that no adequate comprehensive theory existed.[22]

Pumpelly and his team of well-trained assistants, several of whom had studied micropetrography in Germany with Rosenbusch, systematically worked out the structure of a section of the Green Mountains in great detail during the summers of 1886, 1887, and 1888. As the region for study, Pumpelly chose the northwest corner of Massachusetts, slightly to the east of the Taconic range itself, a region now better known as the northern Berkshires. His section included some of the areas previously studied by Emmons, Dana, and others. He centered his work on an east-west belt extending through the main ridges, Mounts Greylock and Hoosac, thinking of this belt as a bridge across the Green Mountains that might provide the starting point for determining the age of all of the New England rocks. Mount Greylock, 3,491 feet high, is the highest point in the state, its massive bulk dominating western Massachusetts. Herman Melville, who had owned a farm at Pittsfield, had dedicated his 1852 novel *Pierre* to "Greylock's Most Excellent Majesty" and had even invited his friend Nathaniel Hawthorne to come and "vagabondize" with him on the mountain. Mount Hoosac is cut through by one of the longest railroad tunnels in the country; Pumpelly had examined the tunnel in 1865 while it was under construction. He knew that the tunnel would provide an excellent opportunity to study the mountain's deep structure. He and his team conducted additional investigations in Vermont, in the Highlands area on the Hudson River, and in the Connecticut Valley to the east.[23]

Pumpelly's principal team members were T. Nelson Dale, John Eliot Wolff, and Bayard Putnam. Pumpelly worked with Putnam and Wolff on the structure of Hoosac mountain while Dale, assisted by William Herbert Hobbs, did most of the fieldwork on Mount Greylock. Putnam had worked with Pumpelly on the Tenth Census and returned with him to the USGS in 1884, when the railroad survey came to an end. Unfortunately, Putnam, whom Pumpelly considered one of the survey's "most accurate and thoughtful geologists," died in an accident on Greylock in 1886 and the work there was continued by Wolff.[24]

Pumpelly's research team is indicative of the close relationship that existed between government and university geologists in these years. His assistants brought their own expertise to the investigations and in return gained valuable field experience, which benefited their teaching and research. Dale, who had spent his early years in Europe with his parents, became interested in geology while attending schools in Paris and Frankfurt am Main. He made geological explorations in Scandinavia under the guidance of the noted Munich professor of geology, Dr. Karl Zittel, and published studies of stratigraphic problems in the Alps that the director of the Austrian geological survey praised for their accuracy. From 1877 to 1879 he taught natural science at Vassar, publishing various papers on the geology of the Poughkeepsie area. Dale had served on Pumpelly's Tenth Census survey and, after working out the geology of Greylock for Pumpelly, continued as a USGS geologist until 1920. He also taught geology from 1893 to 1901 at Williams College, in the heart of the Green Mountains.[25]

Wolff had studied geology with Shaler at Harvard and had done fieldwork with him in Kentucky and Virginia before joining Pumpelly's Tenth Census team in 1880. He had also worked on the Northern Transcontinental Survey, doing microscopical studies of the rocks of the Crazy Mountains that stimulated his interest in micropetrography. He then went to Heidelberg to study with Rosenbusch and returned to Harvard as a graduate student and instructor in petrography. Wolff did the fieldwork on Mount Hoosac and most of the petrographic work for the Green Mountain monograph. He was Harvard's first professor of microscopic petrography and later became the curator of its mineralogical museum. Wolff married Pumpelly's niece, the daughter of his sister, Antoinette Loder.[26]

Other young geologists joined Pumpelly's team as assistants for a summer or a year, most of them graduate students or instructors of geology. The work gave them an opportunity to conduct independent research under Pumpelly's general direction. William Hobbs was a graduate student in chemistry at Johns Hopkins but had decided to change his major to geology because of his fascination with petrography, taught at Hopkins by George Huntington Williams, another Rosenbusch student. Williams recommended Hobbs for a summer position with Pumpelly in the Green Mountains, a job that proved to be "a most valuable education, the equal of several semesters in the university." Hobbs spent two seasons working as assistant to Dale, after which he too went to Germany to study micropetrography with Rosenbusch. Hobbs later became head of the geology department at the University of Michigan.[27]

One of Wolff's graduate students in petrography, August Frederick Foerste, became his part-time assistant, working with Wolff on Mount Hoosac during the summers. Although Foerste's earlier interests had been in paleontology, he received his Ph.D. degree from Harvard in 1890 with a thesis in petrography. Foerste, like Wolff and Hobbs, did advanced work with Rosenbusch and hoped for a permanent career with the USGS, but that career failed to materialize after the cutbacks of 1892. At that time Pumpelly gave Foerste a job as tutor to his son Raphael, and Pumpelly and Foerste did some studies together on the Tertiary rocks of Georgia near Pumpelly's winter home in Bainbridge. Foerste later became a high school science teacher and devoted his spare time to paleontological research.[28]

William Morris Davis, Pumpelly's former student, had been with him on the Northern Transcontinental Survey and since 1879 had been an instructor in geology at Harvard. Davis was doing structural studies in the Connecticut Valley, using his work there as a summer school for his students, and Pumpelly asked him to join the USGS on a temporary basis as a field assistant to determine the age of the younger rocks that lay east of the Green Mountains. Davis published several papers in scientific journals on the Triassic formations of the Connecticut Valley, his final report being for the USGS.[29]

Pumpelly's research team was the equivalent of a research school in a laboratory science. Jack B. Morrell, in a study of the research schools of chemists Justus von Liebig and Thomas Thomson, identified factors that seem to be characteristic of such schools: a charismatic director with an established reputation, strong institutional support, a well-defined research program that required a supply of students "keen to apprentice themselves to a recognized . . . master of his subject," and an opportunity for students to publish under their own name. These characteristics also apply to other kinds of organizations that conduct research, as James A. Secord found in a study of the British survey of the mid-1850s under Henry de la Beche.[30]

Pumpelly and his team might also be thought of as such a research "school." He had the support of the U.S. Geological Survey with its publication facilities behind him; he was a recognized authority on the Archean rocks and the methods of micropetrology; he formulated the plan for the working out of the structure and age of the rocks of the Green Mountain region. He expected his assistants to be able to work independently toward a common goal and allowed Wolff and Dale to publish their reports under their own names, while he provided the overall coordination and interpretation. Pumpelly was a charismatic director with whom the group felt a strong rapport. He and his wife made members of his team feel at home when they worked at his house, either in Dublin during the summers or in Newport or Bainbridge in the winters, when reports were prepared, providing hospitality and a social ambience that led to Wolff's meeting his future wife and Foerste later becoming almost a part of the family as tutor to young Raphael.

As Martin J. S. Rudwick, Thomas S. Kuhn, Michael Polanyi, and others have pointed out, the day-to-day practice of a science is based on shared assumptions about what constitutes research and on "tacit" knowledge gained "not from textbooks but by working alongside a more experienced practitioner within a living communal tradition."[31] This relationship was as true of Pumpelly's group as it was of many of the other USGS teams then working in the field. Pumpelly and his research team knew that the study of structure must be based on such routine procedures as observation of strata and their contacts, careful measurement of exposed sections, the collection and microscopic study of appropriate specimens, and the mapping of results. What his assistants learned in the field from their director, from each other, and from the rocks was assimilated into a report that was later cited as a textbook example of how to conduct a structural study.

Pumpelly made his first reconnaissance of the region in 1885, leaving his summer home at Dublin on July 18 with a wagon, team, and driver hired at survey expense for four dollars a day. He planned to center the summer's activities around the town of North Adams, in the northwest corner of Massachusetts. Within a ten-mile radius of North Adams were Mount Greylock and the Hoosac Mountains to the south and east, the Green Mountains of southern Vermont to the north, and the Taconic range to the west. With one or another of his assistants, Pumpelly visited all of these areas during the summer of 1885. Although the first summer's work was primarily a reconnaissance, and although the metamorphosed and contorted condition of the rocks and the absence of fossils made the work extremely difficult, Pumpelly did enough detailed fieldwork that season to enable him to establish tentative relationships between some of the rocks of Hoosac and Greylock. At first he concentrated on locating, describing, and measuring as many exposed rocks and outcrops as possible. These he found in brook beds, riverbeds, road cuts, quarries, and gullies and on cliffs and ridges. He would follow an outcrop far up the side of a mountain or along a ridge to see if it topped or dipped below another formation. He took measurements of the degree of slope (dip) and the direction (strike) of the exposed layers of strata and noted the amount of folding or faulting of the strata and whether they appeared to be synclinal or anticlinal in structure.[32]

Over the next few years, similar painstakingly thorough fieldwork by Pumpelly and his assistants made possible the preparation of many detailed maps and cross sections of the region that appeared in the final report. USGS topographers prepared new and more accurate topographic maps especially for the Green Mountain work and on them each geologist recorded the observations he had taken. (Dale recorded 1,850 observations on Mount Greylock alone.)[33]

In the field, Pumpelly looked particularly for ways to identify the Archean rocks and tried to find places where they made contact with a more recent formation, for that would be the dividing line between the Cambrian and the Precambrian. His field notebooks are filled with descriptions of the various kinds of crystalline gneisses, schists, and granites that abound in the region. He also noted the condition of the rocks—the effect of weathering, their state of disintegration, and the nature of the contact with other strata. He carefully observed the effect of large-scale folding, because it often caused extensive plication, or intense small-scale folding, within a layer of strata. Although earlier geologists had thought that all crystalline rocks were of Archean age, Pumpelly knew that many of those he observed were more recent, deformed by metamorphism during periods of orogenic movement. The work of his team for the next few years was to try to determine as precisely as possible the age of the deformed rocks.[34]

During the first summer, Pumpelly and his assistants found places on Hoosac and on Clarksburg Mountain, near the Vermont border, where a coarse granitoid gneiss was in contact with overlying schists. It was clearly distinct from the schists yet seemed to be conformable with them.[35] The fact that the beds of the granitoid gneiss graded into the overlying rocks in many places and appeared to be a conformable series had confused earlier investigators, but Pumpelly was able to determine that the gneiss was of Precambrian age and unconformable with the overlying rocks. The most convincing proof that a time break had occurred was the evidence Wolff obtained at a spot just over the state line at Stamford, Vermont, where the more recent Cambrian conglomerate had filled irregularities in the older rock. Pumpelly made repeated visits to the site and obtained conclusive evidence by digging that

> the Cambrian transgression found here a fissure, either open or filled with a rotten dike, which was washed out to a depth of several feet and refilled with beach sand and pebbles. . . . The sudden thickening and sagging of the quartzite over the fissure, taken in connection with the mixture of dike material and sand, and the stopping of the dike at the quartzite, prove sufficiently the pre-Cambrian age of the granitoid gneiss.[36]

The Stamford dike of Pumpelly's report has become the classic locality illustrating the division between the Precambrian and the Cambrian in the eastern part of the Taconic region and continues to be cited as such.[37]

The Hoosac Tunnel, which Pumpelly had examined in 1865, proved to be a productive means of access to the deeply buried rocks. Geologists had apparently not made use of it before in connection with the Taconic question. Much of the tunnel's five-mile length had been bricked over and the rock was covered with thick soot, but by examining the interior and studying the waste piles at the ends of the tunnel Pumpelly and his team were able to determine that the central core of the mountain was made up of the Precambrian granitoid gneiss overlain by a Cambrian white gneiss, which was in turn overlain by what came to be called the "Hoosac schist" of Silurian age.[38]

Early in the investigation, Pumpelly had realized that it would help to determine "the true order of bedding" if his team could avoid faulted areas and concentrate on finding places where the structure "should show folds with pitching axes." Putnam and Wolff found an anticlinal fold on the west side of Mount Hoosac that Wolff believed resembled the great Glarus fold of the Alps, which Albert Heim had been studying for several years and had made famous in his *Mechanismus der Gebirgsbildung*. On this part of Hoosac, as earlier observers had noticed, a bed of granitoid gneiss was superimposed over beds of younger white gneiss, the reverse of the order that Pumpelly and Wolff found in the tunnel. Wolff's analysis showed that this seemingly anomalous position could be explained by an overturned fold, which had reversed the original position.[39]

Extensive microscopic analysis of thin sections of rock samples provided important clues to the changes in structure the mountains had undergone. Pumpelly and his assistants collected many representative rock specimens, and the microscopic work supplied examples for others of how to detect large-scale orogenic processes through the study of small samples. Only by applying the results of the most recent petrographic research of European and American geologists was it possible to classify and correlate the crystalline rocks, Pumpelly reported in 1891. He thought that the petrographers of the USGS and the Archean Division had themselves "contributed greatly" to advances in petrographic methods.[40]

Wolff believed that, "improbable as it may seem at first sight," the Green Mountain work had proved that it was possible, "by proper methods of work," to determine the stratigraphy of the older contorted and metamorphosed rocks. His fieldwork and microscopic analysis of the rocks of Hoosac Mountain helped to demonstrate that metamorphism could cause rocks that were originally of the same age and similar in appearance to become different when subjected to different conditions and those that were originally dissimilar to become like each other. Wolff conducted thorough studies of the lower Cambrian rocks that overlay the granitoid gneiss and found that the fossiliferous quartzite of Clarksburg Mountain, called the "Vermont Formation," changes laterally in an infinite series of gradations into a series of white gneisses and a metamorphic conglomerate as it passes into other localities.[41]

Dale made important contributions to the study of the cleavage and foliation in metamorphic rock, basing his work on that of Heim, Sorby, George F. Becker, and others. Earlier investigators had frequently confused bedding with foliation. Dale's studies on rock deformation helped him detect the difference between stratified beds and the foliated structures produced in gneisses and schists by metamorphism. Dale drew up seven principles regarding rock deformation, adapted from Heim, which he applied to the construction of ten complete and three partial sections across the Greylock mass. According to Bailey Willis, Dale's work provided classic examples of the structures to be looked for in metamorphosed sediments.[42]

Although he relied mainly on petrographic methods, Pumpelly also found paleontology to be an indispensable tool. Charles D. Walcott, one of the survey's most skilled paleontologists and director of the USGS after Powell, identified the primitive trilobite *Olenellus* in the rocks of western Massachusetts that verified Pumpelly's identification of the "Vermont Formation" as lower Cambrian. On a reconnaissance of New England limestone areas, Dale collected several fossils, which Walcott and Carl Rominger used in assigning a limestone formation near Littleton, New Hampshire, to an earlier period than other geologists had thought. Wolff, Dale, and August Foerste discovered other Cambrian fossils that helped to determine the age of limestone beds near Rutland, Vermont.[43]

Pumpelly's exceptional ability to visualize the continual breakdown and regrouping of the materials of which mountains are composed is evident in the passages in his monograph in which he attempts to form a comprehensive picture of the geological age of the region. In correlating the work of Wolff on Hoosac with that of Dale on Greylock, Pumpelly found that not all of the formations were present on both mountains; a large section of the geological column present in Greylock, consisting partly of limestone beds, was missing on Hoosac. Pumpelly explained the difference by hypothesizing that a Precambrian ridge had remained dry land during the period when a Paleozoic ocean covered much of the country to the west. He referred to his earlier paper on rock disintegration in picturing the advance of the sea onto the ridge, which he believed was already deeply disintegrated before the sea reached it. The advancing sea, he wrote, "found ready prepared the materials which the water assorted and distributed to form the great sheet of Cambrian rocks. While these deposits of detritus were accumulating over the shallow seas, the materials for the future limestone were gathering offshore to the west." These deposits were deeply buried under later sediments until the pressure and temperature, combined with the "action of a great lateral pressure," were sufficient to satisfy the conditions of metamorphism, changing the sedimentary deposits to crystalline schists, quartzite, and gneisses and folding them into their present form. In 1891 Pumpelly included this Green Mountain work in his second paper on the subject of rock disintegration, which he read at a meeting of the Geological Society of America.[44]

While Pumpelly was working with his team in the Green Mountains, members of the Lake Superior and Appalachian divisions were studying similar problems related to structure and the identification of the crystalline rocks. Pumpelly frequently visited other regions to share his experience and expertise with the other division heads. In July 1887, with Roland Duer Irving, director of the Lake Superior Division, he visited sites where the ancient rocks were exposed in pits and mines and consulted with Irving and Irving's young assistant, Charles R. Van Hise, on the age, mode of origin, and subsequent alteration of various Precambrian rock formations. When Van Hise became head of the Lake Superior Division in 1888, after the death of Irving, he and Pumpelly made a number of trips together, traveling to Canada, northern Michigan, Missouri, and the southern Appalachians to coordinate work on the crystalline schists. In the spring of 1889, Pumpelly spent several days with Bailey Willis, who had succeeded Grove Karl Gilbert as head of the Appalachian Division and was working in Tennessee and North Carolina. Willis wanted Pumpelly's opinion on the quartzite and granite formations and took him to various locations where Pumpelly found similarities to formations in the Green Mountains. Both Willis and Van Hise, who later wrote authoritative monographs and textbooks that dealt comprehensively with the broad principles of structural geology as well as with the specifics of structure in their own regions, acknowledged their debt to Pumpelly's insight and suggestions.[45]

On January 18, 1892, Pumpelly submitted his completed monograph, *Geology of the Green Mountains in Massachusetts,* to Powell. Willis and Van Hise praised Pumpelly's report for its contribution to the field of structural geology and referred their readers to the Green Mountain monograph as a report to be emulated. Willis, who has been called "one of the grandfathers of structural geology" for his original research and extensive writing on the subject, later cited the work of Pumpelly's team as a classic illustration "of the skill with which such investigations should be executed."[46]

Some reviewers thought Pumpelly's work had resolved the Taconic controversy. J. F. Kemp, for example, reviewing *Geology of the Green Mountains* for *Science,* was of the opinion that the monograph was "the most detailed and valuable contribution yet made to the solution of the much debated 'Taconic question.'" Willis paid tribute to Pumpelly's "capacity for patient, conclusive investigation" that enabled him to "open a new era in the geology of New England and to settle a controversy which had lasted for half a century." Pumpelly himself made no claims that his five years of struggle had settled the obscure stratigraphic and structural problems. "Did we solve them?" he asked rhetorically as he wrote his *Reminiscences* in 1918. "Who knows? An old half-breed guide in the Northwest always decided weather predictions with 'probably yes, probably no.'"[47]

Even though Pumpelly and his team had worked out the structure of the region in considerable detail, debate continued over matters of terminology. Some geologists had promoted the use of the term *Taconic* for the lower Cambrian as a way of inserting an American term into international stratigraphy, but English terms prevailed. Part of the strata that Emmons had called "Taconic" Pumpelly referred to as lower Silurian or Cambro-Silurian. Pumpelly's Cambro-Silurian is the equivalent of what is known today as the Ordovician, the period immediately above the Cambrian. Although Charles Lapworth had suggested the name "Ordovician" for the period between the Silurian and the Cambrian in 1879, it was 1960 before the term was adopted internationally. The term *Taconic* survives today in geology as the "Taconian orogeny," the period during the Ordovician when the mountains of the western Massachusetts–New York border region were formed.[48]

Much work has been done in western Massachusetts since the appearance of Pumpelly's monograph, and later investigators have added to or modified some of his team's findings. Nevertheless, part of his work still stands in spite of the advent of plate tectonic theory, which is used today to explain the formation of the Appalachians. Pumpelly greatly expanded the efforts of the earlier geologists who had worked separately in the region for many years, and by applying the latest work of the Alpine geologists he made the *Geology of the Green Mountains* a contribution to structural geology comparable to the best European work and a classic example of the way the methods of structural geology could be applied to a particular mountainous region.

As a modern geologist has said, speaking of the Rocky Mountains: "We should dissect all these mountain ranges before we get diarrhea of the pen trying to clue them in to plate theory. . . . Until we know the anatomy of each mountain range, how are we going to say what came up when?"[49] Pumpelly's study of the anatomy of the Green Mountains was independent of any overriding theory as to their formation. At the time of his work no general agreement existed on orogenic theory, but his scrupulous attention to the details of structure and stratigraphy ensured that his report would continue to be useful to a later generation of geologists by helping to provide a solid foundation upon which new theory could be based.

Defining the Precambrian

Pumpelly's work as head of the Archean Division represented a new interest in the Precambrian era made possible by micropetrologic techniques and geophysical studies of crystalline rocks. By the 1880s geologists had classified most of the fossiliferous strata, but the rocks below the Cambrian were still a mystery and remained so long after publication of the Green Mountain monograph, which dealt primarily with the Paleozoic formations. Pumpelly did extensive consulting work on these primordial rocks, particularly with Charles R. Van Hise, who became one of the foremost authorities of his generation on the Precambrian formations.

Henry Adams became aware of this new interest in the Precambrian in 1901, when his friend Samuel Franklin Emmons brought Van Hise, Canadian geologist Frank Dawson Adams, and USGS director Charles Walcott to "a geological dinner."

When I was young, geology began with fossils and shells and the signs of life. Nowadays it ends there. Not one of these four men, whose names are all of the highest authority all over the world, will look twice at a fossil except to throw out the rock they find him in. All they touch is granites and things that lie at the bottom. There they have about five times as much rock as there is above it, and all they study is to know what made it. The youth from Canada has been squeezing it like butter.[50]

When Pumpelly became head of the Archean Division in 1884, most geologists used the term *Archean* for all rocks below the Cambrian. During the next eight years they began to realize that the Archean rocks were much more complex than they had thought, and Pumpelly and other USGS geologists began to make some progress toward breaking them down into more precise subdivisions. In 1893 Powell reported that, thanks to the introduction of new methods, the Archean and Lake Superior divisions had determined that the Archean was made up of several very thick rock series. And, instead of being completely without fossils, as they had supposed, survey geologists now agreed, based on the fact that the oldest Cambrian fossil, *Olenellus*, was already a well-developed organism and far advanced in the time scale, that these rocks must contain at least one life-bearing subdivision representing a period "probably longer than all succeeding time." They suggested the word *Proterozoic* for the life-bearing period (*Agnotozoic* and *Eparchean* had also been proposed) and agreed on the name Algonkian for the rocks of that period, the term in use today. They suggested reserving the term *Archean* for the oldest division, below the Algonkian.[51]

During the time Pumpelly was working in the Green Mountains, the International Geological Congress, which was trying to unify geological nomenclature and standardize the colors for geological maps, took up questions relating to the classification of the Archean era. As a member of the American Sub-Committee on the Archean, Pumpelly participated in the preparation of a report for the 1888 London meeting of the IGC. His answers to fourteen questions circulated to committee members regarding the desirability of subdividing the Archean indicate his cautious support for the subdivision. He had "positive personal knowledge of non-conformability" between two formations in the Lake Superior region, he reported. For this reason he recommended that the term *Archean* be confined "to the rocks below the top of the Laurentian," the name used for the oldest crystalline rocks of the Canadian shield. He thought that the interval from the top of the Laurentian up to the bottom of the Cambrian (for which he felt the term *Agnotozoic* would be "unobjectionable") be left open "for the freest exercise of local classification until a much more advanced state of our knowledge" permits a more "absolute terminology."[52]

The editor of the subcommittee's report, Persifor Frazer, worried about the dangers of premature classification, especially "the establishment of artificial lines, which become in time real barriers to that free ebb and flow of conception which has always preceded the establishment of a permanent theory." Grove Karl Gilbert, then in charge of a series of USGS "Correlation Papers," agreed. He worried that both the IGC and the USGS were too enthusiastic in their efforts to classify formations and standardize nomenclature: "I am now convinced that unless the conservatives make themselves heard geology may be saddled with a tyranny of authoritative classification that will seriously hamper its development." Pumpelly was on the side of the conservatives; he made recommendations only when they were based on the results of personal investigation. In spite of his great experience in this area he readily admitted that there was still too little knowledge of the Precambrian rocks to make any international correlations. Even today, with new radioactive dating techniques, the Precambrian is generally divided into local series of rock sequences, because too little is known to determine their relations to each other.[53]

The last paper Pumpelly wrote as a member of the U.S. Geological Survey, a collaboration with Charles R. Van Hise on the subject of divisions within the Algonkian, was based on their joint investigations on the north shore of Lake Huron. The two men spent the summers of 1890 and 1891 together in the field, confirming to their satisfaction the claim of

N. H. Winchell, state geologist of Minnesota, that the Algonkian formation in Minnesota, there called Huronian, consisted of two distinct series. They also were able to show that the base of the Huronian rested on the basement complex, or Laurentian as it was called in Canada.[54]

The interaction between Pumpelly and Van Hise is an example of the mutual stimulation and inspiration that can occur when scientists with the same interests are working together—an interaction that is very real but difficult to assess. The times spent in the field with Van Hise, who was twenty years his junior, were "cherished memories" for Pumpelly. Van Hise's personality and working style complemented Pumpelly's in many ways. Unlike Pumpelly, whose geological insight enabled him to perceive geological relationships quickly, Van Hise was systematic and methodical, working out geological relationships through the use of three-dimensional models, for example. Van Hise later became president of the University of Wisconsin, but as a young man he was uncomfortable in social situations, shy, and awkward in conversation. Nevertheless, Pumpelly found Van Hise "charged with mental lightning" and a good traveling companion whatever the hardships. Van Hise must have found Pumpelly equally stimulating, for, as Bailey Willis remembered, it was "in conversation in the field face to face with the facts or in talks of an evening between days' work" that Pumpelly made his greatest contributions to the solution of Precambrian problems.[55]

Willis, who was with them on at least one occasion in the Appalachians, observed that while Van Hise systematically collected specimens and planned how he would use them to work out a complex problem of metamorphism, Pumpelly could imaginatively recreate the geologic history of a region by analogy with settings he knew from past experience. Pumpelly inspired the more down-to-earth Van Hise with "his penetrating insight into the intricate relations and processes" involved. Van Hise acknowledged his special debt to Pumpelly as well as to Irving in a monograph-length paper for the USGS on the Archean and Algonkian: "I have been much in the field for the last two seasons and have received many pregnant ideas. What part of the thoughts . . . come from these two friends I am unable to specify in detail, but I am conscious that the debt is a heavy one."[56]

When Willis, in 1924, requested an opinion of Pumpelly's work from Van Hise's co-worker, Charles K. Leith (Van Hise having died in 1918), Leith replied that Van Hise

spoke often of the inspiration he got from him, particularly along the lines of structural geology. By the time I became active Pumpelly had practically retired, with the result that I could judge only from his writings, where I found many suggestive things but not enough to develop the enthusiasm which came from personal contact.[57]

The enthusiasm that comes from personal contact with a mentor, whether in the laboratory or the field, is an important source of inspiration to younger co-workers in any science but is probably especially important for geologists, who must necessarily spend much informal time together when on extended field trips. The influence of Pumpelly, who never wrote a comprehensive treatment of the subjects he knew so well, on Van Hise and on other geologists who worked with him was apparently often due to the perceptions and suggestions they received from him during day-to-day discussions over an actual problem in the field.

Pumpelly was fifty-five years old and might well have expected to serve several more years as a USGS geologist when, in January 1892, he submitted the final report on the Green Mountains to Powell. Unfortunately, that year Powell was coming under personal attack for his supposed extravagance, for placing too much emphasis on pure science, particularly paleontology, and for his irrigation survey, which displeased western congressmen. It was also the beginning of a period of economic decline that preceded the great Panic of 1893, and in July a congressional investigation concluded with a vote that reduced the appropriation for the geological survey to $376,100, a sharp cut from the $800,000 it had received in the late 1880s. When the budget cuts became law, all activity in the field was suspended and many positions were cut. Of five geologists receiving the top salary of $4,000 a year, Pumpelly, George F. Becker, and Henry Adams's friend Emmons were let go. Ironically, the three were Powell's best economic geologists. Becker and Emmons were reinstated in 1894 but Pumpelly never returned to the survey.[58]

As a member of the USGS during its early years, Pumpelly contributed to the prestige of the survey, considered one of the best in the world. His division was, of course, only one of several that were investigating and mapping the diverse geology of the country, but it represents the professionalism with which the survey teams conducted their research. Never just a desk administrator or closet theorizer, Pumpelly enjoyed being in the field where he could study the rocks at firsthand, analyze relationships and processes, and see what his assistants were up to. He remained a generalist at a time when geology was becoming more specialized and when more and more geologists were turning to experimental work in the laboratory to supplement work in the field. Willis, for example, was conducting a series of structural experiments, trying to recreate in the laboratory the forces that caused crustal folding. Becker was turning from economic geology to geophysics, conducting experiments and writing technical papers on rock deformation and other subjects that few people could understand. Both Becker and Van Hise played an important part in the establishment of the Geophysical Laboratory of the Carnegie Institution of Washington.[59]

After leaving the survey, Pumpelly became again the gentleman geologist, although geology gradually took a less important place in his activities. In 1893, his finances weakened by the panic, he and his family left for Europe because he thought they could live more economically there. The children, who had never had to worry about money, now became "strict mentors," taking seriously the spending of every nickel. When the family returned in 1895, Pumpelly's affairs had improved but he could find no permanent position. He took occasional consulting jobs in the West, and with his son-in-law (Margarita's husband) Henry Lloyd Smyth, a professor of mining at Lawrence Scientific School, he explored for iron in the Lake Superior region and for gold in Colorado, Nevada, and California but with little success.[60]

In 1898 Pumpelly's daughter Elise married Thomas Handasyd Cabot, whose family had been summering nearby in Dublin. In a letter written in 1932 to a friend who had been reading Pumpelly's *Reminiscences*, Thomas's brother Hugh recalled his first meeting with Pumpelly in Dublin. He had been alone reading when Pumpelly, "an apparition with a long double-barreled beard, appeared at a French window. This window he partly opened, the wind blew his beard into it, and the door then slammed locking itself securely so that the beard was on one side and he on the other." It was a most appropriate introduction, Cabot thought, "since he was the wildest of wild Indians who I ever saw in quasi respectable society." To his friend, who wanted to know whether to believe Pumpelly's life story, Cabot replied:

He was an extraordinary raconteur telling the most wonderful and lurid stories in the most attractive fashion and the extraordinary thing about it was that . . . most of the stories were true. If you had heard him, sitting before his fire in Dublin with the stage very nicely prepared, you would have put him down for a monumental liar with a most attractive personality, but the fact of the matter was that he was not a liar. . . . You need not add more than the normal quantity of salt.[61]

Sitting by the fire and telling stories of his adventures was not yet to be the final chapter of Pumpelly's life, however. In a few years he would begin a new experience that would be for him the most interesting part of his life.

7 Explorations in Turkestan

In 1903, at the age of sixty-five, Pumpelly became once again the Humboldtian explorer. That year he organized the first of two expeditions to Central Asia, hoping to shed light on a question that had fascinated many nineteenth-century gentlemen and scholars. With a grant from the newly established Carnegie Institution of Washington and the help of geographers and archaeologists, he set out to investigate sites east of the Caspian Sea that he thought might prove to be the original home of the Aryans—the people who, according to a popular theory, had brought their language and the civilizing arts of agriculture, domestication, and metal working to Europe.

Pumpelly's theory, which had grown out of his years of exploration and study of the Aryan question (the word *Aryan* did not then have the overt racist implications that it has today), was that Central Asia, which is now arid, had once been wetter and capable of supporting a larger population than now lives there. Toward the end of the ice ages, the water from the melting of the Russian ice cap and the glaciers of the eastern high mountain ranges would have filled the region now occupied by the Caspian and Aral seas, creating a sea larger than the Mediterranean. Around this sea, Pumpelly thought, might have lived a people who developed the use of agriculture, the domestication of animals, and the art of working metals. Changing climatic conditions at the end of the last glacial epoch would have brought about progressive desiccation and sent waves of migration westward to Europe and eastward to India and the Orient.[1]

All of Pumpelly's past experience had prepared him for this quest, on which he spent the happiest and most satisfying years of his life. His youthful explorations in China and Japan, his interest in foreign cultures, his studies of glaciers and loess, and his conversations with geologist friends and gentlemanly companions all contributed to the adoption of his theory as a working hypothesis. The organizational and administrative ability he had demonstrated while working on the Tenth Census, the Northern Transcontinental Survey, and the USGS enabled him to carry out the testing of his theory. Pumpelly integrated research from several disciplines in his geoarchaeological approach to the question of Aryan migrations. He drew from contemporary studies in archaeology, anthropology, ethnology, philology, physical geography, and geology. At a time when many geologists were specializing in ever narrower fields such as geophysics, geochemistry, and petrology, Pumpelly was broadening his knowledge in a way that is reminiscent of Humboldt in order to use the methods of several sciences to study the effect of climatic change on prehistoric cultures. To understand his interdisciplinary approach it is necessary to look at the way other nineteenth-century scholars were dealing with the "Aryan question."

The Aryan Question

The question of Aryan (or Indo-European, as it is called today) origins had fascinated scientists and philologists since 1786, when the noted British Orientalist, Sir William Jones, pointed out similarities between Sanskrit, Latin, Greek, Celtic, and modern European languages and suggested that they all must have sprung from a common ancestor. If such a common language had existed, scholars reasoned, an ancestral race that spoke that language must have existed as well. The question was: Who were these people and where did they come from? The existence of an Indo-European language was confirmed by philologists, but the original home of the people who spoke it was still in doubt at the end of the nineteenth century, the question confused by proposals that the Aryans had come from North Africa, northern Europe, the Steppes of Russia, the Pamir, the Hindu Kush, or Central Asia.[2]

Pumpelly had been interested in the location of the Aryan homeland ever since his travels in China and Mongolia in 1863–64. The scholars who had helped him gather information for the preparation of his geological map of China had provided him with old maps on which were notes referring to a place where lived "a people with red hair and blue eyes" and to cities long since buried by sand. Perhaps, the young Pumpelly had thought, this was the place of origin of the Aryan peoples.

In 1891, at the International Geological Congress held in Washington, D.C., he discussed the question with the head of the Russian geological survey who told him that Russian geologists had recently found Caspian shells of the Pleistocene epoch in sediments above the present level of the Caspian Sea. This seemed to Pumpelly proof that a great sea had indeed once covered much of Central Asia and that this region could have been the Aryan cradleland.[3]

During the last decades of the nineteenth century, while Pumpelly was involved with geological work, the literature on the Aryan question had grown tremendously. Some of the world's most distinguished scientists had discussed the problem, calling for more rigorous application to it of the new, more scientific methods of archaeology, comparative ethnology, and anthropology.[4] British biologist Thomas Henry Huxley, for example, complained that too many theorists had done too much unscientific speculation on the subject and he doubted that the makeup of primitive racial stocks would ever be determined. Nevertheless, he was excited by the "vast amount of positive evidence" that prehistoric archaeologists and anthropologists were finding. Huxley vigorously defended northern European origins and cited evidence from prehistoric sites in Europe showing that people were already living in many parts of Europe at the end of the ice ages. Huxley was convinced that these prehistoric inhabitants of Europe had developed metal working and other arts independently rather than through migrations from the east, as Pumpelly and many others thought.[5] The debate between diffusion and independent invention continues among archaeologists and anthropologists to this day. Although Huxley and Pumpelly held different opinions about origins, both recognized the problem as an important and challenging one to which the sciences could make positive contributions.

The German philologist Otto Schrader, who based his extensive research on Indo-European origins on etymological studies, argued that philology alone was not enough to solve the problem. Archaeological investigations, the comparative study of the objects used by prehistoric peoples, and analysis of the language and customs of surviving primitive societies must be applied to bring about a better understanding of early origins. The German geographer Friedrich Ratzel, who has been called "the greatest single contributor to the geography of man," emphasized the role of geographic barriers that isolated one group from another and allowed a separate evolution of the different races. Ratzel supported the theory of Central Asian origins but thought that the Aryans had spread to North Africa, where the Sahara acted as a barrier separating them from the black race. As the northern ice sheets retreated from the European continent, he argued, the Aryans migrated into northern Europe by

Explorations in Turkestan 167

various routes, bringing with them agriculture and the arts of polishing stone, building houses, breeding cattle, and making pottery and metal objects.[6]

Inspired by the Aryan question, the American anthropologist and ethnologist William Z. Ripley studied the physical characteristics of the races of Europe, using statistics and maps to show the geographic distribution of three principal racial types: the short, dark Mediterranean type, the round-headed Alpine type, and the tall, blond, long-headed Teutonic type. Ripley rejected the idea that the language of the Aryans could be identified with any race, however, and deplored contemporary theories of Germanic superiority. No race has a monopoly on intellect or virtue, he said.[7]

Racism was, of course, the most infamous ramification of the Aryan question, although it should be made clear that Pumpelly was not a racist. Several American geologists, Nathaniel Shaler for example, did write extensively on the environmental aspects of Aryan or Anglo-Saxon superiority, and Huxley gave his tentative support to the idea that the speakers of the Aryan language were a blond, long-headed race from northern Europe. Some geologists and biologists thus contributed to the acceptance of the racist Anglo-Saxonism that became prevalent in England and the United States in the nineteenth century. Pumpelly, however, believed that his own early experience in Corsica, Arizona, China, and Japan—his "broader field of education," as he called it—had taught him that human nature was the same whatever a person's race and had "made clear the dangers of racial prejudice." He read and enjoyed Ripley's *Races of Europe,* another indication that he did not see his investigations as proving racial superiority, for Ripley had discredited the racial aspects of the Aryan question.[8]

In preparing for his travels and in writing the reports of his expeditions, Pumpelly read widely in anthropology, ethnology, geography, and linguistics; it was the kind of study he wished he could have taken up at Freiberg. Bailey Willis remembered a visit when he found Pumpelly absorbed in reading Ripley's *Races of Europe.* "I never could read books on geology; I had to see the facts to become interested, but I can read this by the hour," he said to Willis, holding up the book. He studied Schrader's *Prehistoric Antiquities,* from which he learned to identify many root words of the Indo-European languages. He also took extensive notes on Ratzel's paper on Aryan origins, and it is obvious from his final reports that he shared Ratzel's views on the relationship of the physical environment to the development and migrations of human societies.[9]

By the end of the century, many scholars thought that the Aryan issue was dead, mired in a welter of conflicting theories and "incapable of clarification because the crucial evidence was lost, apparently forever."[10] The question was not dead, however. The study of Indo-European origins is, in fact, very much alive today, without overtones of racism, as indicated by the publication and controversial reception of Colin Renfrew's recent *Archaeology and Language: The Puzzle of Indo-European Origins*.[11] Pumpelly was tackling a very big problem, the most ambitious project of his life and typical of the imaginative endeavors of a Humboldtian explorer. He continued to believe in the Asiatic origins of civilization, and he seemed to be confident that by application of the latest scientific methods and with the help of expert assistants, as had been his approach to the Taconic controversy, he could throw light on the Aryan question.

Pumpelly had discussed his Aryan theory with Henry and Brooks Adams and other friends, but it remained only an armchair hypothesis until the establishment of the Carnegie Institution of Washington in 1902. In December of that year, with the encouragement of Brooks Adams, he applied for a grant. His proposal, "Trans-Caspia: A Field for Archaeological Research," gave his reasons for assuming that a large inland sea had once existed in the Caspian-Aral basin; that a large population had lived around its borders; that the sea had dried up, leaving only the Aral, Caspian, and the Balkash seas, causing "the dispersion of these peoples to China, India, Western Asia and Europe"; and "that the cities, already old at the dawn of history—Samarkand, Bactra and others on the great ancient trade routes between the far East and India, Persia, Western Asia and Egypt, were in more remote antiquity, the sites of centres of these dispersed populations." Pumpelly proposed to study the "past and present physico-geographic conditions of this basin and its archaeological remains; the physical and archaeological studies to be correlative factors of an apparently well defined historical problem."[12]

For his final report for the CIW, Pumpelly wrote a chapter on the Aryan migrations but withheld it because he thought the hypothesis was still unproven.[13] The expedition's value would lie not in the solution of the Aryan problem but in the introduction of exact methods to the prehistoric archaeology of Central Asia and in the interdisciplinary study that treated a particular arid region as an organic whole.

The Carnegie Institution

Andrew Carnegie had founded the Carnegie Institution of Washington in 1902 with $10 million in U.S. Steel bonds for the purpose of encouraging original "investigation, research, and discovery, and the application of knowledge to the improvement of mankind." It was similar in purpose to the new Rockefeller Institute, founded in 1901 to support medical research. As prototypes of twentieth-century research foundations, these institutions enabled individuals within universities to do basic research freed from the responsibilities of teaching and also funded independent researchers, like Pumpelly, who did not have other means of support for large research projects.[14]

The new institution quickly set up advisory committees and sent out circulars inviting proposals, arousing great interest and debate among members of the scientific community. As the *New York Independent* reported, only slightly tongue in cheek, the country's leading scientists were divided as to how the new institution should best distribute its grants. Should it "establish large and well-equipped laboratories at Washington"? or "waste no money on buildings"? Should it give "small sums to many individuals"? or "give at least $100,000 at a time"? Should it assist "unknown and struggling men in small colleges"? or make grants only to "tried and proved investigators"? Should it publish "a handsome series of quarto and folio memoirs"? or "waste no money on big books and wide margins"?[15]

Some members of the CIW executive board argued that money should go to fund laboratories in Washington. Charles Walcott, who was director of the USGS as well as secretary of the Carnegie Institution and member of its executive board, was a powerful force behind the establishment of the institution's Geophysical Laboratory in 1905. In these early years money also went to establish the Mount Wilson Observatory, the Marine Biological Laboratory at Tortugas, Florida, and C. B. Davenport's Station for Experimental Biology at Cold Spring Harbor on Long Island.[16]

Carnegie's own intention was to promote original research, not by putting up large buildings and laboratories, but by supporting existing institutions and enabling "the exceptional man in every department of study . . . inside or outside of schools . . . to make the work for which he seems specially designed his life work." As he later told Walcott, "My own opinion is that no big institution should be erected anywhere, but the exceptional men should be encouraged to do their exceptional work in their own environment." In the first years the trustees spent much time discussing the problem of finding the exceptional man whose ability was well documented. As one trustee said, "If something is proposed, we say Yes that is a very good thing—who is your man? That has been the dominating question. We did not take up the $5,000 proposal for digging a hole in the side of a hill proposed by Miss X—that did not strike us properly."[17]

The Carnegie Institution did not find it easy to identify the exceptional man—it was much easier if the applicant had already produced work of recognized quality. Because Pumpelly was clearly an "exceptional man," the trustees received his proposal favorably; at a trustees' meeting John S. Billings remarked that Pumpelly was "a mining engineer capable of doing that kind of thing." Not only did Pumpelly have an excellent reputation for his previous experience in conducting explorations and surveys, but he was also known personally, because of their association on the USGS, to Walcott and members of the Carnegie Institution's Advisory Committee on Geology, Charles R. Van Hise and Thomas C. Chamberlin. Walcott was very supportive of Pumpelly, perhaps remembering the turmoil within the USGS in 1892–93 when Pumpelly lost his job and he himself had become head of the survey after Powell resigned. When Pumpelly's request for $5,000 for the first year was approved on December 16, 1902, Walcott wrote that it was "done on my statement that you would take personal charge of the work for the first year."[18]

Brooks Adams was also very enthusiastic about Pumpelly's project. Although Pumpelly had at first "hesitated and made excuses," possibly because he knew he would be getting into a field that was new to him, Adams urged him to submit a proposal and called on Walcott personally to promote the expedition. When the grant was approved, Walcott asked Pumpelly to notify Adams, "in order that he may be less pessimistic as to the future of investigation in the Trans-Caspian region."[19] Adams was delighted at the news and congratulated Walcott for his influence at the CIW: "I take it as an indication that you have obtained full control of the Carnegie Trust. With you to direct I have little doubt that the Institution will do great work. Were it left in academic hands it would be pure waste."[20]

The reason for Adams's special interest in Pumpelly's project can be found in his book *The New Empire,* published in 1902, a further development of the economic theory of history that Adams had introduced with *The Law of Civilization and Decay* in 1896. Since ancient times, Adams argued, civilizations have followed trade routes. The great commercial centers grew up where trade routes intersected, and trade routes depended on geography. Traders were always looking for the shortest, cheapest route, "the line of least resistance," as Adams put it. When a cheaper route was found, the empires built upon the older ones began to decline. Because Pumpelly's plan was to explore and excavate abandoned sites in Central Asia, the heart of the ancient silk route, Adams must have been aware of the possibility of finding clues to the geographic changes that had caused a shift in the arteries of trade.[21]

In general, the Carnegie Institution did not follow a policy of supporting geographic exploration; most of the grants large and small went to the physical and natural sciences. The chairman of the Advisory Committee on Geography, William Morris Davis of Harvard, had recommended that "the expense of exploring expeditions had best be left, as a rule, to governmental and individual funds." Bailey Willis, with Walcott's support, received a grant of $12,000 for geological exploration in China, but large-scale proposals such as biological surveys of the Paleoarctic region and of South and Central America were not funded. The Carnegie Institution at first agreed to support Alexander Agassiz's proposed "Exploration and Study of the Tropical Pacific Ocean" with a grant of $40,000 but later dropped it; nor did it approve an Antarctic expedition proposed by the Carnegie Institution of Pittsburgh or an application from Capt. Robert Peary for Arctic exploration.[22]

The advisory committees on archaeology and anthropology, however, gave serious consideration to proposals in their fields. The Advisory Committee on Anthropology, which submitted its report in October 1902, recommended support for research in physical anthropology, ethnology, and archaeology, particularly in the Americas, and suggested that research in archaeology begin with a systematic study of aboriginal remains with the help of geologists in order to establish a chronology of early man. For a few years the CIW made small grants to the American schools of classical studies at Athens and Rome, research schools founded by the Archaeological Institute of America and supported by university and private funds. The CIW also gave grants to a few individuals doing research in classical archaeology and later established a department of archaeology for the study of Precolumbian sites in Central America.[23]

Pumpelly proposed to combine archaeological with geographic and geological exploration in a region not previously studied by American archaeologists. Although the Transcaspian basin had been a part of Russia since 1865, the Russians had done little archaeological work there and what work had been done was at sites of a later period than that in which Pumpelly was interested. Pumpelly told Walcott that the Russian government had at one time offered to aid him "in the way of facilities and topographers" in the search for signs of the ancient Central Asian sea but that he preferred the work to be American.[24] The Carnegie trustees evidently were convinced not only that they had an exceptional man but also that they had a project that could enhance the Carnegie Institution's international standing.

Geographic Influences: The Expedition of 1903

Although the best-known aspects of Pumpelly's work in Turkestan were his archaeological excavations at Anau, the physiographic and geological research was just as important to him as the archaeology. He and the members of his expedition devoted much effort to the study of glaciers, uplift, erosion patterns, shorelines, and the stratigraphy of the site selected for excavation in order to detect signs of past climatic change that might have affected the life of the people who had lived there.

Pumpelly's conviction that the earth's changing environment had affected human history was an area of interest he shared with several of his fellow geologists as well as with some nineteenth-century historians like Brooks Adams and Frederick Jackson Turner. Pumpelly certainly believed, as Shaler did, that "geographic conditions may greatly affect the struggle for existence in most important ways." Shaler's *Nature and Man in America,* based on a series of lectures at the Lowell Institute, was a very popular exposition of the influence of geography on American history. Charles R. Van Hise and Thomas C. Chamberlin, who were Frederick Jackson Turner's mentors at the University of Wisconsin, both believed that physiography played an important role in the development of industry and civilization. As William Coleman has pointed out, Turner's frontier thesis, which treated society as a biological organism affected by environmental conditions, probably owed much to their ideas. In 1903, the year of Pumpelly's first expedition to Turkestan, two influential works appeared, Ellen Church Semple's *American History and Its Geographic Conditions* and Albert Perry Brigham's *Geographical Influences in American History,* both prime examples of the application of physical geography to the interpretation of American history.[25] Pumpelly's study of environmental influences on the growth of civilizations was therefore timely and in keeping with current trends in history and geography.

Once the Carnegie grant was approved, Pumpelly began the planning and organization of his expedition with characteristic thoroughness. He studied the literature, selected expert assistants, and spent some time in Saint Petersburg making arrangements for travel in Russia. At age sixty-five he was an experienced traveler, tactful and friendly in his relations with representatives of foreign governments. The first year of the Transcaspian work, during the spring and summer of 1903, was a preliminary reconnaissance during which he did wide-ranging physiographic studies and selected a site for excavation the following year.

Pumpelly began to gather all the information he could find about Russian Turkestan, frankly admitting that in the past he had done little reading about the region and was "ignorant of the amount of thought and effort that during forty years had been devoted to Central Asia." As a start he made notes from the works referred to in Prince Peter Kropotkin's articles on Turkestan in the *Encyclopedia Britannica* and consulted books in French, German, and English on travel, geography, geology, history, archaeology, and anthropology. He even taught himself enough Russian to read some of the works that the Russians had done on the geology and geography of Turkestan. It was a "new education," which he pursued until he finished the final report in 1908. "For five years it was my life by day and . . . my dream by night," he wrote later.[26]

To Walcott he soon admitted that many workers had mined the field before him: "Since the matter formulated itself clearly in my mind, between 1863 and 1870, others have got the priority as I have not been willing to publish a *schreibtisch* [desk] theory. However this is merely a personal disappointment and the work done by others is so much gain toward facilitating the exploration."[27]

The assistants Pumpelly chose for his expeditions were experts in their fields, people with interests of their own for whom the expedition was an opportunity to investigate new phenomena, develop their own ideas, and publish independently. Most of them shared his ideas about the influence of the environment and were sympathetic to his aims. Pumpelly felt he had made an especially important move in persuading William Morris Davis to join him. "He is as enthusiastic over the whole scope and importance of the problem as I am," Pumpelly wrote Walcott, "and has agreed to take charge of the physico-geographic and climatological part of the work."[28]

Since the 1890s, Davis had been actively promoting the teaching of physiography as a science distinct from geology. Physiography, or geomorphology as it is called today, was becoming a popular branch of geology concerned with the evolution of the earth's surface features, and Davis was then the recognized leader in this field. Davis was also attempting to redefine the content of geography to include Darwinian adaptation, coining the term *ontography* to mean "all those responses by which the inhabitants, from the lowest to the highest, have adjusted themselves to their environment." He suggested that even forms of language and habits of thought might be determined by environment.[29] Pumpelly's expedition gave Davis many opportunities to observe examples of physiography and ontography as an integrated relationship.

The expedition also gave Davis a chance to study his concept of the cycle of erosion that he had first formulated while on Pumpelly's Northern Transcontinental Survey. During the cycle, according to Davis, a region undergoes a process of uplift followed by dissection and erosion by streams, wind, glaciers, or other forces until the original landmass is eventually reduced to a featureless plain, which he named the "peneplain." The concept, a model for analyzing landscape formation as an evolutionary process, was to dominate the study of geomorphology for many years. In the summer of 1902 Davis had taken some of his students to Arizona and Utah, where they had observed stages in the cycle of erosion in the deserts, the Grand Canyon, and Lake Bonneville. In Central Asia, Davis could apply the cycle model to both arid and glacial environments.[30]

Davis took with him one of his most promising graduate students and a devoted disciple, Ellsworth Huntington, who later became known as a leading proponent of environmental determinism. The son of a Congregational minister, Huntington had studied geology and other sciences at Beloit College and in 1897 went to Harpoot, Turkey, as assistant to the president of Euphrates College. In addition to his other duties there, he taught geology, recorded climatological data, mapped the upper Euphrates River, worked with a German archaeological expedition, and learned Armenian and some Turkish. Asia held a lifelong fascination for Huntington. When he left to enter Harvard in the fall of 1901 he was sure he would "come back to the Orient. I cannot help it. It has seized hold of me." Pumpelly gave him the chance to go back in 1903 and 1904, and his experience on both expeditions was to have a lasting effect on his career. Huntington's report for Pumpelly on his exploration of the basin of Sistan in Persia concluded with a section on "Climate and History" that was his first writing on the subject for which he would become famous. His chapter on the Merv oasis proved to be "one of the steps," he added in a footnote at the time of publication in 1908, that had led to the development of his theory of the effect of climatic pulsations in historic times. Huntington's theory was presented in full in his popular *Pulse of Asia*, published in 1907.[31]

Pumpelly knew that the inclusion of an experienced archaeologist in the party was crucial to the success of his expeditions, and he invited Richard Norton, son of Charles Eliot Norton of Harvard, to accompany him to advise on selecting promising sites for excavation. The senior Norton had been editor of the *North American Review* when Pumpelly wrote his article on China for the journal in 1868. Richard had taught the history of fine arts at Bryn Mawr and was now, at age thirty-one, the director of the American School of Classical Studies in Rome, which conducted archaeological excavations of classical sites. Norton did not return in 1904.[32]

The archaeologist with the 1904 expedition was Hubert Schmidt, curator of ceramics at the Museum für Völkerkunde in Berlin and experienced in the archaeology of the Mediterranean region. He had previously studied and worked with Wilhelm Dorpfeld, the archaeologist who had revolutionized Heinrich Schliemann's methods at Troy by introducing the latest excavation techniques. The museum agreed that Schmidt could join the expedition if it could receive duplicates from the dig.[33] Also with the expeditions of 1903 and 1904 was Pumpelly's son, Raphael Welles Pumpelly, a Harvard junior who had studied geology with his father and at Harvard with Shaler. With a better background in mathematics and physics than his father, young Raphael was able to assist Pumpelly in studying the geology of archaeological sites and the physiography of the plains and mountains. The principal reason Pumpelly brought his son along, however, was to give him field experience. Young Raphael expected that his work on the expeditions would be applied toward his degree.[34]

Pumpelly now had his grant, his plans, and his personnel, but he did not yet have permission to travel and explore in Russian Turkestan. He must have been confident that the backing of the Carnegie Institution, his own reputation, and all of his past experiences in dealing with scientists and government officials of various nationalities would help him as he made arrangements for the journey to Russia.

Pumpelly and his son Raphael sailed for Europe on March 18, 1903, their destination Saint Petersburg by way of London and Berlin. The others met them in Turkestan.[35] Henry Adams helped in getting the necessary letters of introduction to Russian authorities from the State Department. Adams, then sixty-four years old, declined an invitation to go along, but he hoped Pumpelly would be able to supply a new theory to account for all the glacial water that had stood on the continents since the "pre-archaic." He wrote: "My geological friends . . . have shown a singular want of interest in establishing the simplest general facts. . . . So good luck to you! may you tell us something about that glacial water. . . . It will bear a heap of study, I am sure; but I've a terrible fear that the early trade routes now run under the Persian Gulf and the Indian Ocean."[36]

Pumpelly spent three weeks in Saint Petersburg, from April 23 to May 15, and found it a very slow process to get "full authority to travel and work away from the main line of railway." Apparently, however, his gentlemanly yet authoritative manner, together with the Carnegie name, gained him a cordial reception wherever he went. In the end, as he wrote CIW president Daniel Coit Gilman, "I have it only because we are all Americans; and today I have the final assurance of authority from the Minister of War who controls Turkestan very jealously." Government officials made it possible for Pumpelly and his party to travel comfortably and safely by sending notice to the heads of the various provinces they expected to visit and by providing a private railroad car, a luxury everyone appreciated, which they could divert whenever they wanted to make stops. Through the intercession of Ferdinand von Richthofen, Pumpelly also received the approval and promise of help from officials of the Imperial Geographical Society and the Russian geological survey. Russia's archaeological commission gave assurances of aid "for this year and in connection with any possible future systematic work."[37]

The deliberateness with which the Russians granted Pumpelly permission to travel may have been due to growing tension between Russia and England and other European nations over Russian expansion into China with the building of the Trans-Siberian Railroad, which crossed Manchuria to Vladivostok. England sided with Japan in opposing Russia's interference with China's internal affairs, and other European countries with imperialistic designs on China also opposed Russia's presence there. John Hay's Open Door policy in China, supported by all countries involved except Japan, had helped to ease the tension and may have had something to do with the approval of Pumpelly's travel requests and his subsequent cordial treatment.[38]

Pumpelly learned from his talks with the Russian geologists and archaeologists that the Russians had studied the geology of Turkestan extensively but had done little work in prehistoric archaeology. As he reported to Gilman:

> They do not seem to have grasped the idea of the possibly extremely remote antiquity of the civilizations and of the interest attaching to the relation between these and their changing environment. . . . The nearer I approach the region, and the more I learn about it, the more the problem seems vast, fascinating and complex. From the Caspian to Eastern Mongolia there seems to be a continuous cemetery of cities.[39]

Archaeology in Central Asia was probably a low priority for the Russian government, which was trying to consolidate its rule over a region half the size of the United States. The Russians had begun their domination of Turkestan with the taking of Tashkent in 1865 but maintained it only by such measures as keeping a large military presence, by settlement, and by the building of railroads. They had completed the Transcaspian Railroad, on which Pumpelly's party traveled two thousand miles or more, from Krasnovodsk on the Caspian Sea to Samarkand only in 1894 and had extended it to Andijan in 1899.[40] Geology and engineering would have been more useful sciences than archaeology in a time of expansion into undeveloped territory, just as they had been in the United States.

As Pumpelly at last reached the shores of the Caspian Sea, the romantic nature of his journey began to affect him. On May 21 he arrived at the port of Baku, "famous in antiquity for its sacred fires of burning petroleum," now an industrial city famous for its "forest of derricks pumping oils." The party crossed the Caspian to Krasnovodsk at night and as Pumpelly watched the sun rise through a "mystic veil" he became intensely aware of the ancient world they were approaching: "There lay the goal of heroes. Beyond were cradled nations, gods, and myths."[41] As Pumpelly well knew, this was the land opened to the West by the march of Alexander the Great, about which Humboldt had written: "In no age, excepting only the epoch of the discovery and opening of tropical America . . . has there been revealed at one time and to one race, a richer field of new views of nature, or a greater mass of materials for laying the foundation of a physical knowledge of the earth, and of comparative ethnological science."[42]

Like Humboldt and other scientific explorers, Pumpelly intended that his expedition would contribute new knowledge about the earth, well-grounded in the exact science of his time. Even though his romantic nature was affected by the mythology and history of the region, he never lost sight of his scientific goals, which were to study the relations between the physiography and archaeology of this long-inhabited region.

Pumpelly treated the Transcaspian basin of Russian Turkestan as if it were a biological organism, each part interactive with every other part. Not only did he feel the close connection between geography and man, but he was also always aware of the physical interrelations of mountains, plains, and seas. Water and wind were the circulating mechanisms that transported and redistributed the loess that was the source of life on the plains. A change in any one part of the organism affected all of the others.

In planning the search for clues to the past climate of the basin and signs of progressive desiccation, Pumpelly had started a Transcaspian notebook and had made a list of "topographic and geologic work to be done."[43] A first step, he thought, would be to prepare a "profile of the critical watersheds of the Caspian-Aral with surface geology and older as obtainable." Next would be to observe the geological character, distribution, and elevation of terraces and to collect their associated fossils. He also wanted to compare the present fauna and flora of the Caspian with fossils collected from the sediments of the vanished sea. He hoped to determine the extent of glaciers in the surrounding mountains and to establish the relation of glacial conditions there to the climate and rainfall of the Transcaspian basin. He thought that the same climatic factors had affected both areas.

A study of loess and other soil deposits and their relation to the prevailing winds could provide clues to the processes and effects of progressive aridity, such as changes in soil fertility and the movement of sand that encroached on cultivated areas. He thought that a comparative study of the loess deposits of Transcaspia and the Great Lakes region might be useful in determining the age of the area.

More detailed planning of the scientific work began as soon as Pumpelly met Davis and Huntington at Baku. "Mr. Pumpelly and I have had various talks about plans, feeling our way, as it were," Davis reported to Gilman. They agreed that their work for the first year would begin with an investigation of Caspian shorelines near Krasnovodsk. Their itinerary included travel on the Transcaspian Railroad to Ashkhabad, Merv (Mary), Samarkand and Tashkent, with stops to visit promising archaeological sites and to take side trips by horseback into the mountains dividing Turkestan from Iran. At the end of the line, at Andijan, they would buy supplies and horses for a journey into the high mountain ranges, Huntington and Davis going to lake Issik Kul in the Tien Shan range, the Pumpellys and Norton to the Pamirs.[44]

The physiographic work centered on three distinct geographic regions: (1) the area around the Caspian and Aral seas, where they looked for old shorelines; (2) the plains and alluvial fans at the edge of the mountains, where they expected to find the remains of ancient settlements; and (3) the mountains to the south and east of the central basin, where they studied erosion features and estimated the number of glacial epochs. Inasmuch as Russian geologists had done extensive work on the geology of the Tertiary period and earlier, Pumpelly and Davis concentrated on the geologically recent Quaternary formations.[45]

Pumpelly seems to have had a good working relationship with Davis and Huntington. Huntington found him very likable: "He is a fine looking tall man with white hair and a long white beard. His eyes have a very kind expression and are full of fun. He has seen lots of the world and enjoys telling about it which he does in a very interesting way."[46]

Davis had worked with Pumpelly before, of course, and knew his ways. Even though Davis was becoming known as "an infallible oracle to whose followers every utterance seemed sacred and immutable," Huntington noticed that Davis deferred to Pumpelly, letting him "go his own way until he gets to the point where he wants advice." Pumpelly, in turn, was willing to let his assistants develop and even publish their own opinions but did not let their inferences interfere with his own.[47]

Caspian Shorelines

Pumpelly's investigation of the ancient Aralo-Caspian Sea has certain parallels with Grove Karl Gilbert's classic study of Lake Bonneville, the ancient Pleistocene lake of Utah, of which Great Salt Lake is a remnant. But where Gilbert had used a mechanical approach that included geophysical studies of waves and crustal warping, Pumpelly was simply attempting to determine former sea levels, and where Gilbert had spent several years of fieldwork and study on Bonneville, Pumpelly and Davis had little more than a week of reconnaissance around the shores of the Caspian. What Pumpelly had in common with Gilbert was an awareness of the climatic factor that had brought about the filling and the subsequent evaporation of these large inland bodies of water. Both men thought that it would be possible to correlate glacial cycles in the mountains with water levels in the seas or lakes. Even on their brief reconnaissance of Caspian shorelines, Pumpelly, Davis, and Huntington were able to confirm some of the previous work of Russian geologists, who had determined that the Caspian and the Aral seas had been confluent during the Pliocene and had covered at least part of what is now the Kara Kum desert. Most of the Russians thought that the Aral and Caspian had become separated during the Quaternary, but they disagreed on when and how often and to what extent the Aralo-Caspian Sea had expanded and shrunk. This question Pumpelly hoped Davis could clarify.[48]

Huntington and Davis had reached Baku in May and had already spent a week looking for old shorelines before Pumpelly and his son arrived. Pumpelly went with them to see one shoreline they had found at about 600 feet above the Caspian near Baku. He agreed that it was a "very well defined beach deposit of gravels" but he did not find enough confirming evidence elsewhere to say positively that the Caspian had ever reached that height. On the eastern side, near Krasnovodsk, the team found and measured elevated beaches and cobble beds at several levels, from 8 to 250 feet, but was unable to determine their age with any certainty. Pumpelly later tried to correlate Davis's shoreline data with the level at which he found kurgans or ruins. He had seen no signs of ancient settlement lower than 250 feet above the Caspian, which seemed to support his theory that people had settled around the shores of the former sea.[49]

Davis believed that the results of their limited study of the shorelines were inconclusive and recommended that further work be done on this "preeminent" problem.[50] The Carnegie Institution apparently did not consider this an important physiographic problem for Americans to investigate, however. Davis did not return the following year, and the efforts of the others were directed elsewhere.

Delta Oases

As they traveled east from Krasnovodsk the members of the party observed from the train the second physiographic province that engaged their interest: the piedmont belt along the base of the Kopet Dagh, the mountains that divide Russian Turkestan from Iran. There, the deposition of the debris washed down from the bordering mountains had formed a long series of alluvial fans at the mouths of valleys. The plains here were being built up or aggraded by gravel, sand, and silt, because most of the rivers coming down from the mountains never reach the sea but end in the desert.

Pumpelly realized that the delta oases, as he called them, provided clues to past geological, climatic, and historical change. On the fans were dry stream channels, remains of abandoned irrigation ditches, the ruins of ancient towns, and many mounds that had clearly once been sites of human occupation. These sloping piedmont plains became the focal point for the next expedition, for here between the mountains and the barren sand of the desert was, or once had been, enough good soil and water to support settled communities, and here the strata could be correlated, Pumpelly thought, with periods of erosion in the mountains.[51]

On this part of the journey Davis found many opportunities to study erosion cycles and examples of ontography. He was fascinated by the efforts of the oasis dwellers to live and raise crops in an arid environment. "The number of ontographic illustrations is endless," he wrote to Gilman. "One gathers them in even from the passing train. The construction of railroad culverts is one of them." The building of flood control channels and irrigation ditches, the method of well digging, and even the route chosen for the railroad, which rose and fell as it crossed successive fans, were for Davis all examples of human responses to the physical environment of the delta oases.[52]

An important objective of the next expedition, Davis thought, would be to investigate the strata of the plains to determine conclusively whether they were formed by sediments from the sea or from river deposits, because it would have made a considerable difference in the way of life of people who had lived there. Davis did not think the sea had extended this far, for he found no shorelines here.[53]

The Mountain Ranges

On his excursions into the mountains, Pumpelly tried to estimate periods of climatic variation by looking for river terraces, loess deposits, and other evidence of past glaciation and erosion that might be correlated with periods of deposition on the plains. At the end of May, Richard Norton joined Pumpelly, young Raphael, Davis, and Huntington at Ashkhabad, where they were entertained by the governor, his wife, and his daughter, who were eager to visit the United States and wanted to know more about it. Then, with cooks and guides, making a group of fourteen in all, they took a five-day side trip on horseback into the Kopet Dagh. They found no glaciers nor any evidence of former glaciation in those mountains, but Pumpelly had a chance to do a brief but useful study of stream terraces that indicated past climatic changes. Davis observed a number of terraces in the high valleys that he believed represented successive cycles of valley deepening, possibly as many as eight "impulses" of erosion in some places, although he wasn't sure whether changing climate or uplift of the land, or a complex interaction of the two, had been responsible. In regard to Pumpelly's aims, Davis was fairly sure that the "successive changes in the behavior of the streams . . . have probably had some recognizable effect in changing the character of the piedmont deposits," but he thought that it would be very difficult to establish a direct connection.[54]

In three separate excursions that provided the first evidence of successive glacial epochs in Asia, Pumpelly's group explored the mountain ranges to the east of the Transcaspian basin, where peaks reach to heights of more than 24,000 feet. In July, Pumpelly, his son, and Richard Norton ascended into the Pamirs while Davis and Huntington explored in the Tien Shan to the north. After Davis returned home early in August, Huntington made a separate journey of reconnaissance over the Tien Shan to Kashgar in China.[55]

For Pumpelly, the journey into the high mountains was exhilarating as well as profitable from a scientific standpoint. With guides and pack train, his party rode about twenty-five miles a day, at times traveling with Kirghiz nomadic tribesmen who were driving their herds to the high valleys for summer grazing, as their ancestors had done for centuries. Sometimes the group camped out, but at other times they were invited to share the warm felt yurts (Pumpelly called them "kibitkas") of the Kirghiz, because the nights were often intensely cold even in July. Pumpelly withstood the trip well. Even after one long day's fifty-mile ride to lake Kara Kul "over high passes and plains swept by winds and whirling columns of dust," he was not tired. "I had borne the long trip better than the others, and felt quite superior to them," he remembered.[56]

Pumpelly's son did most of the fieldwork on the glaciated areas, subject to his father's review and confirmation. Near the shore of lake Kara

Kul, in a scoured and barren landscape more than 12,000 feet above sea level, young Raphael had seen that older moraine material was covered by thick beds of finely layered clay sediments. The sediments were strewn with erratic blocks and in some places had been pushed up into ridges by an advancing glacier of later date. (From Raphael's description of the fine clay lake sediments, it seems that what he had seen might have been varves, the annual layers of sediments that the Swedish geologist, Gerhard de Geer, discovered after the Pumpelly expedition in the glacial lakes of Sweden and that geologists and archaeologists have since used as an aid to geochronology and the prehistoric archaeology of glaciated regions.)[57] Pumpelly found confirmation of his own theories in Raphael's observations:

> From these facts we may perhaps assume that there were at least 2 moraine forming periods. 1st that in which Karakul clays were formed . . . 2nd that in which erratic blocks were dropped on the Karakul clays or perhaps same as that in which the Karakul clays were pushed before the glacier. . . . I think there can be little doubt that a relation existed between the glacial period producing these moraines and the expanding of the Aralo-Caspian seas.[58]

In the Tien Shan ranges and around lake Issik Kul, Davis and Huntington saw evidence in moraines, terraces, and lake deposits of two and possibly three glacial epochs, confirming the Pumpellys' findings. In his subsequent reconnaissance across the Tien Shan to Kashgar, Huntington thought he saw indications of at least five successively milder glacial epochs with warmer interglacial periods. These discoveries expanded upon the work of Thomas C. Chamberlin and James Geikie, who in the 1890s had determined that not one period of glaciation but several periods had occurred. In the mountains, Davis also found some of the best examples he had seen of the cycle of erosion and recommended that further study of the structure of the Tien Shan would be of outstanding importance for theoretical geology.[59]

The extent of the loess deposits impressed Pumpelly. The mountains "are being buried in the products of their own disintegration," he wrote in his field notebook. He thought he had found the "missing link" in his 1879 theory of the origin of the materials for loess. He agreed with Richthofen that the materials were windblown, but he now thought they "must have passed through a desert stage," which would answer the criticism that his former explanation of loess did not account for its alkali content. He now thought that the fine material, which was apparently produced by the breaking up and disintegrating of rocks by the extreme changes of temperature in the mountains, was then either by wind or water "brought into the desert region, spread out on the fans and plains, impregnated by capillary attraction in moist periods with the desert salts, and thence carried by the winds to be deposited on grassy surfaces beyond the desert as loess."[60]

These ever-evolving ideas about loess played an important part in the development of Pumpelly's efforts to correlate the deposits of mountains and plains with the activities of the prehistoric plains dwellers, for the climatic conditions that brought about the formation of the grassy loess plains had once supported, he believed, the herds of wild animals that prehistoric man learned to domesticate.

Pumpelly's emphasis on physiography was due to his conviction that the glacial period had played a crucial role in modifying the climate of Central Asia and making possible "the evolution of the intellectual and social life of man." He was optimistic about being able to correlate the glacial timetable of the mountains, the expansions and contractions of the ancient Aralo-Caspian Sea, and the deposits of the plains. If he could accomplish this correlation it would give him a geological chronology that would help to unravel the archaeological chronology. Davis, in sympathy with Pumpelly but perhaps more realistic about the difficulties, thought that the correlation might be accomplished "with much time and patience . . . if the valleys were examined at intervals of 30 or 40 miles all around the border of the plains on the south and east." Or, as he suggested in a letter to Gilman, it might be possible to date piedmont deposits "by digging a shaft or well, and making careful note of the succession of strata there seen."[61]

In his report on the 1903 expedition, Pumpelly expressed confidence that his findings warranted the renewal of the grant for another year. What was needed now, he said, was a detailed study that would apply "all the comparative sciences that relate to the history of man." He believed that a scientifically conducted excavation of the sites he had located, "with the idea that everything met with—the earth itself, the character, position and association of fragments—is part of history" could not fail to produce fruitful results relating to prehistoric man.[62]

Although the Carnegie Institution awarded Pumpelly a new grant for the next year, he did little further work on physiography. The board may have thought that the previous summer's physiographic reconnaissance was merely repeating work done by the Russians or that Pumpelly's program to correlate glacial phenomena with the development of a culture was too ambitious. It is also possible that increasing emphasis on specialized research at the institution and in the country's universities discouraged support for a study that was intended to combine "all the comparative sciences" relating to man. The next expedition, the trustees agreed, should concentrate on archaeology.

Geology and Archaeology: The Expedition of 1904

That Pumpelly should take up archaeology is not surprising, for both geology and archaeology are historical sciences; the data with which geologists and archaeologists work come from the analysis of materials deposited over long periods of time. Archaeologists and geologists both look for recognizable layers of strata and clues that allow division into named periods or epochs. And both geological and archaeological sequences have long been used as evidence of evolution and progress.[63]

In writing about his archaeological excavations at Anau, Pumpelly more than once spoke of thinking geologically, as when he pointed out that fragments of different styles of pottery provide the main clues to changing cultures just as fossils help to determine the age of different geological strata. He was also fascinated with the study of the roots of Indo-European languages, comparing it to the study of fossils: "In the paleontology, if we may use the term, of the Aryan languages . . . names of domestic utensils, animals, and plants correspond to the petrifications in geological reasoning."[64] His work at Anau, where he conducted a geological study paralleling the archaeological excavations, brought the two disciplines even closer together. It interwove the findings in a way that proved to be a pioneering investigation in geoarchaeology.

One of the objectives of the expedition of 1903 had been to find an appropriate site for archaeological excavation during the following year. As Pumpelly had said, "There seems to be a continuous cemetery of cities" along the route, and whenever possible he arranged to stop for two or three days to investigate the most promising sites, visit museums, and consult with local archaeologists. The sites were of two types, the ruins of ancient towns, which had been occupied in historical times but now were "more or less buried in sands beyond the mouths of retreating rivers, in places once fertile and now desolate," and the weathered tumuli or kurgans, as he called them, which seemed to be the remains of prehistoric settlements. Pumpelly visited Afrosiab, the city founded by Alexander the Great, according to legend, and he examined promising ruins and mounds at Tashkent, Samarkand, Paikent, Bokhara, and Old Merv, near the modern city of Mary on the Murg-Ab River. The extensive abandoned ruins near Samarkand interested him because the city had once been a major commercial center on the old East-West trade routes. Pumpelly paid special attention, however, to the kurgans of "made earth," composed of disintegrated sun-dried brick, for it was obvious to him that they were sites of much older occupation.[65]

The site he chose for excavation in 1904 was on a delta oasis at the foot of the Kopet Dagh, near Ashkhabad, the capital of Turkmenistan. On the site were two large mounds and the ruins of the abandoned Muhammadan city of Anau, in which part of a blue-tiled mosque was still standing. Not only was the site convenient to the railroad, but a Russian general had several years earlier dug a deep trench through the top of one of the mounds and Pumpelly could see in the exposed walls of the trench fragments of broken vases, animal and human bones, ashes, charcoal, and other material. The material of the mound was stratified into well-defined zones, each containing different types of pottery, which made him think that the kurgan was the result of long occupation.[66]

In order to convince the Carnegie Institution to renew his grant, Pumpelly made a point of assuring Walcott that he would be doing original work in archaeology, because the chairman of the executive committee, John S. Billings, had told him that he did not think any more Carnegie money should be spent on physiography. The nearest and most closely related archaeological excavating, he told Walcott, was being done by a large French expedition under Jacques De Morgan at the ancient Chaldean site of Susa in Persia. The Russians had done no systematic digging in Central Asia, Pumpelly said, although they had indicated the locations of ruins and tumuli on their maps. Pumpelly claimed that the collection and analysis of animal bones, which, to his knowledge, no archaeologists had done before, would provide evidence to support his thesis that the people of Central Asia had been the first to domesticate animals. At his request a paleontologist had analyzed a few fragments of bone from the lowest level of the north kurgan at Anau and identified them as being from domestic species of horse, sheep, and other animals.[67]

On November 23, 1903, the Carnegie Institution approved his application for renewal of the grant and awarded him $18,000 to continue his Transcaspian exploration "especially with reference to archaeological excavation." At the end of December, accompanied this time by his wife Eliza, he left for London and Saint Petersburg to negotiate with the Russian authorities for permission to excavate. Russian archaeologists were becoming more interested in excavating their own sites and perhaps feared that Pumpelly's work might destroy important remains, but his discussions with the head of the Russian archaeological commission finally resulted in agreement that he would be allowed to excavate for research purposes and to take what was needed for study after inspection by the commission.[68]

Pumpelly's dignified but unpretentious demeanor and his wife's charm seem to have made the couple unofficial ambassadors of goodwill at a time of tense international relations. On February 8, 1904, the Japanese attacked Port Arthur, setting off the Russo-Japanese War of 1904–05. In Moscow, in February, Pumpelly and Eliza saw soldiers leaving for the war and watched patriotic demonstrations in support of the czar. This support for the government declined during the spring and summer when the Japanese proved surprisingly well equipped for war and inflicted heavy losses on the Russian army and navy. The tension of war seems not to have interfered with the Pumpellys' travels, however. They were frequently entertained by fellow scientists or government officials and met many "cultured and refined" ladies and gentlemen whom they joined in toasts to harmonious Russian-American relations. A party at Tiflis (Tbilisi), the capital of Georgia, given for the whole group by a Prince and Princess Begtabegoff, included singing and dancing and "toasts to the alliance of Georgia with America." The Georgians performed traditional dances for their guests and afterward young Langdon Warner, the newest member of the expedition, danced the cakewalk, "followed by loud applause."[69]

In Berlin, on a visit to the Museum für Völkerkunde, Pumpelly had met Hubert Schmidt, curator of the Schliemann Collection, who so impressed Pumpelly with his knowledge of ceramics that he asked Schmidt to join the expedition as archaeologist. The success of the 1904 expedition owed much to Schmidt's expert planning and execution of the dig at Anau. Richard Norton, the archaeologist with the 1903 expedition, did not contribute to Pumpelly's final report on the explorations of 1903 and did not return in 1904. Instead, possibly to Pumpelly's dismay but perhaps by mutual agreement, Norton published the results of his work in the *Supplementary Papers of the American School of Classical Studies in Rome,* of which he was the editor. Norton was apparently more interested in the art and archaeology of the classical period. Although he agreed with Pumpelly that the ruins of the abandoned cities near Merv and Samarkand would yield important discoveries "that would help to fill a gap in the earliest history of civilization," he did not share Pumpelly's belief that progressive desiccation had caused the abandonment of cities. Norton favored instead a theory that the founders of new cities had abandoned the old ones because they wanted "to avoid the ghosts and traditions of their predecessors and to get the first draw of the river water for their new gardens."[70]

A larger group made up the expedition of 1904 than had been with Pumpelly on his reconnaissance of 1903. Although he was not able to take a physiographer as an official member of his team, he hired Ellsworth Huntington to serve as Schmidt's archaeological assistant, to supervise the laborers. Huntington managed to do physiographic studies around Anau, however, which probably supported his own developing theory of climatic pulsation more than they contributed to Pumpelly's theory of progressive aridity. Young Raphael, who was not paid a salary from Carnegie funds, assisted his father with the geological and physiographic investigations of alluvial strata in the vicinity of the Anau kurgans. Pumpelly's encouragement of the young is evident in his invitation to Hildegarde Brooks, daughter of his old friend Thomas Benton Brooks, and Langdon Warner, a Harvard friend of Raphael's, to join the party as volunteer archaeological assistants. Warner, who became a noted Orientalist, attributed the beginning of his career to his participation in Pumpelly's expedition. Budding archaeologist Homer Kidder also spent part of the season with the group.[71]

In a move that was very unusual in archaeology at that time, Pumpelly called on several specialists to analyze materials from the kurgans and to contribute reports to the Carnegie volumes. These specialists were Yale chemist and metallurgist Frank A. Gooch, who analyzed metal objects; comparative anatomist J. Ulrich Dürst of the University of Bern, who spent three years studying and classifying the many animal bones Pumpelly collected; physical anthropologists Giuseppe Sergi of the University of Rome and Thomas Mollison from the Zurich Anthropological Institute, who studied human skulls and bones; and Swiss botanist H. C. Schellenberg, who determined that grain hulls, straw, and chaff from cultivated varieties of wheat and barley had been used in pot making.[72]

The excavating at Anau began on March 24 under Schmidt's supervision, using the most advanced methods of scientific archaeology, which Schmidt fully described in his final report. Schmidt agreed with Pumpelly that the two kurgans were composed of superimposed layers of debris representing a long habitation and that the pottery visible on the surface of the north kurgan indicated that it was much older than the south kurgan. The first digging, using Turkomen workers hired at Ashkhabad, began on the older north kurgan and proceeded at about one foot a day. After two weeks, work was shifted to the south kurgan. In order to expose as many parts of the kurgans as possible, Schmidt excavated a series of terraces at different levels on the top of the kurgans and sank shafts that allowed access to the middle and lower levels. He and Pumpelly established a datum point at the level of the plain and labeled all items, no matter how small, noting their position and depth above or below the datum point. Hildegarde Brooks took many photographs of items in place and in the evenings everyone would gather around the table in the main "kibitka" to discuss the day's finds and speculate about their meaning.[73]

Schmidt classified the pottery according to technique, form, and decoration. Using the various pottery types as criteria, but also taking into consideration other important finds such as hearths and cooking methods, skeletons of children who had been buried in the houses near the hearths, and many objects of metal and stone, both useful and ornamental, Schmidt determined that four major Anau culture periods had occurred. These began with the late Neolithic (at the bottom of the north kurgan), evolved through a stone and copper period (now called the Chalcolithic), and culminated in an Iron Age culture, represented by the culture strata at the top of the south kurgan. Pumpelly added Anau V, represented by the abandoned city of Anau with its blue-tiled mosque. Schmidt was reluctant to assign absolute dates to these cultures, but estimated that Anau I dated from 3000 to 2000 B.C., Anau II from 2000 to 1500 B.C., Anau III from 1500 to 1000 B.C., and Anau IV from 1000 to 500 B.C.[74]

Pumpelly thought Schmidt was too conservative in his assignment of dates but in his generous way allowed full publication of Schmidt's conclusions. In a footnote to Schmidt's report, however, Pumpelly commented that Schmidt had "an unexpressed inclination to seek Western origins" for the Anau culture and too often based his estimates on analogies with European and Mediterranean finds with which he was familiar.[75] Pumpelly believed the cultures were of Central Asian origin and much older than Schmidt's estimates and that the Central Asians had influenced European cultures, not the reverse.

Pumpelly's own chronology was based on what he called "a simple geological study." He knew from the physiographic work of the previous year that the piedmont belt where the kurgans were located had undergone periods of buildup and erosion. According to his "geological reasoning," the growth of alluvial strata during wet periods would parallel the growth of the culture strata, and a decline in the growth of the delta during dry periods could be matched with a period of abandonment or culture change in the kurgans. While Schmidt supervised the archaeological dig, Pumpelly and Raphael sank twenty-four shafts on and near the kurgans and in the city of Anau, hoping to obtain data that would indicate climatic change, establish the rate of growth of the geological strata relative to that of the culture strata, and help to determine an absolute chronology.[76]

Shafts dug in a low extension of the south kurgan, away from the main archaeological pit in the center, revealed that a thin layer of culture strata containing worn fragments of lower culture pottery had apparently been washed down into an irrigation ditch and buried under nineteen feet of natural and irrigation sediments and then covered by culture strata of the higher period. Pumpelly calculated that the nineteen feet of natural sediment found in the shafts had grown to that height during the same period of time that the main kurgan had grown fifty-two feet. Other measurements and calculations led to his adoption of an average ratio of one foot of natural growth to two and one-half feet of culture strata growth. He used this ratio to make rough estimates of the time gap between the cultures of the north and south kurgans and between the copper and the iron cultures on the south kurgan.[77]

Pumpelly also used this ratio to attempt an absolute chronology for the Anau culture. He had two known dates. One was the date when the mosque at the city of Anau was built; the other was obtained from coins of the third century A.D. found in the Merv oasis associated with a green glazed ware that was also found in Pumpelly's Anau city shafts. Pumpelly assumed a uniform rate of growth for towns built of sun-dried brick, calling this rate the "law of proximate uniformity of growth of city mounds in dry climate." He estimated that the city of Anau had grown at a rate of two and one-half feet per century and the kurgans two feet per century. During a visit to Egypt in 1906–07, he consulted with the eminent British archaeologist Sir Flinders Petrie, who had pioneered in the development of better methods of sequence dating. Pumpelly's final report put the founding of the Anau I culture far back in the postglacial period, to the ninth millennium. Culture II he estimated to have begun about 6000 B.C. and Culture III to have lasted from 5200 to 2200 B.C. On Anau IV he was more in agreement with Schmidt, dating it at about 450 B.C.[78]

Attempts to determine chronology by estimating the number of feet of growth of culture strata per century are very uncertain because so many factors affect that growth, but before the discovery of radiocarbon dating this was one of the few ways to do it. Pumpelly admitted later, after he had had a chance to study the completed work of De Morgan at Susa, that his chronological estimates in the Carnegie report had been too high. His mistake, he thought, was in applying to the kurgans the rate of growth of the city of Anau. The city had been built of longer-lasting burned bricks that were reused for new building, while the sun-dried bricks of the kurgans deteriorated and more earth had to be brought for new building. His revised estimate put the Anau II and III cultures between 3500 and 1000 B.C. but left the date for Anau I unchanged.[79]

More important to him than the chronology was his use of the data obtained from the various shafts to correlate climatic cycles with changes in the Anau cultures. He had found "evidence of three separate growths of alluvial strata between the founding of the North Kurgan and the beginning of irrigation, and of two intervening degradations." He prepared a remarkable diagram for his Carnegie report that related depth of shafts to time, to cultural development, and to climatic change. The five cultures of the two kurgans and the city are shown one above the other, with gaps left for periods not represented by culture strata. The relation of the climatic cycles to the periods of different cultures is indicated on the right side of the chart by lines of maximum and minimum periods of aggradation on the plains. During the major dry periods, represented by dotted lines, the plains were dissected and the kurgans were abandoned. During the three wetter periods, represented by solid lines, silt was brought down to nourish the plains, and cultures flourished.[80]

Pumpelly's report on the early Anau culture added to the growing body of evidence showing that agriculture had preceded domestication rather than the reverse, the view that had previously been generally accepted. Data supplied by comparative osteologist Dürst and paleobotanist Schellenberg proved, Pumpelly believed, that "in Anau I . . . we have the oldest instance of an organized agricultural civilization at present known." Schellenberg detected fragments of cultivated wheat and barley in a piece of clay pot from the lowest level. Dürst reported that the bones from the lowest culture were those of only wild species of sheep, ox, and pig but that those from the upper level of Anau I became progressively smaller and more porous, indicating the appearance of domesticated species. The fact that the earliest people of Anau cultivated grains and had no weapons seemed to confirm a then-current theory that domestication had occurred among agriculturists who were not hunters. Dürst tended to agree with Pumpelly's chronology, accepting 8000 B.C. as the approximate period of the oldest culture, although he expressed reservations as to whether the people of Anau I had actually originated domestication or had received domesticated animals from elsewhere.[81]

The anthropological and metallurgical evidence supplied by Sergi and Gooch enabled Pumpelly to make further inferences about the Anau culture. Sergi reported that the skulls from the north kurgan were dolichocephalic. "We are therefore justified in assuming," claimed Pumpelly, "that domestication and the forming of the several breeds of domestic animals at Anau . . . were effected by long-headed people." The analysis of metal objects showed that the people of Anau II–III were not yet of the Bronze Age. They used copper extensively but not alloyed with tin,

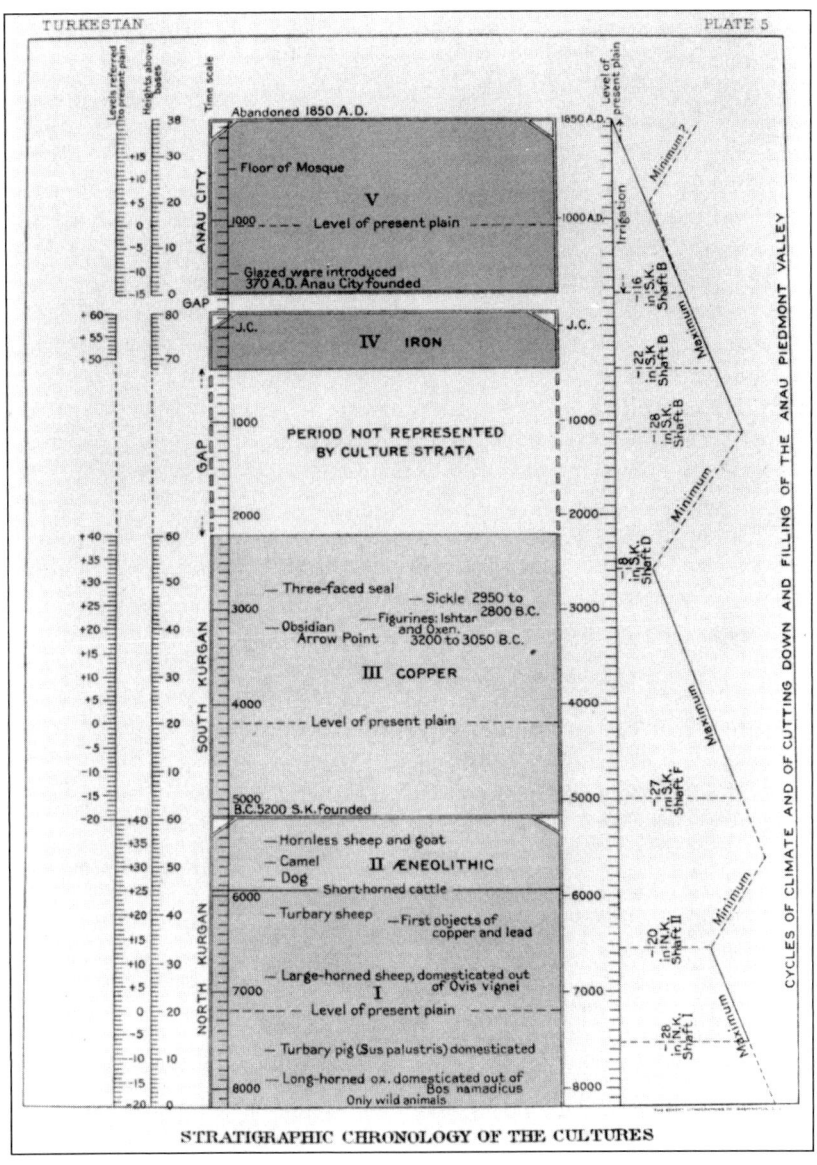

Chronology of the culture strata at Anau showing relation to climatic cycles. From *Explorations in Turkestan, 1904*, vol. 1, plate 5. (Courtesy of Carnegie Institution of Washington)

except for a few items in which tin appeared in small amounts, probably accidentally.[82]

In May an infestation of grasshoppers that filled the shafts, attacked the crops, and caused the governor to recall many of the Anau workers to help destroy the insects brought an end to Pumpelly's work at Anau. Knowing better than anyone how much more work remained to be done, Pumpelly planned another expedition for 1905, but, although the Carnegie Institution granted him an additional $26,000, he was unable to return to Central Asia because of the unrest during the Revolution of 1905, which followed Russia's defeat in the Russo-Japanese War.[83] Pumpelly's accomplishments in archaeology rest, therefore, with the results of the 1904 expedition.

On his return from Turkestan, Pumpelly was elected to the presidency of the Geological Society of America and a large and receptive audience listened with great interest as Pumpelly summed up the results of his work in Central Asia at the Ottawa meeting in December 1906. His presidential address, which in a revised and expanded version became the introductory chapters of his final Carnegie report, provided an overview of the changing cultures of Anau, set not only in the context of a changing environment but also in the context of history. To set the stage for man, Pumpelly surveyed the "organic whole" of the inner-continental arid basin, cinematically telescoping time and space in a way that gave his listeners and his readers a vivid picture of the evolving landscape. The Austrian geologist Eduard Suess had used a similar technique in the opening pages of his classic synthesis, *The Face of the Earth,* which Pumpelly must have read.[84]

Imagine yourselves . . . looking down over this great expanse and, foreshortening space and the vista back through untold centuries, able to view the successive phases of its life during a short period of geological time. First you are in the Glacial period. . . . You see the giant mountains . . . far-reaching glaciers . . . the cap of continental ice . . . the blue waters of a sea greater than the Mediterranean . . . rivers building great deltas. . . .

While you look . . . the Glacial period has passed . . . the ice cap is gone . . . evaporation is now more rapid than inflow of water . . . the rivers grow smaller . . . the dried silts have become the prey of the winds.[85]

Pumpelly describes the interrelated processes of the region much as a physiologist might regard the processes of the biological organism while at the same time visualizing the evolution of the arid environment. He invites his readers to watch "all the controlling agencies that are the life of the great geographic organism that we call an arid inner-continental region." The wind classifies the fine material, carrying the finest in "massive yellow clouds that are darkening these plains," and deposits it as loess while moving the coarser sands along the surface to form dunes. The dust remains on the protected grassy plains to nourish the grass that feeds teeming herds of wild ruminants and horses. The zone of the loess plains lies between the dunes and the delta oases, which are being formed by the streams emerging from the mountains. As the climate becomes more arid the loess steppes shrink and are broken up into disconnected areas by the advancing dunes, the herds decline, and life is "restricted to the mountains and to the borders of the few remaining streams and the deltas." Now animals and prehistoric human societies are isolated from each other, allowing the evolution of different but fundamentally related regional cultures.[86]

Pumpelly's emphasis on the influence of the arid environment on man might be seen as an example of environmental determinism. The whole inner-continental region was "predestined," he wrote, "to a definite course of life history." The geographic features became the "motivating factors in the evolution of the intellectual and social life of man," who, "under the spur of Necessity, the relentless goddess of evolution," built the "foundations of civilizations." The increasing desiccation stimulated the inventiveness of these early oasis dwellers, inventiveness that allowed them to survive by developing irrigation agriculture and raising herds.[87]

Determinism is perhaps too strong a word, however. Pumpelly's position is closer to William Morris Davis's concept of ontography—the response of the organism to the physical environment—that Davis developed while working with Pumpelly. Pumpelly's interpretation is perhaps closest of all to Arnold J. Toynbee's later theory of "challenge and response." Toynbee, in fact, used the results of the Pumpelly expedition to show that the nomads of Central Asia developed their way of life in response to the challenge of the arid environment. "The clearest light that we have as yet on the origins of Nomadism has been thrown by the researches of the Pumpelly Expedition in the Transcaspian oasis of Anau," Toynbee wrote. Toynbee admitted that he was "enormously influenced" by Ellsworth Huntington, who in turn had acknowledged the inspiration of Pumpelly and Davis in his own work. Toynbee did not think of himself as a determinist and did not think Huntington was either, although Huntington's work was long ago dismissed with that label when the applications of environmental influences to the study of history went out of fashion.[88]

The Migrations and the Aryan Problem

In the end, Pumpelly did not offer any solution to the Aryan question. He wrote a chapter entitled "The Migrations and the Aryan Problem," but he did not include it in his final report "because it seemed a premature as well as a hazardous venture for one not already an authority on the subject." He hoped that what he did include in his published report might provide data that would be useful to those who continued the search.[89] The unpublished manuscript is with the Bailey Willis papers at the Huntington Library, along with the papers that Pumpelly's son sent to Willis for use in writing the "Memorial." Because the origin of the Indo-European languages is still a lively question today, the chapter has interest as a reflection of the ideas of his time, if not as a solution of the "Aryan problem."

Pumpelly believed that geographic isolation was as crucial to the development of the Aryan language as climate change was to the increasing sophistication of a culture. The oasis world of which Anau was an example seemed to him to provide the necessary conditions under which a new language could evolve: a "long-continued inner-continental isolation" during the last Ice Age, the evolution of a settled civilization, and the challenge of an increasingly arid environment. In this oasis world, he believed, the Aryan language had developed among a peaceful, settled people who were cut off from outside contact by high glacier-covered mountains and the Central Asian sea.[90]

Most of Pumpelly's arguments for why the more highly developed language should have belonged with the more advanced culture of the oases, rather than in Neolithic Europe or among roving nomadic tribes, were not original with him, but he used them persuasively in combination with the results of his geoarchaeological work to develop a plausible, if not fully supported, picture of human migrations. His arguments included the long-held idea that because Aryan is still spoken by isolated Galcha tribes in the Pamirs and in other areas of central and western Asia, primitive forms of Aryan speech must have originated somewhere in that region. He also thought that the development of organized society and of new industries in the oasis communities, of which he found evidence at Anau, "must necessarily be accompanied by progress in vocabulary and probably also in grammatical construction" (14).

The roots of words had always had a fascination for Pumpelly, even as a young student in Germany, and as he worked on the reports of his expeditions he spent much time in the comparative study of the paleontology, as he called it, of the Aryan languages. He paid particular attention to the similarities in various Indo-European languages of the ancient words for metals, especially copper and gold, and familiarized himself with the cultures that archaeologists had shown had used these metals. He even studied Chinese characters for gold and silver. These methods were among those he used to try to show that the earliest cultures at Anau must have used copper, or at least some metal, before the steppe nomads or the Neolithic cultures of Europe. Otto Schrader thought that the words *ayas* in Sanskrit, *ayah* in Avesta, *aes* in Latin, and *aiz* in Gothic referred to copper, which he believed was known to the primitive Aryan-speaking peoples. Pumpelly, however, who was convinced that the first Aryan-speaking culture was much earlier than Schrader thought, suggested the possibility "that this metal may have been gold, and the primitive designation have stood simply for 'metal'" (16–18).

Pumpelly challenged the claim of Schrader and "the present German school" that the Aryans were long-headed conquering invaders from the steppes north of the Black Sea, those belonging to the world using celts and stone arrow- and spear-points, of whom, Schrader thought, one branch moved west, another to the south, to Irania, creating the division that had brought about the *centum* and *satem* branches of the Indo-European languages. But, Pumpelly objected, an invasion from that region in Neolithic time would have introduced these implements throughout Central Asia, and no such weapons were found in the earliest culture strata at Anau or at Susa. A later invasion would not have allowed enough time for differences in physical type and for the differentiation of so many varieties of Asiatic Aryan languages (19–20).

As Pumpelly knew, archaeological excavation at the site of prehistoric lake dwellings in Switzerland had revealed the remains of a round-headed people, Asiatic turbary sheep and cereals, and traces of copper, and he assumed that this round-headed Alpine type must have originated in Asia, where the predominant skull shape was round. At the same time he faced the problem of accounting for the dolichocephalic skulls found at Anau (15, 33).

In trying to reconcile the skulls of Anau with the round-headed Alpine type of Europe, he adopted the views of the Italian anthropologist Giuseppe Sergi and the English ethnologist A. H. Keane, "who make dolichocephalic Africa the source of the Iranian long-headed stock." Thinking as a geologist in terms of "myriads of years," he argued that the earliest Anau culture must have originated in Africa, migrating to Central Asia in interglacial times. These people would have become isolated into separate areas by the conditions of the last Ice Age.

Later social development and differentiation of cranial types could have taken place in any of four physiographic provinces "potentially capable of forcing man out of the hunting stage and giving him the impetus towards advancing culture," but because the only evidence at that time of early man in these regions was at Anau and Susa, he limited himself to discussing the conditions in the mountain valleys of the Iranian plateau and on the lowland plains of western Turkestan, "two physically distinct major potential ethnic provinces . . . that must necessarily have impressed correspondingly marked differences in type on their inhabitants" (20–23). According to his hypothesis, the region had remained isolated by a "glacial epoch proper" for a period "measurable by some scores of milleniums," providing "sufficient time for environment to operate in developing man socially and intellectually and in changing the physical type" (24–26).

In the highland areas the change toward aridity at the end of the ice ages forced man "into the struggle which initiated the transition from the hunter stage into one that was to expand into civilization," while in the lowlands the hunting stage persisted longer because the grass supported herds of wild ruminants and horses. But, thanks to topographic and climatic conditions, continued Pumpelly, the desert oases along the base of the Kopet Dagh and in the east, which received water from the mountains, formed a transition zone between the highlands and the lowlands (26–27).

This extensive zone of moderate elevation, offering easy intercourse between countless oases, was well adapted to long-continued intercourse between the nomadic and settled peoples. Such intercourse as exists today between Persian and Turkish peoples in Central Asian cities. Here I imagine the Aryan language to have been evolved. (27–28)

The growing aridity would have forced the plains nomads to move south, where they would have come into contact with the people of the oases, receiving from them the Aryan language and the domestic animals that inaugurated a new phase of nomadic life. During the "long period of environmental molding" that followed, the people of the "innumerable oases" of Central Asia and of the isolated mountain valleys of Irania developed settled communities and social organization.

In the oasis world, at the same time that the camel made wider communication possible, added Pumpelly, deteriorating climate and increasing population stimulated the movement to better districts. The frontier moved slowly, at first only from oasis to oasis, forcing others to move on. "Through this slow-moving tidal displacement, wave after wave of migrations from the eastern oases and mountain valleys" passed south of the Caspian and through the Caucasus, through the Armenian highlands to the Black Sea or through Asia Minor to the Aegean.

And now, on the extreme western confines of the continent, the product of purely Asiatic evolution was brought some 6000 or 7000 years ago face to face with that of another world center, with the Mediterranean race, having a Neolithic culture which had, perhaps, itself originated in the oases of the Sahara and had already the beginnings of a written language. (31)

Pumpelly then asked, "Do our investigations at Anau throw any light on the question of Central-Asiatic contributions to prehistoric European culture?" (33). In trying to answer this question he confined himself to discussing the first two cultures of the north kurgan. The presence of copper in the first culture, before its existence in Europe, was strong evidence, he thought, to support the theory of Asiatic origin for the use of copper. Spindle whorls and painted pottery were also found both at Anau and at Susa before their use in Europe.

To Pumpelly the most important contributions, apart from the Aryan language, were cereals, agriculture, and domestic animals. He cited Dürst's lengthy research on the bones of the first and second cultures proving that the first culture had domesticated ox, sheep, horse, and pig from the wild forms; that three breeds of sheep and two of cattle appeared during the first two cultures; that the dog, goat, and camel appeared in the second culture as importations; and that a breed of sheep and pig from Anau were the same as those of the Neolithic lake dwellings of Switzerland. This evidence, Pumpelly believed, "established a well-defined relation in one direction between the cultures of the oasis world and that of the eastern intruders into neolithic Europe" (34–35).

Pumpelly proposed that the "beginning of the unrest" occurred during the end of the first and the early part of the second culture of the north kurgan, or about 6000 B.C.: "There is, I think, little doubt that these migrations were necessitated by the progress towards the dry extreme of the climatic cycle which, as I have shown from our physiographic studies, culminated towards the end of culture I, and which is confirmed by the stunting of the breeds of sheep and cattle" (37).

The inhabitants of many oases participated in these earliest migrations, he thought, the movement resulting in peaceful displacements, substitutions, and amalgamations of peoples along the routes before their later infiltration among the native Europeans. Because evidence exists that Europe was later invaded in a much more warlike manner, Pumpelly ventured a tentative hypothesis to explain these armed invasions. The increasing desiccation toward the end of the second culture, around the fifth millennium B.C., he thought, would have caused some offshoots from the oases to become nomads, who gradually differentiated on independent grazing regions. According to his theory, "a nomadic people, shifting its habitat with the changing seasons and seeking to extend its grazing areas at the expense of other nomads, would develop warlike habits." It is these nomadic tribes that gradually covered the steppes of western Asia and southeastern Europe with Aryan-speaking branches, Pumpelly thought. He left to students in anthropology, archaeology, and comparative philology "to decide whether it is not possible that in these scattered hordes we may see the ancestors of the later prehistoric conquering invaders of Europe and of the historic peoples of the *centum* speeches" (39–40).

Even though he chose to withhold the chapter from publication, Pumpelly remained convinced that the migrations had been stimulated by deteriorating climate combined with population increase beyond the ability of the oases to support it. In an appendix to his *Reminiscences,* he again tied the emigrations to periods of increased aridity. By this time (1918) Ellsworth Huntington had published his *Pulse of Asia,* perhaps influencing Pumpelly to place slightly greater emphasis than he had earlier on the cyclic nature of climatic change.

The significant result of this investigation was the discovery that the North Kurgan was founded during an aggrading—increasing flow of silt-bearing water—that reached its maximum toward the end of Anau I, and then turned toward dryness. The South Kurgan—Anau III—was founded during the aggrading of a later climatic cycle, which reached its maximum near the end of the culture. So again with Anau IV (iron) culture. . . . The life of each culture was confined to the favorable part of the climatic cycle. The trend toward dryness made emigration necessary.[91]

Pumpelly's arguments for Central Asian origins are much like those of Colin Renfrew, who proposes in his *Archaeology and Language* (1987) that Indo-European languages originated with an Anatolian culture that cultivated grains, did not have weapons, and migrated peacefully westward into Europe, although Renfrew does not emphasize the role of climate. The dominant theory today, however, among students of Indo-European languages is that of Maria Gimbutas, who holds that the proto-Indo-Europeans were warlike nomads of the Eurasian steppes north of the Caspian who spread their language through conquest. Gimbutas and her followers unconditionally reject Renfrew's proposal. The debate continues, using new linguistic and archaeological evidence, as scholars still ponder the Indo-European homeland problem. As J. P. Mallory has said, "One does not ask 'where is the Indo-European homeland?' but rather 'where do they put it *now*?'" The modern "consensus" still puts the homeland anywhere from southern Greenland to the Aral Sea.[92]

Pumpelly's decision not to publish his Aryan homeland theory is an indication of his high standards of scientific work. He was also aware that those whose specialty was in philology or archaeology might be unwilling to accept the conclusions of a nonspecialist. Bailey Willis admired the "ideal of truth" that caused Pumpelly to suppress the chapter on Aryan migrations but regretted that he had done so. "Might not the old man, who had cherished that dream for forty-four years, have put his statement of its realization more strongly?" Willis wondered. In 1936 Willis sent the chapter to John C. Merriam, then president of the Carnegie Institution, because he thought it might still have scientific value. Merriam replied that the opinion of his "best expert" was that Pumpelly's doubt about the validity of his conclusions was justified. "It seems that the results of recent excavations have given an entirely new orientation on this problem and that the time scale advocated by Professor Pumpelly would not now be accepted by any modern scholar," Merriam said.[93] By that time many archaeologists and anthropologists had abandoned migration theories like Pumpelly's in favor of theories of independent evolution of cultures.

Pumpelly's friend, Henry Holt, thought Pumpelly had resolved the Aryan question: "The report of this expedition . . . put Pumpelly's reputation as an archeologist on a level with the high one he already achieved as a geologist. An Austrian authority declared that he had destroyed at a stroke the megalomaniac claim to be the cradle of civilization that Germany had lately been cooking up."[94]

Henry Adams, who had been so supportive of the expeditions, was disappointed that Pumpelly had not included a discussion of his findings relating to Aryan origins. As it was, Anau appeared to be only a remote outpost,

> without mother country; without a beyond; without trade; and without enemies, dangers, or even wild animals of any serious peril. Yours is a sort of Garden of Eden; it realises the Book of Genesis. . . . The trade-route theory, as I understand it, seems to be killed. There was no trade! The oasis theory takes its place, and this oasis civilization is barren at both ends.

"We are thrown back on Nippur and Persepolis" as a place of origin, Adams thought, and he more than half-seriously suggested that if they were both forty years younger he would love nothing better than to go to Persia with Pumpelly and "make a new start there. . . . I should delight to set up a Persian establishment and live on sherbet and poetry, while watching you dig for pots."[95]

Although the Aryan problem remained unsolved, both the scientific and the popular press commented favorably on Pumpelly's physiographic and archaeological results. A *Geographical Journal* reviewer

(A. H. M.) praised the final report on the 1903 expedition (published in 1905, after the completion of the second expedition) for its high level of research that produced so much new information in such a short time. The reviewer did not agree with all of Pumpelly's conclusions but called the report a "remarkable advance in the scientific treatment of the physico-geographical problems of a country." In commenting on the 1903 *Yearbook* of the Carnegie Institution, in which Pumpelly's preliminary report was published, the *Nation* singled out for praise Pumpelly's seventeen-page summary of the first Transcaspian expedition, calling it a "historical mystery" the solution of which would be just as important as "the investigation of double stars or cryptogams." The year before, the *Nation* had criticized the Carnegie Institution for its "one-sidedness" in emphasizing investigations of "the physical phenomena of the world" and neglecting studies that would contribute to better understanding of history and the arts. More research of the kind Pumpelly was doing was what was needed to correct the imbalance.[96]

L. W. King, a reviewer for *Nature,* thought that in *Explorations in Turkestan, Expedition of 1904* Pumpelly had produced "a work of the first importance to students of archaeology." He believed that Pumpelly had confirmed Richthofen's theory of the wind-blown origin of loess and had added valuable insights of his own to it, but he had reservations about Pumpelly's climatic theory and his efforts to show that the Central Asian oases were "the fountain-head of Western Asiatic culture." Although he did not approve of Pumpelly's method of dating the growth of a city site from geological methods and thought some of his dates were "fanciful," he claimed that this dating problem did not affect the accurate establishment of the relative chronology of the different cultures at Anau. On the whole he was impressed with the success of the expedition and thought that the "admirable volumes" in which the results were presented "are a striking testimony to Mr. Pumpelly's enthusiasm and powers of organization, and at the same time show the high scientific aims and standards which inspire American archaeological and geological research at the present time."[97]

Until the 1920s, Anau was considered a major Middle Eastern archaeological site and Western scholars "treated it almost as the equal of those that appeared in more famous areas," such as Mesopotamia. Pumpelly's interpretations predated by several years those of V. Gordon Childe's *Dawn of European Civilizations,* an important and influential work published in 1925 that synthesized all of the archaeological work in the Middle East up to his time. Like Pumpelly, Childe believed that European civilization had originated with the arrival from Asia of agriculture, domestication, and metal working, although he favored a different place of origin. The Europeans, Childe thought, built upon these arts and evolved far beyond the cultures of the Middle East through an inventiveness that culminated in the industrial revolution.[98]

Archaeologists did little further excavation of any importance in Central Asia until after World War II. Today, dozens of sites have been excavated west of the Caspian Sea, along the piedmont belt of the Kopet Dagh, and on the western flanks of the Pamirs and the Tien Shan, confirming Pumpelly's conviction that a populous, complex civilization emerged in southern Central Asia in prehistoric times. Archaeologists from Russia have excavated sites at Djeitun, northwest of Anau near the Caspian, and elsewhere that have conclusively demonstrated the development of a Neolithic food-producing economy in southern Turkmenistan. Djeitun is the type-site to which the lowest level at Anau is compared, its date comparable to Pumpelly's estimate of 6500 B.C. The Namazga culture, named for a large site first excavated in 1916 on the piedmont belt of the Kopet Dagh, about midway between Anau and Merv, is now the major type-site of a Chalcolithic and Bronze Age peasant culture of which Anau II and III are important examples. The Namazga culture is thought to be closely related to those of Baluchistan, Harappa, and other sites of the Indus Valley civilization, the origins of which are still obscure. Pumpelly's vision of a Central Asian culture that spread outward to the east and west seems to be shared by prehistoric archaeologists Grahame Clark and Stuart Piggott, who have suggested that "we appear to see" in northwest India "the eastern frontiers of a group of related cultures stretching from the Caspian Sea to the Khyber Pass."[99]

Pumpelly's geological-geomorphological approach to archaeology was an unusual collaboration for his day and the last of its kind for several decades. Recently, geological archaeology has become a new discipline within geology, or rather "a melding at an interdisciplinary boundary," according to geoarchaeologists John A. Gifford and George R. Rapp, Jr. They consider Pumpelly a pioneer in their field and call Pumpelly's excavations at Anau a "remarkable manifestation of interdisciplinary field archaeology for their time." Geologists and geomorphologists today are making important contributions, as Pumpelly did, to the reconstruction of cultures and to the understanding of how geomorphic processes have affected an archaeological site. Philip L. Kohl calls for "more sophisticated cooperation with specialists" in Central Asia in order to "distinguish natural from human induced environmental changes," as Pumpelly used his knowledge of soils to distinguish between natural erosion and irrigation sediments.[100]

Why was Pumpelly able to bring about so much interdisciplinary cooperation in archaeology and why did it take so long for others to see its value? One explanation is that Pumpelly, as an individual with no academic affiliations, was better able to transcend the boundaries that were forming in graduate departments of geology, geography, and archaeology, where scholars were defending their territory rather than cooperating with those from other disciplines. Because of his reputation as a scientist-explorer he could call upon specialists from many fields to work with him. In the twentieth century, prehistoric archaeology became more closely associated with anthropology rather than with geology.[101] The older geologists who had been interested in investigating human remains and the antiquity of man were dying and the younger ones were forming new specialties, many of them, such as petroleum geology, associated with rapid economic development. Most of the new specialists had neither the time nor the interest to pursue research that required a broad view like Pumpelly's which perceived prehistoric man's relationship to his environment as an organic process to be studied with all the scientific methods available.

8

The End of Geology's Heroic Age

In spite of his initial disappointment at not being able to return to Turkestan, Pumpelly spent the years from 1905 to 1908 happily researching, editing, and writing his final report on the expedition of 1904. He went to Europe every year with Eliza to visit museums and consult with his contributors and to Egypt during the winter of 1906–07 to measure the growth of mounds. For part of each winter they rented a villa on Capri, where they enjoyed the company of a congenial group of artists and writers, and one year Pumpelly took his wife to Germany to show her his youthful haunts. In 1913 they traveled in North Africa with a niece and a granddaughter before going on to Naples and Rome to show the young people the sights of Italy.[1]

About 1911, as something to occupy his active mind, Pumpelly began writing his *Reminiscences,* which kept him busy until its publication in 1918. The death of his youngest daughter Pauline in 1911 was a sad loss, but the greatest blow was the death in 1915 of his beloved Eliza, who had been, "throughout the forty-six years of our joint life, the most important factor in my environment," he wrote. Bailey Willis sent his condolences, no doubt expressing the sentiments of all the young men who had worked with Pumpelly: "The beauty of Mrs. Pumpelly's nature in all her relations with your boys gave us a sense of the exquisite happiness and inspiration with which she filled your life."[2]

On August 10, 1923, in his eighty-sixth year, after only a few months of ill health, Pumpelly died and was buried with Eliza in the churchyard of Berkeley Memorial Chapel in Middletown, near Newport. A week later a moving memorial service was held on the hill at his Dublin home

Raphael Pumpelly at about age eighty (Courtesy of Raphael Pumpelly III)

overlooking Lake Monadnock, attended by "some hundreds of us who loved him," Henry Holt remembered. Pumpelly's friends and family gathered to listen to music and the reading of classic passages on immortality. Then three little girls in white placed an evergreen wreath in the open space before the mourners, who were facing the view of the distant Green Mountains to the west. When the service was over, no one wanted to leave, Holt said: "We watched until the last edge of the sun had disappeared behind the mountains, as, we felt, a great soul had passed beyond the barriers of the earth." It was a fitting tribute to a man who had written, "It is in the great wildernesses, on lofty heights and on desolate deserts, that one feels the greatness of Nature's mysteries."[3]

One memorialist called Pumpelly "the last survivor of the Heroic age in American exploration." Historians of geology have frequently used the term *heroic* in referring to the last forty years of the nineteenth century, the years covered by Pumpelly's career. These were the years when geologists like Powell, Gilbert, and King were exploring and studying the mining regions and physiographic features of the West, when geologists were tackling a wide range of problems that stimulated both theoretical and applied research, and when the United States Geological Survey was formed and the geology of the whole country was opened to federally supported investigation. Those who followed the geologists of this period came to see them as having had the broad vision and imagination needed to deal with new problems in previously unstudied regions. "The older geologists made our geology," thought one who had lived through that time. "The share of recent geologists is like that of workmen who fill up cracks . . . and put on the finishing touches."[4]

Pumpelly's life offers a good cross section of the kinds of work geologists were doing for pay and the kinds of organizations that supported geological research during this period. It also illustrates some of the new trends in the practice of geology that were taking place and shows what a major force economic and political factors could be in shaping a career. An important aspect of Pumpelly's career was exploration, because it led to his achieving a "name," but equally important was his work as an economic geologist and as a scientific administrator in the service of government.

Bailey Willis thought Pumpelly "belonged to the great explorers"—a Marco Polo or a Humboldt, "traveling in quest of an understanding of the world." Scientific exploration in the Gilded Age enabled the late Victorians to combine their fascination with distant places with their expectations of the role science would play in improving their lives. Pumpelly's experiences as an explorer were not just a fulfillment of his own love of adventure and devotion to science; they provided a vicarious experience for many others as well, as the popularity of his travel book *Across America and Asia* indicates. From his childhood days, when he searched the Owego hills for fossils or watched the log rafts set out down the Susquehanna for unknown places, to his old age when he explored the mountains of Central Asia, Pumpelly was indulging in an activity that appealed to the Victorian imagination.[5]

Much of the appeal of exploration was to escape the routine and familiar things of everyday life. It demanded such heroic qualities as courage and physical endurance—qualities Pumpelly had in abundance. The prospect of adventure, danger, and physical challenge attracted him to the deserts of Arizona and Turkestan or the mountains and rivers of China's interior as much as their strangeness appealed to his romantic nature. No doubt his readers admired him more for his bravery in withstanding Apache attacks in Arizona than they did for his ability to determine the quality of the silver ores. It was a rare person, as the *North American Review* observed, who had the stamina for this strenuous life, the opportunities to investigate faraway places, and the scientific knowledge to profit from their exploration. Pumpelly, like Powell in the canyons of the Colorado, Clarence King in the Sierras, or Peary in the Arctic, had the physical ability, the opportunity, and the knowledge, and like them he received public acclaim for his accomplishments.

His urge to explore was in keeping with the nineteenth-century tendency to romanticize the strange and unfamiliar, whether it was the Arctic, the Alps, darkest Africa, or the Far East. There was an element of mystery in these places, but the scientific explorers who set out to investigate the unfamiliar often succeeded in clearing away the mystery. As Pumpelly named mountain systems or studied the stratigraphy of the Yangtze gorge, discovered glaciers in northern Montana or described the physiography of Turkestan, he was contributing to the demystification of the unfamiliar. By the end of the century, most of the previously unknown regions had been explored, their features studied, mapped, and "domesticated with names."[6]

Pumpelly was acutely aware of the changes that had come through industrial development and population growth to the regions he had explored when they were still unfamiliar and wild. In 1907, with Eliza, he revisited the Rhine Valley, where he had taken a romantic walking tour in his student days, "when, tramping and dreaming, I had led a charmed life in a languid atmosphere of ruined castles and their legends. . . . Alas, railway trains rushed along both shores, the air was full of smoke, and the grand old castles had been hideously 'restored' by millionaires. Even Nature was no longer congenial."[7] He returned to the deserts of Arizona in 1915, after his wife's death, traveling this time with his children in three chauffeur-driven automobiles. He found that, while the desert still had its "mysteries and dangers" and was still a source of spiritual strength, much of it had "lost its mystery and charm" through the growth of cities, the building of railroads and highways, and other "evidences of vulgarization."[8]

Despite whatever romantic or mystical feelings Pumpelly may have had about exploration, it is important to remember that his explorations were always undertaken with a scientific purpose. It is for his scientific travels that his fellow Freiberg graduates called him the "American Humboldt." Pumpelly's explorations in China, the Northwest, and Turkestan can be seen as an example of the Humboldtian approach to science. The scientific explorers of the first part of the nineteenth century studied geology, climatology, botany, zoology, and ethnology, not just to accumulate facts but to find their interrelations and apply them to an understanding of the total environment. They were interested in everything about the regions they explored. Later, increasing specialization broke down the Humboldtian approach, and these sciences became more technical and isolated into separate disciplines.

Like others of his generation Pumpelly resisted "narrow specialization," even while his own work contributed to it, and he continued to be interested in the broader questions related to geology. The persistence of this "Humboldtian" tradition among geologists helps to explain John Wesley Powell's parallel interests in geology and ethnology, for example, and his efforts to relate the geology of arid regions to the classification of land for agriculture. Nathaniel Shaler, Eugene W. Hilgard, and Thomas C. Chamberlin all are known primarily as geologists but also studied geology's interrelations with other sciences. It is not surprising, therefore, to find that Powell, Shaler, Hilgard, and Pumpelly are regarded as geographers as well as geologists. Humboldt was trained as a geologist but is credited with being one of the major founders of modern geography.[9]

Pumpelly's explorations in Turkestan, where he combined the methods of geology, physical geography, climatology, archaeology, and anthropology in an interdisciplinary study of the effect of the environment on the development of a primitive culture, perhaps best exemplify the Humboldtian approach in the sense William Goetzmann defines it. Like Humboldt, Pumpelly generalized from the data obtained from all of these sources in trying to explain a complex period of human prehistory. Pumpelly does not entirely fit Susan Faye Cannon's definition of what it meant to be Humboldtian, however. He did not collect specimens of plants and animals, as Humboldt did, or do comparative studies of the climate or hydrography of different regions, nor was he particularly interested in geomagnetic measurement or the use of isothermal lines.[10]

But the making of accurate measurements and the necessity of presenting data visually are also marks of a Humboldtian, and these activities were of great importance for Pumpelly. As Cannon has said, "If you find a 19th-century scientist mapping or graphing his data, chances are good that you have found a Humboldtian."[11] Starting with his work in China, Pumpelly's first concern was to have maps prepared on which to present his data. The maps for the Northern Transcontinental Survey and the Green Mountain study were the epitome of the best and latest procedures in geologic mapping, and the diagrams he prepared to present the results of his archaeological and geological investigations in Turkestan were skillful graphic representations that organized his findings to support his climatic hypothesis.

Pumpelly's career also indicates the extent to which geologists were becoming involved in the development of the mineral industries in the Gilded Age. The employment of a trained mining engineer or geologist not only provided for expert identification of quality ores and the means of extracting them, it also added prestige and a sense of reliability to a mining venture, as Pumpelly's work in Arizona has shown. Pumpelly felt strongly that well-conducted scientific surveys would enable this country to use its resources wisely. Through his work as head of the Missouri Bureau of Mines and Geology he helped to raise the quality of economic geology done by state surveys by bringing in a specialist in iron ores and hiring other highly qualified geologists and analytical chemists to survey the state's coal, iron, and other minerals. His survey of the iron ores and other nonprecious metals for the U.S. Tenth Census—a massive use of scientific experts by the government—was an unprecedented attempt to assess the nation's resources. But, just as booming economic conditions encouraged the establishment and growth of geological surveys, so could panics and depressions affect their decline. Henry Villard's bankruptcy meant the cancellation of Pumpelly's Northern Transcontinental Survey, and the cutbacks in the United States Geological Survey that occurred in 1892 not only ended Pumpelly's career with the USGS but also brought about a redirection of the survey's activities under Charles Walcott.

Well before the end of the century, Americans were also serving as consultants to foreign governments. As Japan and China began to emerge from their centuries-long isolation, they looked to America for technological assistance. The work of Pumpelly, Blake, Louis Janin, and Benjamin Smith Lyman in Japan demonstrates the role economic geologists played in technology transfer. A technical geological report like that of Pumpelly's on China's coal mines could generate great interest. His was considered important enough to be included in Anson Burlingame's diplomatic dispatches to Washington and to be published in England and France. In their service abroad, mining geologists also observed the people and customs of the countries they visited, sometimes becoming interpreters of foreign cultures, as Pumpelly and Lyman did for the Japanese at a time when Americans knew little about them and were eager to know more. Pumpelly tried to portray China as a nation that, in its own time, would join the other nations of the world as a modern power, and he thought of his investigations as a contribution to Burlingame's policy to help China develop its own resources, although Pumpelly also promoted China as a market for American goods and a source of labor supply for American industry.

Private work as a mining expert could be a lucrative form of employment, Pumpelly found. Consultants were well paid for their expertise in evaluating mining properties or testifying in legal cases. Mining geologists also occasionally had the opportunity to invest in mining properties they thought promising. Pumpelly's income from investments and consulting fees enabled him to build large homes, to travel, and to support his family in a generous life-style. On the other hand, Clarence King resigned as director of the USGS hoping that with his knowledge of the mining industry he could become a rich man, but his investments in Mexican mines were in general not successful and he spent his last years ill and burdened by financial worries.[12]

During the years when Pumpelly served as director of the Missouri survey, the Tenth Census survey, and a USGS division, he became a respected scientific administrator, learning to grasp the essence of a problem quickly, analyze it, and draw up a plan for working it out, although sometimes his plans were too ambitious for the resources available to him. He was extravagant in his personal financial affairs, as his son admitted to Bailey Willis,[13] but he always took the long view, thinking of what would be good for his grandchildren. He was the same in his working life. He wanted to investigate a subject in depth, using the best people and the latest methods to provide a comprehensive solution that would anticipate the needs of the country in the future. In Missouri he embarked on an ambitious plan to reorganize the survey and received a generous appropriation from the governor for mapping and publication, but the coming of the depression of 1873, combined with his illness, brought an end to his plans. His organization and administration of the Tenth Census survey were admirable, but he seemed to expect the government to spend money as generously as he would spend it. Although he achieved some of his goals and produced a well-received report, he was not able to accomplish such worthwhile aims as having all the iron ores analyzed in order to find those best suited for the Bessemer process.

As a research director, Pumpelly was an inspiration to his co-workers and assistants, many of whom testified to the stimulation they received from working with him. A geological survey usually consists of teams that go into the field where much of the scientific work is done, then spend the winter at headquarters analyzing the data and writing reports. Almost all survey work is group work. To direct the work successfully requires a clear perception of the problems to be solved, recruitment of assistants who are able to work independently on related problems, and coordination of effort by the director.

Some of the surveys Pumpelly directed resembled a "research school," an analogy that James Secord found useful in assessing the organization of the early Geological Survey of Great Britain. Secord's analysis of the British survey under Henry de la Beche has much in common with studies of William Harvey's followers at Oxford and Justus von Liebig's laboratory at Giessen, which emphasize the importance of social interaction among researchers who share an interest in a common problem. The British survey had a strong research director, a "single guiding presence," who inspired his assistants and provided a work environment that stimulated the interaction of ideas. Even though dispersed geographically during the months of fieldwork, members of the British survey often felt an enthusiasm for working together on a common problem and a loyalty to their director that is perhaps more common in a laboratory science.[14]

The members of the Tenth Census survey reported feeling a sense of pride as they worked with Pumpelly at his headquarters at Newport on a project of national importance. Willis remembered Pumpelly's "generous confidence in the loyalty and capacity of the young men" whom he had recruited and the way Mrs. Pumpelly had made "his boys" feel at home.[15] Pumpelly set the problems to be worked out but he expected his men to be able to think for themselves, and he gladly let them develop their ideas and gave them credit for it. The young men who came from Freiberg, Harvard, the Columbia School of Mines, and elsewhere to work with him on the Missouri and Northern Transcontinental surveys had good academic preparation, but he gave them the opportunity to develop further under his expert guidance.

The structure of the USGS under Powell allowed for even greater opportunities for young assistants to do research with an experienced survey director. Powell granted each of his division heads considerable freedom to conduct their surveys in their own way. When he appointed Thomas C. Chamberlin to head the Glacial Division in 1881, Powell gave him only general instructions to study the terminal moraine and related deposits that extended in a "sinuous course" across the northern part of the country. The assistants whom Chamberlin trained and guided in this work until his retirement in 1904 constituted a veritable "school" of glacial geologists, whose research and publication reflected the thought and interpretations of their director.[16]

Pumpelly's Green Mountain survey was a similar "school," in this case a research group that combined meticulous fieldwork with micropetrological analysis to study mountain structure. His research group consisted of assistants who followed their director's plan of work and used his methods but, with his encouragement, followed independent lines of research. William Hobbs, who spent the summer of 1885 working for Pumpelly in western Massachusetts, found the experience was the equivalent of several semesters in a university. John Eliot Wolff and T. Nelson Dale, who wrote the separate reports on Hoosac and Greylock mountains, spent much time in the mountains on their own, but Pumpelly visited them often, consulting, checking their work, and coordinating their results. Although not regularly working together with daily contact, Pumpelly and his assistants were as bound by the joint investigation of a well-defined scientific problem as research scientists in a laboratory would be.

Not least of the binding factors was the personality of the research director. Pumpelly's encouragement and interest inspired his assistants to do their best work; he was the "single guiding presence" that is characteristic of a research school. Charles Keyes remembered meeting Pumpelly—"a great, blue-eyed giant, with long, flowing beard"—at a Geological Society of America meeting in 1890, where Keyes had given a paper. Pumpelly "stalked across the hall and sat down beside me . . . and at once entered upon a lively conversation, accompanied by a running fire of questions," and offered Keyes an opportunity to work with him in the Green Mountains the following summer. Keyes always had some feelings of regret "that I did not avail myself of the pleasure of spending at least one field season under the Pumpellian afflatus."[17]

Pumpelly saw many changes in geology during his lifetime. From a period when geology was practiced by naturalists, clergymen, physicians, and gentlemen geologists, it had become, by the end of the century, a field with academic departments in many universities, a thriving professional society, a number of journals, and several subspecialties. Pumpelly's life highlights the fact that geologists of this transitional period cannot always be separated into those who did geology "for the love of it," on their own time (the word *amateur* would be misleading because of its connotation that there is a lack of skill), and those who were paid professionals. Pumpelly was involved with geology in both ways during the progress of his career, at times the paid professional and at other times the gentleman of leisure who supported his own research.

Most geologists of his time, whether they were self-supported, taught geology, or served as professional survey men, cultivated many interests. Many of the older geologists were explorers, Willis thought, "not only in the sense that they traveled widely in little known lands, but also in that they reasoned widely on little known subjects. They were broad men, who grasped strongly the whole scope of earth science, and developed their speculations with corresponding daring."[18]

Willis must have been thinking of Pumpelly as he wrote these lines in the last year of Pumpelly's life and suggested that the field geologist needed something of these qualities. In a brief tribute, published before his longer memoir, Willis called Pumpelly an explorer of the "great vista of knowledge" he saw stretching out before him. Other geologists of the Heroic Age might have come to mind as well. Many who died in the early twentieth century were thought of as being the last of the nineteenth-century generalists. It was with an obvious nostalgia that the memoirs were written of the men who lived through this period. "The scope of his studies was broad; he belonged to the old school to which most geologists of fifty years ago belonged," wrote N. H. Winchell of Edward Claypole in 1901. Herman L. Fairchild called Joseph LeConte "perhaps the last distinguished representative of the general geologist" when he died in 1901, LeConte and James Dwight Dana being "the noblest American representatives of the passing type."[19]

Geological knowledge had been accumulating throughout the nineteenth century at an ever-increasing rate, and for a time it was possible for geologists to encompass most aspects of it. The Heroic Age of exploration came to an end as much because of the impossibility of keeping up with the knowledge explosion as it was because of the closing of geographical frontiers.

Pumpelly was both a generalist and a specialist. His interests were broad but he also investigated a few subjects in depth. His work in these areas suggests the way the transition from the generalist to the specialist came about. Generalists and specialists were not necessarily separate groups; individuals at various times in their careers could represent both old and new phases. In petrology, Pumpelly's work, as Waldemar Lindgren told Willis, "showed a great originality, and in this direction of the microscopic study of minerals, he was as much of a pioneer as he proved to be in geological explorations."[20] His *Geology of the Green Mountains* remains a classic study in mountain structure. He was the first to give a geological description of the loess deposits of China and was instrumental in the acceptance of the eolian hypothesis of loess distribution. On his expeditions to Turkestan he brought specialists to study the glaciers and physiography of a previously unexplored region and pioneered in the application of geological techniques to archaeology, the specialty known today as geoarchaeology.

Pumpelly's exploring nature delighted in going into new intellectual fields or applying new tools to old problems. It was perhaps his commitment to field-based work that held him back from publishing on other subjects in which he was interested but on which he may have felt that he did not have the hands-on experience. He did not have the prolific publishing record that some of his contemporaries had, nor was he as concerned about establishing priority or entering into scientific controversy as some other scientists were. He was not a success as a teacher because he had no taste for the codification of geologic knowledge for systematic presentation in the classroom; he preferred to be out in the field pursuing new interests rather than organizing old ones.

Of all American geologists in the last part of the nineteenth century, Pumpelly was perhaps the most cosmopolitan. Many geologists had international connections, because the correlation of the geology of different countries was an important aspect of their work, and this cosmopolitanism increased with the establishment of the International Geological Congress, which first met in Paris in 1878. Pumpelly and other Americans attended some of these meetings, and he served as a vice-president at the Washington meeting in 1891, "probably because I was supposed to speak French."[21] He had always been comfortable with foreign travel, ever since his student days, and he maintained friendships with Richthofen, Suess, and other Europeans. His lifelong experience of world travel and his ease with the people of other countries at all levels of society contributed in an important way to the success of his expeditions to Turkestan.

These expeditions were the culmination of all of Pumpelly's varied interests. They constituted the most absorbing endeavor of his life. They show how prepared he was to take up a broad, discipline-bridging question that had occupied several generations of scholars. The critics who thought he did not follow through on his fertile ideas must not have been familiar with this work, for he spent several years of study and consultation with experts in preparing the final volumes on his 1904 expeditions.

To some, Pumpelly's archaeological investigations may have seemed like a radical departure from his work in geology, but in fact the two were closely related in his mind, as his son, who had worked closely with him in Central Asia, realized:

I know of no man who has equalled him in attaining the geological attitude of mind. In viewing all problems he maintained a purely detached and impersonal point of view with a perspective of space and time that seemed a second nature to him, or rather a first nature. . . . When he took up archaeological work it was from the purely geological point of view. . . . To him it was always a geological problem, the most fascinating of all horizons because it contained the early civilizations of man. His attitude was that every least thing—be it the clay or the dust of the excavation if it could only be properly studied in its associations—contained much of the secret of the unknown.[22]

Central Asia was Pumpelly's laboratory to test the popular belief that physical geography and climate had influenced history. While others studied environmental influences to prove racial superiority, Pumpelly did it to discover the factors that had set early man on the path to civilization. He believed that at that stage man and nature were a unity and that any changes in the environment would have effected changes in man's development. The Turkestan expeditions illustrate the two sides of Pumpelly's nature: the romantic explorer in search of the mysteries of the cosmos and the detached investigator using the methods of science to unravel them.

By the early twentieth century, geology was one of several sciences with fairly well-defined career paths that became increasingly open to the middle class. Little room was left for the gentleman explorer-scientist who could afford to investigate a variety of problems. Once a person was established in a scientific discipline, the knowledge and experience that were necessary to succeed in it meant that a scientist who prepared for one career would find it hard to leave for another line of work.

The Gilded Age, as Pumpelly's career has shown, was a time of rapid change and growth in the country as a whole as well as in geology. It was seen by the new capitalists as a period of unlimited opportunity, and it must have seemed so to geologists as well. By the end of the century geology's Heroic Age was over. Frederick Jackson Turner's announcement, in 1893, of the closing of the frontier was a sign that the age of the great explorations was also coming to a close. Coming to an end as well was the time when geologists could encompass the intellectual content of the field. The emergence of new specialties and the restrictions of the profession meant that the geologist of broad scope like Pumpelly was a disappearing species. As participants in American geology's Heroic Age, geologists of Pumpelly's generation lived through a period when new problems as well as new territories were being explored, and they were excited by the challenges of pioneering in new fields. By the time of Pumpelly's death in 1923, and until the revolution brought about by the acceptance of the plate tectonic theory in the 1950s, geology was a more restricted discipline, less romantically exciting and more limited to following the well-marked paths of those who had gone before.

Notes

Preface
1. Larry McMurtry, *Anything for Billy* (New York: Simon and Schuster, 1988), 57–64.
2. Mark Twain and Charles Dudley Warner, *The Gilded Age* (1873; reprint, Garden City, N.Y.: Doubleday, N.d.), 382–84.

1. Education of a Geologist
1. Raphael Pumpelly, *My Reminiscences*, 2 vols. (New York: Henry Holt, 1918), 1:10–11 (hereafter cited as *Rem.*).
2. Ibid., 3.
3. Ibid., 3–4, 2:785–88; Leroy Kingman, ed., *A Memorial History of Tioga County, New York* (Elmira, N.Y.: W. A. Ferguson, ca. 1897), 273–74.
4. Kingman, *Tioga County*, 273; Joseph Henry to Jabez D. Hammond, Oct. 15, 1825, in *The Papers of Joseph Henry*, ed. Nathan Reingold and Marc Rothenberg, 6 vols. to date (Washington, D.C.: Smithsonian Institution Press, 1972–), 1:108–09.
5. Kingman, *Tioga County*, 73, 273–74; "Harmon Pumpelly," *National Cyclopedia of American Biography*, 63 vols. (New York: J. T. White, 1898–1984), 8:124 (hereafter cited as *NCAB*).
6. Kingman, *Tioga County*, 274; *Rem.*, 1:6–8.
7. *Rem.*, 1:6–7, 2:787–88; Mary Welles Pumpelly, *Poems* (New York: Scribner's, 1852).
8. *Rem.*, 1:10–18.
9. Hugh Miller, *The Old Red Sandstone; or, New Walks in an Old Field* (Edinburgh: J. Johnstone, 1841; Boston: Gould and Lincoln, 1851, from 4th Edinburgh edition). At least thirty editions of *Old Red Sandstone* were published in English. Quotations are taken from the Boston 1851 edition.
10. John Challinor, "Archibald Geikie," in *Dictionary of Scientific Biography*, ed.

Charles C. Gillispie, 16 vols. (New York: Scribner's, 1969–80), 5:333 (hereafter cited as *DSB*).
11. Miller, *Old Red Sandstone*, 2–3; Martin J. S. Rudwick, "Hugh Miller," in *DSB*, 9:388–90; Murchison's address was reported, probably by editor James Dwight Dana, in "Address Delivered at the Anniversary Meeting of the Geological Society of London, Feb. 18, 1842," *American Journal of Science* 43 (1842): 197–99.
12. Miller, *Old Red Sandstone*, 7.
13. Ibid., 10.
14. Ibid., 11, 30; Lardner Vanuxem, *Geology of New York*, vol. 3 (Albany: White and Visscher, 1842); *Rem.*, 1:15.
15. Murchison, "Address," 199; Peter J. Bowler, *Fossils and Progress: Paleontology and the Idea of Progressive Evolution in the Nineteenth Century* (New York: Science History Publications, 1976), 79–80.
16. Miller, *Old Red Sandstone*, 11.
17. Wallace Stegner, *Beyond the Hundredth Meridian: John Wesley Powell and the Second Opening of the West* (Boston: Houghton Mifflin, 1954), 8–17.
18. David N. Livingstone, *Nathaniel Southgate Shaler and the Culture of American Science* (Tuscaloosa: University of Alabama Press, 1987), 14–30.
19. Michael L. Prendergast, "James Dwight Dana: The Life and Thought of an American Scientist" (Ph.D. diss., University of California at Los Angeles, 1978), 12–16; Louis V. Pirsson, "James Dwight Dana, 1813–1895," *National Academy of Sciences Biographical Memoirs* 9 (1919): 44–45.
20. *Rem.*, 1:19–23.
21. Pumpelly's term report is in the Pumpelly Collection, pt. 2, box 2, Henry E. Huntington Library, San Marino, Calif.; Dirk J. Struik, *Yankee Science in the Making* (Boston: Little, Brown, 1948), 299–300. Struik calls Paley's book a "small scientific encyclopedia," which was read by many pre–Civil War scientists.
22. *Rem.*, 1:23–27; Struik, *Yankee Science*, 337–40; Muriel Rukeyser, *Willard Gibbs* (Garden City, N.Y.: Doubleday, Doran and Co., 1942), 96–97; Henry Holt, *Garrulities of an Octogenarian Editor* (Boston: Houghton Mifflin, 1923), 34.
23. Leonard G. Wilson, ed., *Benjamin Silliman and His Circle* (New York: Science History Publications, 1979).
24. Russell H. Chittenden, *History of the Sheffield Scientific School of Yale University, 1846–1922* (New Haven: Yale University Press, 1928); Struik, *Yankee Science*, 337–47; Samuel Eliot Morison, ed., *The Development of Harvard University Since the Inauguration of President Eliot, 1869–1929* (Cambridge: Harvard University Press, 1930), 414; Thurman Wilkins, with the help of Caroline Lawson Hinkley, *Clarence King: A Biography*, rev. and enl. (Albuquerque: University of New Mexico Press, 1988), 30–38.
25. *Rem.*, 1:24–28.
26. Gerald D. Nash, "Josiah Dwight Whitney," in *DSB*, 14:315; Edwin Tenney Brewster, *Life and Letters of Josiah Dwight Whitney* (Boston: Houghton Mifflin, 1909); Edward S. Dana, "George Jarvis Brush," *American Journal of Science*, 4th ser., 33 (1912): 389–96; Frederick Slate, "Biographical Memoir of Eugene Woldemar Hilgard, 1833–1916," *National Academy of Sciences Biographical Memoirs* 9 (1919): 93–155.

27. John Pumpelly to his mother, Mary Welles Pumpelly, July 30, 1854; Mary Welles Pumpelly to William Pumpelly, Aug. 16, 1855, Pumpelly Collection, pt. 2, box 1.
28. Rem., 1:29–31.
29. Ibid., 33–37.
30. John Pumpelly to his mother, Mary Welles Pumpelly, Oct. 29, 1854, Jan. 21, Feb. 18, Mar. 18, 1855, Pumpelly Collection, pt. 2, box 1.
31. Rem., 1:37.
32. See *Sociètè Gèologique de France Bulletin*, vols. 12–13, 1855–56.
33. Rem., 1:44.
34. Ibid.; Martin J. S. Rudwick, *The Meaning of Fossils; Episodes in the History of Paleontology*, 2d ed. (Chicago: University of Chicago Press, 1985), 124–29.
35. J. F. Noyes to Mary Welles Pumpelly, Feb. 23, Mar. 1, 1855, Pumpelly Collection, pt. 2, box 1; Adolph Pabst, "Karl Friedrich Rammelsberg," in *DSB*, 11:270–71.
36. Rem., 1:37; Heinz Tobien, "Friedrich Adolph Roemer," in *DSB*, 11:501–02.
37. Rem., 1:37–38.
38. Mary Welles Pumpelly to William Pumpelly, May 29, 1855, Pumpelly Collection, pt. 2, box 1.
39. *Sociètè Gèologique de France Bulletin*, meeting of Dec. 17, 1855, 13:124.
40. Mary Welles Pumpelly to William Pumpelly, Dec. 2, 1855, Pumpelly Collection, pt. 2, box 1.
41. Rem., 1:40–43.
42. Raphael Pumpelly to William Pumpelly, Dec. 6, 1855, Pumpelly Collection, pt. 2, box 1.
43. Rem., 1:48–50; Fred M. Bullard, *Volcanoes in History, in Theory, in Eruption* (Austin: University of Texas Press, 1962), 129–30, 162–63.
44. Rem., 1:52–54.
45. Ibid., 63–109.
46. Louis Agassiz, *Études sur les Glaciers* (Neuchâtel: H. Nicolet, 1840).
47. Raphael Pumpelly, "Über einige Gletscher-Überreste der Insel Corsica," *Neues Jahrbuch für Mineralogie, Geognosie, Geologie* (1858): 273–77.
48. Rem., 1:173; Raphael Pumpelly, "Sur Quelques Traces de Glaciers dans l'île de Corse," *Sociètè Gèologique de France Bulletin*, 2d ser., 17 (1859): 78–82.
49. Rem., 1:48–51.
50. John Pumpelly to Mary Welles Pumpelly, Mar. 27, 1856; William Pumpelly to John Pumpelly, Nov. 25, 1856, Pumpelly Collection, pt. 2, box 1.
51. Rem., 1:113–15.
52. Ibid., 115–16.
53. John A. Church, "Mining Schools in the United States," *North American Review* 112 (1871): 62–81; Clark C. Spence, *Mining Engineers and the American West: The Lace-Boot Brigade, 1849–1933* (New Haven: Yale University Press, 1970), 25.
54. Church, "Mining Schools," 69.
55. Alexander Ospovat, "Abraham Gottlob Werner," in *DSB*, 14:256–64; Archibald Geikie, *Founders of Geology*, 2d ed. (1905; reprint, New York: Dover Publications, 1962), 201–03. Geikie's disparaging assessment of Werner has been revised by Mott T. Greene, *Geology in the Nineteenth Century: Changing Views of a Changing World* (Ithaca, N.Y.: Cornell University Press, 1982),

19–68, and by Rachel Laudan, *From Mineralogy to Geology: The Foundations of a Science, 1650–1830* (Chicago: University of Chicago Press, 1987), 87–112, 224–25.
56. Freiberg, 1791; English translation by Charles Anderson under the title *New Theory of the Formation of Veins, with its Application to the Art of Working Mines* (Edinburgh: Encyclopedia Britannica Press, 1809).
57. Quoted in Ospovat, "Werner," 262.
58. Helmut De Terra, *Humboldt* (New York: Alfred A. Knopf, 1955).
59. Spence, *Mining Engineers*, 26; *Rem.*, 1:118; Alexander Ospovat, "Der Einfluss ehemaliger Studenten der Bergakademie Freiberg auf die Entwicklung des nordamerikanischen Bergbaus und Hüttenwesens," *Bergakademie* 18 (1966): 548–54.
60. George P. Merrill, "James Duncan Hague," in *Dictionary of American Biography*, ed. Allen Johnson and Dumas Malone, 11 vols. (New York: Scribner's, 1958–64), 8:87 (hereafter cited as *DAB*); "James Putnam Kimball," in *NCAB*, 11:91–92; "Louis Janin," in *NCAB*, 18:11–12.
61. Henry Janin to his father, Louis Alexander Janin, June 15, 1857, Janin Family Collection, Huntington Library.
62. Henry Janin to Louis Alexander Janin, Feb. 11, 1857, ibid.
63. Louis Janin to Louis Alexander Janin, Sept. 24, 1856, ibid.; *Rem.*, 1:120, 128–29; Lester D. Stephens, *Joseph LeConte, Gentle Prophet of Evolution* (Baton Rouge: Louisiana State University Press, 1982); Stephen J. Pyne, *Grove Karl Gilbert: A Great Engine of Research* (Austin: University of Texas Press, 1980), 98.
64. Henry Janin to Louis Alexander Janin, Nov. 25, 1857, Mar. 17, Dec. 19, 1858, Apr. 4, 1859; Louis Janin to Louis Alexander Janin, Mar. 21, Nov. 14, 1858, Janin Family Collection.
65. *Rem.*, 1:128; Henry Janin to Louis Alexander Janin, Feb. 1, Oct. 28, 1859, Janin Family Collection.
66. Church, "Mining Schools," 69; George Brush, *Manual of Determinative Mineralogy with an Introduction on Blowpipe Analysis*, 16th ed. (New York: Wiley, 1909).
67. Hunter Rouse, "Julius Ludwig Weisbach," in *DSB*, 14:232; *Rem.*, 1:120–21.
68. *Rem.*, 1:121–22.
69. Adolph Pabst, "Johann Friedrich August Breithaupt," in *DSB*, 2:440–41; Johann Friedrich Breithaupt, *Die Paragenesis der Mineralien* (Freiberg: J. G. Engelhardt, 1849); *Rem.*, 1:126.
70. In crystallography a twin is a "symmetrical intergrowth of two or more grains of the same crystalline species"; a twin law states the relation between the two parts of a twin. *Glossary of Geology* (American Geological Institute, 1957), 307.
71. Raphael Pumpelly to Jeremiah Loder, [1857], Pumpelly Collection, pt. 2, box 2.
72. *Rem.*, 1:124–25.
73. Hans Prescher, "Carl Bernhard von Cotta," in *DSB*, 3:433–35; Henry Clifton Sorby, "Carl Bernhard von Cotta," *Quarterly Journal of the Geological Society of London* 36 (1880): 40–42; Henry Janin to Louis Alexander Janin, Feb. 1, 1859, Janin Family Collection.
74. Carl Bernhard von Cotta, *Die Gesteinslehre*, 2d ed. (1855); 3d ed. (1862);

idem, *Rocks Classified and Described,* an English edition translated by Philip Henry Lawrence (London: Longmans, 1866).
75. Cotta, *Rocks Classified and Described,* 394.
76. Sorby, "Cotta," 42; *Bernhard von Cotta. Sein geologisches und philosophisches Lebenswerk,* Berichte Geologische Gesellschaft DDR Sonderheft, no. 3 (Berlin, 1965), 118–19.
77. *Rem.,* 2:541–42.
78. Carl Bernhard von Cotta, *Die Lehre von den Erzlagerstätten* (1855); 2d ed., 2 vols. (Freiberg: J. G. Engelhardt, 1859–61), translated into English by Frederick Prime, Jr., as *A Treatise on Ore Deposits* (New York: Van Nostrand, 1870).
79. *Rem.,* 1:125; Greene, *Geology in the Nineteenth Century,* 61–68; Thomas Crook, *History of the Theory of Ore Deposits* (New York: Van Nostrand, 1933), 69–71.
80. Henry Janin to Louis Alexander Janin, Dec. 19, 1858, Janin Family Collection. The work by the German paleontologist Friedrich Quenstedt was probably his *Handbuch der Petrefaktenkunde* (Tübingen: H. Laupp, 1852). John G. Burke, "Friedrich Quenstedt," in *DSB,* 11:235–36.
81. Martin Guntau, "The Mining Academy of Freiberg—A Centre of Geoscientific Teaching and Research," *Journal of Mines, Metals and Fuels* 22 (1974): 223–27; *Rem.,* 1:126.
82. *Rem.,* 1:173–76.
83. Louis Janin to Louis Alexander Janin, Jan. 17, 1860, Janin Family Collection.
84. *Rem.,* 1:126–27; Henry Janin to Louis Alexander Janin, Dec. 19, 1858, Janin Family Collection.
85. *Rem.,* 1:122–23; Sorby, "Cotta," 41.
86. Louis Janin to Louis Alexander Janin, Aug. 13, 1860, Janin Family Collection; *Rem.,* 1:166–69.
87. Louis Janin to Louis Alexander Janin, Mar. 21, 1858; Henry Janin to Louis Alexander Janin, June 2, Dec. 19, 1858, Janin Family Collection.
88. *Rem.,* 1:122–23, 134–38.
89. Ibid., 145–64.

2. Geology in America, 1835–1860

1. On science in the antebellum period see Robert V. Bruce, *The Launching of Modern American Science, 1846–1876* (New York: Alfred A. Knopf, 1987), 1–268. Two works that survey the history of geology in the United States before the Civil War are George P. Merrill, *The First One Hundred Years of American Geology* (New Haven: Yale University Press, 1924), and Mary C. Rabbitt, *Minerals, Lands, and Geology for the Common Defence and General Welfare,* vol. 1, *Before 1879* (Washington, D.C.: Government Printing Office, 1979). Others that discuss the geology of the period in a less comprehensive way are Leonard G. Wilson, "The Emergence of Geology as a Science in the United States," *Journal of World History* 10 (1967): 416–37; Cecil J. Schneer, ed., *Two Hundred Years of Geology in America* (Hanover, N.H.: University Press of New England, 1979); Markes E. Johnson, "Geology in American Education: 1825–1860," *Geological Society of America Bulletin* 88 (1977): 1192–98; Ellen T. Drake and William M. Jordan, eds., *Geologists and Ideas: A*

History of North American Geology (Boulder, Colo.: Geological Society of America, 1985).
2. Douglass C. North, *The Economic Growth of the United States, 1790–1860* (New York: Norton, 1966), 205; United States Bureau of the Census, *Historical Statistics of the United States, Colonial Times to 1970*, 2 vols. (Washington, D.C.: Government Printing Office, 1975), 1:590–93; Rabbitt, *Minerals, Lands*, chap. 6, "The Touchstone is Gold," 1:91–113.
3. Rabbitt, *Minerals, Lands*, 1:84; Henry Darwin Rogers, *The Geology of Pennsylvania*, 2 vols. (Philadelphia: Lippincott, 1858). References to coal and iron ores are found throughout, but see especially vol. 2, pt. 2, 795–811.
4. John W. Foster and Josiah Dwight Whitney, *Report on the Geology and Topography of a Portion of the Lake Superior Land District in the State of Michigan*, pt. 1, "Copper Lands," U.S. 31st Cong., 1st sess., H. Exec. Doc. 69, 1859; pt. 2, "The Iron Region, together with the General Geology," U.S. 32d Cong., spec. sess., S. Exec. Doc. 4, 1851.
5. Ibid., 39–46, 146–51.
6. Josiah Dwight Whitney, *The Metallic Wealth of the United States* (Philadelphia: Lippincott, 1854); Brewster, *Life and Letters of Josiah Dwight Whitney;* Robert Henry Block, "The Whitney Survey of California, 1860–1874: A Study in Environmental Science and Exploration" (Ph.D. diss., University of California at Los Angeles, 1982).
7. Louis Janin to Louis Alexander Janin, Jan. 11, 1860, Janin Family Collection; *Mining Magazine* 2 (1854): 24–27, 253–64, 353–70, 854; Rossiter W. Raymond, "Memoir of William Phipps Blake," *Geological Society of America Bulletin* 22 (1911): 36–37.
8. William P. Blake, "Silver and Copper Mining in Arizona," *Mining Magazine*, 2d ser., 1 (1859): 1–15.
9. Louis Janin to Louis Alexander Janin, Jan. 23, 1859; Henry Janin to Louis Alexander Janin, Apr. 4, 1859, Jan. 24, 1860, Janin Family Collection.
10. Ospovat, "Der Einfluss," 548–54; Rossiter W. Raymond, "James Duncan Hague," *AIME Bulletin* 26 (1909): 109–17; "James Putnam Kimball," in *NCAB*, 11:91–92.
11. "Louis Janin," in *NCAB*, 18:11–12; Wilkins, *Clarence King*, 167–85.
12. William H. Goetzmann has written about the antebellum exploring expeditions of the West in *Exploration and Empire: The Explorer and the Scientist in the Winning of the American West* (New York: Alfred A. Knopf, 1966) and *Army Exploration in the American West, 1803–1863* (New Haven: Yale University Press, 1959). The reports of the railroad surveys were published in several volumes as United States War Department, *Reports of Explorations and Surveys, to Ascertain the Most Practicable and Economical Route for a Railroad from the Mississippi River to the Pacific Ocean*, 12 vols. in 13 (Washington, D.C.: A. O. P. Nicholson, 1855–60) (hereafter cited as Pacific Railroad Reports).
13. Louis Janin to Louis Alexander Janin, Dec. 5, 1858; Henry Janin to Louis Alexander Janin, Dec. 19, 1858, Janin Family Collection.
14. Raymond, "Memoir of William Phipps Blake," 36–47; Charles A. White, "Biographical Memoir of John Strong Newberry," *National Academy of Sciences Biographical Memoirs* 6 (1909): 1–24.
15. Goetzmann, *Army Exploration*, chap. 8, "The Savants and the Surveys," 305–37.

16. Frederick William True, "The United States National Museum," in *The Smithsonian Institution, 1846–1896: The History of Its First Half Century*, ed. George Brown Goode (Washington, D.C.: Smithsonian Institution Press, 1897), 313–15; Pacific Railroad Reports, 5:pref. to pt. 1.
17. James Schiel, "Geological Report of the Country Explored," in Pacific Railroad Reports, 2:102.
18. John S. Newberry, Pacific Railroad Reports, 6:pt. 2, 5–68.
19. William P. Blake, "Geological Report," in Pacific Railroad Reports, 5:pt. 2, 1–310.
20. Clifford M. Nelson, "Geologic Maps of American West: Hall Vs. Marcou," in 28th International Geological Congress, *Abstracts* (Washington, D.C.: N.p., 1989), 2:504–05; Goetzmann, *Army Exploration*, 323–26; Merrill, *First One Hundred Years*, 308–10, 315–17. Letters relating to the controversy over Marcou's map are in Merrill's appendix, 675–81.
21. A. Hunter Dupree, *Science in the Federal Government* (1957; reprint, Baltimore: Johns Hopkins University Press, 1986), 99–100.
22. Goetzmann, *Army Exploration*, 3–61. Humboldt's kind of scientific travel was best described in his *Personal Narrative of Travels to the Equinoctial Regions of the New Continent During the Years 1799–1804*, trans. Helen Maria Williams (Philadelphia: M. Carey, 1815). His cosmic view of nature is presented in *Cosmos: A Sketch of a Physical Description of the Universe*, trans. E. C. Otté, 5 vols. (London: Bell and Daldy, 1871–72).
23. Susan Faye Cannon, *Science in Culture: The Early Victorian Period* (New York: Dawson and Science History Publications, 1978), chap. 3, "Humboldtian Science," 73–110.
24. Goetzmann, *Army Exploration*, 422–23.
25. John Hays Hammond, *Autobiography of John Hays Hammond* (New York: Farrar and Rinehart, 1935), 63; Frederick Gleason Corning, *A Student Reverie: An Album of Saxony Days* (New York: Privately printed, 1920).
26. George P. Merrill, *Contributions to a History of American State Geological and Natural History Surveys*, U.S. National Museum Bulletin 109 (Washington, D.C.: Government Printing Office, 1920); Walter B. Hendrickson, "Nineteenth-Century State Geological Surveys: Early Government Support of Science," *Isis* 52 (1961): 357–71; Michele L. Aldrich, "Geological Surveys, State," in *Dictionary of American History*, rev. ed., 8 vols. (New York: Charles Scribner's Sons, 1976–78), 3:164–66; Stephen P. Turner, "The Survey in Nineteenth-Century American Geology: The Evolution of a Form of Patronage," *Minerva* 25 (1987): 282–330.
27. Wilson, "Emergence of Geology," 435; Michele L. Aldrich, "New York Natural History Survey, 1836–1845" (Ph.D. diss., University of Texas at Austin, 1974). The geological results of the survey are found in *Geology of New York*, 4 vols. William W. Mather is author of vol. 1 on the first district (Albany: Carroll and Cook, 1843); Ebenezer Emmons of vol. 2 on the second district (Albany: White and Visscher, 1842); Lardner Vanuxem of vol. 3 on the third district (Albany: White and Visscher, 1842); James Hall, Jr., of vol. 4 on the fourth district (Albany: Carroll and Cook, 1843).
28. Aldrich, "New York Natural History Survey," chap. 4, "Selection of the Scientists," 92–122.
29. John W. Wells, "William W. Mather," in *DSB*, 9:172–73; C. H. Hitchcock,

"Sketch of W. W. Mather," *American Geologist* 19 (1897): 1–15; Cecil J. Schneer, "Ebenezer Emmons and the Foundation of American Geology," *Isis* 60 (1970): 439–50.
30. Aldrich, "New York Natural History Survey," 119–20; John W. Wells, "Lardner Vanuxem," in *DSB*, 13:581; "Sketch of Professor Lardner Vanuxem," *Popular Science Monthly* 46 (1895): 833–40.
31. C. C. Abbott, "Timothy Abbott Conrad," *Popular Science Monthly* 47 (1895): 257–63; Aldrich, "New York Natural History Survey," 116–18.
32. Donald W. Fisher, "James Hall, Jr.," in *DSB*, 6:56–58; John M. Clarke, *James Hall of Albany* (Albany, N.Y.: E. E. Rankin, 1921).
33. Wilson, "Emergence of Geology," 427; Martin J. S. Rudwick, *The Great Devonian Controversy* (Chicago: University of Chicago Press, 1985), 107–13. One of the key points in the Devonian controversy was the debate over the reliability of fossil criteria.
34. Fisher, "James Hall," 57; Josiah Dwight Whitney to William D. Whitney, July 15, 1850, in Brewster, *Life and Letters of Josiah Dwight Whitney*, 111–12.
35. Aldrich, "New York Natural History Survey," 99–103.
36. Merrill, *State Geological Surveys*, 351.
37. George H. Daniels, *American Science in the Age of Jackson* (New York: Columbia University Press, 1968).
38. Wilson, "Emergence of Geology," 432–33; James A. Secord, *Controversy in Victorian Geology: The Cambrian-Silurian Dispute* (Princeton: Princeton University Press, 1986); Rudwick, *Great Devonian Controversy*.
39. Aldrich, "New York Natural History Survey," 295–98; Merrill, *First One Hundred Years*, 223–35.
40. Greene, *Geology in the Nineteenth Century*, 124–27; Robert H. Dott, "James Hall's Discovery of the Craton," in Drake and Jordan, *Geologists and Ideas*, 157–67.
41. Ebenezer Emmons's Taconic system was reported in his *Agriculture of New York*, vol. 1 (Albany, N.Y.: Van Benthuysen, 1846); Merrill, *First One Hundred Years*, 594–614; Cecil J. Schneer, "The Great Taconic Controversy," *Isis* 69 (1978): 173–91. Pumpelly's work in the Taconic region is discussed in chapter 6.
42. William Buckland, *Reliquiae Diluvianae; or observations on the organic remains contained in caves, fissures, and Diluvial gravel, and other geological phenomena, attesting the action of an Universal Deluge* (London: J. Murray, 1823).
43. Merrill, *First One Hundred Years*, 622 (see chap. 13, "The Development of the Glacial Hypothesis"); Martin J. S. Rudwick, "The Glacial Theory (An Essay Review of *Studies on Glaciers* by Louis Agassiz, translated and edited by Albert V. Carozzi, 1967)," *History of Science* 8 (1969): 139.
44. Nicholaas A. Rupke, *The Great Chain of Being: William Buckland and the English School of Geology, 1814–1849* (Oxford: Clarendon, 1983); Merrill, *First One Hundred Years*, 624–26.
45. Mather, *Geology of New York*, 1:158–228; Hitchcock, "Sketch of Mather," 4.
46. Emmons, *Geology of New York*, 2:422–26.
47. Hall, *Geology of New York*, 4:324–31.
48. Vanuxem, *Geology of New York*, 3:246–47.
49. Stanley M. Totten and George W. White, "Glacial Geology and the North American Craton," in Drake and Jordan, *Geologists and Ideas*, 127–31.

50. Nathan Reingold, "Definitions and Speculations: The Professionalization of Science in America in the Nineteenth Century," in *The Pursuit of Knowledge in the Early American Republic,* ed. Alexandra Oleson and Sanborn C. Brown (Baltimore: Johns Hopkins University Press, 1976), 33–69.
51. Roy Porter, "Gentlemen and Geology: The Emergence of a Scientific Career, 1660–1920," *Historical Journal* 21 (1978): 809–36.
52. Bruce, *Launching of Modern American Science,* 149; Alexis de Tocqueville, *Democracy in America,* 2 vols. (New York: Schocken Books, 1961), 2:52.
53. Patsy A. Gerstner, "Henry Darwin Rogers and William Barton Rogers on the Nomenclature of the American Paleozoic Rocks," in Schneer, *Two Hundred Years,* 178–79.
54. Sally Gregory Kohlstedt, *The Formation of the American Scientific Community: The American Association for the Advancement of Science* (Urbana: University of Illinois Press, 1976), 59–77.
55. Ibid.; "Organization of the Geological Society of America," *Geological Society of America Bulletin* 1 (1890): 1–7.

3. Exploring "Across America and Asia"

1. Rodman W. Paul, *The Far West and the Great Plains in Transition, 1859–1900* (New York: Harper and Row, 1988); idem, *Mining Frontiers of the Far West, 1848–1880* (New York: Holt, Rinehart and Winston, 1963); Spence, *Mining Engineers;* Thomas A. Rickard, *A History of American Mining* (New York: McGraw-Hill, 1932).
2. Diane M. T. North, *Samuel Peter Heintzelman and the Sonora Exploring and Mining Company* (Tucson: University of Arizona Press, 1980); Ida Reid Leonard, "Charles Debrille Poston," in *DAB,* 8:121–22; Raphael Pumpelly, "Mineralogical Sketch of the Silver Mines of Arizona," *Proceedings of the California Academy of Natural Sciences* 2 (1863): 127–39; Sylvester Mowry, *Arizona and Sonora: The Geography, History and Resources of the Silver Region of North America,* 3d ed., rev. and enl. (New York: Harper and Brothers, 1864); W. F. Witherell, *Arizona as a Silver Country* (Saint Louis: J. McKittrick, 1878).
3. Otis E. Young, Jr., *Western Mining* (Norman: University of Oklahoma Press, 1970), 143; Sonora Exploring and Mining Company, *Fourth Annual Report, March, 1860* (New York: W. Minns, 1860).
4. *Rem.,* 1:182–91.
5. Raphael Pumpelly, *Across America and Asia,* 3d ed., rev. (New York: Leypoldt and Holt, 1870), 12–28; *Rem.,* 1:194–221. In writing about his Arizona and Asian experiences in *My Reminiscences,* Pumpelly reused verbatim much of his material from *Across America and Asia,* although with many deletions and additions. In general, citations here are to *Across America and Asia,* unless his later volumes have significant additions.
6. Pumpelly, "Mineralogical Sketch," 134–35; *Rem.,* 1:199.
7. *Rem.,* 1:198.
8. Pumpelly, "Mineralogical Sketch," 132–33. The Freiberg barrel amalgamation method as used at the Heintzelman Mine is described in Frederick Brunckow's report to stockholders, abstracted by William P. Blake, "Processes for the Extraction of Silver," *Mining Magazine,* 2d ser., 1 (1859): 17–18. See also Young, *Western Mining,* 199–200.

9. William Wrightson to Mary Welles Pumpelly, Oct. 20, 1860, Pumpelly Collection, pt. 2, box 1.
10. *Rem.*, 1:197–99, 2:764; Raphael Pumpelly, "Arizona Notebook," Pumpelly Collection, pt. 1, box 1.
11. Pumpelly, *Across America and Asia*, 16–28; Douglas D. Martin, *An Arizona Chronology, The Territorial Years, 1846–1912* (Tucson: University of Arizona Press, 1963).
12. William Wrightson to Mary Welles Pumpelly, June 12 and 21, Aug. 3, Sept. 20 and 25, 1861, Pumpelly Collection, pt. 1, box 1.
13. *Rem.*, 1:266–67; William H. Brewer, *Up and Down California in 1860–1864*, 3d ed., ed. Francis P. Farquhar (Berkeley and Los Angeles: University of California Press, 1966), 196–98.
14. William H. Emory, *Report on the United States and Mexican Boundary Survey*, U.S. 34th Cong., 1st sess., S. Exec. Doc. 108 and H. Exec. Doc. 135, 1857.
15. Pumpelly, "Arizona Notebook"; idem, "Mineralogical Sketch."
16. H. J. Jones, *Live Machines: Hired Foreigners and Meiji Japan* (Vancouver: University of British Columbia Press, 1980). Pumpelly's accounts of his activities in Japan are found in Pumpelly, *Across America and Asia*, 68–194; *Rem.*, 1:267–341; and Raphael Pumpelly, *Geological Researches in China, Mongolia, and Japan, During the Years 1862 to 1865*, in Smithsonian Contributions to Knowledge, vol. 15 (Washington, D.C.: Smithsonian Institution, 1867), 79–108.
17. J. P. T. Bury, ed., *The New Cambridge Modern History*, 14 vols. (Cambridge: Cambridge University Press, 1957–79), 10:710–13.
18. Muragaki Awaji-no-Kami, "Diary of the First Japanese Embassy to the United States," in America-Japan Society, *The First Japanese Embassy to the United States of America*, comp. C. Shibima (Tokyo: America-Japan Society, 1920), 1–76. I thank Kathleen Dorman, assistant editor of *The Papers of Joseph Henry*, for bringing this Japanese mission to my attention.
19. Patterson Du Bois, "The Great Japanese Embassy of 1860. A Forgotten Chapter in the History of International Amity and Commerce," in *First Japanese Embassy*, 288–95; Kamikawa Hikomatsu, ed., *Japan-American Diplomatic Relations in the Meiji-Taisho Era*, trans. Kimura Michiko (Tokyo: Pan-Pacific Press, 1958), 49.
20. Harmon Pumpelly to Raphael Pumpelly, Nov. 8, Dec. 3, 1861; Harmon Pumpelly to Mary Welles Pumpelly, Dec. 4, 1861, Pumpelly Collection, pt. 2, box 1.
21. *Rem.*, 1:267; "Private Diaries, 1861," William Phipps Blake Papers, Arizona Historical Society, Tucson.
22. Raphael Pumpelly, "Japan Notes, 1861–1862," Pumpelly Collection, pt. 1, box 1; *Rem.*, 1:287–88.
23. *Rem.*, 1:304.
24. Pumpelly, *Across America and Asia*, 78–113, 128–42; idem, "Japan Notes, 1861–1862."
25. Raphael Pumpelly to His Excellency, Governor of Hakodate, May 19, 1862, Pumpelly Collection, pt. 2, box 2.
26. Pumpelly, *Across America and Asia*, 144, 154–55. Dutch scientific books reached into many parts of Japan; Hakodate was only one of at least thirty-five centers of Dutch learning. See Allan B. Cole, ed., *A Scientist with Perry in*

Japan, The Journal of Dr. James Morrow (Chapel Hill: University of North Carolina Press, 1947), 284, n. 6.
27. Pumpelly, "Japan Notes, 1861–1862," "Japan Notes, 1862," Pumpelly Collection, pt. 1, box 1; idem, *Geological Researches*, 80–81; idem, *Across America and Asia*, 143–57, 169–91.
28. Pumpelly, *Across America and Asia*, 189–90.
29. William P. Blake, "Abstract of the Report of Professor Blake," in Horace Capron, *Reports and Official Letters to the Kaitakushi* (Tokyo: Kaitakushi, 1875), 9–10.
30. Pumpelly, *Geological Researches*, 82–86.
31. Pumpelly, *Across America and Asia*, 191–94; Hikomatsu, *Japan-American Diplomatic Relations*, 51–55; Bury, *New Cambridge Modern History*, 10:711–13; Governor of Hakodate, Kasooja Chikoogano Cami, to Raphael Pumpelly, Dec. 1, 1862, Pumpelly Collection, pt. 2, box 2.
32. "Louis Janin," in *NCAB*, 18:12; Merrill, "James Duncan Hague," 87; H. Kobayashi, "Benjamin Smith Lyman," in *DSB*, 8:576–77.
33. E. J. Hobsbawm, *The Age of Capital, 1848–1875* (New York: Charles Scribner's Sons, 1979; New American Library, 1984), 144.
34. Bury, *New Cambridge Modern History*, 10:704–07; Pumpelly, *Across America and Asia*, 269; "Anson Burlingame," in *DAB*, 2:289–90; Frederick Wells Williams, *Anson Burlingame and the First Chinese Mission to Foreign Powers* (New York: Scribner's, 1912).
35. Pumpelly describes his travels in China in *Across America and Asia*, 203–427; *Rem.*, 1:342–438, 2:439–504; "Thomas Wright Blakiston," in *Dictionary of National Biography*, ed. Leslie Stephen and Sidney Lee, 22 vols. and suppl. (London: Oxford University Press, 1951–), 22:214–15; Thomas Wright Blakiston, *Five Months on the Yang-Tsze* (London: J. Murray, 1862). Pumpelly referred to Blakiston's book several times in *Geological Researches*.
36. Pumpelly, *Geological Researches*, iii–iv, 1–79; Raphael Pumpelly, China Notebooks covering the years 1862–65, Pumpelly Collection, pt. 1, box 1.
37. Martin J. S. Rudwick, "The Emergence of a Visual Language for Geological Science, 1760–1840," *History of Science* 14 (1976): 149–52; Pumpelly, *Geological Researches*, 51, 156, pl. 6. For a discussion of the subjective nature of geologic maps, see J. M. Harrison, "Nature and Significance of Geological Maps," in *The Fabric of Geology*, ed. Claude C. Albritton, Jr. (Reading, Mass.: Addison-Wesley, 1963), 225–32.
38. Pumpelly, *Geological Researches*, 6, 54–55, 62–64; John S. Newberry, "Description of the Plants from the Chinese Coal-Bearing Rocks," app. 1 in Pumpelly, *Geological Researches*, 119–23, reprinted in *American Journal of Science*, 2d ser., 42 (1866): 151–54.
39. Pumpelly, *Geological Researches*, 56–61.
40. *Rem.*, 1:434.
41. Pumpelly, *Geological Researches*, 46–50, pl. 4 and 5, "Maps Representing the Historical Changes in the Course of the Yellow River, or Hwang Ho," 151–54; George P. Merrill, "Eugene Woldemar Hilgard," in *DAB* 9 (1932): 22–23.
42. Pumpelly, *Geological Researches*, 67–69. For a discussion of the debate in North America about the origin of mountain ranges, see Greene, *Geology in the Nineteenth Century*, 122–43.

43. Pumpelly, *Geological Researches*, 40–45, 78; idem, China Notebook, "Trip to Coal Fields of Chihli and Journey Along Southern Edge of Mongolian Plateau, 1864," Pumpelly Collection, pt. 1, box 1.
44. Pumpelly, *Geological Researches*, 70–77, pls. 3 and 7, 149–50, 157–58; idem, China Notebook, "Pekin to St. Petersburg via Mongolia and Siberia," Pumpelly Collection, pt. 1, box 1; Charles P. Berkey and Frederick K. Morris, *Geology of Mongolia: A Reconnaissance Report Based on the Investigation of the Years 1922–1923*, Natural History of Central Asia, vol. 2 (New York: American Museum of Natural History, 1927), 16.
45. Pumpelly, *Geological Researches*, 76–77.
46. Ibid., 39–45; Totten and White, "Glacial Geology," 137–38.
47. Pumpelly, *Geological Researches*, 40. Compare the definition in, for example, Charles C. Plummer and David McGeary, *Physical Geology* (Dubuque, Iowa: W. C. Brown, 1979), 244.
48. Pumpelly, *Geological Researches*, 42–45.
49. Tim Wright, *Coal Mining in China's Economy and Society, 1895–1937* (Cambridge: Cambridge University Press, 1984), 5–9.
50. Pumpelly, *Across America and Asia*, 287.
51. Anson Burlingame to Secretary of State William H. Seward, Nov. 4, 1863, Dispatches from United States Ministers to China, Record Group 59, microcopy no. 92, roll 22, National Archives.
52. Raphael Pumpelly, "Report to the Chinese Government on a Preliminary Examination of the Coal District of the Se-Shan in the Province of Chihli," in ibid., Jan. 4, 1864.
53. Ibid.; Pumpelly, *Across America and Asia*, 303.
54. Pumpelly, *Geological Researches*, 14–21; Sparrow Knight, "The Coals from Se-Shan (the Hills West of Peking)," *Friend of China*, Dec. 27, 1867, 1–2; Raphael Pumpelly, "Combustibles du Se-Shan, Chine," *Annales des Mines* 9 (1866); Bury, *New Cambridge Modern History*, 12:334.
55. Minutes of Fourth Session of the National Academy of Sciences held in Northampton, Aug. 23–26, 1865, National Academy of Sciences Archives, Washington, D.C. On the history of the academy see Rexmond C. Cochrane, *The National Academy of Sciences: The First One Hundred Years, 1863–1963* (Washington, D.C.: National Academy of Sciences, 1978).
56. Raphael Pumpelly, "Notice of an Account of Geological Observations in China, Japan and Mongolia," *American Journal of Science*, 2d ser., 41 (1866): 145–49. During the early years of the academy little money was available for publication; the first volume of *Memoirs*, which appeared in 1866, included only five of the papers given during the first three years of the academy's existence.
57. *Rem.*, 2:550.
58. Raphael Pumpelly to Louis Janin, n.d. [1865], Pumpelly Collection, pt. 2, box 2.
59. Thomas Coulson, *Joseph Henry, His Life and Work* (Princeton: Princeton University Press, 1950), 191–92; Joseph Henry, quoted from preface to Smithsonian Contributions to Knowledge, 15:iv; Cyrus Adler, "Smithsonian Publications," in Goode, *Smithsonian Institution*, 481–500.
60. Smithsonian Institution, Office of the Secretary, 1863–1879, Incoming Correspondence, box 11, folder 12; Office of the Secretary, 1865–1869, Out-

going Correspondence, vols. 3 and 4, Feb.–Sept. 1866, Record Unit 33, Smithsonian Institution Archives, Washington, D.C.
61. Smithsonian Institution, *Annual Report* (Washington, D.C.: Smithsonian Institution, 1866), 37; *American Journal of Science*, 2d ser., 43 (1867): 408–09; Raphael Pumpelly, "On the Delta Plain, and the Historical Changes in the Course of the Yellow River," *American Journal of Science*, 2d ser., 45 (1868): 219–24; Daniel Coit Gilman, "Geographical Notices: Notes on China, by Rev. W. A. Martin, D.D.," *American Journal of Science*, 2d ser., 47 (1869): 98–102; "Age of the Coal-Formation of China," *Geological Magazine* 3 (1866): 507.
62. Brewster, *Life and Letters of Josiah Dwight Whitney*, 240; Robert P. Beckinsale, "Ferdinand von Richthofen," in *DSB*, 11:438–41. Richthofen's letters in the *American Journal of Science* were: "Geological Explorations in China," 2d ser., 50 (1870): 410–13; "On the Existence of the Nummulitic Formation in China," 3d ser., 1 (1871): 110–13; "On the Porcelain Rocks of China," 3d ser., 1 (1871): 179–81. Richthofen's major work on China is *China: Ergebnisse eigener Reisen und darauf gegrundeter Studien*, 3 vols. (Berlin: Dietrich Reimer, 1877–1912).
63. Richthofen, "On the Existence of the Nummulitic," 112.
64. Josiah Dwight Whitney to William D. Whitney, July 15, 1874, in Brewster, *Life and Letters of Josiah Dwight Whitney*, 313–14.
65. Clarence King, *Mountaineering in the Sierra Nevada* (Boston: James R. Osgood, 1872); John Wesley Powell, *The Canyons of the Colorado* (New York: Flood and Vincent, 1895).
66. *Rem.*, 2:594–95; "Pumpelly's *Across America and Asia*," *North American Review* 110 (1870): 224–28.
67. John S. Haller, *Outcasts from Evolution: Scientific Attitudes of Racial Inferiority, 1859–1900* (Urbana: University of Illinois Press, 1971).
68. Pumpelly, *Across America and Asia*, 35.
69. Ibid., 33–35; Hubert Howe Bancroft, *History of Arizona and New Mexico, 1530–1888*, vol. 17 of *The Works of Hubert Howe Bancroft* (San Francisco: History Co., 1889), 518; *Weekly Arizonan*, Mar. 5, 1870, 2.
70. Raphael Pumpelly, "Western Policy in China," *North American Review* 106 (1868): 592–612 (included as a chapter in *Across America and Asia*, 339–58).
71. Pumpelly, *Across America and Asia*, 316, 317.
72. Livingstone, *Nathaniel Southgate Shaler*; Sorby, "Cotta," 42.

4. Economic Geologist of the Gilded Age

1. Hobsbawm, *Age of Capital*, xx.
2. Frederick L. Ransome, "The Present Standing of Applied Geology," *Economic Geology* 1 (1906): 1–10. The journal was established before a professional society existed; the Society of Economic Geologists was not organized until 1920.
3. Ibid., 2–4.
4. Ibid., 2.
5. *Rem.*, 2:553.
6. Ibid., 549, 553–54; Raphael Pumpelly to President Thomas Hill, Feb. 16, 1867, Corporation Papers, Harvard University Archives, Cambridge;

George E. Pumpelly to Raphael Pumpelly, Oct. 2, 1868, Pumpelly Collection, pt. 2, box 2.
7. William B. Gates, Jr., *Michigan Copper and Boston Dollars* (Cambridge: Harvard University Press, 1951), 43–45; *Rem.*, 2:554–56.
8. *Rem.*, 2:564–79, 589; Raphael Pumpelly, *Prospectus of the Portage Lake and Lake Superior Ship Canal Company* (New York: W. L. Stone and J. T. Barron, 1868).
9. *Rem.*, 2:589–91; Bailey Willis, "Thomas Benton Brooks," *Science* 13 (1901): 460–62.
10. Rabbit, *Minerals, Lands*, 1:162, 204; *Letters and Recollections of Alexander Agassiz*, ed. George R. Agassiz (Boston: Houghton Mifflin, 1913), 53–90; *Rem.*, 2:596–603.
11. Agassiz, *Letters*, 192; *Rem.*, 2:791; Bruce, *Launching of Modern American Science*, 154.
12. Turner, "Survey in Nineteenth-Century American Geology," discusses the various ways survey geologists presented their requests for support to government bodies.
13. Alexander Winchell, "Michigan: First Geological Survey Under Douglass Houghton," in Merrill, *State Geological Surveys*, 158–203; Roland C. Allen and Helen M. Martin, "A Brief History of the Geological and Biological Survey of Michigan, 1837–1920," *Michigan History Magazine* 6 (1922): 675–750.
14. Merrill, *State Geological Surveys*, 230–31.
15. Quote is in Spence, *Mining Engineers*, 70; Merrill, *State Geological Surveys*, 228; David J. Krause, "Testing a Tradition: Douglass Houghton and the Native Copper of Lake Superior," *Isis* 80 (1989): 622–39.
16. Thomas Benton Brooks, "Iron-Bearing Rocks (Economic)," in Board of Geological Survey, *Geological Survey of Michigan, Upper Peninsula, 1869–1873*, 2 vols. and atlas (New York: Julius Bien, 1873), vol. 1, pt. 1.
17. Raphael Pumpelly, "Copper-Bearing Rocks," in ibid., vol. 1, pt. 2, x–xi.
18. Raphael Pumpelly, "The Paragenesis and Derivation of Copper and its associates on Lake Superior," *American Journal of Science*, 3d ser., 2 (1871): 188–98, 243–58, 347–55; Raphael Pumpelly and Thomas Benton Brooks, "On the Age of the Copper-bearing Rocks of Lake Superior," *American Journal of Science*, 3d ser., 3 (1872): 428–32.
19. Allen and Martin, "Geological and Biological Survey of Michigan," 700; Reginald E. Hore, "Michigan Copper Deposits," in Roland C. Allen, ed., *Mineral Resources of Michigan*, Michigan Geological and Biological Survey, no. 19 (Lansing, Mich.: Wynkoop Hallenbeck Crawford, 1915), 31–37; Charles Palache and Helen E. Vassar, "Some Minerals of the Keweenawan Copper Deposits: Pumpellyite, a New Mineral," *American Mineralogist* 10 (1925): 412–15.
20. *Rem.*, 3:657; Eliza Shepard Pumpelly to her sister, Rebecca Shepard, Sept. 9, Oct. 25, Nov. 6, 1871, Pumpelly Collection, pt. 2, box 4.
21. *Rem.*, 2:592; Harvard University, *Annual Report* (1865–66), 4, and (1874–75), 34–35; Harvard University, *Annual Catalogue* (1869–70), 72–74, Harvard University Archives, Pusey Library, Cambridge; William Morris Davis and Reginald A. Daly, "Geology and Geography, 1858–1928," in Morison, *Development of Harvard*, 307–09.

22. *Rem.*, 2:596; Eliza Pumpelly to her sister, Nellie Shepard Hill, Mar. 7, 1871, Pumpelly Collection, pt. 2, box 4.
23. William E. Parrish, *A History of Missouri*, 3 vols. (Columbia: University of Missouri Press, 1971–73), 3:227–30; Merrill, *State Geological Surveys*, 274–90.
24. *Rem.*, 2:603; Eliza Pumpelly to her mother's friend, Mrs. Fox, June 5, 1872, Pumpelly Collection, pt. 2, box 10; Arthur Winslow, "Geological Surveys in Missouri," *Journal of Geology* 2 (1894): 214–18; Raphael Pumpelly, ed., *Geological Survey of Missouri; Preliminary Report on the Iron Ores and Coal Fields, from the Field Work of 1872* (New York: Julius Bien, 1873), x–xiv.
25. Garland C. Broadhead, Fielding B. Meek, and B. F. Shumard, *Reports on the Geological Survey of the State of Missouri, 1855–1871* (Jefferson City, Mo.: Regan and Carter, 1873), 3; Turner, "Survey in Nineteenth-Century American Geology," 315; *Rem.*, 2:603–04.
26. Raphael Pumpelly, "Notes on the Geology of Pilot Knob and its Vicinity," in Pumpelly, *Geological Survey of Missouri*, 3–28; *American Journal of Science*, 3d ser., 7 (1874): 61–62; Thomas Sterry Hunt, "The Geological Survey of Missouri," *American Naturalist* 9 (1875): 240–45.
27. Gerald D. Nash, "The Conflict Between Pure and Applied Science in Nineteenth Century Public Policy: The California State Geological Survey, 1860–1874," *Isis* 55 (1963): 217–28; Pyne, *Grove Karl Gilbert*, 32.
28. Ellis Yochelson, "Fielding Bradford Meek," in *DSB*, 9:255–56; Charles A. White, "Biographical Sketch of Fielding Bradford Meek," *American Geologist* 18 (1896): 337–50; Raphael Pumpelly to Fielding B. Meek, Apr. 11, June 5, Oct. 25, 1872, Fielding B. Meek Papers, 1843–77, Smithsonian Institution Archives.
29. Fielding B. Meek to Raphael Pumpelly, Apr. 18, June 6 and 16, 1872, Pumpelly File, Archives of the Missouri Department of Natural Resources, Division of Geology and Land Survey, Rolla, Missouri.
30. Fielding B. Meek to Raphael Pumpelly, Nov. 3, 1872, in ibid.
31. Dupree, *Science in the Federal Government*, 277–79; A. Ross Eckler, *The Bureau of the Census* (New York: Praeger, 1972); Carroll D. Wright, *The History and Growth of the United States Census* (1900; reprint, New York: Johnson Reprint, 1966), 58–69.
32. United States Bureau of the Census, *Tenth Census Reports*, 22 vols. (Washington, D.C.: Government Printing Office, 1883–86); Eckler, *Bureau of the Census*, 113.
33. Clarence King, *First Annual Report of the United States Geological Survey* (Washington, D.C.: Government Printing Office, 1880), 75–79. On the establishment of the USGS and the events leading up to it, see Thomas G. Manning, *Government in Science: The U.S. Geological Survey, 1867–1894* (Lexington: University of Kentucky Press, 1967); Rabbitt, *Minerals, Lands*, 1:263–88.
34. Wilkins, *Clarence King*.
35. King, *First Annual Report*, 13–14; Wilkins, *Clarence King*, 300.
36. Biographies of the three men found in *National Academy of Sciences Biographical Memoirs* are: George P. Merrill, "George Ferdinand Becker," 11 (1924): 1–19; Arnold Hague, "Samuel Franklin Emmons," 7 (1913): 307–34; Joseph P. Iddings, "Arnold Hague," 9 (1919): 19–38.

37. Rabbitt, *Minerals, Lands,* 2:25, 29–31, 47–50. The results of the two mineral surveys were Samuel Franklin Emmons and G. F. Becker, *Statistics and Technology of the Precious Metals,* Tenth Census Reports, vol. 13 (1885), and Raphael Pumpelly, ed., *Report on the Mining Industries of the United States (Exclusive of the Precious Metals),* Tenth Census Reports, vol. 15 (1886), hereafter cited as Pumpelly, *Mining Industries.*
38. Raphael Pumpelly to Clarence King, Feb. 22, 1880, Letters Received by the United States Geological Survey, 1879–1902, Record Group 57, National Archives; Pumpelly, *Mining Industries,* "Introductory Remarks," xxi–xxiii.
39. Pumpelly, *Mining Industries,* xxv, 855–988.
40. Ibid., xxi. The questions are reprinted in Wright, *History and Growth,* 538–45.
41. Wright, *History and Growth,* 549–79; Pumpelly, *Mining Industries,* xxiv.
42. King, *First Annual Report,* 4, 69–79.
43. Raphael Pumpelly to Clarence King, Sept. 10, 1880, in ibid., 58–59; Pumpelly, *Mining Industries,* xxii. Pumpelly summarized the work on the iron ores in his article "Geographical and Geological Distribution of the Iron Ores of the United States," in *Mining Industries,* 3–36.
44. Bailey Willis, "Memorial of Raphael Pumpelly," *Geological Society of America Bulletin* 36 (1925): 72; *Rem.,* 2:618–23; Andrew A. Blair, "The Methods Employed in the Analysis of Iron Ores," in Pumpelly, *Mining Industries,* 509–27.
45. Bailey Willis, *A Yanqui in Patagonia* (Palo Alto, Calif.: Stanford University Press, 1947), 5–6; Willis, "Memorial," 72.
46. Raphael Pumpelly to Bailey Willis, Oct. 13, 1879, Bailey Willis Collection, Huntington Library.
47. Willis, *Yanqui in Patagonia,* 6–8; "Diary of a Trip to Vermillion Lake, Minn. Oct. 3–Nov. 23, 1880," Bailey Willis Collection; Willis, "Memorial," 72–73.
48. Ralph S. Tarr, *Economic Geology of the United States* (New York: Macmillan, 1894), 119.
49. Rabbitt, *Minerals, Lands,* 2:57–60.
50. Charles R. Wood, *The Northern Pacific: Main Street of the Northwest* (Seattle: Superior, 1968).
51. Ibid., 18–28; James Blaine Hedges, *Henry Villard and the Railways of the Northwest* (New Haven: Yale University Press, 1930).
52. Hedges, *Henry Villard,* 64–66; *Memoirs of Henry Villard, Journalist and Financier, 1835–1900,* 2 vols. (Boston: Houghton Mifflin, 1904), 2:503; *Rem.,* 2:624.
53. *Rem.,* 2:624; Raphael Pumpelly to John Wesley Powell, n.d., USGS Letters Received, roll 11.
54. Raphael Pumpelly, *Northern Transcontinental Survey, First Annual Report* (New York: E. Wells Sackett and Rankin, 1882); part of the NTS annual report was included in Merrill, *State Geological Surveys,* app. 2, 539–44; a copy of the report is in the Bailey Willis Collection; *Rem.,* 2:626.
55. NTS annual reports for 1882 and 1883.
56. Richard J. Chorley, Robert P. Beckinsale, and Antony J. Dunn, *The Life and Work of William Morris Davis,* vol. 2 of Chorley, Dunn, and Beckinsale, *The History of the Study of Landforms* (London: Methuen, 1973), 160–63; William Morris Davis, "Relation of the Coal of Montana to the Older Rocks," in Pumpelly, *Mining Industries,* 711.

57. Chorley, Beckinsale, and Dunn, *William Morris Davis*, 160–62.
58. Waldemar Lindgren, "The Eruptive Rocks of Montana," in Pumpelly, *Mining Industries*, 719–37; Kirtley Mather, "Waldemar Lindgren," in *DSB*, 8:370–71.
59. Frank A. Gooch, "The Conversion of Lignite into Fuel of High Heating Power," in Pumpelly, *Mining Industries*, 791–96; Pumpelly, *NTS, First Annual Report*, 11; *Rem.*, 2:626.
60. John Wesley Powell, *Report on the Lands of the Arid Region of the United States*, 2d ed. (1879; reprint, ed. Wallace Stegner, Cambridge: Harvard University Press, 1962); Stegner, *Beyond the Hundredth Meridian*, chap. 3, "Blueprint for a Dryland Democracy," 202–42. Quotations on 219 and 212.
61. Pumpelly, *NTS, First Annual Report*, 7–8.
62. Ibid., 7.
63. Ibid., 11; W. W. Campbell, "Edward Singleton Holden," *National Academy of Sciences Biographical Memoirs* 8 (1916): 358–72.
64. Pumpelly, *NTS, First Annual Report*, 4, 11–12; Rabbitt, *Minerals, Lands*, 2:160.
65. Pumpelly, *NTS, First Annual Report*, 4; Slate, "Eugene Hilgard," 93–155; Eugene W. Hilgard, *Map Bulletin No. 1: Yakima Region, Colville Region, Washington Territory* (New York: Julius Bien, 1883). Copy seen at the Huntington Library.
66. Alfred Rehder, "Charles Sprague Sargent," *Journal of the Arnold Arboretum* 8 (1927): 69–86; Stephanie B. Sutton, *Charles Sprague Sargent and the Arnold Arboretum* (Cambridge: Harvard University Press, 1970); Pumpelly, *NTS, First Annual Report*, 13–14.
67. Gilbert Thompson, Acting Chief Topographer, USGS, to John Wesley Powell, Jan. 26, 1882, USGS Letters Received; Pumpelly, *NTS, First Annual Report*, 6.
68. Pumpelly, *NTS, First Annual Report*, 4, 8–9; Allen D. Wilson, *Map of the Crazy Mountains and Vicinity*, and *Maps of Judith Basin*, and *Map of Yakima Region* (New York: Julius Bien, 1882). Copies seen at the Huntington Library.
69. Raphael Pumpelly to John Wesley Powell, May 10, 1882, USGS Letters Received.
70. Quoted in Slate, "Eugene Hilgard," 138–40.
71. Sutton, *Charles Sprague Sargent*, 145.
72. Raphael Pumpelly, "First N.T. Survey Trip, 1881," Pumpelly Collection, pt. 1, box 1.
73. *Rem.*, 2:628–37; Raphael Pumpelly, "NTS Notebook, 1882," Pumpelly Collection, pt. 1, box 1.
74. Pumpelly, "NTS Notebook, 1882," entry for July 7.
75. *Rem.*, 2:642–43.
76. Raphael Pumpelly, "NTS Notebook, 1883," Pumpelly Collection, pt. 1, box 1.
77. Willis, "Memorial," 73; Hedges, *Henry Villard*, 110–11; Villard, *Memoirs*, 2:317–18.
78. Pumpelly, *NTS, First Annual Report*, 6; Raphael Pumpelly, "The Northern Transcontinental Survey," in Merrill, *State Geological Surveys*, app. 2, 543–44; Raphael Pumpelly, *Northern Transcontinental Survey, Second Annual Report of the Director* (N.p., 1883), 3; Willis, "Memorial," 73. A copy of Pumpelly's 1883 report is in the library of the Arizona Historical Society.

79. Rem., 2:645–46.
80. Pumpelly, Mining Industries, 689–796; Merrill, State Geological Surveys, 544.
81. Slate, "Eugene Hilgard," 146–48; Bailey Willis, "Stratigraphy and Structure of the Puget Group, Washington," Geological Society of America Bulletin 9 (1898): 2–6.
82. Rem., 2:606.

5. Gentleman Geologist

1. Porter, "Gentlemen and Geology," 809–36.
2. Ibid., 811–15. See also Roy Porter, The Making of Geology: Earth Science in Britain, 1660–1815 (Cambridge: Cambridge University Press, 1977); David E. Allen, The Naturalist in Britain (London: Allen Lane, 1976); Charles C. Gillispie, The Edge of Objectivity (Princeton: Princeton University Press, 1960, fourth paperback printing, 1973), 295.
3. Porter, "Gentlemen and Geology," 817–25; Rudwick, Great Devonian Controversy, 17–41; Jack B. Morrell and Arnold Thackray, Gentlemen of Science: Early Years of the British Association for the Advancement of Science (Oxford: Clarendon, 1981).
4. Porter, "Gentlemen and Geology," 825–36. Humphry Davy quoted on 821.
5. Nathaniel S. Shaler, The Autobiography of Nathaniel Southgate Shaler, With a Supplementary Memoir by His Wife (Boston: Houghton Mifflin, 1909), 348–51.
6. Tamara Plakins Thornton, Cultivating Gentlemen: The Meaning of Country Life Among the Boston Elite, 1785–1860 (New Haven: Yale University Press, 1989).
7. Rem., 2:608, 656–59, 664–68.
8. Ibid., 664.
9. Ibid., 606.
10. Henry Clifton Sorby, "On Unencumbered Research—A Personal Experience," in Essays on the Endowment of Research, ed. Charles Appleton (London: H. S. King, 1876), 149–75.
11. Charles Keyes, "Raphael Pumpelly: Premier Explorer," Pan-American Geologist 40 (1923): 247.
12. Livingstone, Nathaniel Southgate Shaler; Rollin T. Chamberlin, "Biographical Memoir of Thomas Chrowder Chamberlin," National Academy of Sciences Biographical Memoirs 15 (1934): 307–407.
13. Brewster, Life and Letters of Josiah Dwight Whitney, 319–21.
14. Willis, "Memorial," 66.
15. Rem., 2:610; Holt, Garrulities, 54.
16. Porter, "Gentlemen and Geology," 833–36; Rem., 1:123.
17. Cyril Stanley Smith, "Henry Clifton Sorby," in DSB, 12:542–46; Norman Higham, A Very Scientific Gentleman: The Major Achievements of Henry Clifton Sorby (Oxford: Oxford University Press, 1963). The full history of the development of micrographic techniques in petrology has not yet been written. At present its history can be found in biographical memoirs, in the introduction to petrography textbooks, and in other scattered writings, such as Merrill, First One Hundred Years, chap. 14, "The Development of Micro-Petrology," 643–47; Arthur Holmes, Petrographic Methods and Calculations (London: Thomas Murby, 1921), 231–34; Beryl M. Hamilton, "The Influ-

ence of the Polarising Microscope on Late Nineteenth Century Geology," *Janus* 69 (1982): 51–68.
18. Merrill, *First One Hundred Years*, chap. 14; G. C. Amstutz, "Ferdinand Zirkel," in *DSB*, 14:625; Paul Ramdohr, "Harry (Karl Heinrich Ferdinand) Rosenbusch," in *DSB*, 11:547–48.
19. Holmes, *Petrographic Methods*, 233.
20. *Rem.*, 2:606–07, 614–15; Charles E. Wright, "Lithology," app. C in *Geological Survey of Michigan*, 2:213–31.
21. Ferdinand Zirkel, *Microscopical Petrography*, vol. 6 (1876) of *Report of the United States Geological Exploration of the Fortieth Parallel*, 7 vols. plus atlas (Washington, D.C.: Government Printing Office, 1870–80); Wilkins, *Clarence King*, 199–200; Samuel Franklin Emmons, "Clarence King," *American Journal of Science*, 4th ser., 13 (1902): 229.
22. Merrill, *First One Hundred Years*, 646; Edward S. Dana, "Abstract of a Paper on the Trap Rocks of the Connecticut Valley," *American Journal of Science*, 3d ser., 8 (1874): 390–92.
23. Willis, "Memorial," 68; *Rem.*, 2:606–07.
24. Raphael Pumpelly, "On Pseudomorphs of Chlorite after Garnet at the Spurr Mountain Iron Mine, Lake Superior," *American Journal of Science*, 3d ser., 10 (1875): 17–21, with pl. 2. A pseudomorph is "a mineral whose outward crystal form is that of another mineral; it is described as being 'after' the mineral whose outward form it has" (*Dictionary of Geological Terms*, 3d ed. [Garden City, N.Y.: Anchor Press/Doubleday, 1984], 409).
25. Raphael Pumpelly, "Metasomatic Development of the Copper-Bearing Rocks of Lake Superior," *Proceedings of the American Academy of Arts and Sciences* 13 (1878): 253–309.
26. Ibid., 254.
27. "Eruptive Copper-Bearing Rocks of Lake Superior" (anonymous review of "Metasomatic Development"), *American Journal of Science*, 3d ser., 16 (1878): 143–44; Waldemar Lindgren, "Metasomatic Processes in Fissure Veins," *AIME Transactions* 30 (1900): 578–692 (historical background on 580–91).
28. Waldemar Lindgren to Bailey Willis, Jan. 9, 1925, Bailey Willis Collection; quoted by Willis in "Memorial," 68–69.
29. Thomas C. Chamberlin, *Geology of Wisconsin, Survey of 1873–1879*, 4 vols. (Madison, Wis.: Commissioners of Public Printing, 1880), 3:vii, 27–49; Frederick A. P. Barnard and Arnold Guyot, eds., *Johnson's New Universal Cyclopedia: A Scientific and Popular Treasury of Useful Knowledge*, 3 vols. (New York: A. J. Johnson and Son, 1875); *Johnson's Universal Cyclopedia: A New Edition*, 8 vols. (New York: Appleton, 1899), 6:328–31.
30. *Rem.*, 2:611–14.
31. Ian J. Smalley, ed., *Loess: Lithology and Genesis*, Benchmark Papers in Geology, vol. 26 (Stroudsburg, Pa.: Dowden, Hutchinson and Ross, 1975), 3–4.
32. Charles A. White, *Report on the Geological Survey of the State of Iowa*, 2 vols. (Des Moines: Mills and Co., 1870), 1:103–17.
33. Raphael Pumpelly, "Richthofen's China," *Nation* 26 (1878): 231–32, 243–44; idem, "The Relation of Secular Rock-Disintegration to Loess, Glacial Drift, and Rock Basins," *American Journal of Science*, 3d ser., 17 (1879): 133–44.
34. Pumpelly, "Richthofen's China," 231.
35. Pumpelly, "Secular Rock-Disintegration," 134.

36. Ibid., 136–44.
37. Eugene W. Hilgard, "The Loess of the Mississippi Valley and the Eolian Hypothesis," *American Journal of Science,* 3d ser., 18 (1879): 106–12.
38. Thomas C. Chamberlin and Rollin D. Salisbury, "The Driftless Area of the Upper Mississippi," in USGS, *Sixth Annual Report* (Washington, D.C.: Government Printing Office, 1885), 205–307; Thomas C. Chamberlin, "Supplementary Hypothesis Respecting the Origin of the Loess of the Mississippi Valley," *Journal of Geology* 5 (1897): 801.
39. Thomas C. Chamberlin, "Studies for Students: The Method of Multiple Working Hypotheses," *Journal of Geology* 5 (1897): 837–48. For a discussion of Chamberlin's methodology see Stephen J. Pyne, "Methodologies for Geology: G. K. Gilbert and T. C. Chamberlin," *Isis* 69 (1978): 413–24.
40. Willis, "Memorial," 55; Bohumil Shimek, "The Distribution of Loess Fossils," *Journal of Geology* 7 (1899): 122–40.
41. Herbert E. Gregory, "A Century of Geology—Steps of Progress in the Interpretation of Land Forms," *American Journal of Science,* 4th ser., 46 (1918): 123–24.
42. Raphael Pumpelly, "Interdependent Evolution of Oases and Civilizations," *Geological Society of America Bulletin* 17 (1906): 637–46; Gregory, "Century of Geology," 124.
43. *Rem.,* 2:678–79.
44. Van Wyck Brooks, *New England: Indian Summer, 1865–1915* (New York: Dutton, 1940), 12–13; M. A. DeWolfe Howe, ed., *Later Years of the Saturday Club, 1870–1920* (Boston: Houghton Mifflin, 1927).
45. *Rem.,* 2:554, 580; Allan Nevins, "The Century, 1847–1866," in Century Association, *The Century, 1847–1946* (New York: Century Association, 1947), 16, 23, 387; membership lists, Century Club archives.
46. *Rem.,* 2:582–83.
47. Henry Steele Commager, "The Century, 1887–1906," in *The Century,* 60.
48. Nevins, "The Century," 24–29; *Rem.,* 2:584; Wilkins, *Clarence King,* 209–10, 256.
49. Rollin T. Chamberlin to Bailey Willis, Nov. 24, 1924, Bailey Willis Collection.
50. *Rem.,* 2:582; John La Farge, "An Essay on Japanese Art," in Pumpelly, *Across America and Asia,* 195–202; Henry Adams, "John La Farge's Discovery of Japanese Art—A New Perspective on the Origins of Japonisme," *Art Bulletin* 67 (1985): 473–82.
51. Holt, *Garrulities,* 282–86.
52. Henry Adams, *The Education of Henry Adams,* private edition of 1907, reprinted in *Henry Adams: Novels, Mont Saint Michel, The Education,* ed. Ernest Samuels and Jayne N. Samuels (New York: Library of America, 1983), 800, 1002, 1130–41. The standard biography of Adams is found in the three volumes by Ernest Samuels, all published by Harvard University Press: *The Young Henry Adams* (1948), *Henry Adams: The Middle Years* (1958), *Henry Adams: The Major Phase* (1964). *Henry Adams* (Cambridge: Harvard University Press, 1989) is an abridgement of the previous three volumes.
53. *The Letters of Mrs. Henry Adams, 1865–1883,* ed. Ward Thoron (Boston: Little, Brown, 1936), 442.

54. Otto Friedrich, *Clover* (New York: Simon and Schuster, 1979); Henry Adams to Raphael Pumpelly, May 21, 1885, in *The Letters of Henry Adams*, ed. J. C. Levenson et al., 6 vols. (Cambridge: Harvard University Press, 1982–88), 2:612.
55. Adams, *Education*, 1004–06; Patricia O'Toole, *The Five of Hearts: An Intimate Portrait of Henry Adams and His Friends, 1880–1918* (New York: Random House, 1990; Ballantine Books, 1991).
56. R. P. Blackmur, *Henry Adams*, ed. Veronica A. Makowsky (New York: Harcourt Brace Jovanovich, 1980), 107–08; Wilkins, *Clarence King*; Adams, *Education*, 1036–39.
57. Wilkins, *Clarence King*, 357.
58. Henry Adams, "A Letter to American Teachers of History," in *The Degradation of the Democratic Dogma*, ed. Brooks Adams (New York: Macmillan, 1920).
59. Henry Adams to Charles Milnes Gaskell, June 6, 1909, in Adams, *Letters*, 6:250–51. The impact of Kelvin on nineteenth-century thought is discussed by Stephen G. Brush, *The Temperature of History: Phases of Science and Culture in the Nineteenth Century* (New York: Burt Franklin, 1978), and M. Norton Wise and Crosbie Smith, *Energy and Empire: A Biographical Study of Lord Kelvin* (Cambridge: Cambridge University Press, 1989). Also see William H. Jordy, *Henry Adams: Scientific Historian* (New Haven: Yale University Press, 1952).
60. Raphael Pumpelly to Henry Adams, May 8, 1910, summarized by Samuels, *Adams: Major Phase*, 487.
61. Henry Adams to Raphael Pumpelly, May 19, 1910, in Adams, *Letters*, 6:339–42. David R. Contosta, in *Henry Adams and the American Experiment* (Boston: Little, Brown, 1980), 98, writes that Adams's "genteel anti-Semitism" was, as for others of his class, an expression of the patrician's insecurity in the face of massive immigration and the new businessman entrepreneur. No evidence whatever of anti-Semitism exists in Pumpelly's writings.
62. Henry Adams to Raphael Pumpelly, n.d., Pumpelly Collection, pt. 2, box 2.
63. *Rem.*, 2:761; Livingstone, *Nathaniel Southgate Shaler*, 6–7, 86–117; James R. Moore, *The Post-Darwinian Controversies: A Study of the Protestant Struggle to Come to Terms with Darwin in Great Britain and America, 1870–1900* (Cambridge: Cambridge University Press, 1979).
64. Henry Adams, *Esther: A Novel* (New York: Henry Holt, 1884), reprinted in Adams, *Novels*, 185–335; quotations on 294–95. King was also a model for Strong, according to Wilkins, *Clarence King*, 350.
65. *Rem.*, 1:14–15, 2:606, 500–501.
66. Ibid., 2:773–74.
67. Rollin T. Chamberlin to Bailey Willis, Nov. 24, 1924, Bailey Willis Collection.
68. Charles K. Leith to Bailey Willis, Nov. 19, 1924, in ibid.
69. Hans Baumgartel, "Alexander von Humboldt: Remarks on the Meaning of Hypothesis in His Geological Researches," in *Toward a History of Geology*, ed. Cecil J. Schneer (Cambridge: Massachusetts Institute of Technology Press, 1969), 20; Willis, "Memorial," 83.

6. With the United States Geological Survey

1. John C. Branner, "The Relations of the State and National Surveys to Each Other and to the Geologists of the Country," *American Geologist* 6 (1890): 295–309; Thomas C. Chamberlin, "Editorial," *Journal of Geology* 15 (1907): 70. On the history of the USGS under Powell, see Stegner, *Beyond the Hundredth Meridian*, 269–367; Manning, *Government in Science;* Rabbitt, *Minerals, Lands*, 2:57–239.
2. Wallace Stegner, "John Wesley Powell," in *DSB*, 11:118–20; idem, *Beyond the Hundredth Meridian*, 249–69.
3. USGS, *Sixth Annual Report*, xxiii–xxvii.
4. USGS, *Seventh Annual Report* (Washington, D.C.: Government Printing Office, 1886), 17–18; idem, *Ninth Annual Report* (Washington, D.C.: Government Printing Office, 1888), 8–10.
5. Manning, *Government in Science*, 122–50; Rabbitt, *Minerals, Lands*, 2:87–126. The complete testimony of the Allison Commission is given in U.S. Congress, *Testimony before the Joint Commission to Consider the Present Organization of the Signal Service* . . . , 49th Cong., 1st sess., S. Misc. Doc. 82, 1886 (hereafter cited as *Testimony*).
6. Alexander Agassiz to Thomas Henry Huxley, Oct. 16, 1888, in Agassiz, *Letters*, 231; Alexander Agassiz to Hon. Hilary A. Herbert, Dec. 2, 1885, in *Testimony*, 1014–16.
7. John Wesley Powell to Hon. William B. Allison, Chairman, Feb. 26, 1886, in *Testimony*, 1070–84.
8. Ibid., 1081; *Rem.*, 2:663.
9. *Testimony*, 1084.
10. Manning, *Government in Science*, 128; *Engineering and Mining Journal* 39 (June 13, 1885): 409.
11. *Engineering and Mining Journal* 39 (June 20, 1885): 420.
12. Grove Karl Gilbert, ed., *John Wesley Powell: A Memorial to an American Explorer and Scholar* (Chicago: Open Court, 1903), 67–68.
13. Pyne, *Grove Karl Gilbert*, 117.
14. Willis, "Memorial," 52.
15. Louis M. Prindle and Eleanora Bliss Knopf, "Geology of the Taconic Quadrangle," *American Journal of Science*, 5th ser., 24 (1932): 301–02.
16. On the history of the controversy, see Merrill, *First One Hundred Years*, chap. 12, "The Taconic Question," 594–614; Schneer, "Taconic Controversy," 173–91.
17. Secord, *Cambrian-Silurian Dispute;* Rudwick, *Great Devonian Controversy;* Schneer, "Taconic Controversy," 191.
18. William North Rice, "The Geology of James Dwight Dana," in William North Rice et al., *Problems of American Geology* (New Haven: Yale University Press, 1915), 26–32; James Dwight Dana to William B. Dwight, Nov. 9, 1886, Dana-Dwight Letters, New York State Library, cited in Prendergast, "James Dwight Dana," 563–65.
19. Third International Geological Congress, Berlin, 1885, *Comptes Rendu* (Berlin: A. W. Schade, 1888), A78, cited in Schneer, "Taconic Controversy," 189.
20. Raphael Pumpelly, John Eliot Wolff, and T. Nelson Dale, *Geology of the Green*

Mountains in Massachusetts, USGS Monograph 23 (Washington, D.C.: Government Printing Office, 1894), xiii. The Green Mountain monograph consists of three parts: pt. 1, Pumpelly, "General Structure and Correlation," 1–34; pt. 2, Wolff, "The Geology of Hoosac Mountain and Adjacent Territory," 35–118; pt. 3, Dale, "Mount Greylock: Its Structural and Areal Geology," 119–96.

21. Albert Heim, *Untersuchen über den Mechanismus der Gebirgsbildung,* 2 vols. and atlas (Basel: Benno Schwabe, 1878); Richard J. Chorley, "Albert Heim," in *DSB,* 6:227–28; Bailey Willis, "American Geology, 1850–1900," *Science* 96 (1942): 169; Greene, *Geology in the Nineteenth Century,* 195–98.
22. Greene, *Geology in the Nineteenth Century,* 259–60, 294. Greene provides the best survey to date of European and American mountain-building theories in chap. 5, "The Debate in North America, 1840–1873."
23. Pumpelly, "General Structure," 7–8; Herman Melville to Nathaniel Hawthorne, July 22, 1851, in *The Norton Anthology of American Literature,* 2 vols., ed. Ronald Gottesman et al., 1:2077 (New York: W. W. Norton, 1979).
24. Pumpelly, "General Structure," xiv.
25. "Thomas Nelson Dale," in *NCAB,* 15:152–53; "Obituary: Thomas Nelson Dale," *Science* 86 (1937): 603.
26. Charles Palache, "Memorial to John Eliot Wolff," *Proceedings of the Geological Society of America for 1940* (1941): 247–53.
27. William H. Hobbs, *An Explorer-Scientist's Pilgrimage: The Autobiography of William Herbert Hobbs* (Ann Arbor, Mich.: J. W. Edwards, 1952), 8–9.
28. R. S. Bassler, "Memorial of August F. Foerste," *Proceedings of the Geological Society of America for 1936* (1937): 143–45.
29. William Morris Davis, "The Triassic Formation of Connecticut," in USGS, *Eighteenth Annual Report* (Washington, D.C.: Government Printing Office, 1898), pt. 2, 1–192; Chorley, Beckinsale, and Dunn, *William Morris Davis,* 153–54.
30. Jack B. Morrell, "The Chemist Breeders: The Research Schools of Liebig and Thomas Thomson," *Ambix* 19 (1972): 1–46; James A. Secord, "The Geological Survey of Great Britain as a Research School, 1839–1855," *History of Science* 24 (1986): 223–75.
31. Rudwick, *Great Devonian Controversy,* 9–10; Thomas S. Kuhn, *The Structure of Scientific Revolutions,* rev. ed. (Chicago: University of Chicago Press, 1970); Michael Polanyi, *The Tacit Dimension* (New York: Doubleday, 1966).
32. Raphael Pumpelly, Appalachian Notebooks, vol. 1, 1885, Pumpelly Collection, pt. 1, box 1.
33. Pumpelly, *Geology of the Green Mountains,* xiv; Dale, "Mount Greylock," 133.
34. Pumpelly, Appalachian Notebooks, vol. 2, Oct. 1885–Sept. 1887; vol. 3, 1887–90.
35. Ibid., vol. 1, Sept. 17–27, 1885.
36. Pumpelly, "General Structure," 11–12.
37. Prindle and Knopf, "Taconic Quadrangle," 271; Rolfe S. Stanley and Nicholas M. Ratcliffe, "Tectonic Synthesis of the Taconian Orogeny in Western New England," *Geological Society of America Bulletin* 96 (1985): 1234.
38. Wolff, "Hoosac Mountain," 69–70; Pumpelly, "General Structure," 8–9.
39. Pumpelly, "General Structure," 7–10; Wolff, "Hoosac Mountain," 106.
40. Raphael Pumpelly, "Report of Mr. Raphael Pumpelly," in USGS, *Twelfth*

Annual Report (Washington, D.C.: Government Printing Office, 1892), 67–70.
41. Wolff, "Hoosac Mountain," 48–59, 106.
42. Dale, "Mount Greylock," 125–27; Willis, "Memorial," 77.
43. Pumpelly, "General Structure," 29; Raphael Pumpelly, "On the Fossils of Littleton, New Hampshire," *American Journal of Science*, 3d ser., 35 (1888): 79–80.
44. Pumpelly, "General Structure," 30–34; Raphael Pumpelly, "The Relation of Secular Rock-Disintegration to Certain Transitional Crystalline Schists," *Geological Society of America Bulletin* 2 (1891); 209–24.
45. Pumpelly, Appalachian Notebooks, vol. 2, Oct. 1885–Sept. 1887, 67–69; vol. 3, 1887–90; "Report of Mr. G. K. Gilbert," in USGS, *Eleventh Annual Report* (Washington, D.C.: Government Printing Office, 1891), pt. 1, 53.
46. Charles R. Van Hise, "Principles of North American Pre-Cambrian Geology," in USGS, *Sixteenth Annual Report* (Washington, D.C.: Government Printing Office, 1896), pt. 1, 830; Bailey Willis, *Geologic Structures* (New York: McGraw-Hill, 1923), 196.
47. J. F. Kemp, "Geology of the Green Mountains in Massachusetts," *Science* 2 (1895): 699–700; Willis, "Memorial," 77; *Rem.*, 2:647.
48. N. H. Winchell, "Some Objections to the Term Taconic Considered," *American Geologist* 1 (1888): 162–72; Stanley and Ratcliffe, "Tectonic Synthesis."
49. USGS geologist David Love, quoted in John McPhee, *Rising from the Plains* (New York: Farrar, Straus, and Giroux, 1986), 152–53.
50. Henry Adams to Elizabeth Cameron, Apr. 8, 1901, in Adams, *Letters*, 5:231–32.
51. John Wesley Powell, "Summary of Work on Algonkian and Archean Rocks," in USGS, *Fourteenth Annual Report* (Washington, D.C.: Government Printing Office, 1894), pt. 1, 102–04.
52. Fourth International Geological Congress, London, 1888, *Comptes Rendu* (London: Delau, 1891), A86.
53. Ibid., A17; Grove Karl Gilbert to Archibald Geikie, in Pyne, *Grove Karl Gilbert*, 121; William B. N. Berry, *Growth of a Prehistoric Time Scale, Based on Organic Evolution*, rev. ed. (Palo Alto, Calif.: Blackwell Scientific, 1987), 116.
54. Raphael Pumpelly and Charles R. Van Hise, "Observations Upon the Structural Relations of the Upper Huronian, Lower Huronian and Basement Complex on the North Shore of Lake Huron," *American Journal of Science*, 3d ser., 43 (1892): 224–32.
55. Maurice M. Vance, *Charles Richard Van Hise: Scientist Progressive* (Madison: State Historical Society of Wisconsin, 1960), 44–46; *Rem.*, 2:678; Willis, "Memorial," 75.
56. Willis, "Memorial," 75–76; Charles R. Van Hise, "Correlation Papers: Archean and Algonkian," *USGS Bulletin*, no. 86 (1892), 16.
57. Charles K. Leith to Bailey Willis, Nov. 19, 1924, Bailey Willis Collection.
58. Manning, *Government in Science*, 204–10; Rabbitt, *Minerals, Lands*, 2:203–11, 243.
59. Rabbitt, *Minerals, Lands*, 2:193; John W. Servos, "To Explore the Borderland: The Foundation of the Geophysical Laboratory of the Carnegie Institution of Washington," *Historical Studies in the Physical Sciences* 14 (1983): 147–85.
60. *Rem.*, 2:680–93.

61. Hugh Cabot to George P. McCallum, Jan. 6, 1932. This letter is with the papers of Dr. Hugh Cabot that have been placed in the temporary possession of Patricia Spain Ward, Chicago, Ill. (with no restriction on their use) by the late Elizabeth Cabot McRoberts and the late Arthur Tracy Cabot, Jr. I am grateful to Dr. Ward for bringing this letter to my attention.

7. Explorations in Turkestan

1. Pumpelly wrote at length about his explorations in Turkestan in *Rem.*, 2:698–744, 793–814. The scientific reports of the two expeditions, both published by the Carnegie Institution of Washington (CIW), are Raphael Pumpelly, ed., *Explorations in Turkestan, With an Account of the Basin of Eastern Persia and Sistan: Expedition of 1903* (1905), and *Explorations in Turkestan, Expedition of 1904: Prehistoric Civilizations of Anau, Origins, Growth, and Influence of Environment*, 2 vols. (1908).
2. J. P. Mallory, *In Search of the Indo-Europeans: Language, Archaeology and Myth* (New York: Thames and Hudson, 1989); Frank H. Hankins, "Aryans," in *Encyclopedia of the Social Sciences*, 15 vols. (New York: Macmillan, 1930–35), 2:264–65.
3. *Rem.*, 2:698–701.
4. Glyn E. Daniel, *A Hundred and Fifty Years of Archaeology*, 2d ed. (London: Duckworth, 1975), 182–86.
5. Thomas Henry Huxley, "The Aryan Question and Prehistoric Man," *Nineteenth Century* 28 (1890): 750–77, reprinted in Huxley, *Man's Place in Nature and Other Anthropological Essays* (Akron, Ohio: Werner, 1915), 272–329.
6. Otto Schrader, *Prehistoric Antiquities of the Aryan Peoples: A Manual of Comparative Philology and the Earliest Culture* (London: Charles Griffin, 1890), 148–49; Robert E. Dickinson, *The Makers of Modern Geography* (New York: Praeger, 1969), 62; Wilhelm Ratzel, "Der Ursprung der Arier in Geographischem Licht," *Die Umschau* 3 (1899): 825–27, 839–41.
7. William Z. Ripley, *The Races of Europe: A Sociological Study* (1900; reprint, New York: Johnson Reprint, 1965); Thomas F. Gossett, *Race: The History of an Idea in America* (Dallas: Southern Methodist University Press, 1963), 126; T. K. Penniman, *A Hundred Years of Anthropology*, 3d ed. (London: Duckworth, 1965), 98.
8. For a history of Aryanism, see Léon Poliakov, *The Aryan Myth: A History of Racist and Nationalist Ideas in Europe*, trans. Edmund Howard (New York: Basic Books, 1971); Haller, *Outcasts from Evolution*; Livingstone, *Nathaniel Southgate Shaler*, 121–57; *Rem.*, 2:548–49.
9. Willis, "Memorial," 79. Pumpelly's notes on Schrader are in his Transcaspian notebook 2, "Turkestan 1903–1904"; extracts from Ratzel are in notebook 1, "Transcaspian Notes, 1902," Pumpelly Collection, pt. 1, box 2.
10. Hankins, "Aryans," 265. The "Aryans" article was not included in the next edition of the encyclopedia.
11. Colin Renfrew, *Archaeology and Language: The Puzzle of Indo-European Origins* (New York: Cambridge University Press, 1987). Renfrew's ideas are presented in brief form in Renfrew, "The Origins of Indo-European Languages," *Scientific American* 261 (Oct. 1989): 106–14. Critiques of Renfrew's book and his reply to them appear in *Current Anthropology* 29 (1988): 437–68.

12. Raphael Pumpelly, "Trans-Caspia: A Field for Archaeological Research," Dec. 12, 1902, Pumpelly File, CIW Archives, Washington, D.C.
13. Pumpelly, *Explorations in Turkestan, 1904,* 1:xxxi.
14. CIW, *Yearbook* (Washington, D.C.: CIW, 1903–), 1 (1902): xiii; Nathan Reingold, "National Science Policy in a Private Institution: The Carnegie Institution of Washington," in *The Organization of Knowledge in Modern America, 1860–1920,* ed. Alexandra Oleson and John Voss (Baltimore: Johns Hopkins University Press, 1979), 313–41; Howard S. Miller, *Dollars for Research: Science and Its Patrons in Nineteenth-Century America* (Seattle: University of Washington Press, 1970), chap. 9.
15. Reported in "The Progress of Science," *Popular Science Monthly* 66 (1904–05): 287–89.
16. See reports in vols. 1, 2, and 3 for 1903, 1904, and 1905 of CIW, *Yearbook*.
17. CIW, *Yearbook* 1 (1903): xiii; Andrew Carnegie to Charles D. Walcott, Dec. 19, 1905, Charles D. Walcott Collection, Record Unit 7004, box 32, Smithsonian Institution Archives; CIW Trustees minutes, Dec. 8, 1903, 191, CIW Archives.
18. Reingold, "National Science Policy," 318–24; CIW Trustees minutes, Dec. 8, 1903, 190; Charles D. Walcott to Raphael Pumpelly, Dec. 17, 1902, Pumpelly File, CIW Archives.
19. Brooks Adams to Charles D. Walcott, Dec. 21, 1902; Walcott to Raphael Pumpelly, Dec. 4 and 17, 1902, Pumpelly File, CIW Archives.
20. Brooks Adams to Charles D. Walcott, Dec. 21, 1902, in ibid.
21. Brooks Adams, *The New Empire* (Boston: Houghton Mifflin, 1902); idem, *The Law of Civilization and Decay: An Essay on History* (New York: Macmillan, 1896; Vintage Books, 1955). In his introduction to this edition of *The Law,* Charles A. Beard commented favorably on Brooks Adams as an economic historian and called the book one of the outstanding documents of American intellectual history.
22. Reingold, "National Science Policy," 325; CIW, *Yearbook* 1 (1903): 73, app. B, 239–84; CIW, *Yearbook* 2 (1904): xxxv; CIW Executive Committee minutes, Dec. 9, 1903–May 18, 1904, 16, CIW Archives. The Peary Arctic Club funded Peary's Arctic expedition of 1905.
23. CIW, *Yearbook* 1 (1903): 174–81; CIW, *Yearbook* 4 (1905): 54–55; Reingold, "National Science Policy," 329.
24. Raphael Pumpelly to Charles D. Walcott, Nov. 25, 1902, Pumpelly File, CIW Archives.
25. Nathaniel S. Shaler, *Nature and Man in America* (New York: Scribner's, 1891), 13; William Coleman, "Science and Symbol in the Turner Frontier Hypothesis," *American Historical Review* 72 (1966): 22–49 (see especially 28–29, n. 19); Livingstone, *Nathaniel Southgate Shaler,* 174–75.
26. Pumpelly, *Explorations in Turkestan, 1904,* 1:xvi; idem, "Transcaspian Notes, 1902," 1–3, 6–12; *Rem.,* 2:746.
27. Raphael Pumpelly to Charles D. Walcott, Jan. 21, 1903, Pumpelly File, CIW Archives.
28. Ibid.
29. Chorley, Beckinsale, and Dunn, *William Morris Davis;* Preston E. James, *All Possible Worlds: A History of Geographical Ideas* (Indianapolis: Bobbs-Merrill, 1972), 350–65; William Morris Davis, "An Inductive Study of the Content of Geography," *American Geographical Society Bulletin* 38 (1906): 67–84, re-

printed in *Geographical Essays*, ed. Douglas Wilson Johnson (Boston: Ginn, 1909), 3–22. A regular column by Davis, "Current Notes on Physiography," had been appearing in *Science* since 1895.

30. Chorley, Beckinsale, and Dunn, *William Morris Davis*, 160–97; Sheldon Judson, "William Morris Davis," in *DSB*, 3:592–96.
31. Geoffrey Martin, *Ellsworth Huntington, His Life and Thought* (Hamden, Conn.: Archon Books, 1973), 3–28; Ellsworth Huntington, "The Basin of Eastern Persia and Sistan," in Pumpelly, *Explorations in Turkestan, 1903*, 219–315.
32. "Professor Richard Norton," in *Who Was Who, 1916–1928* (London: A. C. Black, 1929); Obituary of Richard Norton, *American Journal of Archaeology* 22 (1918): 343–44.
33. *Rem.*, 2:716; Pumpelly, *Explorations in Turkestan, 1904*, 1:xxvii; Daniel, *Hundred and Fifty Years of Archaeology*, 168–69; "Hubert Schmidt," in *Wer Ist's* (Berlin: Verlag Herrmann Degner, 1928), 1373.
34. *Rem.*, 2:694–96.
35. Ibid., 702–03.
36. Henry Adams to Raphael Pumpelly, Mar. 6, 1903, in Adams, *Letters*, 5:467–68.
37. Raphael Pumpelly to Daniel Coit Gilman, May 14, 1903, Pumpelly File, CIW Archives.
38. *The New Cambridge Modern History*, vol. 12, *The Shifting Balance of World Forces, 1898–1945*, ed. C. L. Mowat (Cambridge: Cambridge University Press, 1968), 335–38.
39. Raphael Pumpelly to Daniel Coit Gilman, May 14, 1903, Pumpelly File, CIW Archives.
40. Edward Allworth, ed., *Central Asia: A Century of Russian Rule* (New York: Columbia University Press, 1967).
41. *Rem.*, 2:703.
42. Humboldt, *Cosmos*, 2:520.
43. Pumpelly, "Transcaspian Notes, 1902," 4–5.
44. William Morris Davis to Daniel Coit Gilman, June 5, 1903, Pumpelly File, CIW Archives; Raphael Pumpelly, *Explorations in Turkestan, 1903*, 3–6; William Morris Davis, "A Journey Across Turkestan," in Pumpelly, *Explorations in Turkestan, 1903*, 23.
45. Davis, "A Journey," 24.
46. Quoted by Martin, *Ellsworth Huntington*, 35.
47. Gordon L. Davies, "Research by Debate: The Geomorphology of William Morris Davis," *History of Science* 13 (1975): 139. Huntington's comment is in a letter to Davis, Mar. 12, 1905, in which he was comparing his experience working in Asia with Robert Barrett to Davis's experience with Pumpelly, quoted by Gary S. Dunbar, "'Geography Rides, Geology Walks': The Barrett-Huntington Expedition to Central Asia in 1905," *Association of Pacific Geographers Yearbook* 45 (1983): 11.
48. Grove Karl Gilbert, *Lake Bonneville* (Washington, D.C.: Government Printing Office, 1890); Pyne, *Grove Karl Gilbert*, 134–45. Pumpelly's Transcaspian notebook, 1902, contains brief notes from various studies of the Caspian and Aral seas.
49. Pumpelly, "Transcaspian Notes, 1902," entrys for May 21–24, 1903; Davis, "A Journey," 24–40; Pumpelly, *Explorations in Turkestan, 1903*, 18.
50. Davis, "A Journey," 117.

51. Pumpelly, "Transcaspian Notes, 1902," May 27, 1903. Pumpelly's best description of the oasis world is in the report of the following year's expedition, "Ancient Anau and the Oasis-World," in Pumpelly, *Explorations in Turkestan, 1904*, 1:3–80.
52. William Morris Davis to Daniel Coit Gilman, May 28, 1903, Pumpelly File, CIW Archives.
53. Davis, "A Journey," 40–43.
54. Pumpelly, "Transcaspian Notes, 1902," May 30–June 4; Davis, "A Journey," 46–54.
55. Pumpelly, *Explorations in Turkestan, 1903*, 4–5.
56. *Rem.*, 2:707–12.
57. Raphael Welles Pumpelly, "Physiographic Observations Between the Syr Darya and Lake Kara Kul on the Pamir, in 1903," in Pumpelly, *Explorations in Turkestan, 1903*, 123–55. For a discussion of varve analysis see Frederick E. Zeuner, *Dating the Past, An Introduction to Geochronology*, 3d ed. (London: Methuen, 1952), and Frank Hole and Robert F. Heizer, *An Introduction to Prehistoric Archaeology*, 3d ed. (New York: Holt, Rinehart and Winston, 1973), 269–70.
58. Pumpelly, "Transcaspian Notes, 1902," July 8, 1903.
59. Davis, "A Journey," 84–117; Ellsworth Huntington, "A Geologic and Physiographic Reconnaissance in Central Turkestan," in Pumpelly, *Explorations in Turkestan, 1903*, 159–216; Thomas C. Chamberlin, "Glacial Phenomena of North America," in James Geikie, *The Great Ice Age and Its Relation to the Antiquity of Man*, 3d ed. (New York: Appleton, 1895), 724–74.
60. Pumpelly, "Transcaspian Notes, 1902," July 8, 1903. Pumpelly incorporated these notes into his report, "Ancient Anau and the Oasis-World," 9–10.
61. Davis, "A Journey," 54; William Morris Davis to Daniel Coit Gilman, Aug. 21, 1903, Pumpelly File, CIW Archives.
62. Pumpelly, *Explorations in Turkestan, 1903*, 13–15.
63. Daniel, *Hundred and Fifty Years of Archaeology*, 116–17; Bowler, *Fossils and Progress*.
64. Pumpelly, "Ancient Anau," 186, 54–55; Raphael Pumpelly, "The Migrations and the Aryan Problem," 6, manuscript in Bailey Willis Collection.
65. Pumpelly, "Transcaspian Notes, 1902," June 13–26, July 24–Aug. 1, 1903; idem, *Explorations in Turkestan, 1903*, 7–12. Technically a "kurgan" is a burial mound and a "tepe" is a town site. Pumpelly used "kurgan" for both.
66. Pumpelly, "Transcaspian Notes, 1902," Aug. 3, 1903.
67. Raphael Pumpelly to Charles D. Walcott, Nov. 12 and 14, 1903, Pumpelly File, CIW Archives.
68. CIW Executive Committee minutes, Jan. 30, 1902, to Nov. 23, 1903, 243; Raphael Pumpelly to Daniel Coit Gilman, Feb. 20, 1904, Pumpelly File, CIW Archives; *Rem.*, 2:716–17.
69. Diaries of Eliza Shepard Pumpelly, 1903–04, vol. 1, Jan. 22–Mar. 14, 1904, entry for Mar. 9, Pumpelly Collection, pt. 1, box 2.
70. Richard Norton, "Report on Archaeological Remains in Turkestan," in American School of Classical Studies in Rome, *Supplementary Papers*, 2 vols. (New York: Macmillan, 1905–08), 1:196–216.
71. Pumpelly, *Explorations in Turkestan, 1904*, 1:xxxiv–xxxv; *Langdon Warner Through His Letters*, ed. Theodore Bowie (Bloomington: Indiana University

Notes to Pages 187–198   **245**

Press, 1966), 5–8, 202; Huntington's field notebooks are with the Ellsworth Huntington Papers, Manuscripts and Archives, Yale University Library, New Haven.
72. Specialists contributing reports to Pumpelly's *Explorations in Turkestan, 1904* were: Frank A. Gooch, "Chemical Analyses of Metallic Implements and Products of Corrosion," 1:235–40; J. Ulrich Dürst, "Animal Remains from the Excavations at Anau, and the Horse of Anau in Its Relation to the Races of Domestic Horses," 2:341–442; Giuseppe Sergi, "Description of Some Skulls from the North Kurgan, Anau," 2:445–47; Thomas Mollison, "Description of Some Human Remains Found in the North Kurgan, Anau," 2:449–68; H. C. Schellenberg, "Wheat and Barley from the North Kurgan, Anau," 2:471–75.
73. Hubert Schmidt, "Archeological Excavations in Anau and Old Merv," in Pumpelly, *Explorations in Turkestan, 1904*, 1:83–210, trans. and ed. Pumpelly, pl. 7, between pp. 84 and 85; diaries of Eliza Shepard Pumpelly, 1903–04, Pumpelly Collection, pt. 1, box 2, entries for Mar. 25–Apr. 26, 1904.
74. Schmidt, "Archeological Excavations," 186.
75. Ibid.
76. *Rem.*, 2:812; Pumpelly, Transcaspian notebook 2, "Turkestan, 1903–1904," and Transcaspian notebook 3, "Turkestan, 1904," entries for Apr. 10–23, 1904, Pumpelly Collection, pt. 1, box 2. A map showing the location of the shafts is in Pumpelly, *Explorations in Turkestan, 1904*, vol. 1, facing p. 18.
77. Pumpelly, "Ancient Anau," 18–22, 50–54.
78. Ibid., 54–55; Pumpelly, *Explorations in Turkestan, 1904*, 1:xxxiv, 57.
79. *Rem.*, app. 2, 2:807–08. On the uncertainties of dating by growth of culture strata, see Hole and Heizer, *Prehistoric Archeology*, 276.
80. Pumpelly, "Ancient Anau," 23, 58–59, color pl. "Stratigraphic Chronology of the Cultures" facing p. 50.
81. *Rem.*, 2:808–09; Dürst, "Animal Remains," 435–36; Schellenberg, "Wheat and Barley"; Pumpelly, "Ancient Anau," 67–68.
82. Sergi, "Skulls," 446; Gooch, "Metallic Implements," 239; Pumpelly, "Ancient Anau," 69, 42–44.
83. *Rem.*, 2:732–33, 745.
84. Ibid., 748. Pumpelly's address was published as "Interdependent Evolution of Oases and Civilizations"; Eduard Suess, *The Face of the Earth*, 4 vols., trans. Hertha B. C. Sollas (Oxford: Clarendon Press, 1904–09), 1:i, 1–6. Greene, *Geology in the Nineteenth Century*, 158–59, describes this part of Suess's work.
85. Pumpelly, "Ancient Anau," 11–13.
86. Ibid.
87. Ibid., 66.
88. Arnold J. Toynbee, *A Study of History*, abridgement of volumes 1–6 by D. C. Somervell (New York: Oxford University Press, 1947), 167; Martin, *Ellsworth Huntington*, xvi.
89. Pumpelly, *Explorations in Turkestan, 1904*, 1:xxi.
90. Pumpelly, "Migrations." Page numbers following in the text refer to pages in the original manuscript.
91. *Rem.*, 2:812.

92. Mallory, *In Search of the Indo-Europeans*, 143, 144 (map). For current research on the subject, see issues of the *Journal of Indo-European Studies*.
93. Willis, "Memorial," 82; Bailey Willis to John C. Merriam, Apr. 8, 1936; Merriam to Willis, June 17, 1936, Bailey Willis Collection.
94. Holt, *Garrulities*, 228–29.
95. Henry Adams to Raphael Pumpelly, Mar. 9, 1909, in Adams, *Letters*, 6:234–35.
96. *Geographical Journal* 27 (1906): 395–97; *Nation* 76 (Mar. 5, 1903): 187, and 78 (Jan. 14, 1904): 26.
97. L. W. King, "Transcaspian Archaeology," *Nature* 83 (1910): 157–59.
98. Philip L. Kohl, ed., "The Bronze Age Civilization of Central Asia: Recent Soviet Discoveries," *Soviet Anthropology and Archeology* 19, nos. 1–2, 3–4 (1980–81): viii; the articles in these special issues are translations from the Russian. V. Gordon Childe, *Dawn of European Civilizations* (New York: Alfred A. Knopf, 1925), 23.
99. Kohl, "Bronze Age Civilization," viii–x; Swarajya P. Gupta, *Archaeology of Soviet Central Asia, and the Indian Borderlands*, 2 vols. (Delhi: B. R. Publishing, 1979), 2:53–132; Grahame Clark and Stuart Piggott, *Prehistoric Societies* (New York: Alfred A. Knopf, 1968), chap. 9, "Peasant Communities of Prehistoric Western Asia," 182–223.
100. John A. Gifford and George R. Rapp, Jr., "History, Philosophy, and Perspectives," in Rapp and Gifford, *Archaeological Geology* (New Haven: Yale University Press, 1985), 1–23; Kohl, "Bronze Age Civilizations," xxxii.
101. Gifford and Rapp, "History, Philosophy, and Perspectives," 10–11.

8. The End of Geology's Heroic Age

1. *Rem.*, 2:745–60.
2. Ibid., 756, 791; Bailey Willis to Raphael Pumpelly, Feb. 17, 1915, Pumpelly Collection, pt. 2, box 2.
3. Holt, *Garrulities*, 230; *Rem.*, 2:773.
4. Keyes, "Raphael Pumpelly," 241; John J. Stevenson, "Geological Methods in Earlier Days," *Popular Science Monthly* 86 (1915): 32. One example of the use of the term *Heroic Age* by a historian is William H. Goetzmann, "The Heroic Age of Western Geological Exploration," *American West* 16, no. 5 (1979): 4–13, 59–61. Keyes's use of the term shows that it was probably current in Pumpelly's lifetime.
5. Bailey Willis, "Memorial Tribute to Raphael Pumpelly," *Geological Society of America Bulletin* 35 (1924): 42–43; U. C. Knoepflmacher and G. B. Tennyson, eds., *Nature and the Victorian Imagination* (Berkeley and Los Angeles: University of California Press, 1977).
6. Chauncey C. Loomis, "The Arctic Sublime," in Knoepflmacher and Tennyson, *Nature and the Victorian Imagination*, 112.
7. *Rem.*, 2:752.
8. Ibid., 777.
9. Dickinson, *Makers of Modern Geography*; James, *All Possible Worlds*. The article on Pumpelly in the *Dictionary of Scientific Biography* lists geography as one of his fields.

10. Cannon, *Science in Culture*, 95.
11. Ibid., 96.
12. Wilkins, *Clarence King*, 365–411.
13. Raphael Welles Pumpelly to Bailey Willis, Jan. 29, 1924, Bailey Willis Collection.
14. Secord, "Geological Survey of Great Britain"; Morrell, "Chemist Breeders"; Robert G. Frank, Jr., *Harvey and the Oxford Physiologists: Scientific Ideas and Social Interaction* (Berkeley and Los Angeles: University of California Press, 1980); Gerald L. Geison, "Scientific Change, Emerging Specialties, and Research Schools," *History of Science* 19 (1981): 20–40.
15. Willis, "Memorial," 73.
16. Chamberlin, "Thomas Chrowder Chamberlin," 316–20.
17. Keyes, "Raphael Pumpelly," 250.
18. Willis, *Geologic Structures*, 189.
19. Willis, "Memorial Tribute," 43; N. H. Winchell, "Memorial of Edward Claypole," *American Geologist* 27 (1901): 247; Herman L. Fairchild, "Memorial of Joseph LeConte," *Geological Society of America Bulletin* 26 (1915): 47–57, quoted in Stephens, *Joseph LeConte*, 270.
20. Waldemar Lindgren to Bailey Willis, Jan. 9, 1925, Bailey Willis Collection.
21. *Rem.*, 2:678.
22. Raphael Welles Pumpelly to Bailey Willis, Jan. 29, 1924, Bailey Willis Collection.

Bibliography

A Note on Archives and Manuscript Sources

Pumpelly's papers are at the Henry E. Huntington Library, San Marino, California. Part 1, box 1 contains his field notebooks on Arizona, Japan, China, the Northern Transcontinental Survey, the Green Mountains, the southern Appalachians, and the Lake Superior region. Box 2 contains Pumpelly's notebooks for the Transcaspian expeditions of 1903 and 1904 and the diaries kept by his wife Eliza Shepard Pumpelly on the expedition of 1904. Part 2 consists of thirteen boxes containing the correspondence of Pumpelly, his mother and father, his brother and sister, and the extensive correspondence of his wife Eliza.

The Bailey Willis Collection at the Huntington Library includes not only the papers of Bailey Willis but also correspondence and records collected by Willis for his memorial of Pumpelly. With the Willis papers is Pumpelly's unpublished chapter entitled "The Migrations and the Aryan Problem," originally intended for inclusion in his *Explorations in Turkestan, Expedition of 1904*. Other sources at the Huntington Library are the Janin Family Collection, boxes 20 and 21, and the William H. Pettee Collection, boxes 1 and 2, both of which contain letters pertaining to mining education at the Freiberg Mining Academy in the 1850s and 1860s.

At the National Archives in Washington, D.C., are letters from and about Pumpelly in Letters Received by the United States Geological Survey, 1879–1902, Record Group 57, Records of the Geological Survey. Material relating to Pumpelly's work in China, including his report on the coal district of the Se-Shan, is in the Dispatches from United States Ministers to China, 1843–1906, Record Group 59, General Records of the Department of State.

The Smithsonian Institution Archives in Washington, D.C., contain rich sources of material on American science. Correspondence relating to Joseph Henry's publication of Pumpelly's report on China, Mongolia, and Japan is in Record Unit 26, Office of the Secretary, 1863–1879, Incoming Correspondence; Record Unit 32, Office of the Secretary, 1865–1879, Incoming Correspondence;

and Record Unit 33, Office of the Secretary, 1865–1891, Outgoing Correspondence. Also in the Smithsonian archives are the Charles D. Walcott Collection (Record Unit 7004) and the Fielding B. Meek Papers (Record Unit 7062).

In the Pumpelly File at the archives of the Carnegie Institution of Washington in Washington, D.C., are Pumpelly's grant proposal, a number of letters from Pumpelly and William Morris Davis to Daniel Coit Gilman and Charles D. Walcott, and other material relating to Pumpelly's expeditions to Turkestan. Also in the CIW Archives are the minute books of the Carnegie Institution's Board of Trustees and the Executive Committee.

With the William Phipps Blake Papers in the archives of the Arizona Historical Society, Tucson, are several volumes of Blake's diaries. Unfortunately, the diary kept while Blake was with Pumpelly in Japan is missing.

Other sources cited or consulted are:

George F. Becker Papers. Manuscripts Division, Library of Congress.
Anson Burlingame Papers. Manuscripts Division, Library of Congress.
William Morris Davis Papers. Houghton Library, Harvard University, Cambridge.
Samuel Franklin Emmons Papers. Manuscripts Division, Library of Congress.
James D. Hague Papers. Henry E. Huntington Library, San Marino, California.
Harvard University Archives, Pusey Library, Cambridge.
Ellsworth Huntington Papers. Manuscripts and Archives, Yale University Library, New Haven.
Clarence King Papers. Henry E. Huntington Library, San Marino, California.
Archives of the National Academy of Sciences, Washington, D.C.
Pumpelly File. Archives of the Missouri Department of Natural Resources, Division of Geology and Land Survey, Rolla, Missouri.
Charles Richard Van Hise letters. USGS Lake Superior Division Correspondence, State Historical Society of Wisconsin, Madison.
Henry Villard Collection. Baker Library, Harvard School of Business Administration, Boston.

Works By Raphael Pumpelly

1858 "Über einige Gletscher-Überreste der Insel Corsica." *Neues Jahrbuch für Mineralogie, Geognosie, Geologie*, 273–77.
1859 "Sur Quelques Traces de Glaciers dans l'île de Corse." *Sociètè Gèologique de France Bulletin*, 2d ser., 17: 78–82.
1863 "Mineralogical Sketch of the Silver Mines of Arizona." *Proceedings of the California Academy of Natural Sciences* 2: 127–39.
1866a "Combustibiles du Se-Shan, Chine." *Annales des Mines* 9.
1866b "Notice of an Account of Geological Observations in China, Japan and Mongolia." *American Journal of Science*, 2d ser., 41: 145–49.
1867a "The Coals from Se-Shan . . . from the dispatch of Raphael Pumpelly to Mr. Seward." *Friend of China*, Dec. 27, 1–2.
1867b *Geological Researches in China, Mongolia, and Japan, During the Years 1862 to 1865*. In Smithsonian Contributions to Knowledge, vol. 15. Washington, D.C.: Smithsonian Institution.

1868a "On the Delta Plain, and the Historical Changes in the Course of the Yellow River." *American Journal of Science*, 2d ser., 45: 219–24.
1868b *Prospectus of the Portage Lake and Lake Superior Ship Canal Company: Description of Canal; Its Commercial Importance; Lands Granted by Congress to the Company; Pine and Timber Lands; Iron and Copper Lands*. New York: W. L. Stone and J. T. Barron.
1868c "Western Policy in China." *North American Review* 106: 592–612.
1870 *Across America and Asia; Notes of a Five Years' Journey Around the World, and of Residence in Arizona, Japan and China*. 3d ed., rev. New York: Leypoldt and Holt.
1871 "The Paragenesis and Derivation of Copper and its associates on Lake Superior." *American Journal of Science*, 3d ser., 2: 188–98, 243–58, 347–55.
1872 With Thomas B. Brooks. "On the Age of the Copper-bearing Rocks of Lake Superior." *American Journal of Science*, 3d ser., 3: 428–32.
1873a "Copper-Bearing Rocks." In Board of Geological Survey, *Geological Survey of Michigan, Upper Peninsula, 1869–1873*. 2 vols. and Atlas of Maps, vol. 1, pt. 2. New York: Julius Bien.
1873b Raphael Pumpelly, ed. *Geological Survey of Missouri; Preliminary Report on the Iron Ores and Coal Fields, from the Field Work of 1872*, New York: Julius Bien.
1873c Review of *Reisen in Indien und Hochasein*, vol. 3, *Tibet*, by H. von Schlagintweit-Sakünlüski. *North American Review* 117: 485–90.
1874 With Thomas B. Brooks and Adolph Schmidt. *Iron Ores of Missouri and Michigan*. New York: G. P. Putnam's Sons.
1875a "On Pseudomorphs of Chlorite after Garnet at the Spurr Mountain Iron Mine, Lake Superior." *American Journal of Science*, 3d ser., 10: 17–21.
1875b "Ore Deposits." In *Johnson's New Universal Cyclopedia: A Scientific and Popular Treasury of Useful Knowledge*, edited by Frederick A. P. Barnard and Arnold Guyot. 3 vols. New York: A. J. Johnson and Son.
1876 "The Iron Ores of Missouri." *Engineering and Mining Journal* 22 (July 1): 1.
1877 "On the Influence of Marine Life and Currents in the Formation of Metalliferous Deposits." In Geological Survey of Kentucky, *Reports of Progress*, n.s., 2: 318–30.
1878a "Metasomatic Development of the Copper-Bearing Rocks of Lake Superior." *Proceedings of the American Academy of Arts and Sciences* 13: 253–309.
1878b "Mines of the Arizona Gold and Silver Mining Company." In W. F. Witherell, *Arizona as a Silver Country*, 13–14. Saint Louis: J. McKittrick.
1878c *Report on the Properties of the Excelsior Water and Mining Company, Smartsville, California*. Boston: T. R. Marvin and Son.
1878d "Richthofen's China." *Nation* 26: 231–32, 243–44.
1879a "The Relation of Secular Rock-Disintegration to Loess, Glacial Drift, and Rock Basins." *American Journal of Science*, 3d ser., 17: 133–44.
1879b Review of *United States Geological Exploration of the Fortieth Parallel*, vol. 1, *Systematic Geology*, by Clarence King. *American Journal of Science*, 3d ser., 17: 296–302.
1880 "Lithology of the Keweenawan System." In Thomas C. Chamberlin, *Geology of Wisconsin, Survey of 1873–1879*, 4 vols., 3:27–49. Madison, Wis.: Commissioners of Public Printing.

1881 "The Relation of Soils to Health; A Preliminary Report to the National Board of Health; Filtering Capacity of Soils." National Board of Health, *Bulletin,* 4th supp. Washington, D.C.: Government Printing Office.

1882 *Northern Transcontinental Survey, First Annual Report.* New York: E. Wells Sackett and Rankin.

1883 With George A. Smyth. "Second Report on the Results of an Investigation into the Filtering Capacity of Soils." In National Board of Health, *Annual Report,* Appendix O, 579–660. Washington, D.C.: Government Printing Office.

1885a "Composite Portraits of Members of the National Academy of Sciences." *Science,* original ser., 5: 378–79.

1885b "Report of Prof. Raphael Pumpelly." In USGS, *Sixth Annual Report,* 18. Washington, D.C.: Government Printing Office.

1886 United States. Census Office. *Report on the Mining Industries of the United States (Exclusive of the Precious Metals).* U.S. Tenth Census, vol. 15. Washington, D.C.: Government Printing Office.

1888a "On the Fossils of Littleton, New Hampshire." *American Journal of Science,* 3d ser., 35: 79–80.

1888b "Report of Prof. Raphael Pumpelly." In USGS, *Seventh Annual Report,* 60–61. Washington, D.C.: Government Printing Office.

1889a "Report of Prof. Raphael Pumpelly." In USGS, *Eighth Annual Report,* pt. 1, 124–25. Washington, D.C.: Government Printing Office.

1889b "Report of Prof. Raphael Pumpelly." In USGS, *Ninth Annual Report,* 75–76. Washington, D.C.: Government Printing Office.

1890 "Report of Prof. Raphael Pumpelly." In USGS, *Tenth Annual Report,* pt. 1, 114–16. Washington, D.C.: Government Printing Office.

1891a "The Relation of Secular Rock-Disintegration to Certain Transitional Crystalline Schists." *Geological Society of America Bulletin* 2: 209–24.

1891b "Report of Prof. R. Pumpelly." In USGS, *Eleventh Annual Report,* pt. 1, 64–65. Washington, D.C.: Government Printing Office.

1892a "Report of Mr. Raphael Pumpelly." In USGS, *Twelfth Annual Report,* pt. 1, 67–70. Washington, D.C.: Government Printing Office.

1892b With Charles R. Van Hise. "Observations Upon the Structural Relations of the Upper Huronian, Lower Huronian and Basement Complex on the North Shore of Lake Huron." *American Journal of Science,* 3d ser., 43: 224–32.

1893a "An Apparent Time-Break Between the Eocene and Chattahoochee Miocene in Southwestern Georgia." *American Journal of Science,* 3d ser., 46: 445–47.

1893b "Memorial of Thomas Sterry Hunt." *Geological Society of America Bulletin* 4: 379–93.

1893c "Reports of Mr. Raphael Pumpelly" (as head of Archean and New Jersey divisions). In USGS, *Thirteenth Annual Report,* pt. 1, 100–103. Washington, D.C.: Government Printing Office.

1894 With John Eliot Wolff and T. Nelson Dale. *Geology of the Green Mountains in Massachusetts.* USGS Monograph no. 23. Washington, D.C.: Government Printing Office.

1903 "Archeological and Physico-Geographical Reconnaissance in Turkestan." Carnegie Institution of Washington, *Yearbook* 2: 271–87.

1904a "Excavations in Turkestan." *Science* 20: 60–61.

1904b "Trans-Caspian Archeological Expedition." Carnegie Institution of Washington, *Yearbook* 3: 75–79.
1905 Raphael Pumpelly, ed. *Explorations in Turkestan, With an Account of the Basin of Eastern Persia and Sistan: Expedition of 1903*. Carnegie Institution of Washington Publication no. 26. Washington, D.C.: Carnegie Institution of Washington.
1906 "Interdependent Evolution of Oases and Civilizations." *Geological Society of America Bulletin* 17: 637–70.
1908 Raphael Pumpelly, ed. *Explorations in Turkestan, Expedition of 1904: Prehistoric Civilizations of Anau, Origins, Growth, and Influence of Environment*. 2 vols. Carnegie Institution of Washington Publication no. 73. Washington, D.C.: Carnegie Institution of Washington.
1918 *My Reminiscences*. 2 vols. New York: Henry Holt.
1920a "The Northern Transcontinental Survey." In George P. Merrill, *Contributions to a History of American State Geological and Natural History Surveys*, Appendix 2, 539–44. U.S. National Museum Bulletin 109. Washington, D.C.: Government Printing Office.
1920b *Travels and Adventures of Raphael Pumpelly, Mining Engineer, Geologist, Archaeologist and Explorer*. (Abridged edition by *My Reminiscences* for young readers.) New York: Henry Holt.
1965 *Pumpelly's Arizona: An Excerpt from Across America and Asia by Raphael Pumpelly, Comprising Those Chapters Which Concern the Southwest*. Edited by Andrew Wallace. Tucson: Palo Verde Press.

Secondary Sources

Abbott, C. C. "Timothy Abbott Conrad." *Popular Science Monthly* 47 (1895): 257–63.
Adams, Brooks. *The Law of Civilization and Decay: An Essay on History*. New York: Macmillan, 1896; Vintage Books, 1955.
———. *The New Empire*. Boston: Houghton Mifflin, 1902.
Adams, Henry. "A Letter to American Teachers of History." In *The Degradation of the Democratic Dogma*, edited by Brooks Adams. New York: Macmillan, 1920.
———. *The Letters of Henry Adams*. Edited by J. C. Levenson, Ernest Samuels, Charles Vandersee, and Viola Hopkins Winner. 6 vols. Cambridge: Harvard University Press, 1982–88.
———. *Novels, Mont Saint Michel, The Education*. Edited by Ernest Samuels and Jayne N. Samuels. New York: Library of America, 1983.
Adams, Henry. "John La Farge's Discovery of Japanese Art—A New Perspective on the Origins of Japonisme." *Art Bulletin* 67 (1985): 449–85.
Adams, Marian ["Clover"] Hooper. *The Letters of Mrs. Henry Adams, 1865–1883*. Edited by Ward Thoron. Boston: Little, Brown, 1936.
Agassiz, Alexander. *Letters and Recollections of Alexander Agassiz, With a Sketch of His Life and Work*. Edited by George R. Agassiz. Boston: Houghton Mifflin, 1913.
Aldrich, Michele L. "Geological Surveys, State." In *Dictionary of American History*, rev. ed., 8 vols., 3: 164–66. New York: Charles Scribner's Sons, 1976–78.

———. "New York Natural History Survey, 1836–1845." Ph.D. diss., University of Texas at Austin, 1974.
Allen, Roland C., and Helen M. Martin. "A Brief History of the Geological and Biological Survey of Michigan, 1837–1920." *Michigan History Magazine* 6 (1922): 675–750.
Allworth, Edward, ed. *Central Asia: A Century of Russian Rule.* New York: Columbia University Press, 1967.
America-Japan Society. *The First Japanese Embassy to the United States of America.* Compiled by C. Shibima. Tokyo: America-Japan Society, 1920.
Barrell, Joseph. "The Growth of Knowledge of Earth Structure." *American Journal of Science,* 4th ser., 46 (1918): 133–70.
Bassler, R. S. "Memorial of August F. Foerste." *Proceedings of the Geological Society of America for 1936* (1937): 143–45.
Bates, Ralph S. *Scientific Societies in the United States.* 3d ed. Cambridge: Massachusetts Institute of Technology Press, 1965.
Bates, Robert L., and Julia A. Jackson, eds. *Dictionary of Geological Terms.* 3d ed. Prepared under the direction of the American Geological Institute. Garden City, N.Y.: Anchor Press/Doubleday, 1984.
Berry, William B. N. *Growth of a Prehistoric Time Scale, Based on Organic Evolution.* Rev. ed. Palo Alto, Calif.: Blackwell Scientific, 1987.
Blackmur, R. P. *Henry Adams.* Edited by Veronica A. Makowsky. New York: Harcourt Brace Jovanovich, 1980.
Blake, William Phipps. "Silver and Copper Mining in Arizona." *Mining Magazine,* 2d ser., 1 (1859): 1–15.
Bowler, Peter J. *Fossils and Progress: Paleontology and the Idea of Progressive Evolution in the Nineteenth Century.* New York: Science History Publications, 1976.
Branner, John C. "The Relations of the State and National Surveys to Each Other and to the Geologists of the Country." *American Geologist* 6 (1890): 295–309.
Brewer, William H. *Up and Down California in 1860–1864: The Journal of William H. Brewer.* 3d ed. Edited by Francis P. Farquhar. Berkeley and Los Angeles: University of California Press, 1966.
Brewster, Edwin Tenney. *Life and Letters of Josiah Dwight Whitney.* Boston: Houghton Mifflin, 1909.
Brooks, Van Wyck. *New England: Indian Summer, 1865–1915.* New York: Dutton, 1940.
Brown, Rollo. "Cosmic Prospector." In *Lonely Americans.* 1929. Reprint. Freeport, N.Y.: Books for Libraries Press, 1970.
Browne, J. Ross. *Adventures in the Apache Country: A Tour Through Arizona and Sonora.* New York: Harper, 1869.
Bruce, Robert V. *The Launching of Modern American Science, 1846–1876.* New York: Alfred A. Knopf, 1987.
Brush, Stephen G. *The Temperature of History: Phases of Science and Culture in the Nineteenth Century.* New York: Burt Franklin, 1978.
Cannon, Susan Faye. *Science in Culture: The Early Victorian Period.* New York: Dawson and Science History Publications, 1978.
Capron, Horace. *Reports and Official Letters to the Kaitakushi.* Tokyo: Kaitakushi, 1875.
The Century, 1847–1946. New York: Century Association, 1947.
Chamberlin, Thomas C. "Seventy-five years of American Geology." *Science* 59 (1924): 127–35.

———. "Studies for Students: The Method of Multiple Working Hypotheses." *Journal of Geology* 5 (1897): 837–48.
———. "Supplementary Hypothesis Respecting the Origin of the Loess of the Mississippi Valley." *Journal of Geology* 5 (1897): 795–802.
Chappell, John E., Jr. "Climatic Change Reconsidered: Another Look at 'The Pulse of Asia.'" *Geographical Review* 60 (1970): 347–73.
Childe, V. Gordon. *The Aryans; A Study of Indo-European Origins*. New York: Alfred A. Knopf, 1926.
———. *Dawn of European Civilization*. New York: Alfred A. Knopf, 1925.
Chittenden, Russell H. *History of the Sheffield Scientific School of Yale University, 1846–1922*. New Haven: Yale University Press, 1928.
Chorley, Richard J., Robert P. Beckinsale, and Antony J. Dunn. *The Life and Work of William Morris Davis*. Vol. 2 of *The History of the Study of Landforms*. London: Methuen, 1973.
Church, John A. "Mining Schools in the United States." *North American Review* 112 (1871): 62–81.
Clark, Grahame, and Stuart Piggott. *Prehistoric Societies*. New York: Alfred A. Knopf, 1968.
Clarke, John M. *James Hall of Albany, Geologist and Palaeontologist, 1811–1898*. Albany, N.Y.: E. E. Rankin, 1921.
Cochrane, Rexmond C. *The National Academy of Sciences: The First Hundred Years, 1863–1963*. Washington, D.C.: National Academy of Sciences, 1978.
Coleman, William. "Science and Symbol in the Turner Frontier Hypothesis." *American Historical Review* 72 (1966): 22–49.
Corning, Frederick Gleason. *A Student Reverie: An Album of Saxony Days*. New York: Privately printed, 1920.
Cotta, Bernhard von. *A Treatise on Ore Deposits*. Translated from the 2d German edition by Frederick Prime, Jr. New York: Van Nostrand, 1870.
Crook, Thomas. *History of the Theory of Ore Deposits*. New York: Van Nostrand, 1933.
Daniel, Glyn E. *A Hundred and Fifty Years of Archaeology*. 2d ed. London: Duckworth, 1975.
Daniels, George H. *American Science in the Age of Jackson*. New York: Columbia University Press, 1968.
Darrah, William Culp. *Powell of the Colorado*. Princeton: Princeton University Press, 1950.
Davies, Gordon L. "Research by Debate: The Geomorphology of William Morris Davis." *History of Science* 13 (1975): 139–45.
Davis, William Morris. *Geographical Essays*. Edited by Douglas Wilson Johnson. Boston: Ginn, 1909.
———. "Pumpelly's Reminiscences." *Science* 49 (1919): 61–63.
———. "A Summer in Turkestan." *American Geographical Society Bulletin* 36 (1904): 217–28.
De Terra, Helmut. *Humboldt: The Life and Times of Alexander von Humboldt, 1769–1859*. New York: Alfred A. Knopf, 1955.
Dickinson, Robert E. *The Makers of Modern Geography*. New York: Praeger, 1969.
Drake, Ellen T., and William M. Jordan, eds. *Geologists and Ideas: A History of North American Geology*. Boulder, Colo.: Geological Society of America, 1985.
Dunbar, Gary S. "'Geography Rides, Geology Walks'; The Barrett-Huntington

Expedition to Central Asia in 1905." *Association of Pacific Geographers Yearbook* 45 (1983): 7–23.
Dupree, A. Hunter. *Science in the Federal Government: A History of Policies and Activities*. Cambridge: Harvard University Press, 1957. Baltimore: Johns Hopkins University Press, 1986.
Eckel, Edwin B. *The Geological Society of America: Life History of a Learned Society*. Boulder, Colo.: Geological Society of America, 1982.
Eckler, A. Ross. *The Bureau of the Census*. New York: Praeger, 1972.
Emerson, Edward Waldo. *The Early Years of the Saturday Club, 1855–1870*. Boston: Houghton Mifflin, 1918.
Emmons, Ebenezer. *Geology of New York*. Vol. 2. Albany, N.Y.: White and Visscher, 1842.
Emmons, Samuel Franklin. "Clarence King." *American Journal of Science*, 4th ser., 13 (1902): 224–37.
Fairchild, Herman L. *The Geological Society of America, 1888–1930; A Chapter in Earth Science History*. New York: Geological Society of America, 1932.
Foster, John W., and Josiah Dwight Whitney. *Report on the Geology and Topography of a Portion of the Lake Superior Land District in the State of Michigan*. Pt. 1, "Copper Lands." U.S. 31st Cong., 1st sess., H. Exec. Doc. 69, 1859; Pt. 2, "The Iron Region, together with the General Geology." U.S. 32d Cong., spec. sess., S. Exec. Doc. 4, 1851.
Friedrich, Otto. *Clover*. New York: Simon and Schuster, 1979.
Gates, William B. Jr., *Michigan Copper and Boston Dollars: An Economic History of the Michigan Copper Mining Industry*. Cambridge: Harvard University Press, 1951.
Geikie, Archibald. *Founders of Geology*. 2d ed. 1905. Reprint. New York: Dover Publications, 1962.
Geikie, James. *The Great Ice Age and Its Relation to the Antiquity of Man*. 3d ed. New York: Appleton, 1895.
Geison, Gerald L. "Scientific Change, Emerging Specialties, and Research Schools." *History of Science* 19 (1981): 20–40.
Gilbert, Grove Karl, ed. *John Wesley Powell: A Memorial to an American Explorer and Scholar*. Chicago: Open Court, 1903.
Goetzmann, William H. *Army Exploration in the American West, 1803–1863*. New Haven: Yale University Press, 1959.
———. *Exploration and Empire: The Explorer and the Scientist in the Winning of the American West*. New York: Alfred A. Knopf, 1966.
———. "The Heroic Age of Western Geological Exploration: The U.S. Geological Survey and the Men and Events That Created It." *American West* 16, no. 5 (1979): 4–13, 59–61.
Goode, George Brown, ed. *The Smithsonian Institution, 1846–1896: The History of Its First Half Century*. Washington, D.C.: Smithsonian Institution Press, 1897.
Greene, Mott T. *Geology in the Nineteenth Century: Changing Views of a Changing World*. Ithaca, N.Y.: Cornell University Press, 1982.
———. "History of Geology." *Osiris*, 2d ser., 1 (1985): 97–116.
Gregory, Herbert E. "A Century of Geology—Steps of Progress in the Interpretation of Land Forms." *American Journal of Science*, 4th ser., 46 (1918): 123–24.

Guntau, Martin. "The Emergence of Geology as a Scientific Discipline." *History of Science* 16 (1978): 280–90.

———. "The Mining Academy of Freiberg—A Centre of Geoscientific Teaching and Research." *Journal of Mines, Metals and Fuels* 22 (1974): 223–27.

Gupta, Swarajya P. *Archaeology of Soviet Central Asia, and the Indian Borderlands.* 2 vols. Delhi: B. R. Publishing, 1979.

Hall, James. *Geology of New York.* Vol. 4. Albany, N.Y.: Carroll and Cook, 1843.

Haller, John S. *Outcasts from Evolution: Scientific Attitudes of Racial Inferiority, 1859–1900.* Urbana: University of Illinois Press, 1971.

Hamilton, Beryl M. "The Influence of the Polarising Microscope on Late Nineteenth Century Geology." *Janus* 69 (1982): 51–68.

Hammond, John Hays. *Autobiography of John Hays Hammond.* New York: Farrar and Rinehart, 1935.

Hankins, Thomas L. "In Defense of Biography: The Use of Biography in the History of Science." *History of Science* 17 (1979): 1–16.

Hendrickson, Walter B. "Nineteenth-Century State Geological Surveys: Early Government Support of Science." *Isis* 52 (1961): 357–71.

Henry, Joseph. *The Papers of Joseph Henry.* Edited by Nathan Reingold and Marc Rothenberg. Washington, D.C.: Smithsonian Institution Press, 1972– .

Higham, Norman. *A Very Scientific Gentleman: The Major Achievements of Henry Clifton Sorby.* Oxford: Oxford University Press, 1963.

Hilgard, Eugene W. "The Loess of the Mississippi Valley and the Eolian Hypothesis." *American Journal of Science*, 3d ser., 18 (1879): 106–12.

———. *Map Bulletin No. 1: Yakima Region, Colville Region, Washington Territory.* New York: Julius Bien, 1883.

Hinton, Richard Josiah. *The Handbook of Arizona: Its Resources, History, Towns, Mines, Ruins and Scenery.* 1878. Reprint. Tucson: Arizona Silhouettes, 1954.

Hobbs, William H. *An Explorer-Scientist's Pilgrimage: The Autobiography of William Herbert Hobbs.* Ann Arbor, Mich.: J. W. Edwards, 1952.

———. "On the Use of the Microscope in Petrography." *American Monthly Microscopical Journal* 9 (1888): 70–74.

Hobsbawm, E. J. *The Age of Capital, 1848–1875.* New York: Charles Scribner's Sons, 1979. New American Library, 1984.

Hole, Frank, and Robert F. Heizer. *An Introduction to Prehistoric Archeology.* 3d ed. New York: Holt, Rinehart and Winston, 1973.

Holmes, Arthur. *Petrographic Methods and Calculations.* London: Thomas Murby, 1921.

Holt, Henry. *Garrulities of an Octogenarian Editor.* Boston: Houghton Mifflin, 1923.

Howe, M. A. DeWolfe, ed. *Later Years of the Saturday Club, 1870–1920.* Boston: Houghton Mifflin, 1927.

Humboldt, Alexander von. *Cosmos: A Sketch of a Physical Description of the Universe.* Translated from the German by E. C. Otté. 5 vols. London: Bell and Daldy, 1871–72.

Hunt, Thomas Sterry. "The Geological Survey of Missouri." *American Naturalist* 9 (1875): 240–45.

Huntington, Ellsworth. *The Pulse of Asia: A Journey in Central Asia Illustrating the Geographic Basis of History.* Boston: Houghton Mifflin, 1907.

Huxley, Thomas Henry. "The Aryan Question and Prehistoric Man." *Nineteenth*

Century 28 (1890): 750–77. Reprinted in T. H. Huxley, *Man's Place in Nature and Other Anthropological Essays.* 1894. Reprint. Akron, Ohio: Werner, 1915.

James, Preston E. *All Possible Worlds: A History of Geographical Ideas.* Indianapolis: Bobbs-Merrill, 1972.

Johnson, Markes E. "Geology in American Education: 1825–1860." *Geological Society of America Bulletin* 88 (1977): 1192–98.

Jones, H. J. *Live Machines: Hired Foreigners and Meiji Japan.* Vancouver: University of British Columbia Press, 1980.

Jordy, William H. *Henry Adams: Scientific Historian.* New Haven: Yale University Press, 1952.

Judd, J. W. "Henry Clifton Sorby and the Birth of Microscopic Petrology." *Geological Magazine,* 5th ser., 5 (1908): 193–204.

Kemp, J. F. "Geology of the Green Mountains in Massachusetts." *Science* 2 (1895): 699–700.

Kevles, Daniel J., Jeffrey L. Sturchio, and P. Thomas Carroll. "The Sciences in America, Circa 1880." *Science* 209 (1980): 27–32.

Keyes, Charles. "Raphael Pumpelly: Premier Explorer." *Pan-American Geologist* 40 (1923): 241–50.

Kingman, Leroy, ed. *A Memorial History of Tioga County, New York.* Elmira, N.Y.: W. A. Ferguson, ca. 1897.

Knoepflmacher, U. C., and G. B. Tennyson, eds. *Nature and the Victorian Imagination.* Berkeley and Los Angeles: University of California Press, 1977.

Kohl, Philip L., ed. "The Bronze Age Civilization of Central Asia: Recent Soviet Discoveries." Special issues of *Soviet Anthropology and Archeology* 19 (1980–81), nos. 1–2, 3–4.

Kohlstedt, Sally Gregory. *The Formation of the American Scientific Community: The American Association for the Advancement of Science.* Urbana: University of Illinois Press, 1976.

Laudan, Rachel. *From Mineralogy to Geology: The Foundations of a Science, 1650–1830.* Chicago: University of Chicago Press, 1987.

LeConte, Joseph. "A Century of Geology." *Popular Science Monthly* 56 (1900): 431–43, 546–56.

Lindgren, Waldemar. "Metasomatic Processes in Fissure Veins." *AIME Transactions* 30 (1900): 578–692.

Livingstone, David N. *Nathaniel Southgate Shaler and the Culture of American Science.* Tuscaloosa: University of Alabama Press, 1987.

Mallory, J. P. *In Search of the Indo-Europeans: Language, Archaeology and Myth.* New York: Thames and Hudson, 1989.

Manning, Thomas G. *Government in Science: The U.S. Geological Survey, 1867–1894.* Lexington: University of Kentucky Press, 1967.

Martin, Douglas D. *An Arizona Chronology, The Territorial Years, 1846–1912.* Tucson: University of Arizona Press, 1963.

Martin, Geoffrey. *Ellsworth Huntington, His Life and Thought.* Hamden, Conn.: Archon Books, 1973.

Mather, William W. *Geology of New York.* Vol. 1. Albany, N.Y.: Carroll and Cook, 1843.

Merrill, George P. *Contributions to a History of American State Geological and Natural History Surveys.* U.S. National Museum Bulletin 109. Washington, D.C.: Government Printing Office, 1920.

———. *The First One Hundred Years of American Geology*. New Haven: Yale University Press, 1924.
Miller, Howard S. *Dollars for Research: Science and Its Patrons in Nineteenth-Century America*. Seattle: University of Washington Press, 1970.
Miller, Hugh. *The Old Red Sandstone; or, New Walks in an Old Field*. 4th Edinburgh ed. Boston: Gould and Lincoln, 1851.
Morison, Samuel Eliot, ed. *The Development of Harvard University Since the Inauguration of President Eliot, 1869–1929*. Cambridge: Harvard University Press, 1930.
Morrell, Jack B., and Arnold Thackray. *Gentlemen of Science: Early Years of the British Association for the Advancement of Science*. Oxford: Clarendon, 1981.
Mowry, Sylvester. *Arizona and Sonora: The Geography, History and Resources of the Silver Region of North America*. 3d ed., rev. and enl. New York: Harper and Brothers, 1864.
Murdoch, Angus. *Boom Copper: The Story of the First U.S. Mining Boom*. New York: Macmillan, 1943.
Nash, Gerald D. "The Conflict Between Pure and Applied Science in Nineteenth Century Public Policy: The California State Geological Survey, 1860–1874." *Isis* 55 (1963): 217–28.
Nelson, Clifford M. "Geologic Maps of American West: Hall Vs. Marcou." In 28th International Geological Congress, *Abstracts* (Washington, D.C.: N.p., 1989), 2:504–05.
The New Cambridge Modern History. 14 vols. Cambridge: Cambridge University Press, 1957–79.
North, Diane M. T. *Samuel Peter Heintzelman and the Sonora Exploring and Mining Company*. Tucson: University of Arizona Press, 1980.
Norton, Richard. "Report on Archaeological Remains in Turkestan." In American School of Classical Studies in Rome, *Supplementary Papers of the American School of Classical Studies in Rome*. 2 vols. New York: Macmillan, 1905–08. 1:196–216.
Ospovat, Alexander. "Abraham Gottlob Werner's Influence on American Geology." *Proceedings of the Oklahoma Academy of Science* 40 (1960): 98–103.
———. "Der Einfluss ehemaliger Studenten der Bergakademie Freiberg auf die Entwicklung des nordamerikanischen Bergbaus und Hüttenwesens. *Bergakademie* 18 (1966): 548–54.
Palache, Charles. "Memorial to John Eliot Wolff." *Proceedings of the Geological Society of America for 1940* (1941): 247–53.
Palache, Charles, and Helen E. Vassar. "Some Minerals of the Keweenawan Copper Deposits: Pumpellyite, a New Mineral; Sericite, Saponite." *American Mineralogist* 10 (1925): 412–18.
Parrish, William E. *A History of Missouri*. 3 vols. Columbia: University of Missouri Press, 1971–73.
Paul, Rodman W. *The Far West and the Great Plains in Transition, 1859–1900*. New York: Harper and Row, 1988.
———. *Mining Frontiers of the Far West, 1848–1880*. New York: Holt, Rinehart and Winston, 1963.
Paul, Wolfgang. *Mining Lore: An Illustrated Composition and Documentary Compilation With Emphasis on the Spirit and History of Mining*. Portland, Ore.: Morris Printing Co., 1970.

Penniman, T. K. *A Hundred Years of Anthropology.* 3d ed. London: Duckworth, 1965.
Pirsson, Louis V. "The Rise of Petrology as a Science." *American Journal of Science,* 4th ser., 46 (1918): 222–39.
Poliakov, Léon. *The Aryan Myth: A History of Racist and Nationalistic Ideas in Europe.* Translated by Edmund Howard. New York: Basic Books, 1971.
Porter, Roy. "Gentlemen and Geology: The Emergence of a Scientific Career, 1660–1920." *Historical Journal* 21 (1978): 809–36.
———. *The Making of Geology: Earth Science in Britain, 1660–1815.* Cambridge: Cambridge University Press, 1977.
Powell, John Wesley. *Report on the Lands of the Arid Region of the United States, With a More Detailed Account of the Lands of Utah.* 2d ed. Washington, D.C.: Government Printing Office, 1879. Reprint, edited by Wallace Stegner. Cambridge: Harvard University Press, 1962.
Prendergast, Michael L. "James Dwight Dana: The Life and Thought of an American Scientist." Ph.D. diss., University of California at Los Angeles, 1978.
"Pumpelly's *Across America and Asia.*" *North American Review* 110 (1870): 224–28.
Pyne, Stephen J. *Grove Karl Gilbert: A Great Engine of Research.* Austin: University of Texas Press, 1980.
———. "Methodologies for Geology: G. K. Gilbert and T. C. Chamberlin." *Isis* 69 (1978): 413–24.
Rabbitt, Mary C. *Minerals, Lands, and Geology for the Common Defence and General Welfare.* 3 vols. Washington, D.C.: Government Printing Office, 1979–86.
Ransome, Frederick L. "The Present Standing of Applied Geology." *Economic Geology* 1 (1906): 1–10.
Rapp, George, Jr., and John A. Gifford, eds. *Archaeological Geology.* New Haven: Yale University Press, 1985.
Raymond, Rossiter W. "Memoir of William Phipps Blake." *Geological Society of America Bulletin* 22 (1911): 36–47.
Rehder, Alfred. "Charles Sprague Sargent." *Journal of the Arnold Arboretum* 8 (1927): 69–86.
Reingold, Nathan. "National Science Policy in a Private Institution: The Carnegie Institution of Washington." In *The Organization of Knowledge in Modern America, 1860–1920,* edited by Alexandra Oleson and John Voss. Baltimore: Johns Hopkins University Press, 1979.
———, ed. *The Sciences in the American Context: New Perspectives.* Washington, D.C.: Smithsonian Institution Press, 1979.
Renfrew, Colin. *Archaeology and Language: The Puzzle of Indo-European Origins.* New York: Cambridge University Press, 1987.
Rice, Marion. "The Contributions of America to Geology." *Science* 25 (1907): 161–75.
Rice, William North, Frank D. Adams, Arthur P. Coleman, Charles D. Walcott, Waldemar Lindgren, Frederick L. Ransome, and William D. Matthew. *Problems of American Geology.* New Haven: Yale University Press, 1915.
Richthofen, Baron Ferdinand von. *China: Ergebnisse eigener Reisen und darauf gegrundeter Studien.* 3 vols. Berlin: Dietrich Reimer, 1877–1912.
———. "Geological Explorations in China." *American Journal of Science,* 2d ser., 50 (1870): 410–13.

———. "On the Existence of the Nummulitic Formation in China." *American Journal of Science*, 3d ser., 1 (1871): 110–13.

———. "On the Mode of Origin of the Loess." *Geological Magazine*, 2d ser., 9 (1882): 293–305. Reprinted in *Loess: Lithology and Genesis*, edited by Ian J. Smalley. Benchmark Papers in Geology, vol. 26. Stroudsberg, Pa.: Dowden, Hutchinson and Ross, 1975.

Rickard, Thomas A. *A History of American Mining*. New York: McGraw-Hill, 1932.

Ripley, William Z. *The Races of Europe: A Sociological Study*. 1900. Reprint. New York: Johnson Reprint, 1965.

Rosenberg, Charles. "Science in American Society: A Generation of Historical Debate." *Isis* 74 (1983): 356–67.

Rudwick, Martin J. S. "The Emergence of a Visual Language for Geological Science, 1760–1840." *History of Science* 14 (1976): 149–95.

———. *The Great Devonian Controversy: The Shaping of Scientific Knowledge Among Gentlemanly Specialists*. Chicago: University of Chicago Press, 1985.

Rukeyser, Muriel. *Willard Gibbs*. Garden City, N.Y.: Doubleday, Doran and Co., 1942.

Samuels, Ernest. *Henry Adams: The Major Phase*. Cambridge: Harvard University Press, 1964.

Schneer, Cecil J. "Ebenezer Emmons and the Foundation of American Geology." *Isis* 60 (1970): 439–50.

———. "The Great Taconic Controversy." *Isis* 69 (1978): 173–91.

———, ed. *Toward a History of Geology*. Cambridge: Massachusetts Institute of Technology Press, 1969.

———. *Two Hundred Years of Geology in America*. Proceedings of the New Hampshire Bicentennial Conference on the History of Geology. Hanover, N.H.: University Press of New England, 1979.

Schrader, Otto. *Prehistoric Antiquities of the Aryan Peoples: A Manual of Comparative Philology and the Earliest Culture*. London: Charles Griffin, 1890.

Secord, James A. *Controversy in Victorian Geology: The Cambrian-Silurian Dispute*. Princeton: Princeton University Press, 1986.

———. "The Geological Survey of Great Britain as a Research School, 1839–1855." *History of Science* 24 (1986): 223–75.

Shaler, Nathaniel S. *The Autobiography of Nathaniel Southgate Shaler, With a Supplementary Memoir by His Wife*. Boston: Houghton Mifflin, 1909.

———. *Nature and Man in America*. New York: Scribner's, 1891.

Slate, Frederick. "Biographical Memoir of Eugene Woldemar Hilgard, 1833–1916." *National Academy of Sciences Biographical Memoirs* 9 (1919): 93–155.

Sorby, Henry Clifton. "Carl Bernhard von Cotta." *Quarterly Journal of the Geological Society of London* 36 (1880): 40–42.

———. "On Unencumbered Research—A Personal Experience." In *Essays on the Endowment of Research*, edited by Charles Appleton. London: H. S. King, 1876.

Spence, Clark C. *Mining Engineers and the American West: The Lace-Boot Brigade, 1849–1933*. New Haven: Yale University Press, 1970.

Stegner, Wallace. *Beyond the Hundredth Meridian: John Wesley Powell and the Second Opening of the West*. Boston: Houghton Mifflin, 1954.

Stephens, Lester D. *Joseph LeConte, Gentle Prophet of Evolution.* Baton Rouge: Louisiana State University Press, 1982.
Stevenson, John J. "Geological Methods in Earlier Days." *Popular Science Monthly* 86 (1915): 25–32.
Struik, Dirk J. *Yankee Science in the Making.* Boston: Little, Brown, 1948.
Sutton, Stephanie B. *Charles Sprague Sargent and the Arnold Arboretum.* Cambridge: Harvard University Press, 1970.
Thornton, Tamara Plakins. *Cultivating Gentlemen: The Meaning of Country Life Among the Boston Elite, 1785–1860.* New Haven: Yale University Press, 1989.
Toynbee, Arnold J. *A Study of History.* Abridgement of vols. 1–6 by D. C. Somervell. New York: Oxford University Press, 1947.
Turner, Stephen P. "The Survey in Nineteenth-Century American Geology: The Evolution of a Form of Patronage." *Minerva* 25 (1987): 282–330.
United States. Bureau of the Census. *Historical Statistics of the United States, Colonial Times to 1970.* Bicentennial ed. 2 vols. Washington, D.C.: Government Printing Office, 1975.
———. Bureau of the Census. Tenth Census [Reports]. 22 vols. Washington, D.C.: Government Printing Office, 1883–86.
———. Congress. *Testimony before the Joint Commission to Consider the Present Organization of the Signal Service, Geological Survey, Coast and Geodetic Survey, and the Hydrographic Office of the Navy Department, with a View to Secure Greater Efficiency and Economy of Administration of the Public Service in Said Bureaus.* 49th Cong., 1st sess. Senate Misc. Doc. 82. Washington, D.C.: Government Printing Office, 1886.
———. War Department. *Reports of Explorations and Surveys, to Ascertain the Most Practicable and Economical Route for a Railroad from the Mississippi River to the Pacific Ocean.* 12 vols. in 13. Washington, D.C.: A. O. P. Nicholson, 1855–60.
Vance, Maurice M. *Charles Richard Van Hise: Scientist Progressive.* Madison: State Historical Society of Wisconsin, 1960.
Van Hise, Charles R. *A Treatise on Metamorphism.* USGS Monograph 47. Washington, D.C.: Government Printing Office, 1904.
Vanuxem, Lardner. *Geology of New York.* Vol. 3. Albany, N.Y.: White and Visscher, 1842.
Villard, Henry. *Memoirs of Henry Villard, Journalist and Financier, 1835–1900.* 2 vols. Boston: Houghton Mifflin, 1904.
Warner, Langdon. *Langdon Warner Through His Letters.* Edited by Theodore Bowie. Bloomington: Indiana University Press, 1966.
White, Charles A. "Biographical Sketch of Fielding Bradford Meek." *American Geologist* 18 (1896): 337–50.
Whitney, Josiah Dwight. *The Metallic Wealth of the United States, Described and Compared with That of Other Countries.* Philadelphia: Lippincott, 1854.
Wilkins, Thurman, with the help of Caroline Lawson Hinkley. *Clarence King: A Biography.* Rev. and enl. Albuquerque: University of New Mexico Press, 1988.
Williams, Frederick Wells. *Anson Burlingame and the First Chinese Mission to Foreign Powers.* New York: Scribner's, 1912.
Williams, George Huntington. "The Microscope in Geology." *Science,* original ser., 5 (1885): 190–91.

Willis, Bailey. "American Geology, 1850–1900." *Science* 96 (1942): 167–72.
———. *Geologic Structures*. New York: McGraw-Hill, 1923.
———. "Memorial of Raphael Pumpelly." *Geological Society of America Bulletin* 36 (1925): 45–84. Reprinted in *National Academy of Sciences Biographical Memoirs* 16 (1936): 23–62.
———. "Memorial Tribute to Raphael Pumpelly." *Geological Society of America Bulletin* 35 (1924): 42–43.
———. "Thomas Benton Brooks." *Science* 13 (1901): 460–62.
———. *A Yanqui in Patagonia*. Palo Alto, Calif.: Stanford University Press, 1947.
Wilson, Leonard G. "The Emergence of Geology as a Science in the United States." *Journal of World History* 10 (1967): 416–37.
———, ed. *Benjamin Silliman and His Circle: Studies on the Influence of Benjamin Silliman on Science in America*. New York: Science History Publications, 1979.
Winchell, N. H. "Some Objections to the Term Taconic Considered." *American Geologist* 1 (1888): 162–72.
Winslow, Arthur. "Geological Surveys in Missouri." *Journal of Geology* 2 (1894): 207–21.
Witherell, W. F. *Arizona as a Silver Country*. Saint Louis: J. McKittrick, 1878.
Wood, Charles R. *The Northern Pacific: Main Street of the Northwest*. Seattle: Superior, 1968.
Wright, Carroll D. *The History and Growth of the United States Census*. 1900. Reprint. New York: Johnson Reprint, 1966.
Wright, George F. *Man and the Glacial Period*. 2d ed. New York: Appleton, 1898.
Wright, Tim. *Coal Mining in China's Economy and Society, 1895–1937*. Cambridge: Cambridge University Press, 1984.
Young, Otis E., Jr. *Western Mining: An Informal Account of Precious-Metals Prospecting, Placering, Lode Mining, and Milling on the American Frontier from Spanish Times to 1893*. Norman: University of Oklahoma Press, 1970.
Zeuner, Frederick E. *Dating the Past, An Introduction to Geochronology*. 3d ed. London: Methuen, 1952.

Index

Abbreviations used in index:
CIW   Carnegie Institution of Washington
NTS   Northern Transcontinental Survey
USGS United States Geological Survey

Academy of Natural Sciences of Philadelphia, 41
Across America and Asia, 73–74, 131, 132, 205, 225 (n. 5); reviews of, 74–75
Adams, Brooks, 168, 172; as economic historian, 242 (n. 21); economic theory of history, 170
Adams, Frank D., 159
Adams, Henry, 133; anti-Semitism of, 137, 237 (n. 61); on death of Eliza Pumpelly, 137; *Esther*, 138; "Letter to American Teachers of History," 136; on Precambrian period, 159; and Pumpelly, 133–37; and Turkestan expeditions, 168, 175, 199
Adams, Marian Hooper ("Clover"; Mrs. Henry), 133–35
Advancement of Learning, 40
Agassiz, Alexander, 121, 131, 171; and Michigan copper mines, 81, 83; opposition to USGS, 144
Agassiz, Louis, 4, 7, 30, 35, 130; *Études sur les Glaciers*, 15, 45
Agricola, Georgius, 53
Agriculture: origin, 190; scientific, 118–19
Alexander the Great, 177
Allison Commission, 144–45
Alluvial fans: geology, 180; as sites for habitation, 180, 196
American Association for the Advancement of Science, 49
American Institute of Mining Engineers, 79, 130
American Journal of Science, 70, 72, 73
American Museum of Natural History: Central Asian expedition (1922–23), 67

American School of Classical Studies in Rome, 171, 174, 186
American West: exploring expeditions, 76–77
Anau: absence of weapons at, 190, 195; chronology of culture periods, 188–89; culture periods and climate, 190–92; excavations at, 185, 187–92; human skulls, 190, 195; use of metal, 190–92, 195; and origin of agriculture, 190
Andrews, Roy Chapman, 67
Apaches, 52, 55
Aralo-Caspian sea, 179, 183
Aral Sea, 164
Archaeological geology. *See* Geoarchaeology
Archaeology: dating techniques, 189
Archean rocks, 143, 154
Aridity, progressive. *See* Central Asia: climatic change; Climatic change
Arizona: geology, 56; joins Confederacy, 55; silver mining, 33, 52–56
Army Corps of Topographical Engineers, 34
Aryan homeland question, 164–68; and philology, 165, 166; and physical anthropology, 167, 195–96. *See also* Indo-Europeans; Indo-European languages
Aryan migrations, 166–67, 193–98
Aryan race, 136, 167. *See also* Indo-Europeans
Ashburner, William, 55
Association of American Geologists, 39, 47, 48–49

Baconian science, 37, 43
Bainbridge, Ga., plantation, 119, 145
Baird, Spencer F., 35–36, 111
Balmville, N.Y., 118–19, 124
Bancroft, Hubert Howe, 75

265

266   Index

Beard, Charles A.: on Brooks Adams as economic historian, 242 (n. 21)
Beck, Lewis C., 42
Becker, George F., 96, 98–99, 162, 163
Begtabegoff, Prince and Princess (of Tbilisi), 186
Benton, Edward R., 101
Bessemer steel process, 99
Beudant, François-Sulpice, 11–12, 13
Billings, Frederick, 104
Billings, John Shaw, 95, 170, 185
Blackmur, R. P., 135
Blair, Andrew A., 92, 100
Blake, William P., 29; appointment to Japan, 57–61; edits *Mining Magazine*, 32–33, 58; with Pacific Railroad survey, 35–36
Blakiston, Capt. Thomas W., 63
Blandet, Emile, 136
Blowpipe, 22, 53
Bowditch, Nathaniel: *Practical Navigator*, 60
Breithaupt, Johann Friedrich, 22–23, 25, 87
Brewer, William H., 55
Brigham, Albert Perry, 172
British Association for the Advancement of Science, 117
Broadhead, Garland, 92, 94
Brongniart, Alexandre, 12, 40, 41
Brooks, Charles W., 58
Brooks, Hildegarde, 187
Brooks, Thomas B.: and Bainbridge plantation, 119; friendship with Pumpelly, 82; and Michigan survey, 84–86, 90, 123
Brown, Gov. B. Gratz, 90–91
Bruce, Sir Frederick, 62, 69, 75
Bruce, Robert V., 48
Brunckow, Frederick, 52
Brush, George J., 9
Buckland, William, 45–46, 117
Bunsen, Robert, 109
Burlingame, Anson, 62, 69, 75
Butterfield Overland Stage, 53

Cabot, Dr. Hugh, 163
Cabot, Thomas H., 163
California Academy of Natural Sciences, 55
California geological survey, 29, 55, 58, 92
Calumet and Hecla copper mines, 81, 83
Cambrian-Silurian controversy, 44, 147
Cambrian system, 43, 154–56
Canby, W. M., 109
Cannon, Susan F., 37, 207–08
Carnegie, Andrew, 168–69
Carnegie Institution of Washington, 164, 168–71; criticism of, 200; Geophysical Laboratory, 163; grants, 170–71
Cascade Range, 36, 111
Caspian Sea, 164, 166, 177; shorelines, 179
Catastrophism, 44, 45, 46
Central Asia: archaeology, 176, 185, 201; as Aryan homeland, 164–66; climatic change, 164, 174, 177–78, 190, 191, 192–93; contributions to European culture, 188, 197; geology, 179–81; glaciers, 181–83; loess deposits, 178, 182–83; mountains, 180–83; physiography, 67, 177–83; prehistoric settlements, 180, 184–85
Central Pacific Railroad, 104
Century Club (New York), 131–33
Chamberlin, Thomas C., 146, 170, 210; *Geology of Wisconsin*, 125–26; on glacial epochs, 182; on influence of geography, 172; on loess, 128–29; on Pumpelly's work, 139; as teacher, 120–21; and theory of multiple working hypotheses, 129; and USGS Glacial Division, 142, 143
Chandler, Charles F., 132
Charvenet, William, 108
Chauvenet, Regis, 92, 108
Chauvenet, William M., 101, 108
Childe, V. Gordon, 200
China: American policy in, 75; and the West, 62; coal, 62, 68–70; geology, 63–68; loess deposits, 67–68; mountain systems, 65–66; railroads, 70
Civil War, 55, 76, 79, 105; and state geological surveys, 84, 91
Clark, Grahame, 201
Classification in geology, 159–61
Claypole, Edward, 212
Clemens, Samuel. *See* Twain, Mark
Climatic change: Central Asia, 164, 174, 177–78, 181, 190, 192–93; in Corsica, 26; and migrations, 193–98; and culture development, 190–91
Coal: of China, 68–70; of New York state, 42; of Northwest, 106–107, 111
Coal mining: Hokkaido, 60; Pennsylvania, 31
Coal production, 31
Coleman, William, 172
Columbia School of Mines, 18, 86, 89, 132
Comstock Lode, 33
Conrad, Timothy, 40, 41, 43
Cooke, Jay, 104
Copper mining, Michigan, 31, 81
Copper ores: origin of, 86–87
Corsica, 14–16, 26
Cotta, Carl Bernhard von, 23–27, 79, 87; on influence of geography, 24, 76; *Die Lehre von den Erzlagerstätten*, 89; and Lyell, 24; and microscopic petrography, 123; and petrology, 23–24; and science of ore deposits, 24–25
Credner, Hermann, 82
Cretaceous period, 41
Crookham, George, 6
Cuvier, Georges, 12
Cycle of erosion, 173–74, 182

Dale, Thomas Nelson, 105; and geology of Green Mountains, 146, 150–51, 153–56, 211
Dana, Edward S., 124
Dana, James D., 7, 8, 72, 212; and *American Journal of Science*, 70; and mountain building, 66, 149; and Taconic controversy, 147, 148
Dana, Paul, 112
Daniels, George H., 43
Darwin, Charles, 73, 117, 136

Davis, William Morris: at CIW, 171; cycle of erosion, 106–07, 173–74, 182; and NTS, 106–07; ontography, 173, 180, 193; as Pumpelly's student, 89, 121; and Turkestan expedition of 1903, 173–83; and USGS, 151–52
Dawes, G. W., 124
De Geer, Gerhard, 182
De la Beche, Henry, 48, 152
De Morgan, Jacques, 185, 189
Delta oases. *See* Alluvial fans
Deluge, The. *See* Diluvial theory
Dennett, J. R., 133
Desor, Edouard, 32
Devonian controversy, 147, 224 (n. 33)
Devonian system, 43–44; of China, 64
Diluvial theory, 45–46
Djeitun culture, 201
Domestication of animals, 185, 190
Dorpfeld, Wilhelm, 175
Drown, Thomas M., 89
Dublin, N.H., summer home, 119, 203
Dunham, George, 9
Dupree, A. Hunter, 37
Dürst, J. Ulrich, 187, 190, 197
Dutton, Clarence: and USGS, 143

Eaton, Amos, 7, 8; students of, 40, 41
École des Mines, 9, 18, 40
Economic geologists: characteristics of, 78–79; and mining industry, 208–09; and technology transfer, 208–09
Economic geology, 31, 42, 78–80; relation to general geology, 79, 80
Economic Geology (journal), 78, 229 (n. 2)
Edgerton, Fay, 7
Education of Henry Adams, 133, 135, 136
Ehrenberg, Herman, 52
Eldridge, George, 106, 114
Élie de Beaumont, Jean, 25
Emerson, Ralph Waldo, 130
Emmons, Ebenezer, 40, 41; and glacial theory, 46; and Taconic controversy, 44–45, 147
Emmons, Samuel Franklin, 96–97, 98–99, 159; and Henry Adams, 135; and Ferdinand Zirkel, 123
Emory, William H., 56
Enriquita quicksilver mine, 33
Environment, influence of. *See* Climatic change; Geography: influence on history; Ontography
Environmental determinism, 76, 174, 193
Environmentalism. *See* Climatic change; Geography: influence on history
Erie Canal, 7
Études sur les Glaciers, 15
Euclid, Burial of (Yale ritual), 8
Exploration, scientific, 34–38, 103–04, 205–08
Exploring expeditions, Western, 34–38, 76–77
Exploring sciences, 37

Foerste, August F., 151

Fort Breckenridge, Ariz., 55
Fort Buchanan, Ariz., 55
Fossils. *See* Paleontology
Foster, John W., 31
Foster-Whitney report, 31–32, 84–85, 96
Frazer, Persifor, 160
Freiberg barrel amalgamation process, 52, 53–54
Freiberg Mining Academy, 17–18, 79; Americans at, 9, 19; chemistry at, 21–22; colloquia, 26; courses at, 21–25; entrance requirements, 20; field trips, 26–27; graduates of, in U.S., 19, 33, 39, 52, 82, 91; mineralogy at, 22–23; mining instruction at, 20, 26; paleontology at, 25; professors at, 22, 27; research at, 25–26
Friend of China, 70
Frontier thesis (Turner), 172

Galcha tribes, 194
Gannett, Henry, 89
Gaskell, Charles Milnes, 136
Geikie, Archibald, 4, 219 (n. 55)
Geikie, James, 182
Gentlemen farmers: characteristics of, 118
Gentlemen geologists, 48; characteristics of, 116–17
Gentlemen's clubs, 130–31
Geoarchaeology, 183, 184, 201–02
Geochemistry, 25
Geographic isolation, 194, 196
Geography: and human migrations, 193–99; influence on history, 24, 75–76, 166–67, 170, 172, 193; and language development, 173, 194. *See also* Climatic change; Ontography
Geological controversies. *See* Cambrian-Silurian controversy; Devonian controversy; Taconic controversy
Geological Researches in China, Mongolia and Japan, 61, 63, 67, 70–73
Geological Society of America, 49, 130
Geological Society of France, 13, 15
Geological Society of London, 48, 117
Geological Survey of Great Britain, 48, 117; as research school, 152, 210
Geological surveys, railroad. *See* Northern Transcontinental Survey; Pacific Railroad surveys
Geological surveys, state, 30, 31, 38–39, 141; California, 29, 55, 58, 92; and government support, 94; Massachusetts, 39; Michigan, 84–87; Missouri, 90–95; New York, 39–49; and paleontology, 41–42, 92–94; Pennsylvania, 31, 32; publication of reports, 85–86, 91
Geologists: education, 6–7, 40; employment, 29; European study, 9; as generalists, 30, 211–12; in Heroic Age, 205; international contacts of, 30, 48, 213; and religion, 118; as specialists, 38, 145, 211
Geology: and archaeology, 184; classification in, 159–61; popularization of, 73–74; professionalization of, 30, 47–49, 121; pure vs. applied, 85–86; specialization, 38, 145; structural,

Geology (continued)
  149–50, 157, 158, 162–63
Geology of New York, 39
Geology of the Green Mountains in Massachusetts, 146, 157–58
Geomorphology, 173–74. See also Physiography
Geophysics, 25
Gibbs, Josiah Willard, 8, 133
Gibbs, Wolcott, 131
Gifford, John A., 201
Gilbert, Grove Karl, 21; on classification, 160; and Lake Bonneville study, 179; and USGS, 143, 146
Gilded Age, xii, 135, 214–15; as period of transition in geology, 211
Gillispie, Charles C., 117
Gilman, Daniel C., 72, 175
Gimbutas, Maria, 198
Glacial epochs, 181, 182
Glacial phenomena: Central Asia, 181–82; Corsica, 15, 25–26; New York state, 45–47
Glacial theory, 15, 43, 46; New York survey geologists on, 45–47
Glacier National Park, 112
Glaciers: and climate, 177–78; and loess deposits, 127–28, 183; in Rocky Mountains, 112
Gobi Desert, 66
Godkin, Edwin L., 132–33
Goetzmann, William, 37–38, 207
Gogebic iron range, 83
Gold Creek, Montana, 113
Gooch, Frank A.: lignite experiments, 107; and NTS, 107, 114; and Tenth Census, 100; and Turkestan expedition, 187, 190
Government and science, 37, 39, 144–45
Grant, Ulysses S., 113
Gray, Asa, 131
Great Diamond Hoax, 34, 82–83
Greely, Horace, 90
Green Mountains, 148–58; Cambrian formations, 154–56; microscopic petrography, 155; paleontology, 156; Precambrian formations, 154–56; structural geology, 153–56
Greene, Mott T., 25, 149
Gregory, Herbert E., 129
Grosvenor, Horace C., 53, 55
Gunpowder: use of in Japanese mines, 60
Guyot, Arnold, 76

Hagan, H. A., 109–10
Hager, Albert D., 90
Hague, Arnold, 96–97, 98–99, 143
Hague, James D., 33, 55, 81; ethics, 83–84; at Freiberg Mining Academy, 19–20; in Japan, 62
Hakodate, governor of, 58, 59, 61
Hall, James, Jr., 29, 32, 35, 49; education, 41; and glacial theory, 47; on mountain building, 44, 66, 149; Paleontology of New York, 41–42, 92
Haller, John S., 74
Hanover, Germany, 10
Hanover polytechnical school, 11

Harris, Townsend, 57, 59
Harvard University: School of Mining and Practical Geology, 80–81, 89, 121
Harvey, William, 210
Hawthorne, Nathaniel, 150
Hay, Clara (Mrs. John), 135
Hay, John, 135, 176
Hayden, Ferdinand V., 38, 93
Hayes, Isaac I., 72
Heim, Albert: Mechanismus der Gebirgsbildung, 149, 155
Heintzelman, Samuel Peter, 52
Heintzelman Mine, 52, 53–54, 56
Henry, Joseph, 2, 35–36; as editor, 71–72; greets Japanese mission, 57
Herbert, Rep. Hilary A., 144
Heredity and environment: Pumpelly's views on, 76
Heroic age of exploration, 205
Hewitt, Abram S., 132
Hilgard, Eugene W., 9, 95, 105; and NTS, 109–11; on eolian hypothesis, 128; and Mississippi delta, 65
Hill, Thomas, 81
Hitchcock, Edward, 39; glacial theory of, 45–46
Hobbs, William H., 150, 151, 211
Hobsbawm, E. J., 78
Hokkaido: mines and mineral resources, 59–60
Holden, Edward S., 108–09
Hollerith, Herman, 95
Holmes, Arthur, 123
Holmes, Oliver Wendell, 130
Holt, Henry, 199; and Century Club, 132–33; opinion of Yale, 8; on Pumpelly's death, 203–04; publishes geology textbook, 121
Hoosac railroad tunnel, 80, 150, 154
Houghton, Douglass, 84–85
Huc, Abbé Évariste Régis, 63
Humboldt, Alexander von, 37–38, 67, 73, 84–85, 139; on Alexander the Great in Central Asia, 177; and Freiberg Mining Academy, 19
Humboldtian science, 37–38, 207–08
Hunt, Thomas S., 70, 92
Huntington, Ellsworth, 193; description of Pumpelly, 178; and environmental determinism, 174, 193; Pulse of Asia, 174, 198; and Turkestan expeditions, 174, 178–82
Huxley, Thomas H., 144, 166

Indo-European languages: origin, 165, 184, 194–95, 196, 198
Indo-Europeans: influence on Neolithic Europe, 197, 200–201; migration of (Pumpelly's theory), 193–98; in northern Europe, 166; origins, 165–68, 198
Industry: and environment, 206
Indus Valley civilization, 201
International Geological Congress, 130, 160, 213
Iron Mountain, Mo., 92
Iron ores: analysis of, 99–100; Michigan, 82–83; statistics, 99

Irrigation: in prehistoric Central Asia, 180, 193; in Northwest, 107–09
Irving, Roland D., 98, 143, 157, 161
Issik Kul lake, 182

Jackson, Charles T., 32
Janin, Henry, 33, 55, 58; career of, 34; at Freiberg Mining Academy, 19, 23, 25, 26, 29; and diamond hoax, 82–83; and Pacific Railroad Reports, 34
Janin, Louis, 33, 34, 55, 58; at Freiberg Mining Academy, 19, 26, 27; in Japan, 62; and Pacific Railroad Reports, 34; Pumpelly's letter to, 71
Janin, Louis Alexander, 20, 33
Japan: American experts in, 56, 61–62; coinage reform, 57; diplomatic mission to the U.S., 57; and Dutch science, 226 (n. 26); Meiji restoration, 57, 61; mining industry, 59–62; mining methods in, 60; and Russo-Japanese War, 186; shogun government, 57, 61; status of experts in, 59
Japanese art, 132
Jardin des Plants, 11
Jewett, Col. Ezekiel, 53
Johnson's New Universal Cyclopedia, 126
Jones, Sir William, 165
Julien, Alexis A., 86, 123

Kara Kul lake, 181–82
Keane, A. H., 195
Keating, William, 19
Kelvin, William Thomson, Lord, 136
Kemp, J. F., 157
Keweenaw Peninsula, 81–82, 86–87
Keyes, Charles, 211
Kidder, Homer, 187
Kimball, James P., 19–20, 33, 58, 131; opens mining bureau, 81
King, Clarence, 8, 142; and Century Club, 132; and diamond hoax, 96; Fortieth Parallel survey, 96, 123–24; and Henry Adams, 135, 237 (n. 64); marriage, 135; and microscopic petrography, 123–24; *Mountaineering in the Sierra Nevada*, 74; and Tenth Census, 95–97; and USGS, 95–99, 103
King, L. W., 200
Kirchoff, Charles, 126
Kohl, Philip L., 201
Kohlstedt, Sally Gregory, 49
Kopet Dagh mountains, 181
Kropotkin, Peter, 172–73
Kuhn, Thomas, 152
Kurgans, 180, 184

La Farge, John, 75, 132
Landed gentry. *See* Gentlemen farmers
Lapworth, Charles, 158
Lawrence Scientific School, 8, 30, 81
Lead mining: Hokkaido, 60
LeConte, Joseph, 21, 74, 212
Leith, Charles K., 139, 161–62

Lesley, J. Peter, 32, 70
Lewis and Clark expedition, 104
Liebig, Justus von, 152, 210
Lignite: conversion to higher grade coal for NTS, 107
Lindgren, Waldemar: on metasomatism, 125; on Pumpelly as micropetrologist, 212; with NTS, 106–07
Livingstone, David N., 76
Loder, Antoinette (sister), 151
Loess, 67–68; of Central Asia, 130, 178, 182–83, 192–93; of China, 67–68, 126–27; description of, 67–68; eolian hypothesis, 68, 126–30; lacustrine hypothesis, 68, 126–27, 128; of Mississippi Valley, 67, 126, 128–29; of Rhine Valley, 67, 127; and rock disintegration, 127–28
Longfellow, Henry Wadsworth, 130
Lyell, Charles, 30, 117; and glacial theory, 46; *Principles of Geology*, 40, 133; rebuffs Pumpelly, 24
Lyman, Benjamin S., 62
Lyman, Theodore, 131

McMurtry, Larry, xi
Mallory, J. P., 198
Maps, geological, 63, 208; of China, 63–65; Marcou's, of U.S., 37
Maps, topographic: Green Mountains, 153; for NTS, 109, 110
Marcou, Jules, 35, 37, 65
Marcy, Gov. William, 40
Marvine, Archibald, 86, 89, 121
Mather, William, 40, 45; and glacial theory, 46
Meek, Fielding B., 38, 92–95
Melville, Herman, 150
Menominee iron range, 82
Merriam, John C., 199
Merrill, George P., 124
Metallic Wealth of the United States, 32
Metasomatism, 125
Metropolitan Museum of Art, 132
Mexican Boundary Survey, 56
Michigan: pine lands, 82
Michigan geological survey, 84–87; Brook's report on iron, 85–86; Pumpelly's report on copper, 86–87
Microscopic petrography. *See* Petrography, microscopic
Miller, Hugh, 4–6
Mineralogy, 42
Miners, Michigan, 85–86
Mining. *See* Coal mining; Copper mining; Lead mining
Mining academies, 18
Mining engineers: characteristics, 78–79
Mining geologists. *See* Economic geologists
Mining geology. *See* Economic geology
Mining industry, 52; statistics, 95–103
Mining Magazine, 32–33
Mississippi River delta, 65

Missouri geological survey, 90–94; paleontology, 92–94; and University of Missouri, 93
Mollison, Thomas, 187
Mongolia: geology, 66–67
Mongolian plateau, 64, 66, 76
Moraines. *See* Glacial phenomena
Morrell, Jack B., 152
Morrill Land Grant Act, 82
Mountain building theories, 44, 149, 158
Mount Baglia Orba (Corsica), 15
Mount Greylock (Mass.), 150, 153
Mount Hoosac (Mass.), 150, 151, 153
Mount Monadnock (N.H.), 119
Murchison, Roderick, 4–5, 43, 46, 117, 147
Museum collections, 35
Museum für Völkerkunde, 186
Museum of Comparative Zoology (Harvard), 35, 83, 121
My Reminiscences, xi, 23, 66, 137, 163, 198, 203, 225 (n. 5)

Namazga culture, 201
Nation, 133; criticizes CIW, 200
National Academy of Sciences, 65, 70–71, 95; *Memoirs*, 228 (n. 56); Pumpelly elected member of, 73
Neo-Lamarckism, 74
Neptunist theory, 18, 25
Nevins, Allan, 132
Newberry, John S., 70, 95; analyzes fossils from China, 64, 72, 73; and Century Club, 132; and Ohio survey, 93; and Pacific Railroad surveys, 35, 36
Newcomb, Simon, 72
New Empire, 170
New Haven Collegiate and Commercial Institute, 7, 9
Newport, R.I., 99
New York Natural History Survey, 5, 34–49; and glacial theory, 45–47; paleontology, 41; stratigraphic system, 43–45
Nöggerath, Jacob, 16
Nomadism: origins of, 193
Nomads: armed invasions of Europe, 197–98; of Mongolia, 76
Nomenclature, geological, 44, 49, 158, 160
North Adams, Mass., 153
North American Review, 74, 75
Northern Pacific Railroad, 103–05; and Clover Adams, 133; last spike driven, 113
Northern Transcontinental Survey, 103–14; benefits of, 113; chemical laboratory, 107; economic geology, 106; forests division, 109–10; irrigation studies, 107–09, 112; land use policy, 108–09; personnel, 106–10; topographic maps, 110
Northwest, exploration, 104
Norton, Charles Eliot, 174
Norton, Richard, 174, 178, 181, 186
Norwood, C. J., 94
Noyes, J. F., 12

Old Red Sandstone (formation), 5, 43
Old Red Sandstone (Hugh Miller), 4–6
Ontography, 173, 180, 193
Open Door policy, 176
Orbigny, Charles d', 11–12, 13
Ordovician system, 147, 158
Ore deposits: origin, 78–79, 125; science of, at Freiberg, 19, 24–25
Oregon Railway and Navigation Company, 104
Orogenesis. *See* Mountain building theories
Owego, N.Y., 2
Owego Academy, 2, 4, 7
Owen, David Dale, 31, 67
Oxford University, 120

Pacific Railroad reports, 34, 38
Pacific Railroad surveys, 29, 34–38, 77, 104
Paleontology: at Freiberg, 25; Missouri survey, 92–94; New York survey, 41–42
Paleontology of New York, 41
Paley, William: *Natural Theology*, 7, 218 (n. 21)
Pamirs, 181
Panic of 1873, 82, 94
Panic of 1893, 135, 162
Paragenesis, 23, 86–87, 123, 124
Pearson, Karl: *Grammar of Science*, 133
Peary, Capt. Robert, 171
Peirce, Benjamin, 70
Perry, Commodore Matthew, 51, 57, 59
Petrie, Flinders, 189
Petrography, microscopic, 122–26; and geology of Green Mountains, 149, 155
Petrology: at Freiberg Mining Academy, 23
Pettee, William H., 89
Physiography: of Central Asia, 173, 177–83
Piggott, Stuart, 201
Pilot Knob, Mo., 92
Plate tectonics, 158
Plattner, Karl Friedrich, 22
Pliny, 53
Polanyi, Michael, 152
Popularization of science, 73–74
Portage Lake and Lake Superior Ship Canal Company, 81–82
Porter, Roy, 48, 116–17
Poston, Charles D., 52, 55
Potsdam sandstone, 44–45
Powell, John Wesley, 6, 66; Allison Commission testimony, 144–45; *Arid Region* report, 107–08; and Bureau of Ethnology, 142; *Exploration of the Colorado River*, 74; and Humboldtian science, 207; as mentor, 146; support of research, 141–45; and USGS, 103, 105, 141–46
Precambrian system, 143, 154; of Green Mountains, 154–56; subdivisions, 159–61
Professionalism in geology, 30, 47–49, 121
Pseudomorph, 235 (n. 24)
Pumpelly, Antoinette (sister), 3, 11
Pumpelly, Charles (uncle), 2
Pumpelly, Elise (Mrs. Thomas H. Cabot), 99, 119, 163

Pumpelly, Eliza Shepard (wife), 118–19, 210; marriage, 87; miscarriage, 89; with husband in Michigan, 88–89; pregnancy, 94; on Turkestan expedition of 1904, 185–86; death, 137, 203
Pumpelly, George E. (cousin), 81
Pumpelly, Harmon (uncle), 2, 55, 57–58
Pumpelly, James (uncle), 2
Pumpelly, John (brother), 3, 10, 11
Pumpelly, John (grandfather), 1–2
Pumpelly, Margarita (daughter), 99, 119
Pumpelly, Mary Welles (mother), 3–4, 5–6, 9, 55, 81; *Poems*, 3; with son in Europe, 10–16
Pumpelly, Pauline (daughter), 99; death of, 203
PUMPELLY, RAPHAEL: *Across America and Asia*, 55, 56, 66, 73–74; ancestors, 1–2; avoidance of controversy, 130; Bainbridge plantation, 119, 145; Balmville farm, 118–19, 124; birth, 3; boyhood, 1–6; called "American Humboldt," 38, 207; and Century Club, 131–33; characteristics, 1, 10, 27, 178; in Corsica, 14–16, 26; death of, 203–05; as director of research school, 152, 210–11; Dublin summer home, 119, 135; as economic geologist, 79–80, 208–09; elected to Geological Society of France, 13, to National Academy of Sciences, 73; ethical standards, 83–84; as explorer, 205–08; extravagance, 12, 209; as generalist, 212; as gentleman geologist, 116, 118, 163; *Geological Researches in China, Mongolia and Japan*, 67, 70–73; and Henry Adams, 133–37; and Hoosac railroad tunnel, 80; and independent research, 119–20, 122–30; and International Geological Congress, 130, 160, 213; investments, 82–83, 118; and Johnson's *Cyclopedia*, 126; and loess, 126–30; marriage, 87; and mathematics, 21; and microscopic petrography, 122–26, 212; as mining engineer, 79; "Metasomatic Development" (1878), 125; mouflon story, 27–28; *My Reminiscences*, xi, 23, 66, 137, 163, 198, 203, 225 (n. 5); offered position at Sheffield, 81; and paleontology, 5, 11–12, 13, 25, 42, 92–94; and Panic of 1893, 163; and philology, 194–95; and politics, 115, 146; president of GSA, 192; "On Pseudomorphs of Chlorite" (1875), 124–25; as raconteur, 163; rebuffed by Lyell, 24; relations with staff, 100–01, 162, 178, 210–11, with Van Hise, 160–62; and religion, 3, 137–38; as religious skeptic in Adams's *Esther*, 138; in Rhine Valley, 13, 206; on Richthofen's eolian hypothesis, 126–27; "Rock-Disintegration" (1879), 127–28, 156; and Saturday Club, 130–31; as scientific administrator, 105–06, 209; as scientific farmer, 118–19; and scientific societies, 130; and social clubs, 130–33; students of, at Harvard mining school, 89; as teacher, 121–22; as textbook writer, 121; urge to explore, 1, 3; views on race, 74–75, 167
—*in Arizona:* Apache attacks, 55; attitude toward Native Americans, 74–75; California Academy paper on silver mines, 55–56; at Santa Rita mines, 53–55; return to, after wife's death, 137, 206
—*in Central Asia:* Aryan homeland theory, 164–68; Aryan migration theory, 193–99; CIW proposal, 168, 171; chronology of Anau culture periods, 188–89; geoarchaeology, 165, 183, 184, 188–89, 201–02; on influence of environment, 172, 192–93; loess, 182–83; in Pamirs, 181–83; physiography, 177–83; Turkestan expedition of 1903, 171–84; of 1904, 174–75, 184–92
—*in China,* 62–70, 209; on age of limestone, 64; Chinese geographers, 64, 165; examines coal mines, 68–70; geographic influences, 75–76; geological map, 63–65; itinerary, 62–63; lacustrine hypothesis, 68; loess deposits, 67–68; on Mongolian plateau, 66, 76; return home from, 70–71, 74; Sinian mountain system, 65–66; sympathy for people, 62, 75; Yellow River delta, 65
—*education:* early years, 4–7; European travel and study, 9–16; Freiberg Mining Academy, 16–27; at Hanover polytechnical school, 11; language study, 10; Russell's New Haven Institute, 7, 9; study with d'Orbigny, 11–12
—*in Japan,* 56–62; attitude toward Japanese people, 74–75; buys scientific instruments, 58; introduces blasting, 60; observes customs, 59; students of, 59–60; studies volcanoes, 61
—*in Michigan:* discovers Gogebic range, 83; with Michigan geological survey, 84–87; partnership with Brooks, 82; report on copper ores, 86–87
—*in Missouri,* 90–95; as administrator, 90–91; corresponds with Meek about paleontology, 92–94; publishes reports, 91–94; resigns from survey, 94
—*Northern Transcontinental Survey,* 103–14; discovers glaciers, 112–13; expense of, 113; land use policy, 108–09; maps, 110, 114; organizes survey, 105–06; reconnaissance trips, 111–12
—*with U.S. Geological Survey,* 141–42, 162; Archean Division, 142, 144–52; fieldwork, 153–54, 213; *Geology of the Green Mountains,* 148–58, 211; rumored to replace Powell, 145–46; Tenth Census *Report on the Mining Industries,* 97, 103; Tenth Census work, 95–103, 210
Pumpelly, Raphael Welles (son), 99, 151; on Pumpelly as geoarchaeologist, 213–14; with Turkestan expedition, 175, 181–82
Pumpelly, William (father), 2–3, 12–14, 16; death of, 118
Pumpelly glacier, 112
Pumpellyite, 87
Putnam, Bayard T., 101, 150

Quenstedt, Friedrich, 25, 221 (n. 80)

Races: evolution of, 74
Racism, 74–75, 167–68

Railroads: in China, 70. *See also* Northern Transcontinental Survey; Pacific Railroad surveys
Rammelsberg, Karl, 9, 12
Ransome, Frederick L., 78
Rapp, George R., Jr., 201
Ratzel, Friedrich, 166–67
Reich, Ferdinand, 25
Reingold, Nathan, 47
Renfrew, Colin, 168; *Archaeology and Language*, 198
Rensselaer School (Rensselaer Polytechnic Institute), 7, 41
Research: endowment of, 120
Research schools, 210–11; characteristics, 152
Richter, Theodore, 22
Richthofen, Ferdinand von, 65, 176; corrects Pumpelly on age of limestone, 73; eolian hypothesis, 68, 126–30; research in China, 72–73
Ripley, William Z.: *Races of Europe*, 167
Ritter, Carl, 76
Rock disintegration: and loess, 127–28; and rocks of Green Mountains, 156
Roemer, Friedrich Adolph, 13
Rogers, Henry D., 31, 149
Rogers, William B., 32, 131, 149
Romanticism, 117–18
Rominger, Carl, 85, 156
Rood, Ogden N., 132
Rosenbusch, Harry: and microscopic petrography, 123; students of, 151
Royal Academy of Mines (Berlin), 18
Royal Academy of Mines (Russia), 18
Royal School of Mines (London), 121
Rudwick, Martin J. S., 46, 147, 152
Russell, William. *See* New Haven Collegiate and Commercial Institute
Russia: archaeological commission, 176, 185; archaeological work in Central Asia, 176, 185, 201; geological survey, 166, 176; Imperial Geographical Society, 176; international relations, 176, 186
Russian-American relations, 186
Russo-Japanese War, 186
Rutherfurd, Lewis M., 131, 132

Sahara Desert, 26
Salisbury, Rollin D., 121
Santa Rita Mining Company, 52–56
Sargent, Charles S.: and Glacier National Park, 112; *Silva of North America*, 111; and Tenth Census, 95; with NTS, 109–11
Saturday Club (Boston), 130–31
Schellenberg, H. C., 187, 190
Schiel, Dr. James, 36
Schliemann, Heinrich, 175
Schmidt, Adolph, 91–92
Schmidt, Hubert, 174–75, 186; excavations at Anau, 187–88
Schrader, Otto, 166, 167, 195
Scientific instruments: for Japan, 58
Secord, James A., 152, 210

Sedgwick, Adam, 41, 43, 117, 147
Semple, Ellen Church, 172
Sergi, Giuseppe, 187, 190, 195
Seward, William H., 69
Shaler, Nathaniel S., 6–7, 74; and Anglo-Saxon superiority, 167; on Century Club, 132; on environmental influences, 76; as gentleman farmer, 118; as Harvard professor, 27, 120, 121–22; and religion, 137; rumored to replace Powell, 145
Shaw, Quincy, 83
Sheffield, Joseph, 8
Sheffield Scientific School, 8–9, 69, 81
Shimek, Bohumil, 129
Silk route, 170
Silliman, Benjamin, 8
Silurian period, 43
Silver mining: Arizona, 33, 52–56
Silver refining: Freiberg barrel amalgamation process, 52, 53–54
Smith, William, 48
Smithsonian Institution, 35–36; Contributions to Knowledge series, 71; foreign exchange program, 34; visit of Japanese mission, 57
Smyth, Henry Lloyd (son-in-law), 163
Social Darwinism, 74, 136
Society of Economic Geologists, 229 (n. 2)
Soils: of Northwest, 108–09, 110–11. *See also* Loess
Sonnenschein, Dr. (Berlin chemistry professor), 12
Sonora Exploring and Mining Company, 52
Sorby, Henry Clifton: and independent research, 120; and microscopic petrography, 122
Spencer, Herbert, 74, 136
Spurr Iron Mining Company, 82
Stamford dike, 154
Stegner, Wallace, 108, 142
Stevens, Isaac, 104
Stiles, William A., 112
Stratigraphy, 30, 41; New York state, 43–45
Suess, Eduard: *The Face of the Earth*, 192
Surveying, 10, 22
Susa: excavations at, 185, 189
Susquehanna Steam Navigation Company, 2
Swallow, George C., 90, 91
Switzerland: Neolithic lake dwellings, 195, 197

Tacit knowledge, 152
Taconian orogeny, 158
Taconic controversy, 44–45, 147–48
Taconic Mountains, 153
Taiping rebellion, 62
Tarr, Ralph S., 103
Tenth Census. *See* U.S. Bureau of the Census, Tenth Census
Thermodynamics, Second Law of (Kelvin), 136
Thin sections, 122–24
Thompson, Gilbert, 110
Thomson, Thomas, 152
Thornton, Tamara P., 118

Tien Shan mountains, 181–82
Todd, Ada (Mrs. Clarence King), 135
Toqueville, Alexis de, 48
Townsend Harris Treaty, 57
Toynbee, Arnold J., 193
Trade routes: influence of geography on, 170
Transcaspian basin: as biological organism, 177, 192
Transcaspian Railroad, 176
Trans-Siberian Railroad, 176
Transition formations, 43
Trowbridge, William P., 95
Tubac, Ariz., 55
Turkestan: expeditions to: in 1903, 171–84; in 1904, 174–75, 184–92
Turner, Frederick Jackson, 172, 214
Turner, Stephen P., 91
Twain, Mark, xii
Twin (crystallography), 220 (n. 70)

Uniformitarianism, 47, 46–47
U.S. Bureau of the Census, Tenth Census survey of mining industries, 95–103; census agents, 97–98; chemical laboratory, 99–100; collaboration with USGS, 95–97; iron ores, 99; schedules, 98
U.S. Geological Survey, 79, 95, 132; Appalachian Division, 157; Archean Division, 143–44; Division of Mining Geology, 95–96, 103; Glacial Division, 128, 210–11; Lake Superior Division, 157; and Powell, 141–46; reduction in staff, 162; and Tenth Census, 95–97; and topographic mapping, 141, 153; and universities, 145, 150
University of California, 109

Van Hise, Charles R., 139, 170; and CIW Geophysical Laboratory, 163; on influence of geography, 172; personality, 161; and Precambrian system, 160–61; relations with Pumpelly, 160–61; and USGS, 157
Vanuxem, Lardner, 40, 41, 43; glacial theory of, 47
Varves, 182
Vesuvius, 14, 61
Villard, Henry: bankruptcy, 113; and NTS, 103–04, 105; and Northern Pacific Railroad, 103, 105; as patron of science, 110–11
Volcanoes: in Hokkaido, 61. See also Vesuvius

Walcott, Charles D.: and CIW, 169, 170; identifies fossils in Green Mountains, 156; and USGS, 208
Walker, Frances A., 95
Warner, Charles Dudley, xii
Warner, Langdon, 186, 187
Weisbach, Julius, 22
Wells, H. G., 121
Werner, Abraham Gottlob, 18–19, 25, 79, 219 (n. 55)
White, Charles A., 127
Whitney, Josiah D., 29; and California Academy of Natural Sciences, 55–56; and California Geological survey, 55, 58, 82, 92; in Lake Superior region, 31–32; as mentor to Pumpelly, 55, 57, 69, 80, 70–71; as paleontologist, 42; paleontology report criticized, 93; supports Richthofen, 72–73; as teacher, 121
Whittlesey, Charles, 47, 72
Williams, George H., 151
Williams College, 40
Willis, Bailey, 167; and Aryan migration manuscript, 199; CIW grant to, 171; on death of Eliza Pumpelly, 203; and Glacier National Park, 112; on microscopic petrography, 124; and NTS, 106, 111, 113–14; on Pumpelly as explorer, 205; on Pumpelly as teacher, 121; on Pumpelly's place in science, 139–40; on Pumpelly's relations with staff, 210; on Pumpelly's relations with Van Hise, 161; on sharing of ideas, 146; and Tenth Census, 100–03; and USGS, 157
Willis, Nathaniel P., 3
Wilson, Allen D., 110
Wilson, Leonard G., 39
Winchell, Alexander, 85
Winchell, Newton H., 161
Wolff, John Eliot, 146, 150–51, 153–56, 211
Wright, Charles E., 123
Wright, George Frederick, 137
Wrightson, William, 53, 54, 55

Yale School of Applied Chemistry. See Sheffield Scientific School
Yale University, 8
Yangtze River, 63, 66
Yellow River, 68; delta of, 65
Yesso. See Hokkaido

Zirkel, Ferdinand, 122; *Microscopical Petrography*, 123–24
Zittel, Karl, 150

About the Author

Peggy Champlin is an independent scholar who lives in Los Angeles, California. She received a bachelor's degree from Wesleyan College, a master of library science degree from Immaculate Heart College, School of Library Science, a master of arts degree in history from California State University in Los Angeles, and a Ph.D. in history from UCLA.